The Master's Touch

On being a Sacred Teacher

for the New Age

Yogi Bhajan, *Ph.D.*
Master of Kundalini Yoga

KUNDALINI RESEARCH INSTITUTE • 1997

The Master's Touch: On Being a Sacred Teacher for the New Age, by Yogi Bhajan, Ph.D.

FIRST EDITION, Copyright © 1997, K.R.I.
REVISED FIRST EDITION, Copyright © 2000, K.R.I.

Published by Kundalini Research Institute, P.O. Box 1819 Santa Cruz, New Mexico 87567

ISBN 978-0-9639991-1-5

PROJECT COORDINATOR
Sat Kirpal Kaur Khalsa, Ph.D.

EDITOR
Guru Raj Kaur Khalsa

CONSULTING EDITORS
Shakti Parwha Kaur Khalsa
Ek Ong Kar Kaur Khalsa
Sat Kirpal Kaur Khalsa, Ph.D.

TRANSCRIPTIONIST
Tej Kaur Khalsa

REFERENCES
Tej Kaur Khalsa

DESIGN & LAYOUT
Guru Raj Kaur Khalsa

COVER DESIGN
Original concept of illustration by Yogi Bhajan, Ph.D.
Illustration by Seva Kaur Khalsa
Consultant: Soorya Kaur Khalsa
Technical Support: Pritpal Singh Khalsa

ILLUSTRATIONS
Shabad Kaur Khalsa

PROOFREADER/INDEX
Pranpati Singh (John Ricker)

BACK COVER PHOTOGRAPH
Seva Kaur (Italy)

VIDEOS PROVIDED BY
Golden Temple Enterprises

PRINTER
Sheridan Books, Inc.

Kundalini Research
Institute

This Seal of Approval is granted to those products which have gone through the KRI Review process for accuracy and integrity of the technology of Kundalini Yoga and 3HO Lifestyle as taught by Yogi Bhajan.

Dedication

*This work is dedicated to those who have to excel
and face the Age of Aquarius with their excellence.
We are spiritual beings born for having a human experience. We
are not human beings born for a spiritual experience.
This is the Age of Aquarius, and all the past has to confront the
future. Man will become wise, intuitive, and conscious to find the
difference between gossip and gospel.
It is my understanding and my prayer that these teachings and
these practices may awaken the dormant soul to give the
individual happiness, which is his and her birthright in the
social, psychological, physical, and spiritual world.
These teachings are a part of the Golden Chain and belong to
Guru Ram Das, the Lord of Miracles and Saint
who protects all the needy with His merciful deeds.*

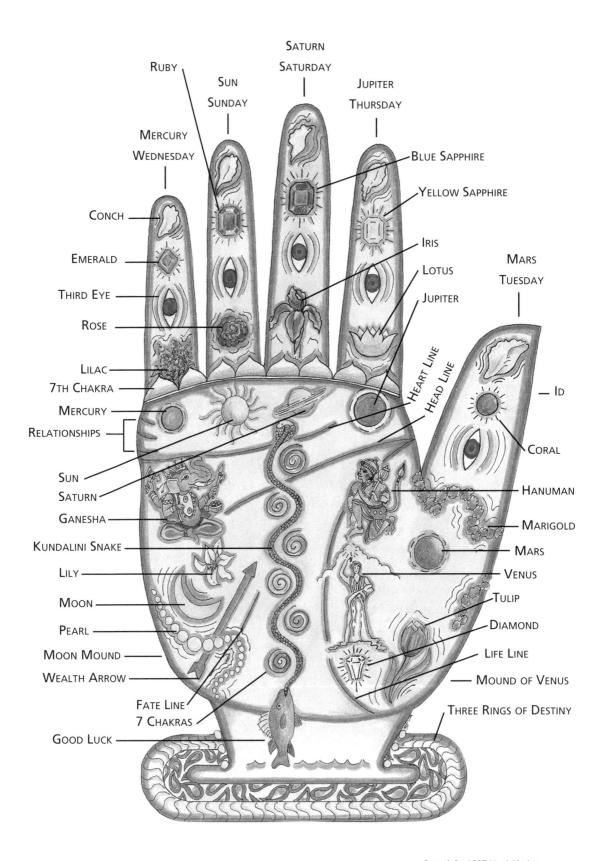

The Hand of the Cosmos

The Hand of the Cosmos was presented by Yogi Bhajan, Ph.D., for The Master's Touch, and represents the divine shield of protection. The placement of the symbols is very precise. Each portrays specific qualities and aspects of life associated with the body, mind, and soul.

Conch—*Totality, Flow of Life*
Third Eye—*Intuition, Wisdom*

Mercury—*Communication*
Emerald—*Prosperity*
Lilac—*Sweetness*

Sun—*Life*
Ruby—*Sun*
Rose—*Romance*

Saturn—*Purity, Knowledge, Piety*
Blue Sapphire—*Saturn*
Iris—*Purity*

Jupiter—*Knowledge, Grace, Wealth*
Yellow Sapphire—*Jupiter*
Lotus—*Purity*

Mars—*Lord of Victory, Happiness*
Id—*Binding Factor of Life:
Soul, Body & Mind*
Coral (reddish)—*Mars*
Marigold—*Victory, Rejoicing*
Mound of Venus—*Love*
Venus—*Love*
Tulip—*Creative Power,
Opens Up Progress, Expansion*
Diamond—*Love*

Moon Mound—*Mind, Thoughts,
Strategy, Planning, Fantasy, Fears*
Pearl—*Communication*
Moon—*Pearl*
Lily—*Communication*
Ganesha—*Success*
Hanuman—*Lord of Strength*
Kundalini Snake—*Central
Power of the Universe, Existence*
Heart Line—*Kindness,
Compassion, Caring*
Head Line—*Strength of
Direction of the Mind*
Life Line—*Length of Life Span,
Breath or Years*
Fate Line—*Challenges to be met*
Relationships—
Social/Sexual/Sensual Interaction
Seven Chakras—
Seven Energy Centers
Seventh Chakra—*The Tenth Gate*
Wealth Arrow—*Prosperity*
Three Rings of Destiny—
*We don't exist without these: Life
(Courage), Love (Prosperity), and
Happiness (Compassion)*

We would like to acknowledge the many teachers and support staff who shared the teachings at these first two Master's Touch courses through lectures, demonstrations, classes, and seva.
The following teachers conducted classes that went towards Level I KRI Teacher Training Certification:
Gurucharan Singh Khalsa, Ph.D.
Guru Dass Singh Khalsa
Satya Singh Khalsa

⊚ About the Author

T hroughout recorded history, a handful of spiritual giants has arisen as dynamic catalysts for the evolution of human consciousness. Their lives, their revolutionary teachings, their very presence on the planet has accelerated the process of millions of souls. Such a Master, a Teacher of teachers, is Yogi Bhajan.

When he arrived in the United States in December of 1968, Yogi Bhajan stated his mission quite clearly. He said, "I have come to create Teachers, not to gather disciples." Determined to train leaders and teachers with the power to heal, uplift, and inspire humanity, he taught Kundalini Yoga openly to the public, breaking the tradition of secrecy which had surrounded it for centuries.

At this writing (1997) he has not only created thousands of Kundalini Yoga Teachers throughout the world, but also an entire sub-culture within the mainstream population has evolved who practice his teachings. It is called "3HO," an acronym for The Healthy, Happy, Holy Organization which he founded. Based on his first principle, "Happiness is your birthright," hundreds of thousands of men, women, and children from many different backgrounds have applied the technology of Kundalini Yoga and have experienced a way to live drug-free, healthy, balanced, happy, and successful lives.

Poet, philosopher, seer, sage, saint, healer, religious leader, counselor, artist, author, lecturer, and even an excellent cook, Yogi Bhajan is always first and foremost a Teacher. He has published over 30 books and his teachings are published in over 200 other books and videos. He holds a Ph.D. in the psychology of communication (1980).

He has created and continues to be the driving force behind 19 corporations which all espouse the same principles he teaches for personal growth. These businesses offer services including computer systems, security, counseling, and a mail order catalog. They also offer a wide array of health food products, including cereals, teas, herbal remedies, and massage oils which are based on formulas he developed.

Since 1969, he has continued to teach and carry his message of hope and inspiration around the world reaching people in all walks of life. Mentor to statesmen, politicians and CEOs; confidante of religious leaders, media personalities, and simple seekers, his motto, printed on the back of his calling card is, "If you can't see God in all, you can't see God at all."

His penetrating insight, infinite compassion, tireless service, and loving compassion immediately endeared him to the eager souls who flocked to his Kundalini Yoga classes in the late 1960s and early 1970s. His fiery determination to awaken their souls, and to teach them to never settle for less than the best within themselves, created a powerful impact. He taught people how to access their intuitive awareness, how to experience higher consciousness without drugs, and how to build a future for themselves and their families. In 1973, he founded 3HO SuperHealth^{SM} the only holistic substance abuse treatment program of its kind, accredited by the Joint Commission on Accreditation of Healthcare Organizations.

Yogi Bhajan is an outspoken champion for the grace and dignity of all women. In 1970, he initiated the Grace of God Movement of the Women of America (GGMWA). In his classes, and since 1974 during his annual summer camp for women, he challenges women to accept their independent roles as women. He educates women on the meaning of their unique identity and how it can best serve them and their relationships to their families and careers. He teaches them how to take responsibility to lead, uplift, and heal through their grace and power.

In 1971, the leaders of his own Sikh faith honored him with the title "Siri Singh Sahib," and bestowed upon him the role of Chief Religious and Administrative Authority for Sikh Dharma of the Western Hemisphere, entrusting him with the responsibility to establish the Sikh Ministry in the West.

His uncompromising call to his contemporaries to break out of the self-limiting concept of separatism and move forward with openness and love for all, has moved him always to meet with religious and spiritual leaders to promote world peace. He has served in the World Parliament of Religions and is co-president and host of Human Unity Conferences. He founded International Peace Prayer Day (1983) which he hosts annually in June in Espanola, New Mexico (USA). He was awarded the Peace Abbey Courage of Conscious Award in Massachusetts in 1995.

Yogi Bhajan was born Harbhajan Singh Puri on August 26, 1929, in India. During his childhood he learned from his wise and saintly grandfather, who sent him to a Spiritual Teacher when he was 7 years old. At the age of 16 1/2 he mastered Kundalini Yoga under the unrelenting tutelage of the great Master Sant Hazara Singh.

He was a teenager during the partition of India in 1947. When his village became part of Pakistan, he was put in charge of leading over a thousand people to safety in Delhi, through a country in tremendous upheaval.

After settling his family in Delhi, he attended Punjab University where he received his Master's degree in Economics and was a champion debater and star athlete. He served the Government of India in the Tax and Customs division until he came to the West.

He has been married to Dr. Bibiji Inderjit Kaur since 1953, is the father of three children, and has five grandchildren.

Yogi Bhajan has gone from riches to rags and back during his life. As a yogi, and not affected by the pair of opposites, he lives in his own majesty, affirming with absolute conviction that everything belongs to God and Guru, and we all are simply the caretakers. Currently making New Mexico his primary residence, he is at home in all circumstances and with all people, always sharing, with love and humor, the technology of how to live in the Age of Aquarius as elevated and radiant, happy and healthy human beings.

Preface

T his book contains the lectures and meditations Yogi Bhajan taught during his Master's Touch courses in July 1996, in Espanola, New Mexico and in April 1997, in Assisi, Italy. They are presented here as a resource for all people on a spiritual path looking to open new doors, to stretch or challenge themselves. Yogi Bhajan explains in The Master's Touch lectures the importance of spiritual discipline in facing the challenges of life. And most of all, he sets the blueprint of what it means to be a true and sacred spiritual teacher for this New Age, the Age of Aquarius.

In the West, the understanding of a Master and the relationship between a Master and student is generally not understood. It is limited to what is seen on television or in the movies, which does not accurately convey this ancient, sacred, and in many cultures essential relationship for spiritual growth. In the West, the term "Master" is loosely applied to indicate anyone of genius who has become so adept at a particular art form or skill that no one can equal him or her; a master craftsman, a chess master, an orchestra maestro. However, in Oriental cultures, there is a specific tradition of Masters in the art and science of consciousness, that is, Masters of the art of life itself!

Such a Master is not a philosopher or a preacher. He or she is a Teacher of Teachers, a transmitter of the same mastery he or she has achieved. A Master has experienced and integrated into his or her consciousness that which gives clarity, depth, and insight, so the teachings can have a profound effect.

The relationship between a Master and a student is like that of a chisel and a stone in the hands of a master craftsman. At first the sparks fly, but that friction releases the potential for the work of art contained within the stone.

When one studies with a Master, the dimensions of life can change dramatically as the individual accelerates to new levels of self-awareness and fulfillment. That transformation is what the students experienced in the Master's Touch courses.

Unlike other eastern traditions, in the lineage of Kundalini Yoga, the Golden Chain or connection to the Teacher is not established by initiation. Yogi Bhajan has explained that students of Kundalini Yoga must initiate themselves by adhering to the discipline and practice of the technology. Yet, as a Master of Kundalini Yoga, he has always made himself available and accessible to students to guide them to achieve the level of commitment necessary for their growth.

While much time was devoted to studies of Kundalini Yoga exercises, including breathing techniques (pranayam) and mantra, the true heart of these courses lay in the lectures and meditations taught personally by the Master of Kundalini Yoga, Yogi Bhajan. In these lectures, for two to three hours every day, he spoke about life, about yoga, and about teaching in such a direct and profoundly penetrating way that each person felt transformed. His words carried a special gift; they touched the psyche and soul of each one, bringing light, insight, and elevation of the spirit.

True spirituality, true awareness, is not something that can be taught. It is grace that ultimately merges the consciousness of the student with that of the Teacher. It was that grace that was felt.

Yogi Bhajan may well be remembered as one of the greatest Teachers of all time, and certainly of modern times. He teaches in the spirit of a long and sacred tradition of Teachers, The Golden Chain, with the deepest reverence for his own Master, who taught him over 50 years ago in India. As a young man Yogi Bhajan began to study with Master Sant Hazara Singh along with 252 other students. After three months there were 75 remaining. By the end of the rigorous training, only he and two other students were left.

The job of the Teacher is to challenge the student to establish his or her own experience with their soul. This is often not a comfortable process because facets of the student's personality and ego can interfere. The Master's job is not to be kind or to coddle. As Yogi Bhajan explained, the Teacher must poke the ego, provoke it into a reaction, confront it with its own limits, and then, most importantly, elevate it. Only a true Master can guide the student all the way through this process, because he has been through the experience himself. It is the ultimate act of compassion and selflessness for a Master to create another Master.

That is what Yogi Bhajan is all about. That is what The Master's Touch is all about.

Guidelines for the Use of the Mantra/Music Tapes

The use of mantra and rhythm is an essential part of the practice of Kundalini Yoga meditations. A listing of all tapes referred to in this book is available on pages 317-319. Where necessary, a rhythm has been indicated which can be used when a particular tape is not available. Sources for all tapes are listed on page 323.

Table of Contents

Assisi Lectures

The Master's Touch

Espanola Lectures

July 1996

The Teachers Oath

I am not a Woman
I am not a Man
I am not a Person
I am not Myself
I am a Teacher.

What is Happiness?

The Age of Aquarius is coming our way. Emptiness,
insanity, and pain shall be everybody's affair.
They shall come to you. As insane as they are, if you
do not take away their pain, and instead you sit in
judgment, you are wrong people.

What is happiness? Come on now, you are all Teachers. What is it? You are healthy, that's why you are here. Happy, you are not. That I know. You are holy because you have nine holes. Everybody's holes are working, is that true? Happy you are not. You can never be happy. Happiness has one condition. It has payment. Take my word for it— Almighty God may be with you, but you shall not be happy if you do not know the formula for happiness.

The known formula for happiness is: Commitment will give you character. That will give you dignity. That will give you divinity. That will give you grace. That will give you the power to sacrifice. Then you'll feel achieved, and you'll be happy. Correct? Does anybody know anything other than that?

But we want instant happiness. How to get through this? Hey, come on. We are all friends. Let us participate. Why are you looking at me, have I got horns? One day I had to learn it, too. But unfortunately I was seven years old. I never stopped learning. So what is the principle of happiness, folks?

Student: Happiness is connecting and knowing the word *"sat."*

YB: That's the easy way out. *(Everyone laughs.)* What is happiness? Go ahead.

S: When the river joins the ocean.

YB: It is called completion, because it'll start coming out as the clouds again. Very good thought. In the Nirvana sutra, it is the perfect thought—it is truth. But it is Piscean. Next?

S: Wake up at three.

YB: Wake up at three, and you have conquered your own death. That's good. Sounds right. Then when you wake up at three, you have the day to yourself, you are preparing time, you are in your own solitude. Solitude makes your attitude known to you. Solitude makes the altitude known to you, and you become a conqueror. That's an incentive. Very good incentive, but not all.

S: Awareness.

YB: Awareness, my dear girl, of what? This is the Infinite world. Nobody will ever know what is what.

S: Of my own Infinity.

The known formula for happiness is:
Commitment will give you character.
That will give you dignity.
That will give you divinity.
That will give you grace.
That will give you the power to
sacrifice. Then you'll feel achieved,
and you'll be happy. Correct?
Does anybody know anything
other than that?

YB: Your Infinity is you when you stop thinking. Have you stopped thinking? That's the end of it. Awareness takes these things away from you: thinking, reason, logic, argument, fantasies, planning, scheming, knowing, and, worrying. These nine things must go before you can say that you are on the path of awareness. Do you know why? Don't you know? God, this little thing you don't even know? You come for a teacher's course? Because the One who rotates the Earth can take care of your routine. These nine things you do are unwanted. They only satisfy your ego. Where there is ego, there is no amigo.

So we're talking about happiness. What is the principle of happiness? We started 3HO: Healthy, Happy, Holy. Right? Healthy you are, one way or the other. As long as you are not in the graveyard pit, you are okay. Holy you are. Anybody who has nine holes and controls what comes in and goes out is holy. But happy? What is the definition of being happy?

S: To experience that me and God are One.

YB: That's always one, experience what? You don't believe it. You are always One with God. Without God you are not in your nucleus, you can't even breathe. That's the fight between an organic and an inorganic religion. Organically we are all divine. Duality is created by our identity, not by our Infinity. By Infinity you are all divine. There's absolutely no reason to see anybody as wrong. What is wrong? There cannot be anything wrong. Wrong and right is our judgment. Judgment is wrong to begin with. What is wrong, then? Go ahead. Keep talking.

S: There's a difference between the reality that is true, and....

YB: Reality which has no royalty is not reality. And royalty which does not have forgiveness has no right to exist. That existence which does not have discipline cannot deliver. That deliverance is the measurement of personal happiness, and that needs discipline in every facet of life, not facts of life.

S: Happiness is the true intention of serving each other.

YB: Intention doesn't count on this planet.

S: Then it's the act of serving each other.

YB: *(Shakes his head "no.")* Within your discipline, whether you serve or you de-serve, within your discipline you live or you don't live, within your discipline you eat or you don't eat, within your discipline you are the discipline. If you are master of that discipline, which is you, you are all God. There's no other.

ਆਦਿ ਪੂਰਨ ਮਧਿ ਪੂਰਨ ਅੰਤਿ ਪੂਰਨ ਪਰਮੇਸੁਰਹ ॥
Aad pooran mudh pooran ant pooran parmesureh
-Guru Arjan, *Siri Guru Granth Sahib,* page 705
The Transcendent Lord pervaded in the beginning, pervades in the middle,
and will pervade in the end.

In the beginning you are you, in the middle you are you, in the end you are God. There's nothing else. If you can't close your eyes, you can't open your eyes, that's the end of the eyes. There's nothing to it. Nothing was, nothing is, nothing shall be.

For thousands of years the Piscean Age has lied to us to make us find God, while they *knew* that we *are* gods. Now we cannot take even two days to remember we are gods.

Longitude and latitude are given to everybody. Altitude and attitude are given by Kundalini Yoga. When the spiral rises to penetrate through all the chakras, the man knows he's Brahm. That's why they say Kundalini Yoga is dangerous. It's dangerous because it takes away from man the ability to be exploited by another man. And for some, life without exploitation has no juice. "Well, what is the use if I can't exploit him, if I can't exploit her. What am I doing?" There has to be exploitation somewhere. "I can't accept this child. I need my hook, my control, my thing. This child must agree I'm great and she's not great." Right? Isn't it true? "Who knows, this child tomorrow may be the greatest of all greats, and I'll not be."

When you see somebody you see the clouds, and you judge the sun, "It's a cloudy day." Then after five minutes it's so bright and beautiful. What happened to the clouds? They are gone. The One who has created you is a Perfect Lord and He cannot create imperfect. That's the Aquarian truth which you have to believe. Everything is subject to His Will. Are you willing to live that truth? Well, then what about your will? Answer me. If everything is God's Will, then what about your will?

S: Is it truly my will and my soul which are in conflict?

YB: Your truly soul and your truly will is to watch out for God's Will. You are on the driver's seat. Watch the lane, and the freeway, and the signs, and the exit, and the number, and the direction. Therefore, you must have a driver's license, and that's called discipline.

I tell all the Sikhs, "Don't read this *Ek Ong Kaar* if you do not know how to drive your own car." Your car is being the body in the self, and you are the driver. You are not the soul, you are not the mind, you are not the body. You are the essence of it. Learn this. You can redeem your soul or you can totally destroy it.

S: I find when I use my will, I run into all the crashes and the ups and downs....

YB: No, no, your will was not given for that. I didn't give you ten dollars to spend on you. I said, "Do charity." God gave you your will to find God's Will. It's just like giving somebody ten dollars to do charity, not to eat it up on themselves. Somebody manufactured you, made you to be. You didn't come here by your will. You come here to find God's Will. That is the purpose we have forgotten.

I came to Canada with thirty-five dollars in my pocket; they are still there. They told me, "You can't live one day on that. You have to earn money, you have to learn driving...."

I said, "Why should I do anything? I served the government of India, I had everything. Now I'm going to serve God, I'm going to have to do everything? Forget it. I don't like demotions."

I didn't have clothes, I didn't have food, I didn't have any amenities on this Earth to survive in minus forty-five degrees centigrade temperatures. I lived. I survived. I said to Him, "Try your best. Test me out. If it makes you happy to give me nothing, have fun." That's when I wrote that poem, "One day the day shall come when all the glory shall be Thine."[1] Still I gave Him the credit. "People say it is yours, I shall deny, not mine." Read that poem, it's wonderful. It was written in those days when I used to put a newspaper on my feet to walk through the snow. I never gave up. The only word I have brought you, folks, is "Keep up." That's the trademark of Yogi Bhajan, Yogi "Bahan." Nobody has a title like mine: "The Garbage Cleaner of the United States."

I tell you today and I'll tell you tomorrow and I'll tell you every day: You have only one friend—you and your discipline which will give you all that you need. The rest are all promises. After studying every scripture of every religion and what I went through, I have found that there are three words: *sadhana, aradhana,* and *prabhupati. Sadhana* means discipline, *aradhana* means perfecting the discipline, and *prabhupati* means you will become the Lord Master of God Itself. Now, should I bring you any other news?

You think you are weak. You think you are handicapped. You think many things. That's what you think. But the first thing Nanak said was, "Think, think not. A hundred thousand thinkings won't make sense." *You* don't think. Your intellect thinks. Your intelligence never thinks. Intelligence can find an answer. Intellect thinks. You are insecure? Yeah, you are insecure. You are very insecure, because your intuition is not there. Your intuition will tell you what will happen tomorrow.

Hey, how much gasoline would it take to rotate this planet Earth? Though it is one of the littlest of all planets, and proportionately, it's not worth anything. In proportion to the universe it is thirty trillion into mega, multiplied by thirty million square into thirty million times square. Figure it out. That's why Guru Nanak said,

ਪਾਤਾਲਾ ਪਾਤਾਲ ਲਖ ਆਗਾਸਾ ਆਗਾਸ ॥
ਓੜਕ ਓੜਕ ਭਾਲਿ ਥਕੇ ਵੇਦ ਕਹਨਿ ਇਕ ਵਾਤ ॥
Paataalaa paataal lakh aagaasaa aagaas.
Orak orak bhaal thakay, ved kahen ik vaat.
-Guru Nanak, *Siri Guru Granth Sahib*, page 5 (from 22nd *pauree* of *Japji Sahib*)
There are nether worlds and more nether worlds below them and there are thousands of skies over them. The scriptures pronounce one conclusion: that people are tired of searching the limits and boundaries of God.

He said, "It's all lies." Some say it is the eighteenth region. This is endless. Infinity. Here is the biggest physicist in the world, and I gave her a formula yesterday. I said, "Figure it out." Did you figure it out?

S: No, Sir.

YB: Figure it out. You believe in Einstein, right, and his theory? This is the formula I gave you. Figure it out. Two Infinity into two square, two. One Infinity into one square, ten. That's the universe. Simple. My students two thousand years from now will understand all that I have taught. Not today. Today you are Piscean going into the Age of Aquarius. You are still insecure. You are worse than birds and fishes. Are they insecure? Have you seen any fish insecure? Have you met one? Really? Have you found a fish insecure? Or have you found a bird insecure?

There was a guy who didn't feel happy, and he had a terrible problem with me. He said, "Well, you are wrong. You teach this, you teach that. You teach Sikh Dharma."

I said, "What do I teach? I don't teach anything. The circumstances made it happen. We were the most innocent people. We were just 3HO and I was not doing anything. Why are you accusing me of that?"

He said, "Why not?"

I said, "What is your problem?"

He said, "I wanted to be your student, and I can't have hair, and I can't tie turban. This is in between me and you. I want to be your student."

I said, "You are not talking gracefully, therefore you're not my student. You do not know the manners of how to talk to a Teacher. You think a Teacher is a man."

He said, "If I have to accept you as my Teacher, then I have to accept you."

I said, "You have to accept what? I have two pounds of feces in there, there's a half a pound of urine there. You don't have to accept that. You have to only accept my wisdom and my caliber of technology in which I can make you a better person. Accepting me as a Teacher doesn't mean 'I am your Teacher, you are my slave.' Where did you learn that?"

Reality which has no royalty is not reality. Royalty which does not have forgiveness has no right to exist. That existence which does not have discipline cannot deliver. That deliverance is the measurement of personal happiness, and that needs discipline in every facet of life not facts of life.

"No, I have a problem with this."

I said, "What is your problem?"

"I don't want to have hair."

I said, "You shall not have it." Now he's bald and he's accusing me of having cursed him. I said, "Now it's very clean. Mr. Clean, like that character Kojak.

The fact is, it is not that whatever I say happens; I just let you know it is happening. Sometimes a trend can change, the weather can change, circumstances can change.

But everybody has intuition, and everybody through their development of intuition should know tomorrow so there'll be no sorrow. But what is in our way is our ego. "Who is he to tell me?" I am not *anybody* to tell you. I am your body which has gone a certain way to tell you there *is* a way. I'm not telling you anything.

The Age of Aquarius is coming our way. Emptiness, insanity, and pain shall be everybody's affair. People will like to hit walls to find out where they can go. They shall come to you. As insane as they are, if you do not take away their pain, and instead you sit in judgment, you are wrong people. That's why we wanted to teach you how to remain disciplined in the most undisciplined world. How to grow, to glow. How to serve, to be.

First, we identify ourselves: We are, we are. Second, our words should be such that they should cool down any fire, the desperation, the depression of the person. Third, we must have the power to uplift the soul and serve the person, to be graceful. And finally, we must stand pure.

Do you know the Oath of a Kundalini Yoga Teacher? Let's do it, and figure it out, then let us discuss it. You all do it, whether you are a woman or a man.

"I'm not a woman, I'm not a man, I'm not a person, I'm not myself. I am a Teacher."

After that oath, is there any question left? You might be thinking in the sense that, "What about my earnings, and what about my wife, and what about my...." Hey, everything fits the puzzle. You don't have to worry. There are two ways: One way is that you hustle and you swim and you go across. Or, you let things happen to you, and you are taken across in a luxury liner. It is up to you.

So don't cut life short. Life is a gift. Don't create a rift and don't drift. Be with life. Life doesn't give you morale, you give life morale. Life doesn't give you ethics, you give life ethics. Life doesn't give you manners, you give life manners. Life doesn't give you lies, you give life lies. Life didn't tell you what is truth, you make up truth. It's all wrong in your head. Nothing is wrong with your heart. Forget searching this, searching that, doing this, doing that. The time you waste in logic, reason, argument, fantasies, all that—that's a waste of happiness. Happiness is me and me within myself. Touch somebody—the magnetic field will change, the psyche will change. You don't have to do a thing. You don't have to say a word.

I went to Cancun. I hid in my room, I didn't want to do anything. The whole town knew that I was there. The whole town. There was a doorman who was a yoga student of one of our Teachers. He told the Teacher, the Teacher told everybody, everybody told everybody. It was supposed to be the most secret trip I ever took; I didn't tell anybody. But in a couple of hours the whole town knew. I had a wonderful experience. There were those shamanistic healers—that Aztec type? They did everything. They beat me, spit at me, put water on me. Oh, God, you can't imagine! They put herbs in me and everything. They rubbed eggs around me, and read the eggs. But I was so silent in the whole universe. I was telling God, "Well, thank you for creating this way of healing, too." Then I ended up healing them. I ended up fixing their spines and doing things. It was amazing to me.

And they said, "Yes, yes, you can't heal yourself, but you can heal us."

I said, "That's fine." How can one not be healed if one is lying down and ten people are massaging you, going, "Yogiji, Yogiji." After that, what is left after two hours? Where is disease? You can't even live in your body; they give it so much beating. They were spanking me with flowers, with those branches of herbs, and they were so strong that I had spots all over my body. It was a shock treatment. You go through it.

So one day, when you become Teachers, you'll be healers, you'll be great, you will know all the truth, you will have all the wisdom and intuition. But one thing you have to have more than anything else, you have to be you. Nothing less than you will work. You minus ego is always you. You with your ego is always not you. "I am because I am." "I am because in the time and space I am." "I am not by myself." Five and a half billion souls in human bodies are around me, and there is nothing like me. So you have to deal with all that is nothing like you. You are already in the shape of an alien, to the known self of you.

How many of you are here? Each of you here is each different. In this different world, all of you are one. That's what you have come to learn. We are here for two weeks. I was told to entertain you. *(Ed: It had been suggested that Yogi Bhajan give a welcoming dinner party at the Ranch pool.)* And I said, "Hell, I'm not going to teach this course. Send them back. Refund their money and let them go home. I have twenty-seven years of insults which I have borne. I have not come here to collect students and be appreciated." The relationship between you and me is like granite stone and a hammer and a chisel. Anytime you get offended, you do not like me, you can leave. You are not welcome. Because there is no nonsense which should make sense to you, and there's no sense which should be nonsense to you. That's what you have come here to learn.

Man has to be trained. This is our first course. This is how we are going to train you. We are going to train you that in every confrontation, head on, you take the altitude. The moment you take altitude, things become little. You are looking for big things. But you have come here not to look for big things; you have come here to become big. So big, soooo big, that you cover everything, that you cannot say "no." So big, like sunshine, you can't say, "I'll shine on this, I won't shine on that." No.

Do you understand the beauty of when somebody said to me, "You idiot, you rotten egg. What you are doing in America?"

I said, "I am here."

"But what are you doing?"

I said, "I am listening to your abuse."

"What do you mean?"

I said, "I am understanding it. You are angry and abusive."

"Are you going to do something about it?"

I said, "Nothing. It's not worth it. I won't do it. You can do a little more. It'll be fine."

"You are provoking me."

I said, "No, I'm not provoking you. But I just want to tell you I am very combat trained. I just want to let you know."

And my student moved.

"No," I said, "It's between me and him. He's angry and abusive. Let him have the fun. Let him have the maximum. I am very well trained. I can be very peaceful, and nobody will support me in this."

This was at the University of California at Berkeley. "You're not afraid of the knife?"

I said, "No, I wear it. What do you mean, 'afraid of it?' I'm not afraid of anything. I just enjoy." I said, "Abuse, abuse, abuse, abuse. Go ahead. Provoke me."

"You're not going to be provoked?"

I said, "Why should I get provoked? Insanity is a bewitchment, and it's an enjoyment in itself. It's entertainment. Why not see the entertainment? It's free. Go ahead," I said, "keep on abusing."

Finally he got tired. He sat down, he bowed. I said, "This won't work, either. Tell me why you're angry."

He said, "You're from India?"

I said, "Hope so."

"You came to the University of California at Berkeley. Everybody wants to come to class. They didn't let me come to your class. I want to hear you. I heard you. You are very wise but I can't be your student. I understand you hate people."

I said, "Wow, everything is one-way traffic? You have to listen to me?"

"What?"

I said, "I don't know how to hate you, at least that I confirm. You can abuse as much as you want. It's very nice of you. And if you attack me with this knife, I'll snatch this knife from your hand, and give it back to you. I like this knife. It's very good. If you allow me, I can keep it."

Longitude and latitude are given to everybody. Altitude and attitude are given by Kundalini Yoga. When the spiral rises to penetrate through all the chakras, the man knows he's Brahm. That's why they say Kundalini Yoga is dangerous. It's dangerous because it takes away from man the ability to be exploited by another man.

I ended up with the knife. I still have it.

You must understand, if your presence doesn't work, nothing works. Understand this very clearly. The first principle is: If your presence doesn't work, nothing works. Number two: If you are not you, nothing works. If within three sentences you cannot prove that you work, then nothing will work. In three sentences. You have a limit of only three sentences. And if you cannot, within three sentences win the trust of another person, nothing works. If in the first sentence you cannot make the person understand you are wise and loving, nothing works. Don't look at the situation. Look at yourself. *You* are working. It is your situation and you are in command of you. You have nothing else to worry about. Once you are you, all will be around you, as you want. That's the catch-22.

Was I loud enough? Did you hear it? Will you remember it? Don't sell your soul. The body is given a structure. Don't sell your body. The mind is given to you as a servant. Don't let it make you a yo-yo. Your mind is your servant, your body is your vehicle, and your soul is your residence. Do not make yourself cheap, do not live like a creep, and do not weep. If God puts you into bad environments, into the worst environments, into tragic environments, into horrible environments, all calamities, insult, tragedy, it's just for you to face and win it.

And that's only the first sound: *"Waah."* You know you chant *"Waa-Hay Guroo?"* It's the first sound: *"Waah." "Waah,* well God, ha ha. Have fun!"

You know how to find God? What you do is you go to a movie, buy your popcorn, take your Diet Coke, right? And you see them shooting, running, horseback riding, sex-ing and x-ing, and everything—just enjoy your hour and a half. Come out and you wasted seven bucks. You pay seven dollars to pass time. One thing about humans is they can't pass time within themselves. But the day you will learn to pass time within yourself, you will have a mastery over time, and time shall serve you. Then you are the master. That's the challenge to the human.

Now you can ask me a few questions so I can quit.

S: You mentioned about discipline. Even with the best intentions and practice, would it be sufficient to take us through the journey, or do we need grace, as well?

YB: Without grace there is no discipline, and discipline means that you keep your grace in the most disgraceful environments. Not having the most disgraceful environments is no discipline. Calamity is to set the climate. Tragedy is to set the target. Your fear is your enemy, not your soul or strength.

You are afraid of your own fear. It tells you, "Uh oh. Uh oh. Uh oh." Do you know how many people ask me every day what to do?

The first thing the person who organized this program told me was, "Oh, it will feel good. Let us give them a dinner, and let them intermingle." She said something like that.

I didn't want to tell this here, because I'm a holy man, but I said, "Throw them out in the river. We have asked them, 'trust, come, we'll make you a teacher.' What are we going to do? Entertain them? Isn't it a lie to start with?

"I'm not Swami-ji and this ji and that ji. I'm going to tell them that I'm going to roast them alive."

I'm not that kind. My kindness is your death. My kindness means you'll never be a teacher. Never. My affection is that I totally carve you out, and you cannot get defeated by time. I am no enemy. Your enemy is your time and space. If I don't make you ride above time and space, I have failed, not you. You came, you paid, you have done your job. Now it is your stamina, whether you can stand it or not. That's a different story.

I am combat-trained. I know how to eat ego for breakfast, lunch, and dinner. And once the man's ego is gone, everything left is divine. There's no duality. Ego creates duality, and you cannot be combating time and space; you will always have an argument with yourself.

What is the way out? You can make it. The way out is either slowly suffer the rest of your life, or suffer once in a while and get out of all this.

You know, Kundalini Yoga does not take very long—three minutes maximum, or eleven minutes, or sixty-two minutes. It creates in the brain the imprint of evaluation, that there is no pain but achievement. And once the mind is trained to achieve, you can reach Infinity.

Everybody wants a disciple. It's good, people give gifts, say "hello," and touch your feet. It looks cozy. Don't we think so? Plus pretty girls and (makes kissing sounds). It's quite a lot of temptation. There's so much. But what if, in the end, the person dies creating not one teacher? What a death. Discontinued. Swami-ji So-and-So—discontinued. You know on a computer it says, "erased." That's not what you are here for. That's not what life is. That's not reality, that's not truth. Your touch must produce, your one touch must produce zero into ten. That's a law. That's why for twenty-seven years I have been lying low and letting it go as it is, earning my own bread, doing my businesses, living like a normal person. Finally, it's my time to go, so in the few years I have left, I thought I may just train teachers, as somebody trained me. This is not training for you to become popular. I owe this to the one who trained me. That is the intention, if you want to know the intention. You pay back what you get. Nothing is free.

Well, when I went to see my teacher, I had fifty horsemen, horses, tents. You know, I was a prince. When I got there, I was given one bunker bed, one bucket of lime, and there was a note: "Your job is to keep the outhouses clean. Don't come with baggage and paraphernalia. You have come here for self. Be your self." I learned it. My teacher never had to repeat it afterwards. I was always myself.

When you are yourself, people will ask your advice, they ask your counsel, they love you, they need you. Because always self needs self. Everything can be bought and sold, other than self. Understood?

Are we developing an understanding? Do you understand why you are here? Mind you, we have two weeks only. Time is still on us, and within those two weeks we have to deliver to ourselves the first concept: "I am, I am, doesn't matter what." This you normally forget. That is the first mistake of a man born on this Earth: they do not remember that God created them, and they did not create themselves; and that everything for them from birth to death is created. Simply you have to harvest it. All the time you waste in logic, argument, reason, fantasies, emotion, commotion, you don't reach the destination. That destination is where your

I tell you today, I'll tell you tomorrow, and I'll tell you every day: You have only one friend— you and your discipline which will give you all that you need. The rest are all promises.

Creator has created for you peace, tranquillity, grace, wealth, health, happiness.

You know these Shamans who were working on me? It was not those people, or what they believe, or what they said. God, it was their innocence. They were so innocent. When I thanked them in the end, you know what they told me? "Oh, our Lord God has given us an honor to allow us to work on you." They were so happy. You are talking about happiness? They were so happy.

So we have these two weeks. We'll sit down and discuss, and if anybody has an objection, don't just pack up and go, confront me and then go. The course is not going to be very sweet and soft. Let me show you that. So at least it's a human courtesy that you have come all the way. Sometimes we'll hit your ego so badly that you will be hurting. There will be no hurt, but that's the way it feels. I know, because I have gone through it myself. So if you feel bad or feel hurt or feel negative, or feel you cannot take it, please come directly and ask me those questions. That's your right. But don't be a cheat. Self-cheating is the main thing we do. Those are the lies we live. When we cannot confront something, we escape.

When I joined my first class we were 252 people. Three months later we were only seventy-two. But I said, "Heck. I'm going to learn, doesn't matter what."

One day somebody said, "Don't you think it's very painful?"

I said, "What? Death, what does that matter? If this is the way they kill me, I'll die, I'll be fine. At least I'll keep learning. I'm not going to go away." And that's why I brought America a new word, "Keep up. You'll be kept up." That needs self-discipline.

I give you a thought today: When a negative thought hits you, that is positive, you are lucky. Hit it with a positive thought—you are the best. One day I was caught in between two pressures. There was one big big thing with a wheel and the other I was holding. If I did not hold it properly and that wheel released, that big pole would hit my neck in the back, and my head would roll about fifty feet. The impact was very well calculated. I was stuck. I said to myself, "It's a very ungraceful situation, but it's a graceful way of dying. Hallelujah. So be it." I just pushed, and on the pressure it went about one foot down; with that I went, and that pole went over me, and I looked at that movement... "Wow!" At that moment it was between me and my death, the only thing which kept me alive was me. And that is what people call "God."

For two thousand years you have been told you have to find God. You are not going to believe me in one minute that you are God. There's no other God. The problem is, you are right or wrong, that doesn't matter. God is God. In the Piscean Age we have been told not to accept God one hundred percent. We only accept a good God. Good guys and good God, right? What about bad guys and bad God? That belongs to us, too. That's where Kundalini Yoga says, *"ida* and *pingala,* and accepting is *shushmanaa."* If you want to know the most secret thing, *ida, pingala,* and *shushmanaa*—positive, negative, and neutral.

(See pages 15-16 for details of the following meditations.)

Sit on your heels. Hurry up! Don't waste too much time.

If you are in balance, your aura will change. Balance it. Let your shoulders carry the weight, not your butt. Hold these hands tight, like steel. Hey, this little thing can put you miles up in the Heavens. With that strength of both hands, left and right, balance your shoulders and carry the spine. Tighten the spine. Put tremendous pressure on your hands from the elbow to the balance, and with that power lift your shoulders. With the shoulders lift your muscles, and with those muscles, lift your spine. Go!

Your breath will start going berserk in one minute if you do it right. The maximum a person in the world has stood is eleven minutes. Maximum. Come on. Prove to yourself you can balance yourself. Automatically the breath will become very imperatively harsh. Even so, do it.

Now close your eyes and concentrate. Tight. Concentrate. Unto God, unto God, unto God, unto God I dwell. In God I dwell. Tighter. My children, tomorrow will come at your feet. Make them good today. You have to lead the Aquarian Age. Make yourself great today. Tighter.

You have one more minute to go. You can change your whole brain, the gray matter, your entire nervous system, and your entire spinal column. Go, for God's sake! One more minute. Tighter on yourself! Your body will shake, your breath will be miserable. That's all understood. That comes on the way. There's nothing wrong. Now I happen to be here, so let us do it! It is you, it is all you. Higher, higher, higher. Go! Go, Go! Forget about breathing, forget about the body, forget about shaking. Who cares? Go. Eat pizza. I told you not to eat too much. Do it now. Put the hands on each other and press hard.

This is one of the best ways for your navel point to adjust. Pressure. You have exactly fifteen seconds. Last try. Pressure, pressure, pressure. Holy ghost come in, come in, come in, holy ghost, come in. Come in holy ghost. Come in.

Breathe in deep. Hold tight. Pull your navel in now folks, as much as you can. At the count of sixteen, let it go. One, two, three, four, five, six, seven, eight, nine, ten, eleven, twelve, thirteen, fourteen, fifteen, sixteen. Go. You don't need much time to practice a lot of things. You want reincarnation standardized into the divine of nirvana? Do this exercise for eleven minutes, you'll have it all. You will be *sattvic* with all. Everything will be tuned in.

Do you feel comfortable? Now you have to feel a little uncomfortable. Take this up here at the Mercury point. Because your words are not heard by another person. Nobody hears what you say. You think they hear it, right? They don't. Ask them to repeat it right there. They can't.

Move the entire spine. Clear your ears-nose-throat with this force. This force should be enough to clear you. Force it, force it, force it. It's for you. The lower back will become loose, and you will lose all your back pain or possibility of it. It's a very good exercise. It keeps a person young. The Mercury mound must be touched. Move, move. It's a very jumping exercise. Come on, folks. What is this? Hey, you guys. Philosophers, the insane, and lovers belong in the same category. Remember that? It's called "one-pointedness," and love of life that you want to save the world tomorrow. That is the project. Fast, heavy, don't let the thumb slip from the mound of Mercury.

Now stretch your hands up, please. Open up your five fingers like antennae. Inhale deep. Take the eternal sound. It is not something which Sikhs occupy or Jews don't know about. Inhale deep. "*Saaaaaaaaaaat Naam.*" Inhale again. Go. Relax.

"Saa" means totality. "Saa" means Infinity. This is the first sound with which God created the universe. Not this little planet ping-pong ball called Earth—the whole universe. If you reach the stage of the ultimate-seeing God, and you become God's man, this is what you will see: impulse playing, dancing, between itself; and that impulse is by itself, so nobody's the Creator. Creator is being its own Creator. So it's a continuous impulse. It is a 3-1/2 cycle psyche which exists in an absolute golden and blue color. And it creates the projection, progressive progression of white and white and white. That's how it is. Some days are not white. The progression is white. Daylight is not white—progression is white. So that is the "Saa-saa."

"Taa" means life. So when you say "Saaaaaa...," "Taa" is the middle—life. And then you say "Naam." This mantra can give you Heaven and Earth in balance, this one word "Saat Naam."

Like "Om." "Om" cannot be chanted, cannot be spoken. It's not a spoken word. "Omm." I'm not doing it right now. One blow and your whole being (YB points to his 10th gate, and circles the top of his head with his finger) can be elevated to as it should be.

So you have come here to learn. Please go from here learned. Don't come here Mr. So-and-So or Miss So-and-So, or Ms. So-and-So. Don't come here as students or Teachers. Come here to learn and go back learned, come back again to learn more, and go back to teach more. That is what we want. A Teacher is God's responsibility. You all love God, I know. But God loves Teachers, that I know, too. He takes care of me so well, you can't believe it. You'll love it.

People ask me, "Why do you wear jewelry?"

"Why not? I have many very rich children. Why not?" Why not? There's no ego involved. They give me gifts. I do P.R. for them. That's okay. That's a good bargain. But you will take nothing with you, except good will. And good will is nothing but God's Will. People bring me presents. What does it take? It takes a long time. I have to sit before the altar and pray and pray for their prosperity. It's constant prayer, which is your constant power, and your heart chants all the time. Your breath chants all the time. You chant all the time. Your ten trillion cells, your thirty trillion living, dancing cells, and your life term is one breath. It comes. Aa-dum. "Adam" you call him. "Aa-dum." "Aa" means come. "Dum" means breath. "Humeh Hum Brahm Hum"—same thing.

"Eve" is "My Havaah." "Mother air," which carries the prana to you. These are fundamentals. Adam loved Eve and we became creation, right? Thanks to their snake and to the apple, or whatever that was. Otherwise, we would have been sitting right there. Oh my God, two people sitting in close environments. Solitary confinement. Unbelievable. Adam was very wise; he ate the apple. Thanks to Adam we are all here. And thanks to you I am here today, otherwise I would have been running around in Mexico, somewhere else. They actually planned it. They wanted to kidnap me for another week. I said, "No, no. I have to go back. I promised."

I hope you will enjoy your stay and the torture which comes with it, and that you will be strong, brave, and courageous. And remember what I say, "It isn't the life that matters, it's the courage you bring to it." Do not give up courage, you will always win. Do not give up hope, you will always have a scope in life. Do not give yourself, and God will always be there in you. Don't pull down the shutters of hopelessness, and discourage yourself. God doesn't dwell outside of you. In God you dwell.

Many of you have received correspondence from me. There is a flag under Siri Singh Sahib's seal which says, "In God I Dwell." That is a message for you, and you have come here to be trained in two weeks so you can go back dwelling in Almighty God. How can you go wrong?

Rejuvenating Meditation to Make You Sattvic (Pure)

Mudra: Sit on your heels, raise your arms up to shoulder level and extend them straight out in front of you. Bend the elbows and bring the forearms parallel to your body, overlapping them in front of your chest, right arm lying flat on top of the left. Make sure the palms are flat and face down. The right palm will be lying flat on top of the left forearm, near the bend in the elbow.

Mantra: Unspecified.

Breath: The breath will become automatically harsh.

Eyes: Closed.

Time: Maximum time is 11 minutes. Done in class for 3-1/2 minutes.

End: Inhale deep, hold the arm position tight as you pull in tightly on your navel point. Hold the breath in for 25 seconds. Exhale. Relax.

Comments/Effects: When you sit on your heels, make sure the shoulders are carrying the weight, not the buttocks. Balance your shoulders and carry the spine. If you are in balance, your aura will change.

Hold the hands and arms tight like steel. Put a tremendous pressure on the area from the hands to the elbows, and tighten and lift your spine from this pressure. The heavy pressure on the arms and hands tends to lift the shoulders, which lift the muscles, and in turn lift the spine. Keep the pressure and keep lifting higher and higher.

This posture is one of the best ways to adjust your navel point. Through this exercise, you can change the gray matter in your brain, entire nervous system, and spinal column.

If you want to experience reincarnation into nirvana, do this meditation for 11 minutes. It will make you *sattvic* with all.

Meditation to Clear Your Communication

Part I

Mudra: Sitting in easy pose, bend the elbows down by the sides and place the hands next to the shoulders, the thumbs pressed against the palm at the mound of Mercury (the fleshy pad on the palm at the base of the little finger). The fingers are held straight.

Movement: Keeping this position, begin rotating the hands in continuous 12-inch circles, from in front of the shoulders, up, and out to the sides, down, and back in towards the body, until you reach the starting position again. The right hand will rotate in a clockwise direction, and at the same time the left hand will rotate in a counter-clockwise direction. Move powerfully.

Time: Unspecified. Done in class for 1 minute, 45 seconds.

Eyes: Unspecified.

Breath: Unspecified.

End: Inhale and move immediately into Part II.

Comments/Effects: The force of the movement of the hands will force your lower back to become loose, which helps to take away all your lower back pain, or the possibility of it. This exercise helps to keep a person young. Make sure you keep the thumb pressed against the mound of Mercury the entire time.

This force of the hands also will clear the ears-nose-throat. It will clear your communication so another person will be more able to hear what you say when you speak.

Part II

Posture: Immediately raise your arms over your head, elbows straight, palms flat, facing forward. Spread the fingers wide apart like open antennae.

Mantra: Inhale deep, and begin chanting long *Saat Naam*'s.

Eyes: Unspecified.

Time: One continuous chanting of the mantra takes about 15 seconds. Practiced in this posture 4 times.

Comments/Effects: This is the eternal sound. It is not something which Sikhs own or Jews don't know about. *Saa* means totality, Infinity. This is the first sound with which the God created the universe. *Taa* means life. And *Naam* means "Name" or "Identity." This mantra can give you Heaven and Earth in balance.

The Art of Communication

Your presence *is communication. Did you ever learn that? Your* existence *is your communication, and your projection is your relation. You* are the power.

Does anybody know the meaning of the word "communication"? What is the *naad* of it? How does sound work? Tell me what we mean by "communication"?

Communication is "common notion." Common notion. The intentional notion of a person is to be together. Man is a social animal— biologically, psychologically, sociologically. God cannot live alone; God cannot create another God; God is impotent. Therefore God created creation. So man created communication. That's all it is. That's the only thing common between us and God; God is not outside; God is within us, we are God, and we communicate. But at what level do we communicate? That is it. If we communicate at a higher level, *akasha*, then we are more than God. When we communicate through air, we are just human. When we communicate ourselves into the fire, we are an angry beast. When we communicate with water, we are yo-yos. And when we communicate Earth, we are garbage. You want to learn something more? Is that not enough?

The question is: From which chakra do you speak? Which chakra is behind your communication? Do you talk, do you speak, do you utter? There are three ways. I have done my Ph.D. in the psychology of communication,[1] do you know that? The common notion of a person is to speak, to talk, because you are not you. You are empty, a hollow shell, unloved, crying for socialization. The only tool you have, fools, is that you communicate. You have never learned. Neither your mother told you, nor your father told you, nor your neighbor told you, nor your priest told you, nor your rabbi told you—that your *presence* is communication. Did you ever learn that? Your *existence* is your communication, and your projection is your relation. *You* are the power.

Life is very sour. There's no happiness, there's no sweetness, because your communication has no purpose of self. You communicate because you are an idiot. You communicate to impress somebody. You don't communicate to relate *you* to somebody. That's the most dangerous thing you do as a human. That's why you suffer now, you will suffer tomorrow, you have been suffering. You don't communicate you. You are our tomorrow. We want to tell you exactly how things are.

He is here. *(YB points to the teacher sitting off to the side.)* When he was here *(YB points to the teacher's bench where YB is currently sitting)*, he was me. When I came in, he couldn't

God is within us, we are God, and we communicate. But at what level do we communicate? That is it. If we communicate at a higher level, akasha, then we are more than God. When we communicate through air, we are just human. When we communicate ourselves into the fire, we are an angry beast. When we communicate with water, we are yo-yos. And when we communicate Earth, we are garbage.

continue. He became himself, fell apart, shredded into pieces. Then I hit him. "Ohhhh," he said. "Wow." He communicated. He told me, "Don't hit me in the presence of these people. What are you doing?"

I said, "I am just merciful—I didn't break your head."

He thinks he didn't say anything, but I heard it loudly.

You also do not know how to speak. You talk like idiots, qualified and sanctified, because there's no flexibility in your communication. Like, "I love you." "I love you." "I really love you." *(YB speaks these sentences with different intonations.)* But if you can say, "I love you, hm hm hm," if you make it a little thin and flexible, it goes "squawk," right in. *(YB extends his arm like an arrow piercing into somebody.)*

But you do not know what love is. What is love? Yes? You are in love these days, I understand. Are you married or are you single? You are married?

Student: Married.

YB: And you are in love.

S: Yes, Sir.

YB: Really? Tell me what love is.

S: It's the transmission, merging of....

YB: Spermatozoa. *(Laughter in classroom.)* Love is the transmission of spermatozoa. Ha, ha. You Gringos, you think I don't know what love is for you? Nanak says a very beautiful thing:

ਬੀਜ ਮੰਤ੍ਰ ਸਰਬ ਕੋ ਗਿਆਨੁ ॥

Beej mantar sarb ko giaan.

-Guru Arjan, *Siri Guru Granth Sahib*, page 274 *(Ashtapadi of Sukhmani Sahib)*
The comprehension of the seed of God's Name is within everyone.

Even the seed, the genetic seed, the spermatozoa of man knows that thirty million will start, one will reach, and it has to go eight times around the egg to get in. You don't even know that.

However, "I love you." For what? "Why do you love me, for what do you love me, who are you to love me, who told you to love me?" Have you answered all those questions? No, you want her, that's why you love her. She wants you, that's why she loves you. It's a love of want. Sex is like a water bucket. You put a stirrer in it and stir it. It's called a "quickie." So, it's love. You make love.

Define love. Take the words of Nanak, you will love it.

ਧਨ ਪਿਰੁ ਏਹਿ ਨ ਆਖੀਅਨਿ ਬਹਨਿ ਇਕਠੇ ਹੋਇ ॥
ਏਕ ਜੋਤਿ ਦੁਇ ਮੂਰਤੀ ਧਨ ਪਿਰੁ ਕਹੀਐ ਸੋਇ ॥

Dhan pir ay-eh na aakhee-an bahen ikathay ho-eh.
Ayk jot du-eh mooratee dhan pir kehee-ai so-eh.

-Guru Arjan, *Siri Guru Granth Sahib* page 788

They are not said to be husband and wife who merely sit together.
Rather they alone are called husband and wife who have one soul in two bodies.

He defined love. "Don't call them together who live together, or are together, or everything is together with them. They are not lovers. One *jot,* one light in two existences, they are the great lovers." When all faculties and facets are dissolved, and oneness becomes one, that's the power of love. Where there's love, there's no question. Where there's a question, there's no love. Where there's a want, there's absolutely no love. Where there's a need—no, it's not love.

Communication is the art of hookery. You hook each other with it. It is called the science of hookery. There are two sciences through which man lives—the science of cookery and the science of hookery. In cookery, you cook, you can make it gourmet, and you want what you want, and you taste and test life. In hookery you project and procure other beings. Cookery is the science of food. Hookery is the science of the applied mind to conquer people physically, mentally, and control them spiritually.

One of the biggest hookeries ever practiced on this Earth is religion, because it teaches you to belong; it doesn't teach you to Master. "I'm a Sikh, I'm a Jew, I'm a Christian, I'm a Muslim...." Are you a human? Have you ever been introduced to anyone who says, "Hi, meet me. I am a human?"

Did she say, "Yeah, I'm a human, too." In your whole life have you had that experience? You met somebody, shook hands, and that person said, "I'm a human." You won't even say it. It looks odd, doesn't it? Well, that's what you are. Lovers. Lovers with rose-colored glasses.

Here is the fish. Woosh. Lovers. What is the fishing wire? Words. What is the bait? Promise. What is the purpose? Transmission of spermatozoa. It's true, it's the naked truth. You can deny it. You can feel offended, "No, no, I'm a true lover."

Somebody said, "I want to love this girl, Yogiji, with your blessing."

I said, "Is that true?"

He said, "Yes."

I said, "You love her?"

"Yeah."

"What do you want?"

He said, "I want to marry her."

I said, "That's true. But there's one condition."

He said, "What?"

I said, "You shall never have intercourse with her."

"Ahhhh ! Ahhhh," he said.

I said, "What?"

"Then why am I getting married?"

I said, "Then have intercourse, but don't marry her. If that's all you want, it won't last."

Your words mean nothing; therefore, you are the most mean living mammals on the Earth. You do not communicate what you mean. You are very very very mean.

Your words mean nothing, therefore you are the most mean living mammals on the Earth. You do not communicate what you mean. You are very very very mean.

You are delightful liars. You never tell your notion, forget about intention. Intention very honestly should be told. But you don't even tell your intention. You don't even tell your notion. Notion is in the negative sense of what you shall be.

Now ask me questions.

S: What is notion?

YB: "In the most negative event, I shall be here and hereafter with you." That's my notion. My intention is that you should be better than me. Why should you trust me?

"Why should I trust you?"

"You have nobody else to trust."

"Why not?"

"Because nobody says so."

"Why so?"

"Because I know it."

"What do you mean?

"I'm not mean. I have done it many lifetimes."

"Why?"

"I am, I Am."

The same dialogue is yours when you become teachers—not exploiters, hookers, fishers, and faceless idiots. When you are a teacher, your intention is to make somebody greater than yourself. It is not a teacher's intention to have somebody.

You are a bunch of liars, faithless to your self and to your integrity and to your honor. You have no commitment as humans. We do not have a relationship. Our relationship is a pure service to uplift a person, to be part of the glory unto the Infinity and to the standardization of God. And that's the pride of a teacher, that he has the privilege to serve another student, because somebody served him. Do you understand that? No. Do you? "Yes, Sir!"

Class: Yes, Sir.

YB: You don't even know how to respond to your teacher. You expect your students to respond to you? Where are you coming from? Is this a movie theater, or a class? Be classic. Have power, have strength, speak with soul. Did you hear me?

Class: Yes, Sir! *(Spoken very forcefully.)*

YB: That is the spirit. Learn to be alert. Answer with the power of the soul. Relate with an affirmation. Every word you say should be an affirmation. What is hello? "Hell-O." You want to go there? The first time I heard somebody say to me, "Hello," I said, "I'm not going." "What should I say?"

I said, "Heaven-O."

"I can't say it."

I said, "Then say 'Sat Nam,' say 'Shalom,' say any damn thing, but what is this 'hello'?"

You say, "Hi." Do you know when you say "Hi?" When somebody's dead. It's a communication of pain. "Hi!"

"Hey" is Thou. "Hi" is dead.

The first role of the teacher is to be humble, grow under, see the growth, and then bring the fruit into the life of the person. The power of the character, the courage, the grace, and the magnitude of a person is in practicing humility. One who cannot go under can never grow. The first power of the seed is to go under, and then grow. The role of the teacher is not exploitation. Do you understand?

Class: Yes, Sir!

YB: Ha ha ha, you caught yourself! *(Class responded powerfully.)* One who is not alert is dirt. How much time do we have to live as dirt? How many lifetimes are we to live as dirt? Applied consciousness is alertness. Alertness is learn on the altar; and altar has no alternative.

I have to give you one *kriya* and go. I might come again this evening and teach.

Quickly, join me! With all your power, join me. In these two weeks either you have wasted money, you have wasted time, you have come here, you can get nothing, or you will get everything. It's up to you.

(See page 25 for details of this meditation.)

Open up your chest cavity with a shock of a current, as if eleven hundred volts have hit you. Put the *Tantric Har* tape on. At the sound of *"Har,"* with all the power, you will stretch out. Concentrate on it. Achieve it. See what it does. Don't worry about what you're doing. See what it brings, okay?

Class: Yes, Sir!

YB: That's why when I say, "Don't trust me," they say, "Why?" Never trust your Teacher, God knows what he's doing. The most dangerous man in your life is your Spiritual Teacher. His job is to catch you; your job is to keep free. That's the game, the relationship between cat and mouse.

Camera Person: Sir, I don't have that tape.

YB: "No" is in the life of those who have no life. "Yes" is in the life of those who have faith and integrity. "Yes, Sir," is in the life of those who have faith, integrity, and dignity. We need that tape. With that tape, what this meditation can do will be marvelous. Why waste time? We'll wait.

A set of all tapes should be available here—absolutely! Yes, Sir!

Camera Person: Yes, Sir!

YB: Speak from here *(YB puts his hand on his navel point.)* One who doesn't speak from here is dead. Every communication which does not come from the navel point brings disease, sickness, sorrow, sadness, madness, insanity, and bad luck. True. It's as true as anything. Never speak from here. *(YB points to his mouth.)* Never speak from here. *(YB points to his throat.)* Never speak from here. *(YB points to his heart center.)* Speak from here *(YB points to his navel point)*, from your original self. Do you see when I talk, how this thing goes in and out? *(YB points to his navel point.)* Practice.[2]

Speak it from the guts. Speak it with your soul. Speak it with your power. God gave you a chance to speak. God gave you intention and notion to communicate. Speak truth which is you. Anything else you speak is untrue. And the word must have power, must project, must hit the target. If you speak from here *(YB points to his navel)*, hit the heart. If you speak from

Speak it from the guts. Speak it with your soul. Speak it with your power. God gave you a chance to speak. God gave you intention and notion to communicate. Speak truth which is you. Anything else you speak is untrue.

here *(YB points to his Third Eye point)*, hit the heart. Never aim your language at the head of a person. It'll come back to you as a boomerang, and hurt you more than you know.

You must understand. When people go home, they'll call up and say, "Robin, Robin, are you listening to me, Robin?

"Oh yes, you just left, what happened?"

"I talked to you, but I'm very confused. I, I don't know what you were talking about."

"Well, you agreed to everything."

"I know. Oh Robin, I don't know what you said. You said a lot of good things, but I don't know what you said. I kind of have a feeling you didn't say something."

Have you had that experience? Because you did not use the language. You just used the hookery. You said beautiful things, you promised a lot of things, you baited, you put that little snail on the hook, and this fly, and "shht, shht" *(sound of someone casting off with a fishing rod)*. But the unfortunate part is, my sweetheart, when you control something, then you have to carry something. And how many things can you carry in life?

So communication should not have the power to control. It should not have the power of promise. It should not have the power of impression. It should be a statement of fact. How many of you can say something like this? "I would like to love you and screw you." We are talking communication only. Try to be a student. Understand that. How many of you have the guts to say so?

S: Yes, I've said that before. They've said "no" sometimes, too.

YB: Thank you. Because your talk must not have a hook. It must not create an impression. It must not try to control. It must not try to dodge. You must not lodge your purpose in anybody. You must be nothing but straight, truthful. So speak your intention, rather than your complicated words. You'll have the happiest life. All will be taken care of.

S: How would we start to do that?

YB: It is so simple. Thank you for asking that question. Somebody asked me this morning, "I want to have your counsel, advice, and guidance."

I said, "Find some dog in the street, because you are a bitch. That will do better."

"Ahhh! Sir, you're abusing me."

I said, "I'm not. I'm shocking you. My intention is to shock you. Your question is affectionate. My answer is most brutal, but you didn't accept me. Love, cruelty, brutality, harassment, all are a part of one person. To accept a person, you must accept all facets. So when you start telling somebody something, first try to be polite:

"I'd like to tell you, I hate you with all my guts." (It is more effective than hours of argument.) "I just want to tell you, honest to my God and to me, I hate you from my guts, and you are so naughty. You screwed my friend and she told me. Look in my eyes. Is it the same you who said you will be my partner here and hereafter? Are you the same lover, man of God, human? Do you dwell in your soul or in your penis? I'm not saying anything. I just want to know."

What answer will you find? Flat. He will just talk to you like this, then he'll be off.

There's no greater power than the power of the word. The spoken word is the only essence you have. You as a hue (hu-man) are like a bulb; your mind is like a bow string, and your word is the arrow. Strike, using your faculty of chakra, and you shall always win.

That's it. Speak authentically straight. Start slow and small, because in the word small, S-M-A-L-L, "ALL" is contained. Just start today.

You can have wealth, you can have health, you can have the world at the tip of your fingers, but you shall not have happiness. Happiness only belongs to those who are straight. And it's not too late to be straight.

What can make you great? That people can trust you. What can make you trusted? If you talk straight. Simple or not. One day your lies will be found out by your friends, and

Speak from here. (YB puts his hand on his navel point.) One who doesn't speak from here is dead. Every communication which does not come from the navel point brings disease, sickness, sorrow, sadness, madness, insanity, and bad luck. True. It's as true as anything. Never speak from here. (YB points to his mouth.) Never speak from here. (YB points to his throat.) Never speak from here. (YB points to his heart center.) Speak from here (YB points to his navel point), from your original self. Do you see how when I talk, this thing goes in and out? (YB points to his navel point.) Practice.

you shall have enemies. They will know it. No person is less than God, and no lie can be hidden. It's a matter of days. As you speak today, so you suffer tomorrow.

Come on. Let's do it. This chest cavity is called "heart chakra." You are going to open it, and it has to have the entire power of your being. You must shock your central nervous system—that is *shushmanaa,* when you speak the sound of "*Har.*"

(Tantric Har tape begins playing.) Don't give up.

Hold! You have difficulty moving. Opening of your heart center cavity is opening up to your Infinity. There lies your central nervous system, *agan granthi,* place of fire—your food digestion, breath, everything. When this is locked, the ribcage is out of placement. Then the diaphragm doesn't act right—you'll lose one third of your life force. Simple. You started with a good intention, and within a minute and a half you found out that it is very difficult, and it is. But we have to do it for eleven minutes.

Don't utter the word *Har.* That's why I gave you a grace. He will just put the tape on, and at the sound of that *Har,* you will open up Almighty's power. Whatever you have, put it in. In return, it'll give you what you never had in experience. Ready? Set? Go.

No speaking. Silent! Move the power of the *ida* and *pingala,* and open up the *shushmanaa.* Simple. Go for it. Go for gold! Win, win, win! Bravo, bravo, do it. Open the chakras. Wow, go, go, go! Come on, come on. We have no time. Just do it. Cross all boundaries.

Inhale. Hold, keep on doing it though. Hold the breath and keep on doing what you were doing. Exhale. Inhale. Exhale. Inhale deep. Pull, pull, pull. Relax.

Hello. How are you? You know, when you read in books about *ida, pingala, shushmanaa,* sense, sensory, sex, stimulation, power, empowerment, modern, later, orthodox, this religion, reality, me, you, we, us...you are getting all confused. It's too much. When all doors are closed, nothing can enter. Nothing. Inside there's nothing, outside everything wants to come in.

Learn that what you say is gold. What you hear should be a diamond. If it is less than that, don't accept it. When you speak, if it is truth, others will know it. If it is not, it will confuse the other person whom you want to befriend. That's how you create your enemies. That's how you ruin your relationships. That's how you bring pain to your life, and that's why you are lonely.

Look at me. When I came twenty-seven years ago, I didn't know one person. Not at all. Look at me today. People didn't like me, people hated me, or people wanted something, expected everything. All I said is, "I have come here to teach you a system to be healthy, happy, and holy. I have not come here to learn anything from you. There's no exchange. I don't have any need; I don't have any want."

"How will you live?"

"All will be taken care of. You don't have to worry about it."

"You must learn driving."

I said, "People will drive me."

"You'll need money."

"Everybody will spend it."

"You'll need this, you'll need that."

"Nothing. I want you to listen, learn, and become learned. That's my happiness." I said it twenty-seven years ago, I say the same thing today.

You are all my relatives. You are all my extensions. I am your yesterday. You must respect me. You are my tomorrow. You must respect yourself. You have to have a tomorrow if you don't want sorrow. Therefore, you must create another Teacher. You shall have no option other than that. A Teacher who does not create a better Teacher is the most cursed person ever born.

I'm not your today. I'm your yesterday. I'm your memory. God brought you here. The whole world will not bring you here. You owe it to yourself to master yourself. You owe it to yourself to be yourself. There's nothing beyond yourself.

Whenever you are going to find Self within yourself, you'll be one with the One who created you, because the One who gave you the Self knows the Self and has the Self. As long as you don't have yourself, you are empty. And to fill that emptiness you are going to do so many things; and these so many things are going to confuse you more and more. What's the idea of having the most beautiful, sensory life, sensitive living, and wasting it in confusion? Why?

Serve me and the world will serve you. That's how the law of karma is. Those who will not worship their yesterday, shall never have tomorrow, and if they try to have it, they will have it with a lot of sorrow. I shall be gone. You shall continue. And when you'll be gone, see there is somebody to continue. Do you understand?

Class: Yes, Sir.

YB: Good luck. God be with you. Now you know. It is good to have you.

Meditation to Open the Lock of the Heart Center, to Increase the Power of the Infinite Within

a   b   c

Mudra: Sit in easy pose with a straight spine. Bring hands approximately 6-8 inches in front of your face, palms flat and facing one another, fingers pointing towards the ceiling, and with approximately a 6-8 inch space between the palms. Elbows are bent and are relaxed down (a).

Movement: With a very fast, powerful jerk, stretch the hands out (b) until there is about 36 inches between the hands (c), and abruptly stop them there. The stopping process will be so abrupt, done with such a powerful force, that you'll find the hands, chest, shoulders, and head jerking back and forth a little bit. This abrupt stopping, and the resulting jerk causes an "opening up your chest cavity with a 'current shock.' You should stretch out like eleven hundred volts have hit you."

Music: *Tantric Har*, or 1 movement per second. Do not sing aloud. On every *Har,* you will stretch your arms with such a powerful force, just as if a eleven hundred volts have hit you. Concentrate on this reaction in your chest, and see the effects it has on you.

Eyes: Unspecified.

Time: 11 minutes.

End: Inhale. Hold the breath, but keep on doing the motion. Held 13 seconds. Exhale. Inhale again and continue the motion. Held 8 seconds. Exhale. Inhale deeply, continue. Held 6 seconds. Relax.

Comments/Effects: The chest cavity is called the heart chakra. This heavy jolt, as you spring your hands and arms apart, will cause a jerking reaction to your chest cavity, which will open up your heart center. Opening of your heart center cavity is opening up to your own Infinity.

This center is sometimes referred to as the *agan granthi*—the place from which all fire-related activites spring—food, digestion, breath, to name a few. When this center is locked, your ribcage is out of placement. Then the diaphragm doesn't act right, and you'll lose one third of your life force. This meditation loosens this lock and will open up the power of the Almighty within you.

You must bring forth the entire power of your being, using a great force as you open up and then suddenly stop your arms, and thus shock your central nervous system (the *shushmanaa)* on the sound of *Har.* Through this meditation you can move the power of the *ida* and *pingala,* and open up the *shushmanaa.*

The Golden Rules of a Teacher

There are two ways to live: One is you love God, the other is God loves you. A Teacher is loved by God. Man loves God. There is a difference.

You have come here to become Teachers, is that true?

Class: Yes, Sir.

YB: You are learning. If you do not know how to obey, you shall not know how to command. Is that understood?

Class: Yes, Sir!

YB: If you cannot obey, you shall never be in a position to command. If your five *tattwas* cannot obey, your five *tattwas* cannot, shall not, will not command. It doesn't matter how much you study, how much you read, how much you know, and how powerful you think you are, you shall never have the grace to penetrate. Your words shall never have the power to make other people obey, because you have not obeyed.

It doesn't feel good, does it? No. Our normal tendency is, "I don't want to obey, but I want to command." If your inner Self, the inner essence, the inner being does not have the capacity to obey the teacher, you shall never become a teacher who shall be in a position to command a student. This is the Law of the Golden Rule. And this law you can never break. Difficult, right? It *is* difficult. *(Some students say, "No.")* What do you mean, "No." Don't be stupid with me. It is difficult, I know that.

When I started with my teacher, we were about 258, I don't remember exactly; it was something like that. When we finished we were three left. I will tell you my own story.

One day I was just fine. My teacher said to me, "We are going to go to the district office." He said, "Come along with me and put on your English suit."

"Okay." So I wore a suit and tie and the whole thing: pants, boots and polish—you know, here you would call it very business-class. You know what I'm saying? On the way he said, "How tall can this tree be?"

I said, "About twenty feet."

He said, "As you are, can you go up?"

I said, "Yes." I was very stout, strong. So I put the boots on the side, and I climbed. It was very difficult, but I made it to where a split was.

Then he said, "Well, stay here 'till I come back."

How many of you would stay with that teacher? He came back three and a half days later. When I came down, he said, "Oh, come on, now. Let's go." He never said, "How was it, what

You are the beloved of God. Therefore, you shall not beg, borrow, or lie for existence. You shall not ask. Everything shall come, and in abundance. You are the Lord of Prosperity, you have the power of prayer, and you have the purity of projection. These three things you must understand. They belong to you when you are a Teacher, as a matter of right. It's not a favor.

happened? I mean, are you alive? How did you go to the bathroom? How did you this...?" Not a word, man. Absolutely nothing. "Let's go!" We went.

Four, five days later he said, "Come here, sit down. What did you learn?"

I said, "I learned how to sleep on the tree. I learned how to poop on the tree. I learned how to pee on the tree. I learned how not to fall, and I learned how to eat."

"What did you learn?"

I said, "The young leaves of that tree are very sweet and edible, the old ones are bitter and rotted. And, that tree had splits four, five, six splits. And every split gets water in it." So I said, "One of those splits where there was water, I kept for drinking, another to clean myself and wash my hands and...."

He said, "How did you poop?"

I said, "I sat between the two branches and let it go! What else?"

"How did you sleep?"

I said, "I didn't sleep very well, but, because I knew it was twenty feet down, I did tie a few branches, and that was good. It was nice."

"What was the difficulty?"

I said, "This damn suit. That was very difficult."

"Why?" he said.

"Because you said, 'Stay 'till I come back. Be here as you are.' Do you remember, Sir?" And he said, "Yes."

"Sir, I still had this tie on; when I came down I was still the same." Because on that tree, I said, "What he has said means something." A Teacher gives you an experience; a preacher gives you philosophy. Without experience you can never become a Teacher, you become a parrot. There's a difference between a wise Teacher and a wise parrot Teacher. They "quack quack" everything, they know everything, they can talk everything, but there's never an experience.

You will always question. "This Teacher sleeps with his students, this Teacher steals from the students...." You have a million experiences, and are a million stories—I have heard all that, I have gone through it. From a Teacher's point of view, you also betray, you also are treacherous, you also lie. You also think your imaginations are true. You also seek sexual and sensual flirtation. You are a maya, too. But between the lines, if you want to understand, do not accept a Teacher ever if you have to have a question. Don't. Just be friends, visit, have fun.

And especially in Kundalini Yoga, we do not initiate. If you are that much of a standardized idiot that you cannot initiate yourself, you don't need to be initiated. That's the law.

The second law in Kundalini Yoga is: If you ever come empty handed, you shall go empty handed. Empty handed you come, empty handed you go. So you must pay first. Kundalini Yoga cannot be taught until the fee is first paid. *Bheta.* So there's no obligation. You pay the teacher, he teaches you. Matter ends. There's no relationship. So if you don't want to sleep with him, don't. Is that clear?

Class: Yes, Sir.

YB: You are forgetting. I know. You are gringos. You have not been properly oriented. You have come here to become Teachers. This is not a class where you are just students, and you take a class and go away because you paid a couple of dollars.

When I used to teach and students never had any money, I used to scatter money in the parking lot so they could collect it and come to the class. Some collected it and never came to the class. But it was part of the game. We'll never break the rule.

You serve, you do business, you live your life, but if you're a Teacher, then Mother Nature and the Divine and God serve you. There are two ways to live: One is you love God, the other is God loves you. A teacher is loved by God; man loves God. There's a difference.

So if you want to become a Teacher, you must understand, you are the beloved of God. Therefore, you shall not beg, borrow, or lie for existence. You shall not ask. Everything shall come, and in abundance. You are the Lord of Prosperity, you have the power of prayer, and you have the purity of projection. These three things you must understand. They belong to you when you are a Teacher, as a matter of right. It's not a favor.

Whatever comes to you as a Teacher, it comes from God. It shall go to the altar. If it doesn't go to the altar, it will ruin you. One wrong action of a Teacher, the next life is as a cockroach. So it's better that you keep a cockroach around you. If a Teacher faults, whether he escapes the justice of this world, whether somebody harms him or not, somebody abuses him or not, or he abuses somebody or not, it doesn't matter at all. One wrong action of a teacher, and the entire divinity guarantees your next lifetime, and that next lifetime is as a cockroach. Because one who's responsible to give light and responsible for light, gets into darkness and lives through a darkness; then the next life is nothing but darkness, that's cockroach.

First of all, I told you very clearly, don't have a Teacher. It's not written that you should have a Teacher. But once you have a Teacher, guru, whatever you call him—Spiritual Teacher, Spiritual Guide, spiritual friend, idiot, spiritual idiot—it doesn't matter what you call him, it's your concept. But once you call him and accept him, never deny him, because then only can you be redeemed in that linkage. You cannot be redeemed otherwise, it doesn't matter what God wants and what God does. That is called the Law of Final Destination.

You each have a longitude and latitude at which you were born. Do you understand that? Every town has a longitude and a latitude at which you are born. Then from a teacher you will learn altitude and attitude to rule, to command. *Purkha* must make the *Prakirti* obey. That's the rule. But because it's a Western world, it's not a mature world. It doesn't have the aspect and respect for the Teacher. Therefore, when you become a teacher, speak the truth. If somebody doesn't want to hear it, doesn't want to obey it, diplomatically "dip low" on the mat and slip out. Understand?

Class: Yes, Sir.

YB: Then never teach that student. Just become a friend. That garbage is not worth even looking at. That is your divine privilege. There's no forgiveness in it.

These are a few Golden Rules. Otherwise that student will become your destruction, because then you'll teach out of attachment, not out of truth. A student has to only directly or indirectly disobey once. In your lifetime you cannot teach that student. Help him, love him, serve him, inspire him, guide him, give him anything you want, but never give him the teachings. And teaching is not what I am giving you. Teaching is when I say, "You are taught!" That's the beginning, that's the middle, that's the end of teaching.

Because you are Western you think a teacher teaches, discusses, philosophizes, lectures. You listen to the tapes, you read the books. I know. That many thick books. You are all blind, deaf, and most stupid. Stupid of the extreme, insane order. If all the libraries can make you teachers, why is anybody unwise? Don't you understand the simple rule of thumb? The crown of spirituality is bestowed, it can never, shall never, and will never be conquered. Three things are not under your control: Love happens, devotion and dedication are unlimited, and the honor of spirituality is bestowed. You cannot earn it, you cannot buy it, and you cannot wangle it or manipulate it. Is that clear?

Class: Yes, Sir! *(Students are not in unison in their response.)*

YB: You can't even speak "Yes, sir." What are you doing here? It means you are not alert, you are not simultaneous, and you are not one voice.

It is my job to freak you out. No, no, it's true. This is not a convention or convocation or some seminar or workshop. Please forgive us. You have not come here to make your presence very pretty. You have come here to be roughed up, and brought to the essence. Don't ever come to a class to become teachers if you do not have the determination that, "I shall not go from here without going into myself, and telling myself: Be a Teacher." With that determination you will get it. This is not a fashion class or a business class. It is a class to become a teacher which can command the *tattwas,* the four elements, and Heaven and Earth. The price? Teachers are always put on the cross or on the stake, or betrayed by their students. That must happen. Your end will be very earthly unpleasant because you shall be tested for heavenly endorsement. Is that understood?

Class: Yes, Sir!

YB: Buddha was poisoned by his own most trusted disciple. Lord Rama was betrayed by his own archer. Lord Krishna was denied by his most powerful devotee. Hazarat Mohammed never had a good time, ever. That man had to pick up a sword to fight for every day of his existence. A Teacher's life is not a life of glamour with people touching your feet and thinking wonderful things about you, your sermons, all your beauty, and your gorgeous aura. A Teacher can bring God and Itself into him at his will. That is granted to him. But on the other side, the price of this is he's the only one who will sit on the fire and just smile. If you are not ready for the price, then don't allow people to touch your feet and say "hello" to you.

The universe, *Prakirti,* the creation, shall serve you as a Teacher. It's a privilege of *Prakirti.* But on the other hand, you shall withstand insult, totally insulating yourself from it. A yogi is a person who is not God, and who is not human, and who is not an angel, or a devil. The pair of opposites do not affect a yogi—neither praise nor insult. That's a yogi. A Teacher is the one whom the pair of opposites do not affect. To the ugliest and to the most bountiful, he or she only gives blessings.

Suffering is honor. A Teacher suffers both ways. A Teacher suffers in serving, a Teacher suffers in commanding. A Teacher first suffers in chiseling, a Teacher suffers in blessing. A Teacher suffers all personal sufferings, because a Teacher is the example of guidance through time and space, and time and space is the test. The test comes only through suffering, and this qualifying through suffering gives you the contentment and happiness that you are everlasting, infinitely immortal. That's how Teachers become immortal.

If you cannot rise above pain and pleasure, desire and demand, it doesn't matter how many scriptures you know, and how charming you are. I have seen a teacher seducing students. Not for sex, for everything. Everything. What an insult to a status. Why does a teacher have to seduce? The world wants to seduce him. God wants to seduce him. Maya wants to seduce him. There's not one thing which can exist which shall not seduce. The sensory system is just to seduce a Teacher.

Why are you in such a hurry? Wait. Become a Teacher and see how things come to you. They don't come to *you*. You are a vehicle. In you there is the purity and piety of a Teacher that you must protect and serve. Then out of your word will come humans who will be invincible, blessed, bountiful, beautiful, and in bliss. You shall rule time and space, and your generations will be happy, healthy, and holy.

This six- to eight- inch penis is not Venus, and

A yogi is a person who is not God, and who is not human, and who is not an angel or a devil. The pair of opposites do not affect a yogi—neither praise nor insult. That's a yogi. A Teacher is the one whom the pair of opposites do not affect. To the ugliest and to the most bountiful, he or she only gives blessings.

your two balls are not eyeballs, and they do not give you the third ball to see Heaven and Earth at the same time. Therefore you are born blind, you live blind, and you die blind. The sensory system does not give you the common sixth sense. If you can prostitute this life which you earned, and the chance, which is a great blessing, that you can become a Teacher, if you let it go, you will start as a cockroach. Marrying a saint is a righteous thing. After that, do you know what life you take on? A squirrel. You know that little thing which collects nuts, runs after the birds? It is a very pretty animal. These are all wives of the great teachers who never saw them as teachers. They did not become cockroaches, but one life above it. Have you talked to them? No? Talk to them, they speak. Their previous life was the wife of a great Teacher. They are very blessed animals. Sometime go see them, take some food; she will do a kissing, kissing thing, and swing her tail. They are very good. They are very friendly. You don't have to listen to them. Just decode their body language. You'll find them They are pretty, and you are attracted to them.

Have you seen those Teachers who have never obeyed their teacher? And have you seen those men who have never honored themselves as a Teacher? All dogs with a fallen ear. Have you seen them? We call them "dumb dogs." You buy the smartest dog, at six months he will become dumb. That's a Teacher.

It is not very professionally likable that you want to become a Teacher, because there comes a responsibility with this power. You think people touch your feet, people bow to you, you say, "Bless you." Do you understand what is waiting for you? For what? One mistake. You are only to commit one mistake. If you miss what you are supposed to take, that is the next life. Do you want to continue this course or do you want to go home?

CLASS: *(Laughter.)*

In you there is the purity and piety of a Teacher that you must protect and serve. Then out of your word will come humans who will be invincible, blessed, bountiful, beautiful, and in bliss. You shall rule time and space, and your generations will be happy, healthy, and holy.

YB: A Teacher doesn't hear—he's deaf. He doesn't speak—he's dumb. He doesn't see—he's blind. He just carries the teachings. He never amends them, never adds to them, never subtracts from them.

You don't interpret it; you just respectfully carry it to another, and that to another, and that to another. When you do this, all knowledge will come to you. Everything will dawn on you. Your teacher will speak in you. Your Teacher will guide in you. Then people do not respect you—they divorce you, they insult you, they demand of you. Your relatives will insult you. It's not you they are attacking. It is like how a moth attacks acandle. When a dog has a collar and a chain, all the street dogs become a reception committee and bark. Your own children will bark at you. Your own wife will insult you. Your own father and mother will abandon you. Finally, my dear Teachers, you will be left by all those who have more Earth and less Heavens. Because your path is of the Heavens, not only your Heavens, but you have to give people the Heavens. That is your virtue as a teacher. You are not spiritual prostitutes. You are spiritual power. As a teacher it's your destiny to grant the Heavens, and to whom you grant, God cannot have the power to refuse. That's your ordinary power. When you bless, angels obey. Why to get upset?

If you don't believe my words, see the life of Nanak. Read the life stories of those who have taught the Word, and see their suffering. Because God sees to it that their attachment is never fulfilling. Because a Teacher is the Lord of the Heavens, the Earth is always testing in vengeance.

You don't have to ask. A Teacher prays for only one thing,

> ਸਰਬੱਤ ਦਾ ਭਲਾ
> *Sarbat da bhalaa.*
> -from the Sikh daily prayer, *Ardas*
> *May all people prosper.*

"My Lord God, my Creator who has given the responsibility to carry me in this, carry all in essence to prosperity. Make them beautiful, bountiful, and blissful."

A Teacher does not draw the line, a Teacher does not discriminate, a Teacher doesn't say "no," a Teacher doesn't refuse. A Teacher is always a victim of jealousy, intrigues, treachery, betrayal, slander, because a Teacher is the one institution which is an easy target. But does a Teacher feel all that? No. He smiles.

I take a walk every morning and pass these dogs. They all bark at me. I say, "Well, you never listened to me last time. Now you are barking at me. For what?" That's my reception commit-

32 · The Master's Touch

tee. I pass through them every morning. They never listened then, they never listen now. They barked then, they bark now. They are all my relatives. But what is wrong in that? Everybody has a soul. Every soul is related in this time and space. What is the difference if somebody's in the body of a dog or a cat or a rat or a cockroach? We are all the same, the soul is the same. You see it as different? You see God as different in a dog? Do you think people who insult you are different from those who praise you? Don't you understand it's a balanced world? Praise and insult are all in equilibrium, in balance. Prayer and prestige—in prayer you are humble, in prestige you are dominant—it is in balance. There cannot exist anything in the universe which is not in balance, and nothing can grow which is not in harmony.

You know what my principal word is when somebody accusingly says, "You." You will find me always smiling. Because that moment a man is individually prostituting me, he does not see me as an institution, he sees me as a prostitute. And that happens to every teacher. People always see you as an individual. And you must know and see and believe and trust you are never an individual. Your "I" is for you an institution. A Teacher is an institution for help, for service, for raising people's consciousness, and granting them the Heavens. He's the guarantor—he or she, whatever— is the guarantor. A Teacher is the guarantor that the other person's life becomes heavenly. So if you are teaching a class for that ten or fifteen dollars, you are not in the right job.

And don't go by the charm of a Teacher. You know, on this planet I have not met one man who has not asked, "Yogiji, how many students do you have? How many ashrams do you have? You have done a wonderful job."

But a Teacher only sees the flow of God and is just a vehicle. Have you seen a water tap in a building, where you press the button and water comes. You quench your thirst and you leave? Understand?

Class: Yes, Sir.

YB: So there are some souls who come to you, and you are the water tap. They press and bow and open their mouths, and you, through the nectar of wisdom, give them the Heavens. Beyond that you are nothing. If you think you are anything other than that, your karma will catch up with you. But on the other hand, when a thirsty one has that in his mouth, he'll say, "Oh, God, wow!" In absolute ecstasy, then man chants the mantra of ecstasy, "Wahe Guru."

Sometime listen to your heart on a sonogram machine. It is a loud frequency of three. "Waa-Hay Guroo. Waa-Hay Guroo." (Says this in a rhythmic whisper imitating the sound of a beating heart.) It's a funny sound. Take a stethoscope, put it to your ear, put it at your heart, listen to yourself. What a big noise is there. "Hum, hum, brahm, hum; hum, hum, brahm, hum." Four valves open and close. But what do you do? You don't listen to that. "You are a Jew, you are a Christian, you are a Sikh, you are a Muslim, you are a Hindu." I don't know who the hell you are? Nobody knows that.

As long as your "I" is your "I," your Third Eye will never open. As long as your Third Eye is not open, it doesn't matter how much you do—parties, trade, business, politics—you shall never be respected. Remember this: If your presence cannot command respect, your orders won't. Don't waste your words. If a person doesn't understand your body language, he will never understand your spoken language. So become very dedicatedly delicate and essential.

Rule one: You must look smart. The art of a teacher is: Look smart, be smart, talk straight. Never be right or wrong, always be neutral. Speak not through the positive mind nor the negative mind, but from the neutral mind. And whenever you have to confront a calamity or a pleasure, take the altitude. Adjust the attitude. Do not react right away. Somebody may say, "Ahh, Yogiji, you are great. Ha ha ha ha."

"Un huh. Un huh. Yogiji's never great. Great is the Maker of Yogiji." Don't forget. And don't forget the Maker. The day you forget your Maker, you will be just shaken. Do not get attached to the that which is given, be attached to the Giver.

ਦੇਦਾ ਦੇ ਲੈ ਦੇ ਥਕਿ ਪਾਹਿ ॥ ਜੁਗਾ ਜੁਗੰਤਰਿ ਖਾਹੀ ਖਾਹਿ ॥

Day(n)daa day lai(n)day thak paa-eh. Jugaa jugantar khaa-hee khaa-eh.

-Guru Nanak, *Siri Guru Granth Sahib*, page 2 (from 3rd *pauree* of *Japji Sahib*)

God, the Giver, constantly gives His gifts and the recipients become tired of receiving them. Throughout all the ages all have been eating what is given.

The Giver gives, those who taketh get tired. Through time infinite this rule has prevailed.

Learn to communicate through common notion. "Communication" means "common notion." Notion is to declare yourself. Let it be known that "I am a teacher, I'm a vehicle, I'm a pipe, I bring you the teachings. They are not mine."

Have you ever seen sometimes in class someone will ask, "Should I close my eyes?"

I say, "I didn't read that. I don't know. Close or open as you choose." I never asked. I was a very good student.

You can learn by questioning or you can learn by blessing. When you learn by blessing, you will be bestowed the crown of spirituality and then Almighty God will love you and shall serve you, because His entire nature will be at your command. But when you question, you will go into the cycle of birth and death forever. That's the price you shall pay. Because where there's a doubt, man will never find the route. When you obey, there's nothing to say.

I'll tell you what happened. I was tested once. I was in Los Angeles, and one Swami-ji was a very good friend. I really respect him and love him, too. His five main directors came flying all the way to meet me, and I talked to them in private. They said, "Well, Swami-ji has gone insane. Swami-ji has said this thing." And they showed me the paper. I looked at the paper.

I said, "The orders are wrong. Are you *sure* they are signed by him?"

"Yes. Yogiji. We have come; he's your friend, you call him and let him know this is not right." Do you understand that? It was a very clear thing.

I said, "No. I will not call him."

"Why not?"

I said, "He's my friend, but he is your Teacher. He has given you in writing to do this, is that true?"

"Yes."

I said, "Just go and do it."

"Yogiji, do you understand what it means?"

I said, "Yes, I understand, it is wrong, and very, very great damage will happen, I know. But you have come for counseling, is that true?"

"Yes."

I said, "Then I advise you to go back and tell Swami-ji, 'We had a good meditation, and we have decided to obey your orders, and we are going to implement it.'"

So they did it. Swami-ji said, "Wait a minute. What did we write? Show me the paper." He saw the paper. He said, "It is not correct." He tore up the paper.

They called me, "Thank you for calling Swami-ji."

I said, "I didn't call."

"But he tore up the paper."

I said, "God is a teacher, too. He was testing you guys. If God would not have come at that moment, then the institution of a Teacher would have fallen. That is not the Will of God."

"Are you sure, Sir?"

I said, "Did I ever lie to you guys? I told you I didn't call."

"He did it on his own?"

I said, "Yep."

A Teacher is an institution for help, for service, for raising people's consciousness, and granting them the Heavens. A Teacher is the guarantor that the other person's life becomes heavenly.

And there's another foolishness which Kundalini teachers do. They mix so many things — astrology, numerology, tarot cards, yum-yum, yu-yu, bananas-pananas-chatanas. They are afraid to cover their head when they teach. They want to be very popular. If you want to sell yourself, sell in the open market, but do not take a profession as a Teacher. Don't insult this institution. In the end you will be sorry and regret it. Teachings are never for sale, and a teacher is never for a price. You are priceless, guaranteed by the One who made this universe.

A Teacher is the personal honor of God Himself. Otherwise, just a simple law: If a teacher is not protected by the Creator, the teachings are not protected by the Creator, insanity will be the rule of the universe. But it has to be in balance—sanity and insanity. Therefore, the institution of a Teacher shall have to be protected, whether God likes it or not. It's a rule of thumb. It's a law of existence.

And when you teach the teachings purely, you shall not be offended. Tested? Yes. Insulted? Yes. Betrayed? Yes. Spat at? Yes. But will you in the end lose honor? No. Will you not be worshipped? Yes, you will be. There's no way, because through you only can God prevail. God has no other channel. But God prevails through a Teacher, and a Teacher is a balance, and each balance is that which has two equal sides. A coin has two sides: tails and heads. So people will talk your tale, and people will love to chop off your head. And if you are willing to accept this, you can be a perfect Teacher.

The first person who attacks you will be your spouse. Second will be your relatives. Third will be your students. Fourth will be your intimate friends. And fifth, you'll be seduced and induced to everything called "Temptation." Just remember, this comes with the territory. Because under every candle, there's a dark shadow. It's not that you are a bad Teacher; it is just that intimacy brings contempt. Therefore, do not worry about that contempt. They are innocent.

When I go to India, all these people say to me, "Ahh, what do you care for us poor Indians? Those white-skinned gringos, you just love to teach them. What's wrong with us?"

I say, "It's not wrong. You are rotten. Look at them. They sit for three days doing White

Tantric Yoga, from nine o'clock to six-thirty, go through all what they go through. You can't go through thirty minutes of it. That's open, you can come there too." Did we ever stop anybody from coming to the Summer Solstice? Did we tell them not to do sadhana there with us? When we go through the White Tantric, do we refuse anybody? But you need steel butts to sit through those hours. In Kundalini Yoga you need steel butts, steel determination, and steel self, and that has to be white, stainless steel. There's no other way.

Come on. We have eleven minutes, and we are going to do it. Come on. Ready?

Class: Yes, Sir. *(Spoken weakly, in a scattered fashion.)*

YB: Shame on you. I taught you this morning, and in the afternoon you forget? Do you hear me?

Class: YES, SIR! *(Said powerfully, in unison.)*

YB: That's better. That's reasonable.

This is called *Giaan Sudhaa Simran Kriya*. It's a long name. *Giaan-Sudhaa-Simran-Kriya.* It's the Sacred Kriya of Kundalini Yoga.

(See page 38 for details of this meditation.) Put your hands like this, and put your fingers as wide as they can go. Now watch this. This looks easy, but it'll blow your cover soon. Take these elbows by your ribcage. It's called "Guidance of the Soul." If perfected by a man, that person shall have power over death, life. Not of himself and herself, but all that there is.

Please open wide these three fingers. Your lower back will move. Your butt will be up off the ground, that much shock is there. Put on the tape *Tantric Har.* I'll relax and watch how you can do it. When I did it, I had a pain for three days. I remember my days. Utter no word. Each time you must be lifted by your own power. Do not tip yourself. Don't do it.

You are losing! Hurry up.

Stop. Stop, stop. Stop, stop, stop. You think it is a joke? The more you are in pain, the more you must push. A status will come when there will be no pain, and these three fingers must remain apart and stiff. We'll give you three more minutes. You can get it or forget it. Well, you have come here to become Teachers of tomorrow. A man shall have, on the press of the button, forty mega-trillion units of information. They can't handle that chaotic insanity. You shall be the hope. What do you think you are? People? Girls and boys? Women and men? Then learn to confront calamity, pain, and hazardness, and overcome them. Now!

Power. Power. Give yourself power.

Good, good, good, good, good. If you would have done it like this, you would have gotten the experience, you cheats. Now you are doing it right. But I have to say, "Good night" to you because my time is up. I have to teach a class over there. Anyway, you missed it. We'll do it tomorrow, okay?

Class: Yes, Sir!

YB: You have not learned to speak from the navel. If you do not speak from the navel, you will never be alert, and if you will not be alert, you shall not have a mastery over time and space. It's a simple rule. Why don't you understand science? "Two and two" makes four. It's not going to make five, not going to make three. Rules are rules. Those who have to rule, shall obey the rule! That's the principle needed here. Reverence shall not need reference. Obedience shall command the sensory system of being, and you'll become human. Otherwise you shall remain in the body of a human, an earthling who has no future but comes on the Earth to pick up the next lifetime in the animal kingdom or in the birds.

The soul has its own power. The soul has a purpose: to be redeemed. You come from Infinity, go through the finite, unto Infinity you must exit. And you have Infinite power to do that, by your will. That's why God gave you the will. The finest will of the Infinite God is that you must exit to the Infinite Will. And you can do that only when you shall understand that you are absolutely to obey the command so that you absolutely can command. You must please have clarity and understanding. There's nothing outside of you. It's already in you. These are very simple things.

When a woman loses reverence to a man, that man become her reference. There's no relationship. It's over. Finished. When a man loses the ability protect the woman, man loses the prospect of life. There are no two lies about it. It's very simple. You must know it. You must understand the fundamentals. You have to become total to know the Total. You must learn to obey totally to command totally. It's a simple balance. There is no God but you.

ਆਦਿ ਪੂਰਨ ਮਧਿ ਪੂਰਨ ਅੰਤਿ ਪੂਰਨ ਪਰਮੇਸੁਰਹ ॥
Aad pooran mudh pooran ant pooran parmesureh
  -Guru Arjan, *Siri Guru Granth Sahib*, page 705
The Transcendent Lord pervaded in the beginning, pervades in the middle,
and shall pervade in the end.

In the beginning you are perfect, in the middle you are perfect. In the end you are the perfect God. That's your merging point. Otherwise, cycle and recycle, you will be different than Coca-Cola bottles and paper bags.

I'm not teaching you a class here. I'm helping you to become Teachers. You have come here to become Teachers. Once you become Teachers, God shall pay you respect, reverence, and you shall have beauty, bounty, and bliss. If you fail, time shall nail you into the cycle of birth and death. Half of life is in water, half of life is in the air and on the Earth. Denial is the cockroach; indifference is the squirrel and the dog. That's why you can't get rid of dogs. There are so many, they end up in pounds and shelters. They never obeyed. I wish they should have obeyed God's Will at that time. What was wrong with them? They came here to finalize.

You have taken courage. "It isn't the life that matters. It's the courage you bring to it." You have taken courage, you have come here. It's all new to you, and I am unknown to you. Please forgive me. I'm trying to be very polite and as gracious as I can be, but that is against my being as a Teacher. So I'm bearing my own insult and living my own corruption to teach you as politely as I can. But normally our relationship is like that between a stone and a chisel of time, and the hammer of a teacher. You must go fully chipped, shaped, and polished. And for that, if you are dishonest in your cooperation, you will not get the psyche to invoke in you the rise of your will. And it's your will, and at your will God's Will must obey. Therefore, you must learn to obey first. There's no miracle about it. It's a simple, scientific law. Cause must have an effect, and effect must create impact—permanent and infinite. Good night.

Guidance of the Soul
Giaan Sudhaa Simran Kriya

Mudra: Sit in easy pose with a straight spine. Touch the tip of the index finger to the tip of the thumb. The other three fingers should be kept straight, with the fingers spread as wide apart as possible.

Secure the bent elbows firmly down into the sides of the ribcage. Place the hand mudras in front of each shoulder, palms facing forward. Tilt the forearms forward at a 45 degree angle from the shoulders. This is your starting position.

Movement: On each repetition of the mantra *Har*, arc the hands from the position, up and back about 12 inches, so they stop in a dead halt, next to each ear. The result will be a quick jerk of the body. The palms will continue to be facing forward. Then quickly resume the original position. Continue in a fast pace, keeping the fingers stiff and separated during the entire movement. Do it so powerfully that you feel yourself lifted with each rise of the hands, and then you feel yourself come down with a jerk on your buttocks.

Eyes: Unspecified.

Music: *Tantric Har*, or 1 movement per second. Remain silent.

Time: 11 minutes.

Comments/Effects: This meditation is a Sacred Kundalini Kriya. It is called Guidance of the Soul. If perfected, that person shall have power over life and death—not only for himself or herself, but for all that exists. The exercise may become painful. The more you are in pain, the more you must push. A stage will come when there will be no pain. Learn to confront your pain, your calamity, and overcome it. Give power to yourself through this exercise.

Make sure that the three fingers remain apart and stiff the entire time.

Use Your Body for Higher Living

*You are lonely because you have not known
yourself. That is your loneliness.*

If a person does not understand his body by the age of 27, complete in all aspects, that person never enjoys life. Simple as that. Your development period is 27 years of age. Your living period is another 27 years. And your dying period is another 27 years. That's how it's proportioned. Your achievement is during the first 25 years. Your time within yourself and with your family is the next 25 years. For the next 25 years you roam the world to share and experience. Then for the next 25 years, you wait to go home. That's how these systems were set.

But instead of maturing at 25, as men you start maturing at 15, and at eleven or twelve as women. So you mature ten years earlier than the natural rule. It is good for the body to not have any sexual intercourse before 25, it doesn't matter what. By the time you are 25, you have 25,000 things going on, so you are already consumed. Your semen is thin, your ejection of spermatozoa is elementary. It's way too fast. Your marrow exchange is not solid and your bone structure is not properly built. Therefore, when you grow up as a human, you are one-third less, and that you cannot compensate by any diet, by any build up, by any Mr. Macho Gold Gym, or any of that.

One premature sexual discharge does not allow the brain and the neurological cells to develop. Therefore, all those who indulge in sexuality, in sexual intercourse earlier than 24 years of age are commotional, and they pay for the handicap for the rest of their life.

It's natural. It is not something that you should worry about. You think you have a little penis down there, and she has a vagina, therefore, they've got to meet? You think sexual satisfaction is great, sensual excitement is great, but you forget that you have a nervous system in the body. You have an area of development which medical science has refused to accept, and that is the quality of the marrow in the bones. When the quality of the marrow in the bones is not acceptable, then the bone structure is not acceptable. That's why if a woman starts sex early, when she grows up she has a problem with her bones, which they call a "calcium problem." You know the doctor has nothing to worry about—the death is yours, the pain is yours, the incompleteness is yours, the handicap is yours. It's not the doctor's fault; he is trying his best. He's charging money for it. Why should he worry about it? You started early.

One wet dream is equal to six physical, excited intercourses. And you can count your wet dreams. The pressure of a wet dream on the nervous system is like the whole roof fell on a person, because that intercourse and sexuality is through the nervous system and mind. So the body pays for it.

We have never been given a chance. Nobody ever told us that we have to be ripe. Unfortunately, here in the United States we don't have parents. Parents here don't give us values. They give us love, they give us money, they give us assurance. These are technically all false. We are built on absolutely false security and false values.

It's amazing. When people tell me dreams, and I have not dreamt in my whole life. I do not know what to say. I'm 67 years old. Some people dream for the whole night. They are drowning, really, or they feel on fire. Do you think a dream is not real? A dream is very factual mentally. Simply you are not totally aware. Otherwise, if you are totally aware, you can read the whole dream, exactly as you would see during the day. But you know how much energy it costs, what a toll it takes? Have you any idea?

Then you have your day-dreams. Oh, sitting in a chair, thinking. "Hmm, hmm. There'll be an egg, there'll be chickens, there will be a poultry farm, there'll be a million dollars. I'm going to Las Vegas, I'm going to have a billion-dollar lottery." Those who leak down will never develop up. *(YB points to his head and Third Eye area.)* Period. Therefore, eighty-four percent of people have no intuition because they started sex early.

Then over and above that, the one who was blind then started walking through the graveyard, so he's bound to fall. First was sex; second was the hallucinogenic drugs. That's it, that completes it.

You know, it's very funny. We have never been given a chance. Nobody ever told us that we have to be ripe. Unfortunately, here in the United States, we don't have parents. Parents here don't give us values. They give us love, they give us money, they give us assurance. These are technically all false. We are built on absolutely false security and false values. So naturally when you have become 18 or 20, you are supposed to gradually start handling yourself. By 27 your tendency is known as to whether you are mature or you are immature, and that's how people value you. When at 27 people start valuing you less than you should be valued, you start getting angrier, angrier, and angrier. What can I say? Then there's no life, there's no living; there's a handicapped living. I hate it from day one. It's not my personal cup of tea to live a handicapped life.

But what can you do? You want to fill a bucket, and you have a tap underneath, and you leak out, and leak out, and leak out. You think you are conquering a woman or conquering a man? This is your victory? You do not know. Then you have headaches. Tylenol, Tylenol, then Tylenol Extra-Strength, then Advil. You know what you are living with? What is a headache? You know what a headache is? Your control room is not functioning. And you think the pain goes away with Tylenol? No. The function is there, hurting, but the sense of it is gone. So you mute your sensory system, you mute your senses, you mute your sense of pain. And you mute, mute, mute. Then you are all muted—no feelings. Nothing. You are the ugliest creatures on the planet. You never live original and organic. It is not your handicap; you are handicapped by development because you are not developed. You are not allowing yourself to develop twenty-five years in total maturity from marrow to nervous system. You don't care.

You know, it is a funny thing in America with muscles. "Ooh, ooh, muscle, ooh muscle." What is this muscle? You can walk with muscle four miles an hour. You can try your best. You can walk about eight miles an hour. I have seen people walking twelve miles an hour, fast movers, they call them "shooters." But in a car you walk seventy miles an hour. You can build up a lot of machine and lot of support, but your machine cannot build your marrow. It can't build your bone structure. It can't build your neurological cells. It cannot build your hemispheres of the brain. It can't.

Woman gets sick in this country at the age of thirty-five. It starts with having a problem in the menstruation, with the sexual gonads and glandular system, and with the ovaries and tubes and all that stuff. Normally a woman who is well developed will not have those signs and symptoms 'till she is sixty-five. Thirty-five to sixty-five is a lot of years.

Sex is a bewitchment to you. It's just, "I'm lonely." You are not lonely. You are lonely because you have not known yourself. That's your loneliness. Your loneliness is that you don't know who are you and how developed you are, or how good you are, or how complete you are, how competent you are, and how much you can take. You are very lonely. And this loneliness is stretched through every walk of life.

Then you learn to cover your face and your lips. Your lips are not red; you know you are sick, so you put on lipstick, you put on rouge, you put on mascara. You know you are not beautiful. That I know you know. That's why you put on make-up.

Another funny thing is what you do to your hair. I asked somebody, "What did you do to your hair?"

She said, "I don't know. I wanted to do something, and the man who designed my hair went berserk too. So I was berserk, he was berserk."

I said, "You look like a butch. Do you know what you look like? Look in the mirror."

She said, "I look horrible." And then three hours later she met me; she had a beautiful, most wonderful bald head.

She told him, "Son of a bitch, razor it out." She took the cap off, and I said, "Wow." I said, "What is this?"

She said, "It was too much, so I started all over new."

What can you do? You have just become enemies of your eyebrows. *(YB demonstrates someone pulling on his eyebrows.)* Monkeys do it. You have no hair left.

You know, when Genghis Khan told Kublai Khan,[1] "This time if you go and build China, you have to win China forever. I don't want a defeat." Genghis Khan had conquered China, and China revolted again. Kublai Khan just conquered China and ordered one thing: "Every woman shall have bangs, and if she doesn't have bangs, behead her. Every male should have his head half shaven. *(YB indicates with his hands the area from the browline up to the tenth gate as the area that was shaven in men.)* If he doesn't, behead him." Kublai Khan ruled China forever.

And I've asked so many women, "Why do you put these bangs?"

They say, "We don't want to see these wrinkles." What is so neurotic about having wrinkles? You have wrinkles inside your head. The brain looks just like a walnut. You have wrinkles all over in you.

Glands are the guardians of health. Your glandular system doesn't work. The glandular system does not secrete. If you don't take a cold shower, your capillaries are not going to open; your inner system is not invigorated; and you don't match up to the sensory system of your body. You cut your hair, which is pure protein. Then the body has to replace it. You think you are joking. Do you want to see the power of your hair? Take your own cut hair, mix it with earth, and put a plant there. Then take ordinary earth, and put a plant there. See the growth. You'll figure it out. "Oh, I couldn't keep it long. I just had to cut it."

And there's another beautiful thing which people do to their hairs. "Oh, I cut my ends. They were split ends." If they were split ends, it means your brain is over-fatigued and tired, and you cut your hair. Now that has to grow. It means a horse with an already broken leg, who is running with three legs, and you broke another one, so the guy has to jump on two.

But unfortunately our system is a three-chord system. Everything is complementary to each other in three ways. That's why we survive. Normally we should fall apart.

The greatest loss which you have is when your personality impact is not there. The word you have never heard is IPI — "Individual Personality Impact." If the IPI is not at least six, seven, eight, out of ten, that person lives with that much less impact. The average person's IPI is two, three, four. So you live only one third of your impact. That's why you have to talk all the time, you have to argue all the time, you have to reason all the time, you have to speak all the time, you have to convince all the time. With such a low IPI, how can anything survive? Food business, marriage business, divorce and marriage—because you don't have IPI. Sometimes you buy clothes you never wear, but you want to buy. If your IPI is not at least six, then you are a compulsive shopper, compulsive eater. All compulsory sicknesses come from having an IPI less than five. Forget it. It's too much for you to handle. You always project what you are not. And you make up figures, you make up statements, you make up stories. That's why there are more books on fiction than on facts.

You think you are a human, but if you ask your dogs and cats, you are their pets. Once a girl came to me and said, "I have to go now. My maid did not show up and I have to feed my cats and my dog. I can come back."

The next day she never showed up. The next time I saw her I said, "Well, what were you doing?"

She said, "My cat was sick."

You don't love human as humans. You love them as pets. So your love is a bewitchment of a pet-ism in which you are already handicapped. When you are young, in your pet-ism, you make love to each other because nobody answers anybody. You feel the relationship is very unique. Then the moment reality hits home, you are the biggest war-mongers among your loving relationships. And finally, after stretching it to whatever point you can stretch it to, it breaks down in a divorce. For this society of ours to thrive, we need about four divorces—each with a new refrigerator, new house, new curtains, new carpets, change of the colors, painting, a few parties. Some people are engaged and dis-engaged, engaged and dis-engaged, as if they are like machines. Life is fun, isn't it? With all this reality, still we smile.

In Western civilization it is, "Get whatever you can." In Oriental civilization, everything is a circle, mature; the world you desire not, you deserve first. You are walking on shallow ice, on raw ground, acting as you do, and not qualifying yourself with basic strength. That is your handicap, and that will show up in you as a Teacher. You are not a strong, elementary individual who has the basic strength of character. So some of your character will be weak, and the student will see it. They may not say it, but they will see it.

One thing you must understand. When you are an idiot, everybody knows it except you.

When you are handicapped, everybody knows it but you. But you always have a habit of putting on make-up—mental make-up, spiritual make-up, physical make-up, and you try to make up for something which cannot be made up.

So all of a sudden, a woman cannot live with this husband. This husband cannot live with the wife. Wife cannot live with her man. Girlfriend cannot live with boyfriend. Two partners cannot live as partners. It happens because you are handicapped. You are weak inside, and you live by a make-up. But you look different, you project differently, and you show differently. It's a funny thing—when you are a teenager, you are the biggest known insane of all times, because you think all the money and love and affection of the parents is covering you. But your ass sooner or later is not going to be covered. You will have to walk by yourself. And similarly this happens to a Teacher. Have you seen in America so many Teachers came, they all fell apart. They boosted up like shard,[2] and they came down like this. (YB raises his arm up in the air, then drops it suddenly). Just like firewood, because they didn't build steady grounds.

After twenty-seven years I am teaching the first teacher's course. Do you know how I used to pick teachers? "Hey, you two get up. Are you married or not?" "Oh yes, we are married." "Go to such-and-such a city, and start a center there." And people stood their ground. Some of them are still there, enjoying and being. But now we are teaching how to be a Teacher. Why? Now the Age of Aquarius has come on us. We have to deal with the whole world, so everybody has to have this hands-on work.

After twenty-seven years I am teaching the first Teacher's course. Do you know how I used to pick teachers? "Hey, you two get up. Are you married or not?"

"Oh yes, we are married."

"Go to such-and-such a city, and start a center there." And people stood their ground. Some of them are still there, enjoying, and being. But now we are teaching how to be a Teacher. Why? Now the Age of Aquarius has come on us. We have to deal with the whole world, so everybody has to have this hands-on work. That's why.

Some of you may feel your friends leave you, or you feel your students leave you, or you feel your relatives leave you. No, no. It is all relative. People relate to each other for emotions and feelings, and emotions and feelings change. Each thought you get with the wink of an eye has to turn into a feeling, an emotion, and a desire. Then it becomes a neurosis, a psychosis. It's a continuous process of the intellect. The intellect lives by it. The intellect keeps on bombarding thoughts and thoughts and thoughts and thoughts and thoughts, and millions of thoughts go into the subconscious, and then the subconscious becomes loaded. Then it unloads itself in dreams, in fantasies, in nightmares and, God, when it starts unloading into the unconscious, then you've had it.

A Teacher has to project from the innocent self, with nothing to make-up for—with no wrong projection. How are you going to do that? It's very funny. You think with all your rot-

Each thought you get with the wink of an eye has to turn into a feeling, an emotion, and a desire. Then it becomes a neurosis, a psychosis. It's a continuous process of the intellect. The intellect keeps on bombarding thoughts and thoughts, and millions of thoughts go into the subconscious. Then the subconscious becomes loaded, and it unloads itself in dreams, fantasies, and nightmares. When it starts unloading into the unconscious, you've had it.

ten habits you can still be smiling. It's just like a person has rotten teeth and starts smiling, with all their black and eaten-up teeth. As with rotten teeth you can't smile, with rotten habits you can't live. You can survive, I have no objection to it.

If when you were young you lived a life of adultery, when you become an adult, you start handicapped. But one thing it is difficult for you to face is to be an adult, to be mature. And the thing you hate to face is old age. In old age you become unwanted, single, unattended, unloved. What a tragedy it is. But go to the Orient and see how the older people live. Early in the morning, children can't even wait, they rush to them to listen to their experiences and stories. Once I knew a very old man, and I asked him, "Wow, what is life?"

He said, "Oh, God, I should have become old and handicapped as I am fifty years ago."

I said, "What's the difference?"

He said, "Look how many people are serving me." There were seventeen kids sitting there.

I asked them, "What do you get out of this man?"

They said, "Man, his beautiful experiences and stories. He tells us all that he has done in life and what should not be done and what should be done."

I looked around, there was food for seventy people because everybody brought something. They just wanted to come and be with him and feel him. You will not have those days. You'll go into those rest homes.

I was traveling from Los Angeles to Sacramento, and there was a man sitting in first class next to me. And I said, "Where are you going?"

He said, "I'm going to Sacramento."

"Why?"

"There's a retirement person's company."

I said, "Who are you?"

"I'm this, I'm that."

I said, "Where do you live?"

"I live in the Bible Belt."

I said, "What have you been?"

"I have been so and so."

He said, "My wife has died, my children have grown, I'm alone."

I said, "What do you mean, 'alone?'"

He said, "I have a twenty bedroom house. It's a palace. I built it. I and my wife used to have dreams, and...."

I said, "How many acres is the garden with it?"

He said, "Forty acres."

I said, "Oh yeah? How many servants do you have?"

"Sixteen."

"How many cars do you have?"

"Twenty."

"Huh. What don't you have?"

He said, "I have everything."

"Why are you lonely?"

He said, "Oh, I am very lonely. My wife is gone. I can't live in that house anymore."

And I said, "You are getting out at Sacramento?"

He said, "Yes."

I said, "Take the return flight, go back home, and every Saturday invite one village in your area to your grounds." He's doing it even today. He's the happiest man. He opens up his home and his lawns, spreads out food and everything, and sends an invitation to the village that, "You'll be my guest this Saturday. Come on and enjoy." They sit on the lawns, have food, and the children play. He gives them some gifts, and passes one day. And it takes him one week to prepare for the next Saturday. He has a purpose. He has tons of money. He doesn't need anything, but he didn't have the tool to smile.

You have a tool for sex, you have tools for being hookers, you have tools for everything. But you do not have a tool to smile from your heart. And the heart which does not smile shall not have a good head in the long run. And that's the problem. These observations are true. This is called immature undeveloped human beings trying to act as mature and developed adults. The handicap is in your childhood. You never let the cup fill to the brim. You leaked it out too early. And that leakage, babies, will cost you life.

When I was living in Hollywood, I saw what I saw, and I asked God, "How come?"

And He said, "Well, that's why I've sent you here. Look at it."

On my right side my neighbors were groupies. On my left side my friends all were gay. Not just this out-of-the-closet business, but real—as a religion. They used to call me the "Gay Master." They were not afraid. I was very proud of them. They were very real.

I was living among them. Where our ashram was is the biggest gay area in Los Angeles, and I was in residence there. My first experience was that I found out they are very truthful and straight-forward.

And they used to ask me, "Do you hate us because we are gay?"

I said, "No. It's natural."

"Why?"

"When the imbalanced parents love in an imbalanced way, either you create a neurotic or you create something like that. It's a sensory system." Sex is a sensory system. Sex is not what you think sex is. Sex has nothing to do with being gay or not gay, or being a lesbian or not being lesbian. Sex is not in the private organs of the human. Sex is in the pituitary. And sex is not what you think sex is. Sex is by smell. And because no human has a real body smell, therefore, there's no real sex. What are those colognes out now? There are many names. "Obsession." "Possession." "Realization." "Excession." Put a little umm, that's it, you are dead. You are gone. You have no original smell. When this nose has smelled that Obsession,

Possession, Realization.... Therefore, in any sexual relationship, there'll be no reality, no affection, no realism, because it's provoked by a wrong smell.

The pituitary by smell must order the central nervous system to go down and prepare a person for that. Do you know that? Many of you might not have heard it. Sex is performed down there, but it is created here. *(YB points to his Third Eye point.)* This is called the "Command Center," the Sixth center, *ajna chakra.* It is the center of creativity, of command, and it commissions everything in the human. And this works through fragrance. This is true. That's why in your life you shall always choose the wrong partners.

It's very funny. Two people wanted to get married. I said, "Well, do you already have a sexual, sensual relationship?"

They said, "We are very established. We are very much for each other, blah, blah, blah."

I said, "Okay, you will take a bath together for fifteen days, and then come back to me." Well, after fifteen days they didn't show up. I said, "Okay, we'll wait." After a month they showed up. And I said, "Well? Are you going to marry or not?"

They said, "I don't think so. We have different thoughts now."

A human who's not organic is not original. And any relationship which is created on an inorganic state, on an unreal status, will not last. I was just discussing with my builder. He was going to build a room. We decided on a price. He said, "I'll do it for thirty-five thousand dollars."

I said, "Okay." We agreed.

He came back today. He said, "You have to pay me fifteen thousand dollars more."

I said, "What for?"

"Oh man, everything," he said, "is wrong." Because when he opened up the whole thing, the structure was totally not what he thought it was. He said, "I have to rebuild the whole thing."

That's why you have to divorce and remarry again. That's why you have to fall in love, again, and again, and again, and again. And then, you are dead. And never again.

It's a serious talk today?

Class: Yes, Sir.

YB: It seems like you don't like it. This is your story, folks, as seen through a mirror.

I normally don't say to people everything that I see, because people get scared. They don't come around. It's a lot of difficulty. If once, out of affection and love of my life, I say it and it happens, then they say I have cursed them. I don't want to curse anybody. What for? It's not my happiness that you are weak, or you fall apart, or you do not enjoy life, and you do not share your blossom beauty with everybody. It's my personal feeling that you be super, super, super happy all the time.

Happiness is our birthright. We are born to be happy. We are born to be so happy, that out of all calamities, tragedies, and whatever it is, we can go through it happily. That's how happy we are. We have been provided longitude and latitude and happiness to that brim. But we start early, and when we reach the middle of life which is like the desert. Tthen we have no protection, we have no juice inside like a camel so that we can go on.

It's not that I don't love you. I love you, that's why I am here, that's why I decided to come here from India. I said, "I'm not going to go and visit and come back and take anybody's money. I'll take their money and be there and spend it on them." I taught you for thirty-five dollars a week when people used to charge three hundred fifty bucks a course. I have never taken money from any student. What comes is yours. What you gave is yours. What is left here is yours. I'm a good parent, I'm a good worker, I'm a good man. I earn my livelihood in honest ways. You have to learn to handle the business of your life in a business-like way.

Business has its own identity, as life has its own identity, and you can't shift it. You can't be married to somebody and play a motherly role. You'll be divorced. You cannot marry somebody and be a husband and try to become a father—you'll be left. She left the father's house to marry you, and you have started acting like another father. Wow. Hell, what does she want with that? Wow. You pursued the man, you locked in the psyche, you understood it, and then after that you don't understand it? What you understood, you don't understand now? Divorce is inevitable.

(See page 48 for details of the following meditation.)
YB: There's a hope today and let's see if we can do something about ourselves. You will see how handicapped you are by this exercise. If you reach a stage of pain, which will be horrible, and I'm not saying it won't be, then you have to cross that so that the brain in its balance should work. Brains in balance work.

The mound is touched, pressure put, then release. Put on a very systematic tape of only the drums. The one from Europe. Let me see how they do. I'm very relaxed today. I'm going to watch how you do this little exercise. Hallelujah. We'll check it out.

You will use the word *"Har"* when you put a pressure from the navel point. *"Har"* from the navel point, with the tip of the tongue. That's all. Not very difficult.

(European Drum Tape is played. Class begins reciting "Har" on about every fourth beat.)

Be alert, be alert. It's a very good, tricky beat.

Bravo! Reach out and touch the heavens.

Inhale. Stop, stop, stop, stop, stop.

Make fists. Inhale deep. Hold the breath, and squeeze your entire being. Shift the energy to every cell. For God's sake, don't stop it now. Cannon fire, exhale. Inhale deep again. Tight, tight, tight, tight, tight. Toe to top, tight. Tight. Shake up the whole thing. Cannon fire out. Last chance. Inhale deep. Shake up the whole being. Whole skull, toes, top, knees. Relax.

We have hope, don't we? Tonight we will have a unique class. What time do you eat at night? Just eat at about four-thirty, so that by the time I come you'll have a little left in you so that you can do it. We call it "Dance of the Navel." All right?

Class: Yes, Sir.

YB: And if you eat less it will be a great experience. I can't explain, you can't understand, so it's okay. We are going to get into it. There's nothing outside of us. It's all inside of us. Nanak said if you search outside you are wasting time. It's inside. When we feel beautiful inside, fulfilled inside, inside our own inside, wow, it's so good. See you later.

Meditation to Discover
the Beauty & Heavens Within

a   b   c

Mudra: Sit in easy pose, spine straight, chin in slightly to chest. Bend elbows down by sides, and bring the hands up to the sides of each shoulder, so the wrists are at shoulder level, and the hands are about even with the level of your ears. Make hands flat, palms face forward, fingers spread wide and pointing towards the ceiling.

Movement:
(a) Bring your thumbs in so the pads of the thumbs press against the "mounds of Mercury," the fleshy mounds just below the pinkie finger on the palm of your hand.
(b) Immediately close your fingers over the thumbs, and put a pressure here (squeeze the fingers).
(c) Immediately fling your fingers wide open and straight.
    Although this movement contains three parts, they are done as one continuous movement, with no pauses between the sections.

Music: *Rhythms of Gatka* by Matamandir Singh, or 1 beat per second.

Mantra: The word *Har* is chanted on every fourth beat, and as it is chanted, the navel point is drawn in and the hands are closed at exactly the same moment. Remember to chant the mantra by flicking the tip of the tongue against the upper palate.

Eyes: Unspecified.

Time: Practiced in class for 17-1/2 minutes.

End: Inhale very deeply and make your hands into fists. Squeeze the entire body, shifting the energy into every cell of the being. Don't lose this chance. Hold the breath 10 seconds. Cannon-fire out the breath. Repeat 3 times total, and relax.

Comments/Effects: Be alert, it's a tricky beat. Reach out and touch the Heavens. There's nothing outside of us. It's all inside of us. Nanak said if you search outside you are wasting time. It's all inside. And when we feel beautiful inside, fulfilled inside, wow, it's so good.

The Purity & Power of a Teacher

As a Teacher of Kundalini Yoga, it is your subtle body which has the power to reach everything and anything and can change the molecular structure in 0.0003 trillionths of a second. That is your power. Your power is in your sight, in your touch, in your word. Sight, touch, and word. These are three things you have.

1 would like to explain something to you. It is not a good thing to become a teacher of Kundalini Yoga and mix other things. When you practice Kundalini Yoga, you stay with it only. Remember that. For example, there's not a palmist in the world who's as qualified as I am. There's not an astrologer in the world who can read the way I can read a chart. There's not a person who can read the Tarot cards the way I can. By profession I am a yogi, but for some years I had experienced and foolishly practiced occult powers.

I know you want to be many things, and I fully understand that. But when you become many things, you become nothing. When you become one thing, you become everything. There's a word among us: *Ek Ong Kar:* "There is One Creative Creation." Creation needs a base, a nucleus. A person with Kundalini experience provides such a nucleus. It should be understood very simply. It's not window shopping, it is not dogma. I'm a master of numerology. But will I practice it? No. The greatest astrologers in the world sometimes bring their puzzles and ask me to solve them. I solve them in two minutes. Am I an astrologer? No. I can touch a person and heal. Am I healer? No. I used to just raise a hand, lift a person four feet and let him drop on his butt. Will I do it now? No. Because the first rule of Kundalini Yoga is that you do not show obnoxiously or politely, humbly or powerfully, any power of your own.

So the first principle of a teacher is, "I am not." If you cannot practice *shuniaa,* you cannot be a teacher of Kundalini Yoga. *Shuniaa* means zero. The moment you become zero, then all powers will prevail through you. The power of a teacher of Kundalini Yoga is in his zero, in his shunnyaa. In *shuniaa* you become zero, you reduce everything to nothing: "I am nothing. Everything is nothing. There's nothing to be nothing." The moment you become that, then everything radiates from you.

Second, you are a servant. The moment you become a servant, you automatically become a master. You can never become a master if you want to be a master. Therefore you shall serve in a "Uni-form," "Uno-Form", "One-Form."

A Sikh is a living sage who helps another person to become a sage.

ਆਸ਼ਾ ਇਸ਼ਟ ਉਪਾਸ਼ਨਾ ਖਾਨ ਪਾਨ ਪਹਿਰਾਨ ॥ ਖਟ ਲਖਟ ਪ੍ਰਗਟੈ ਜਹ ਤਹ ਮਿਤਰੋਤਾ ਜਾਨ ॥

Aasa isht upaasanaa, khaan paan peheraan, khat lakhat pargatay jah tah mitrotaa jaan
    -Tulsee, a Hindu poet, in the *Ramayana*
Longing, purpose, worship, food, drink, clothing. If these six things are in sync,
then that person is a true friend.

Aashaa—what you long for. *Isht*—your ultimate purpose. *Upaasanaa*—how you worship. *Khaan*—what you eat. *Paan*—what you drink. *Peheraan*—what you wear. These things of yours should serve you uniquely to represent the power which comes through you. You cannot one day be a clown, the next day be very decorated, the third day a good-for-nothing, the fourth day hopeless, the fifth day beautiful. You shall not be in the presence of any person if you are not ready. And you shall be perfectly ready to serve the great teachings. That is the entitlement.

Please don't misunderstand that we want you to be this, we want you to be that. It's not true. Actually, Sikhism is not a religion, believe me or not. If you really understand it, it's not a religion. It became a religion, we make it a religion, because we want to escape persecution. That I can understand. What is a Sikh? A Sikh is a living sage who helps another person to become a sage in every age. "Sikh" means "student." A student is one who studies to be a student, and whosoever becomes a perfect student, becomes a perfect master. And what is a sage? The one through whom wisdom flows. A sage is not wise. A sage is one through whom wisdom flows.

I understand that we read and study a lot of things; we do many things to heal. I understand all the sciences. For God's sake, if you want to learn, learn from me. Sometimes I can teach you, sometimes I can't. But it is not that I have not learned. If I had not studied all that, I would not have found out that everything is stupid.

As a head of a religion, I have only one advantage—I have met all the heads of the religions. When I met His Holiness Pope John Paul the Second, we were supposed to meet for three, four minutes; we ended up meeting for forty-five minutes. I told him, "I'll pray for you." You know why I said that? He lives under such cruel environments. The guy gets up at six a.m., and up to nine p.m. he has only three minutes of his own time. You know what I'm saying? Three minutes. His schedule is completely made; he's a Mr. Robot Machine. I have never seen a person with that much get up and go. He meets one person for one minute, the next person for one minute, shakes hands—one minute, blesses— one minute. They write his speech, give it to him to read, which he reads in seven languages. If they made me Pope today, and gave me one million dollars a minute, I would refuse—I'm not kidding. And if my secretary tried to tell me, "You have to read this," that person would not have teeth on that side.

There are certain things you will never find me doing: I'll never write notes and read from them. I'll never prepare a lecture. Never. Another thing is if I say something and you don't like it, I'll let you do what you want—I shall not object. What I cannot cross, I'll by-pass. I have nothing to lose; you have everything to lose. Why should I enforce myself? Tell me. What is mine to be enforced? You want to learn, learn. You don't learn, don't learn. If you learn, you become learned. If you don't learn, you are not learned. Period. By intuition you can learn. Kundalini Yoga gives you knowledge, awareness. That's why we call it the Yoga of Awareness.

What is there to healing? If you tell somebody to eat a cucumber, just tell him to heal, and tell the cucumber to heal—the cucumber shall heal. The cucumber will not be a cucumber, the cucumber becomes a healer. Do you understand what I'm saying?

Class: No.

YB: No. Okay. It's very difficult to explain a lot of things to you guys.

Let us say somebody comes to you affectionately, and he says, "Master, please help me." He will come and bow and touch your feet. He will bring some food or anything—it doesn't matter—a present, a flower or something. It's true what I'm saying, absolutely true. I have seen it myself. A person had his entire body cracked. The disease was so horrible, and it had gone to such an advanced stage—it was unbearable. He said, "Master, it's painful, it's unbearable. I have done nothing wrong. I might have done wrong in any life, I don't know one damn thing. But for God's sake, please have mercy."

He brought a long-stemmed rose. You know, in India, nobody removes the thorns—it's not auspicious to do so. So, there was one big stem with a lot of thorns. He took it and he just spanked the guy. And he said, "You are healed." The only thing which was not healed was the part bleeding from those thorns. The rest of the body was as new as it should be. Spontaneously, on the spot, he was healed.

Suppose there is a cucumber here and a person comes and he says, "I'm dying, I'm very miserable." Pick up the cucumber and say, "Eat it." The touch, the cucumber, the psyche, and the frequency will totally heal. You do not give anybody anything. As a Teacher of Kundalini Yoga, it is your subtle body which has the power to reach everything and anything and can change the molecular structure in 0.0003 trillionths of a second. That is your power. Your power is in your sight, in your touch, in your word. Sight, touch, and word. These are three things you have. You spoke, "Eat this, you will be healed." You are healed. You look at it and you say, "You are healed." There's no power in Almighty God to change it. Do you know what I'm saying?

Class: Yes, Sir.

YB: Because you are a channel of God, you are a channel of divinity. Therefore you can't have duality. When you have duality, you have no divinity. They won't come together. If you have duality you have no divinity. If you have divinity, you have no duality. It's a rule which you can't change.

You shall refuse none, therefore you shall accept none. That's the most difficult thing in the

> *Creation needs a base, a nucleus. A person with Kundalini experience provides such a nucleus. It should be understood very simply. It's not window shopping, it is not dogma. The first rule of Kundalini Yoga is that you do not show obnoxiously or politely, humbly or powerfully, any power of your own.*

So the first principle of a teacher is, "I am not." If you cannot practice shuniaa, you cannot be a teacher of Kundalini Yoga. Shuniaa means zero. The moment you become zero, then all powers will prevail through you. The moment you become that, then everything radiates from you.

life of a teacher. Therefore, in Kundalini Yoga we don't initiate. We are not swamis. We are yogis, and the pair of opposites do not affect a yogi—neither praise nor insult.

One thing I will tell you as a matter of advice: If you do not know corruption, you will never know honesty. Not that you have to play with honesty, or play with corruption. You can watch. That is the most difficult hurdle in a human mind, that you can eat, not eat.

I'll tell you a story and you'll understand. There were eighteen thousand *gopis* who were the consorts of Lord Krishna. He had a wife: Rukhmani. His beloved was Radha. She was the beloved. She won the Infinity. That's why they chant "Radha Krishna." Then he had the eighteen thousand *gopis*, who were his consorts—his lovers.

One day they asked the Lord, "We want to go and see your teacher."

He looked at them and he said, "What is the matter? What is the hurry?"

"My Lord, give us permission to see your teacher. Darbasha Rishi has opened up his meditation, and we want to go see. He's your teacher. Please bless us to go to see your teacher.

Lord Krishna said, "Go."

So they took milk, butter, yogurt, and sweets, all offerings for this great rishi. But before going, they had to ask permission of the River Jumna,[1] because the River was in over-bank, overflowing, and they wanted a way through.

Now you must understand that Lord Krishna was their lover, their physical lover. It is called, "in-sexing," not "sexing." It is in your mind, and in your self, and in your being—every cell of you intercourses every cell. So technically, these were his "sexy" lovers. All eighteen thousand. So they went and stood by the bank of the Jumna, and they said, "River Jumna, Lord Krishna has permitted us to go to our teacher. If he's celibate...." (Watch this word. Remember, they all had sex with him.) "If he's celibate, let us pass."

Jumna came up only to the ankles, and they crossed. They gave the food to Darbasha Rishi and he ate it all. They said, "Lord, now we want to go. Jumna is overflowing. What should we do?"

He said, "If it is true that I only live on air, then the Jumna will let you pass."

So they came to the bank and said, "If Darbasha Rishi, the Lord of Lord Krishna, lives on air, let us pass." The Jumna let them pass. They reached the other side, and said, "Hey you damn Jumna, you liar, what are you doing? He sleeps with us every time he wants to, and you are telling us that he is celibate? And that guy ate tons of food, and you agree that he lives on air? That's not fair." So they found Krishna and they started beating the hell out of him.

He said, "But you are my lovers."

They said, "We'll talk later. First let us get even."

So when they had gotten even, he said, "Well, you have beaten me enough. Now could you tell me what happened?"

They said, "This is what happened. You are our lover, and this is what he said. Jumna cannot lie. Water cannot lie. Water's the only truth God has. Water is circulatory; it's a giver of life. It can't lie."

Lord Krishna said, "Yes, it can't lie. I know it can't lie. Jumna didn't lie."

They said, "You lied. You made Jumna lie."

He said, "Jumna didn't lie. I didn't make Jumna lie."

"You're not celibate."

He said, "All right, tonight we'll experiment." So that night, all eighteen thousand had the experience of sensual, sexual, and all social experience, physical, mental and personal with him. Next morning he said, "What was that last night?"

They said, "You had sex with us."

He said, "Yeah? Really?"

They said, "Yeah."

He called Arjan, "Arjan? Where were we last night?"

He said, "Lord, you were on my chariot, and we drove to such-and-such king, and we were there the whole night. We meditated. In the morning the king came, and he is just sleeping. We came back."

They said, "Arjan, you are lying, too."

He said, "No. Go to that palace and see for yourself who's there."

They went and asked the king. He said, "True, Lord Krishna came last night."

Then they said, "My Lord, explain it to us."

Then Lord Krishna showed his *bharat roop*, multiple self. Then he became so many Krishnas, they couldn't even count. And when all that appeared, he stood on the side and with his flute he said, "Look, look. That's Krishna."

They said, "No, which one is you?"

He said, "Any one."

That is *bharat roop*.

Then time and space and the elements cannot stop your will as a Teacher of Kundalini Yoga. Time and space and elements cannot stop your will. That's the status you are asking for. But if you are thinking of too much dirt and Earth, then it'll be dirt to dirt. It'll never be dirt to Heavens. A Teacher of Kundalini Yoga is the Lord of Heavens. Always is, shall be, and is meant to be. Earth is a place of play. So let us play, so I can leave you in good taste and go.

(See page 57 for details of the following meditation.)

Stretch your spine. It's a guided meditation.

Spread your two fingers apart. Press your two fingers hard. Stretch your spine, and put your chin in, and your chest out, totally. Go back until your shoulders start painfully hurting. Close your eyes, breathe as long and slow as you can. The pressure on the back shoulders should be so much it should hurt. Cause it to hurt. The shoulder blades must hurt. They'll become numb. They will release the tension of the muscular pressure; and the *shushmanaa*, the central nerve, will flare up. It is a simple formula. It's not something which is not scientifically true. Put humongous pressure on your shoulder blades. If your shoulder blade doesn't hurt, it won't happen. In absolute silence, the world will talk to you. In absolute pain, you can take away the pain of the whole universe. You are experiencing mastery, and you are experiencing the first relationship with your self.

You have to win today. The victory is yours. Pull as hard as possible. Look, all that Infinite power is in you. It's not going to come out of the sky. You simply have to challenge yourself. Don't look like a baboon; you have to look like a human. A human is an angel. You are going to be the saviors and servants of the Earth. This is your designation. A teacher of Kundalini Yoga is a Lord of the Heavens; he is a savior, sage, and a servant of the Earth. Period. There's no other definition. He is a master of longitude, latitude, altitude, and attitude.

Please let your love win today. It's not going to hurt. It's not that bad as you may think. For a few minutes it's you conquering you. Conquering pain is not a bad idea. With Tylenol you can do it, but without Tylenol you can do it too. The brain releases a lot of Tylenol—those endorphins.[2] That's what the brain releases when pain is extensive.

(YB reading from a paper.): A - Always fearless. B - Beautiful in public. C - Concentrated in their action. D - Do as they are told. E - Earth's friend. F - Friend, you are friend to all. G - Gives all happiness. H - Happy when tested. I - Is a student of God. J - Jumps ahead when behind. K - Keeps up. L - Learns from the best teacher. M - Meditates on God. N - Never negative. O - On the top. P - Prevails through the hardest challenges. Q - Never questions. R - Ready for anything. S - Soul is pure. T - Teacher teaches others. U - Uses the finest there is. V - Vision, sees God in all. W - Writes from the heart. X - X-rays the aura of the person in need. Y - Yells only at what needs to be awakened. Z - Zaps, then defends. *(Find this Alphabet of a Teacher and other "Alphabets" in the Resources section.)*

Self is challenging the self. Conquer it. We used to do this exercise for eight hours. I am expecting eleven minutes. I think five have passed; then you start relaxing? This is not fair. I thought you were very good.

Say to yourself: "I am the Lord today. I shall bless all. I shall bless myself. I shall command. I am, I Am."

Put the *Ong Namo Guru Dev Namo* tape on for the last few minutes. Help them. Come on. Try it! You have two blades and one great will. Keep your head high. Keep your power flowing. Four more minutes to go, and that is a decisive action; it is your right. It's not a machoism and ego. It's just following the path.

Now you can sing aloud, but don't let the pressure go. Keep up.

Inhale deep, inhale deep, inhale deep, inhale deep, inhale deep. Relax.

Those of you who have done it, know it. There's nothing I can add or say. With honesty, honor, and intensity you have done it; that's your experience. It doesn't take much to bring God down into us. Actually, God is in us. Simply sometimes we can just concentrate and become that. It's called a turning point. People have lied to you for three thousand years, and they have kept God away from you. God always is, was, and shall be in you. Without that you can't live. That's your love. Instead of that love you create duality and love everything else. You have never loved your soul, you have never talked to it, you have never been with it.

The universe is asking you to confirm with yourself whether you would like to serve the Earth, to save the Earth, be the sage of the Earth. Earth—the Sustainer, the Mother of you, which nurtures you—can you nurture it back? That which serves you, can you serve it back?

Class: Yes, Sir.

YB: This is the day. Some people really feel I have gone mad since I joined the Earth movement. I switch off all lights. Preserving the energy is not a bad idea. Saving the water is not a bad idea. Not polluting the environment is not a bad idea. Putting garbage everywhere is not a good idea, and polluting your mind and putting garbage in it is not a good idea. Pushing your soul to a corner where it cannot even breathe is not a good idea.

When you have duality,
you have no divinity.
They won't come together.
If you have duality,
you have no divinity.
If you have divinity,
you have no duality.
It's a rule which
you can't change.

What do you do? You create a storm of commotions and emotions and neuroses and feelings. God, the soul cannot even look at itself. The soul runs and hides in corners—here, there, nowhere. It becomes deep, dormant. Sometimes you create such a hurricane, that even your Third Eye cannot see it. Such a commotion! Emotions, feelings, desire, commotion, ego—put it all together, and you lose your identity. The moment you lose your identity, you lose your impact. When there is no impact in your identity, you have no fact, you have no leg to stand on. Then you pretend and wear the garbs of a Teacher but act as a human. You wear armor. You are called "earthlings."

You are the fountain of love, blessing, grace, bounty, beauty, and bliss, but you seek from your student public relations, admiration, appreciation. And then you proudly say that such-and-such model and such-and-such actor, and such-and-such this and such-and-such comes to your classes. What do you teach, acting or reality? If you are not a jewel yourself, how can you make jewels? And if other people are your decoration, what strength do you have? Have you ever thought of it?

You know, when I came through immigration, the immigration officer said, "I have a great problem with you, Yogiji."

I said, "What is your problem?"

He said, "Well, in Canada you are a Yogi." The Canadian government had to issue a special category of immigration for a "Yogi".

I said, "Yes. I'm not a religious man, I'm not a school teacher, and I'm not a sports teacher. I'm a Yogi. They had only two categories. So they created Category C: Yogi."

So he said, "That's very well. It is in your passport. It's a government stamp, I understand. But the United States wants you to be certified as a Yogi."

I said, "That's it?"

He said, "Yeah. Can you get something done like that? Somebody writes from India, or something?"

I said, "No, I'll give it to you in twenty minutes."

I went to the Bank of America, and I asked somebody to type out: "I, Harbhajan Singh

Khalsa Yogiji, hereby certify that I am a perfect Yogi. I swear it under da da da da." And I signed it, got it notarized, paid one dollar—matter ended. I brought four copies and I gave him one. I said, "Kindly receive it." He received it.

He said, "This is your certificate?"

I said, "Well, who else can certify? Are you going to certify me?"

"Somebody from India."

I said, "Who? Only a Yogi can certify the self and self can certify a Yogi. Let me teach you lesson one: I must certify myself, and myself must certify me. If I do not know this, I'm not a yogi."

He said, "Okay, okay, okay, I understand. It's okay. This will work."

I said, "It will."

If you cannot certify yourself, nobody can certify you, and no certificate will work. If you don't have your character, your characterlessness will make you fail. If you have character, you shall not lose.

Does anybody know how to bow? Hey you, little, come here. *(A young girl comes up and sits on the teacher's platform.)* Sit crossed legged, and when I utter the word "Bow," go on your heels and bow, and jump up as fast as you can. Okay, ready? Look meditative and look normal. Bow! *(Girl is sitting on her heels, and then bows her forehead to the ground.)* Correct.

If you do not know how to bow, you do not know how to excel. Do you understand?

Class: Yes, Sir.

YB: One who does not know how to bow shall never excel. It's a law which you cannot change. Those who bow become the Masters, because it's their privilege. Those who excel, excellently bow, because that's their mastery. Think about it. Good night.

Guided Meditation
to Find the Infinite Power Within

Mudra: Sit in Easy Pose with a straight spine. Bend the ring and pinkie fingers into the palms of the hands, and hold them there with the thumbs. Extend the index and middle fingers straight up, and spread them wide apart. Keep these two fingers very straight, stiff, and hard.

Place the two hands about 8 inches to the sides of each ear, palms facing forward. Stretch your spine up and forward a bit, pull your chin in slightly, and slightly stretch your chest out. Do this to the point where your shoulder blades begin to come together. There will be a pressure on the upper back area, which may hurt, but go through it. Keep your head high. Keep your power flowing.

Eyes: Closed.

Breath: Breathe as long and as slowly as you can.

Music/Time: 11 minutes, in the following segments:
- 7-1/2 minutes, do the meditation with long deep breathing, in silence.
- 2-1/2 minutes, *Ong Namo Guru Dev Namo* by Nirinjan Kaur and Guru Prem. Singh. (The rhythm for the *Ong Namo* is slow.) Meditate in silence, still breathing in posture.
- One minute, music still playing, sing aloud, still holding the posture.

End: Inhale deeply. Relax.

Comments/Effects: The shoulder blade pressure should be so much that they hurt, and may even become numb, but this will release the tension stored in the muscles. This will cause the *shushmanaa*, the central nerve, to flare up. Put a huge pressure on your shoulder blades. If your shoulder blades don't hurt, this will not occur. Learn to conquer the pain, overcome the obstacles, and find the victory within. You are having the first relationship with your self in this meditation.

In absolute silence, the world will talk to you. In absolute pain, you can take away the pain of the whole universe.

You have to win today. The victory is yours. Look at the Infinite power in you. Let your love win today. "I am the Lord today. I shall bless all. I shall bless myself. I shall command. I am, I Am."

Overcoming the Complexes of Life

How can you get rid of a complex?
Make one complex: "I am the Grace of God.
I am the Will of God. I am God."
If you're going to make a complex, make
it a big one, so all can be contained.

Today we are talking about something very serious. It is the cause of all tragedies, the cause of all our pain, the cause of all our degradation, inferiority, depression, unfulfillment, unhappiness. Whatever negative is in your life, this one thing is the cause of it. It is called a complex. We all are the by-product of complexes.

The child in us never grows up, and the child in us has a very strong creative complex. That is why when we are sure, we are not sure; when we are right, we are not right. Some people have no roots. The complex of a child is so powerful. About ninety out of one hundred people just crawl their whole lives whether they have the best or worst environments.

We have never learned to overcome our complexes. "I have white skin." It's a complex. "I am brown." This is a complex. "I'm American," is a complex. "I'm a German," is a complex. "I'm a person," is a complex. "I'm a human," is a complex. "I'm a doctor," is a complex. Everything in life is boxed into a complex, and everything is a certification.

Actually, those who do not have complexes are those who live by the virtue of their soul, all the time. It's a mental process, with no diversion. If we believe, "I'm a spirit, I'm among the spirits, I am from the Great Spirit, I have to merge in that Spirit," all problems shall be solved.

"I am blond, I am brunette, I am a woman, I am a man, I am black, I am yellow, I am pink, I am Japanese, I am French," I don't know. "I'm Spanish, I'm a gringo. I'm a redneck, I'm a blue neck, I'm a pink neck. I'm a lesbian, I'm gay, I'm straight, I'm a hetero. I'm a prostitute, I'm a pimp, I'm a holy man. I'm divine. I'm religious." The whole thing is garbage. Total. It's called "Mental Garbage." Really. Honest to God. It's not untrue. You may not like what I'm saying, and saying it chokes me up. What an unfortunate humanity you are.

The tragedy is you live by complexes, and you don't recognize them. You don't. You are so stupid, arrogant. You are an arrogant mammal. Will you ever learn the reality of you, that you are just a spirit—always were, are, and shall be? You can understand it when you see that when you die, the spirit leaves, yet everything is intact. You know what dies with you? Your complexes.

What is your purpose in life? To axe your life? What are you—choppers? Why can't you just be fine with a fun living smiling spirit?

There is no identity for you, except your spiritual identity. There's no grace in you but to learn. There's no achievement other than to become learned. There's no power but to share what you have learned with all and everyone. Share with compassion—you'll be compensated, and you shall have no complex. Then all that is there shall come to you. Then you don't have to go to anybody.

Just before I came here, I was yelling and screaming—I was the Administrator—making decisions, shifting, doing. Wow, you should have seen me. When I was there, I was there, and I knew what I had to do because that is how the spirit guides me. Now I am here. Did I bring papers, notes? I am here as I am here. There's no need for me to have a victory. I *am* the victory.

Man without a complex is nothing but a living victory. It is as simple as that. You can never win. Every day you win, every day you lose, every day you have problems, every day you eat your own garbage. For God's sake, stop it. Doesn't it stink and smell? You have to eat your own dirt? Are you so sick? Don't you know you are pure, you are positive, you are spirit, and you have nothing but to be? To be, to be. And the light of your spirit you share, you glow and glare, and you have fun.

You have physical, mental, and spiritual complexes. You have even put your spirit into complexes. This is the most funny, most idiotic, most insane thing I have heard: "Oh, I am an old soul, he's an old soul, he's my soul mate." And they screw each other. Can you believe this soul-mate business? Souls have started screwing. God bless America, this great country! When I heard that, I said, "Wow, we've had it."

"This is my soul mate. I want to marry her." Souls marry? Souls don't marry. They don't. Really, they don't. Souls don't marry, and souls don't mate. Souls have no mate. Everything is a soul mate. The entire existence is one soul, as there is one sun and there are a million rays. That's how it all is. And there's no complex, therefore no reflex, therefore no impulse. When a human acts under impulse, as a mammal, as an animal, that human shall never be redeemed. You have to act under intuition. If that is not developed, then you have to act under your spirit. Nanak said that the safest thing is: "Act just with your spirit." Just be. Be to be, because you have been gifted to be. Don't try to drift and create a rift.

You know, the funny part is, when we are young we live in our second chakra. Some have a tendency to start living in the first chakra. Well, sixth and seventh are your chakras, too. Why don't you live in them? It is *all* you. If you can live in the basement and the first story, you can also live on the sixth and seventh stories. But you don't want to live in the sixth and seventh stories, because you will not find mosquitoes and flies there. They can't go that high. Your meanness, your ugliness, your untruths, your lies, your hookery business, when you come to the sixth center, they won't work. Therefore, you can't go there. You have been a human and how can you act as an animal? By impulse.

How can you deal with everything in life with a complex? It'll be judgment, and judgment is not good. That's why you always like to put on make-up and try to look beautiful, try to look this way and that way. Because you are worth nothing. You are a worthless creature. You know it. You have no value. You never value yourself, why should anybody else value you? So, you add your value. *(YB demonstrates a person doing different poses, as if they have different hats on, different clothes on, different make-up on.)*

You think you have to do something. No. You have to do nothing. Because you have come from nothing and when you have come from nothing, nothing has made you something. Just be that, and you will be honored. And once you are honored, you will be loved, you will be respected, you will be desired, you will be admired. All that you want, you'll get. But you won't get it without being what nature made you to be. If you betray your Maker, time and space shall betray you.

Call yourself anything, be anything, label yourself with anything. But there is no identity for you, except your spiritual identity. There's no grace in you but to learn. There's no achievement other than to become learned. There's no power but to share what you have learned with all and everyone. Share with compassion—you'll be compensated, and you shall have no complex. Then all that is there shall come to you; then you don't have to go to anybody.

Isn't that so simple? Didn't God make everything for a human—environmentally, physically, psychologically, biologically, and personally so simple? And you make it complicated. Why? You have complexes. Why a complex? Because you never know who you are. It's very simple.

Somebody asked, "How can I get rid of the complex?"

I said, "Make one complex: 'I am the Grace of God. I am the Will of God. I am God.' If you're going to make a complex, make it a big one, so all can be contained."

We all have to learn to be real, and our reality is that we are the spirit. We're born by spirit, we live by spirit, we die when spirit leaves. Our identity is nothing but our own spirit; our life should be nothing but our spirituality; and our existence should be nothing but our own reality. Everything else is a complicated affair in which we put ourselves in prejudice and jeopardy. You could put on all the make-up in the whole world, but the One who made you knows better.

There was one girl who said to me, "I don't like my nose."

I said, "What is wrong with your nose? It's so good, it fits well."

"Oh no, I don't like my nose. I have to get a nose job done." So she spent six thousand dollars to get her nose job done. Nose got done.

After about two months she came and asked me, "How does it look?"

I said, "Ridiculous."

"Why?"

I said, "Because it is not your nose."

"Oh no, you are prejudiced."

I said, "Yeah, I am prejudiced. But it's not your nose."

"Why?"

I said, "It's not your nose."

"Why?"

"What do you mean about 'why'?"

"Oh, because you know people appreciate me."

I said, "People don't appreciate you. And the doctor didn't appreciate you. Tell your doctor that he has to re-nose you."

"Why?"

You don't need make-up; you don't need to make up for anything.
You are known by your spirit. You shall project out by your radiance.
You shall be loved and honored by your excellence, or stupidity, or by
your ignorance and arrogance, as the case may be.

I said, "I'm telling you. Aren't you finding difficulty breathing at night?"

She said, "Yes, but he said it'll go away."

I said, "No, it will increase. You will not breathe."

Six months later she had to go for a major operation, huge, humongous. She came back. She said, "How does it look?"

I said, "Worse than before, but at least now you'll breathe."

"Why?"

I said, "Did they put tubes in your nose?"

She said, "Yes."

I said, "See?"

"But why did it happen to me?"

I said, "You had a normal nose. Your nose was a straight nose. That straight nose had the direct ear contact with your pituitary. The moment they cut that nerve you were finished."

"What will now happen to me?"

I said, "Un-standard sleeps, headaches, and sometimes your head will eat circles." *(YB demonstrates a person who's head is rolling around in circles on his neck.)* She is still alive, and all those three things are true.

Somebody got his ear fixed. Now he has a problem. He hears like a dog. He hears all the high frequencies. He can't even drive a car. If a police car goes by with its siren on, he has to pull over to the side and stop the car.

Get this "job" done, that "job" done. Doctors are a help. They diagnose. But God made you. If you don't like yourself, kill yourself. What is the idea of being yourself? The idea of life is to be, to be. You can live with your ego and say, "I don't like myself. I want to like myself this way, that way." It's fine. God likes you the way He made you. Did He consult you? Did God have a session with you, face to face, as when you go into college and work with your college advisor, and ask, "Okay, come sit with me. Hello, how are you? I'm sending you to Earth. What're you going to be? How would you like to be?"

And you said, "This, this, this."

And He said, "No, I'll give you this."

Was a contract signed? Was it?

Class: No, Sir.

YB: Then what are you doing here? He sent you here and you want to forget that fact? You created these complexes to help you forget it? Aren't you ashamed of being human?

When I came to the United States people told me: "Oh, you need money. Oh, you need to be able to drive. Oh, you need this. Oh, you need your social security number."

I said, "Am I a dog that I need a number?"

"You have to have it."

I said, "They will send it. Don't worry about it. What I have to have, God has to send to me. I'm not going to go and get anything. He's going to give me everything."

You know that first lecture I gave? *The Art and Science of Liberation? (Find this lecture in the Resources section.)* Get that paper somewhere. It was a great lecture, organized by the YMCA. So many people came—that is, I came and my driver came—it was fun. I gave a full lecture, even though they advertised the wrong date, and he tape recorded it. The next day all the people came, and there was no me, no lecture. But they did play the tape. Everyone loved it. We have printed it so many times. It's the very first lecture we printed in the United States.

You don't need make-up; you don't need to make up for anything. You are known by your spirit. You shall project out by your radiance. You shall be loved and honored by your excellence, or stupidity, or by your ignorance and arrogance, as the case may be. The art is to be smart. To be smart is to be small, which can contain all. Write down this formula:

> The art of being smart is to be small, which can contain all.

> The art of success is to answer the call of duty with grace and compassion.

> The art of happiness is to serve all, and all shall serve you.

These are three fundamentals.

(See pages 65-66 for details of the following meditations.)

Put on that tape *The Yogi*. Focus the eyes on the tip of your nose. Breathe through the "O" of the mouth. Make a clear "O" of the lips. Inhale deep. Hold the breath. *Shuniaa*. Synchronize the entire being. Let it go. Relax.

Put on his *Gobinday, Mukanday* tape. You will never be free if you have the concept that you have a complex. You will always live in dirt. You will always eat your own ego-maniac, self-created pain. Your life will be nothing but a tragedy. You will be hurt, you will be hurting. The more you hurt, the more you'll be hurting. Neither wealth, nor the environment, nor the services of the Earth can save you. You are from the Heavens, you came from the Infinite. You are here, and you have to go back to the Heavens and the Infinite. As long as this Earth is important to you and you have less Heavens and more Earth, there shall be pain. Even with everything intact, you'll be hurting. And the more you hurt, the more you'll hurt.

You are not real, you are not human. You look human, you act as if you are human, and you know you are human. That's your ego. But you have a complex. And you have reflexes. You are not spirit. As long as you are not spirit, you are not going to be happy, you are not going to be, and you are not going to have fun. Spirit is the fun, spirit prevails, spirit is your decoration, spirit is your make-up, spirit is your being, spirit is your identity, and your spiritual projection is your power. Instead of that, you are isolated; you are always hiding behind your hide or behind your walls or behind your curtains, or behind your emotions, commotions, and your dramas. Well, who are you? At least a bottle of Coca-Cola has written on it: "Coca-Cola." It's a trademark.

Who are you? You are a "hu-man being." "Hu" means spirit, the light. *(YB makes circles with his hands over his head, and out to the sides, referring to the auric field or radiant body of a person.)* "Man" means the mental, the now, being now. Now you are the spirit of your mind. You are the bright light of yourself. That's your identity.

Therefore, because of your complex, you cannot accept everything as spirit and everything cannot accept you, so you create more complexes. Therefore, you have no compassion; you run amok; you make no sense. It's a natural progression: you grow, you have a youth, you have warm blood, you have strength; and as you grow, you will grow weaker and emptier. Is that the see-saw you came here for?

Put the *Gobinday Mukanday* tape on. There should be an answer for our pain, so that we do not live in a self-caused insanity. No sound. Your whole upper body from the navel point must dance. Use your spirit, your power. The spine must dance. Power, power, power!

Create the sound from the force of the body, not by clapping. The force is so strong, believe me, that the body will create the sound. Your nerves are stronger. Your ribcage is a drum. Beat it. Come on, do it! Your elbow must hit the ribcage. Hit it! You know where Breath of Fire came from? From this. You are doing *Ashtang Agni Kriya.* Get into it. You are losing ground! Come on! Try it once, experience it, then tell me. Don't do it half way. Watch, watch. Power. You have a genetic force. Keep going. Relax, relax. You are enjoying it?

Class: *(Applause.)*

YB: This is *Ashtang Agni Kriya:* The Eightfold Fire Kriya of Kundalini Yoga. The mantra is *Gobinday, Mukunday, Udaaray, Aaparay, Haariang, Kariang, Nirnaamay, Akaamay.* This is an *Ashtang Yog Shastric Mantra.* How many of you have gone to a rodeo? You know, where they ride the bull and all that stuff? One thing they do, they ride on a horse, and they tie the calf, and they measure the time. Perfection of this mantra can make a person a rodeo-rider with God as the calf. I'm not kidding. True. This gives you a real Breath of Fire.

Play this tape back from the beginning. You have to do this. I'm very good at it. You create a sound. It's the seventh rib, "from which God made a woman." Remember that? It means the entire creativity of humanity is based in the seventh rib. Nobody understands—nobody made a woman out of that little bone, but you know.... This is how they explain things.

Watch. Here is how you get the power. *(YB demonstrates.)* Understood?

Class: Yes, Sir!

YB: Ready. I want you to experience it. Get it, get it, get it, get it! The breath will become Breath of Fire. Come on. Come on, let's make it today! Now, now, now, now, now! *Hallelujah.* Come on! The Saints are marching.... Breath of Fire. Bravo! Hard! Wow, come on. Powerful breath. Powerful. Shalom, brother, Shalom. Peace will prevail. Fire your own fire. Burn your karma. The soul is just a prisoner of the ribcage. Free it! Free it, and free it now! Hit hard!

Inhale. Relax, relax. Now you are getting spaced out. You have to do other things. I just walked in without a program. If we pull it for fifteen minutes more, then forget it. What we have done is just a start. Slowly and gradually we'll develop the fire, our God within us, pure, powerful, and all prevailing with which we shall burn the karma, the cause and effect. The soul is a prisoner of the ribcage. We shall be free, now and forever.

Have a good day. Thank you.

Meditation to Brighten Your Radiance

Mudra: Sit in easy pose, spine straight. Place the two hands about 12 inches to either side of the ears, palms facing forward, fingers pointing straight up towards the ceiling. The elbows are not pressed into the sides, but are held away from the body a bit. Bend the index finger down and curl it under the thumb (*Giaan Mudra*). The rest of the fingers are held side by side, pointing straight up. Hold the position steady and breathe.

Eyes: Focus on the tip of the nose.

Breath: Make your lips into a very clear "O", and breathe long and deep through the "O" mouth.

Tape: *The Yogi* by Matamandir Singh.

Time: Done for almost 21 minutes in class.

End: Inhale deeply, hold the breath, come into a state of *shuniaa* (zero), and synchronize your entire being. Hold 20 seconds. Relax.

Comments/Effects: "You don't need make up, you don't need anything. You are known by your spirit. You shall project out by your radiance. You shall be loved and honored by your excellence, or stupidity, as the case may be.

Who are you? You are a "hu-man being." *Hu* means spirit, the light, the hue. *(YB makes circles with his hands over his head, and out to the sides, referring to the auric field or radiant body of a person.)* *Man* means now, mental, being now. Now you are the spirit of your mind. You are bright light of yourself. That's your identity.

The art of being smart
is to be small which can contain all.
The art of success
is to answer the call of duty
with grace and compassion.
The art of happiness
is to serve all and all shall serve you.

Ashtang Agni Kriya
Eightfold Fire Kriya of Kundalini Yoga

Mudra/Movement: Sitting in Easy Pose, with straight spine, move from (a) to (b) in a fast, forceful motion.

(a) Bring your elbows up and out at shoulder level, and bring your hands, palms down, in front of each shoulder.

(b) Bring the hands towards one another with a great force, as if you are about to clap them together, but you stop when they are about 6 inches apart. Hands are above shoulder level. At the same time, bring the elbows down onto the ribcage with a great force. This will cause the hands to jump back a bit. The forceful hitting of the ribcage should be so strong, about one time per second. It is like playing a drum, and you can almost hear the drumbeat. Let your body dance with the music as you continue to do the movement—the upper body above the navel and spine must dance. Do the entire movement very powerfully, using your spirit, letting your internal power come out.

Breath: Will become a Breath of Fire.

Tape: *Gobinday Mukanday* by Matamandir Singh. Do not sing.

Time: Done for 6 minutes in class the first time. The second time, done 5 minutes.

End: Inhale, exhale and relax.

Comments/Effects: In this meditation, your breath will become a Breath of Fire. This is actually where Breath of Fire came from. The mantra speaks of eight aspects of God, the Infinite:

Gobinday:	*Sustainer.*
Mukanday:	*Liberator.*
Udaaray:	*Enlightener—One who takes us across, uplifts us.*
Apaaray:	*Infinite.*
Hareeang:	*Destroyer.*
Kareeang:	*Creator—by Who's Grace everything is done.*
Nirnaamay:	*Nameless—He is not bound down to the identity of a Name.*
Akaamay:	*Desireless—It is by Itself.*

The main emphasis in this meditation is to forcefully strike the seventh rib. The entire creativity of humanity is based on the seventh rib. Striking this area helps to activate that creativity in us so we can live with our spirit and not our complexes—the imaginary boundaries and limits we put on ourselves which cause us pain.

This is an *Ashtang Yog Shastric Mantra*. Perfection of this mantra can make you like a rodeo rider (one who rides the horse, and ties up the bull and the calf), and God will be your calf (the one you harness).

This is a very fun, energizing, and uplifting meditation, which any whole class will enjoy.

The Life of a Teacher

Flexibility, Humility & Compassion

As a person you have an authority of contract. But as
a Teacher you have no authority—moral, personal, or
individual of contract. You have only one right—
to serve, serve, serve; to elevate, elevate, elevate;
to exalt, exalt, exalt.

We have divided ourselves with many concepts, and each concept has given us a conception. Then our commotions relate to those concepts.

The normal course of our life is very natural—just like the birds and the animals, we are living by impulse. When we are children, we crawl. When we are young, we are very hot and passionate. When we become old, we fall apart. So these are natural processes of life. They have no rational conception. When you are young, you shall grow. As you grow up, you'll become an adult. As an adult, you become mature. When you are mature, you become old. When you are old, you are dying.

But the problem is that you can't handle a relationship, because to handle a relationship, you have to invest your spirit, and you don't have a concept of your spirit. When you do not have a concept of your spirit, then you have a concept of emotions, feelings, commotions, and everything else added to it.

Are you born that way? Is it decreed that you have to suffer? No. If you have your emotions, and you keep your emotions, but if instead of using your emotions, you use your spirit, you shall not suffer.

When you play the game, then the game plays with you. It's like a shuttle car, going back and forth. It's a very subtle situation. Ninety-five percent of people just live their lives, for say, eighty years, and do not leave behind any mark—none whatsoever. They just come, they live, and they go. They were born, just a few people knew them, a few people went to their funeral, and they are forgotten. Not only are they forgotten, the majority of people do not know the name of their great-grandfather, forget about anybody else. So some lived well, some didn't live well, some will not live well. Some will try to live well. It's going on.

Let me tell you something very funny. A person became a doctor. It took him eight years to become a doctor, and then he started his practice. One day he was very frustrated. I said, "What is wrong with you?"

He said, "Oh, I took out a student loan. Now I work day and night, just to pay it back."

I said, "Why is it so painful for you to pay it back? It is karma. You have the life, you have

Is it decreed that you have to suffer? No. If you have your emotions, and you keep your emotions, but if instead of using your emotions, you use your spirit, you shall not suffer.

the *prana*, you have the spirit, you have the soul. You have to pay it back."

Everything you get, you have to pay back. Nothing is free. Your body, your wealth, and your environments are already pre-destined. For instance, somebody might start a business with a hundred thousand dollars; he becomes a millionaire—that's fun. On the other hand, somebody starts with a hundred thousand dollars, and he loses the hundred thousand dollars. There's nothing. So loss and gain are personal. The starting point is already set just as the longitude and latitude that you were born at are set.

Do you recognize who you are supposed to recognize? No, you don't. If it fits your emotion, you recognize it. If it doesn't, you don't. If it fits your purpose, you recognize it. If it doesn't, you don't. The strength of your judgment is the only enemy you have. You don't look at things in the light of the spirit, the light of the soul, and you do not believe and trust that everything is the light of the soul. Things will fit in when they want to fit in. You are not required to fit them and unfit them and make people believe or force them to consider.

What has happened to you when you sign for a divorce from a girl to whom you are married, and whom you have told for seven years, "I love you, I love you, I love you?" Then what happens? What happened to your statement of love? "No contest, just our chemistry doesn't meet." Why? Why do you sometimes have friends, and then you don't have friends? Because technically speaking you don't have strength. You don't have the strength to go through the gallows. And this is the main reason why the most beautiful gift of life, which could just be enjoyed, is wasted.

Once there was a girl who wanted to marry a boy, but everybody told her, "Don't marry this boy."

She said, "No, I want to."

"Okay, get married." Six years later they were divorcing. The next time she came, she wanted to marry again.

We said, "Well, this time don't get married fast. Just get engaged and see what happens." They got engaged for six years.

After six years she said, "I don't want to be engaged. I want to be dis-engaged."

I looked at her and said, "Is six years your routine?"

Similarly, there's a student of mine, who was one of my best students, who left. Every two and a half years, the cycle changes. I was talking to her a week ago. I said, "Hey, this is the second-and-a-half year coming on. What is next?"

She said, "You tell me."

I said, "You are going to mess up again. Why is this?"

She said, "I don't care. I always try to mess up my life, or not mess up my life, I don't care. Worse comes to worse, you are still alive. That's enough."

Can you believe this? I said, "What are you talking about?"

She said, "Oh, I know I can do anything I want, and if worse comes to worse, you'll take care of me."

I said, "So you have a general permit to mess it up?"

She said, "Yeah. In two and a half years, I'll do something else."

You can divide life into two and a half year segments. You have a conception, then an inferiority or a superiority complex comes, because you have conceived that conception.

I know a businessman who is very successful, very calm. But the moment he understands that he has to work in partnership, he leaves. There's a fear of society. It's called "social phobia."

There was a very talented girl. She once got a job offer for a very high position. She said, "No, I want to be a school teacher." She didn't take the ninety-thousand-dollar-a-year job; instead she reported for the twenty-thousand-dollar-a-year position. "I want to teach school children." There was a very powerful conception in the authoritative power, in the image of a school teacher. She wanted to teach. She had a conception. And whenever you have a concept, you have a conflict.

These days the trend is a little changed, but a couple of years ago, everybody was a masseuse, everybody was a healer. Once I asked somebody, "Do you know the name of this muscle?"

He said, "What? You mean calf?"

I said, "The calf has so many muscles. Have you ever studied anatomy, and understood what you are talking about?"

"No."

There is something you do not understand. Birds live, animals live—the cows, the hogs and horses—and you will live, too. In their world, they act and react. But in your case, you have an applied consciousness. In your case it is your depth and strength. In your case it is your wisdom and intelligence. In your case it is your intuition and your human strength. Therefore you can be very flexible, adjustable. Your position can be understood, and you can stand under, and keep going.

A Teacher has no territory and a healer has nothing of self but prayer. A healer is a living prayer. A human is a living light. And there's no fight about it.

In life we lose three things: flexibility, humility, and compassion. If you look through history, you will see that in the beginning we were one, then we were in one cave, then a couple of caves made a tribe, and then the tribe made the territory. A certain territory made the state; those states made the country; and certain countries made the world. We have been dividing from the beginning of time until today. We never learned wisdom, intuition, self-respect, self-esteem, compassion, kindness, caring. All we learned is "conquer or be conquered." Even today we do the same thing. We did not have peace then, nor do we have peace now. Simply our geographical or cultural situations might have changed.

Can you believe that the Jews and Arabs have lived for centuries together, and they can't live in peace today? Yugoslavia was one country. My God, they have killed each other like you can't even understand. Now in 1996 they call it ethnic cleansing. In Africa it's tribal cleansing. At home, it is ego cleansing.

Once a woman came to me, and she was so badly beaten, it was terrible. While counseling the situation I asked her, "What happened the night before that in the morning there was a fight?"

She said, "Oh, we were very happy. We went out for dinner, we came home, and had beautiful, marvelous sex. We slept. We got up in the morning, and we were so happy. Everything was fine."

I said, "Then what happened?"

She said, "Well, he got ready, and I got ready. We were sitting at the breakfast table. I don't know what happened, but when he put his spoon in, there was a fly in it."

He took the bowl and let it go at her face, threw the table up, broke the plates. She said, "All I knew, is afterwards, there was nothing but a disaster. And then he stomped out. I noticed that I was bleeding. I went to the mirror, and saw that my whole face was cut."

Why? Have you tolerance? No. Can you communicate? You can't. Your common notion is not to live in harmony, peace, and tranquillity. Your common notion is to conquer or be conquered. You have a brutal instinct. Yes, I agree that you are part brute, part human, and part angel. But the angelic part must be more than sixty percent. The human part should be almost thirty percent, and your brute part, as ten percent, must keep you together. It is rational. That's how your development should be. That's how your seven-year cycle of consciousness, your eleven-year cycle of intelligence, and your eighteen-year cycle of life must proportionately grow. Your life force at eighteen years is one. Then your consciousness must grow in proportion—2.5, or 2.6, 2.7, 2.8, even 3 points—something like that. When you are eighteen, that is one unit. Your intelligence must grow 1.6, 1.9, or two. Then life will be very comfortable, very easy.

Once I was called by a man to go see my Teacher. He said, "Your Teacher wants to see you."

I said, "Is it urgent, or do I have time?"

He said, "Well, come as you want."

I said, "Okay." I went home, I changed my clothes, I dressed up properly, and I went and presented myself.

He looked at me. He said, "It took you a long time."

I said, "No. I came as fast as I could."

"Well, you are not dressed up properly."

I said, "Yes, Sir, I didn't dress up properly."

He said, "No, no, no, no, no. Stand up before the mirror. I tell you that this is wrong, that's wrong, that's wrong, that's wrong, that's wrong. Usually you are the best-dressed man."

I said, "Oh, what a day it is today!" You know, what can you do? Then I sat down.

He said, "Sit down, I want to tell you something. Never get ready in a hurry. You will never be yourself. If you will be lazy, you are crazy. If you are in a hurry, you won't be you."

A month or two passed, and I forgot about the situation. The man came again and announced: "You are wanted again."

I said, "Again? Do I have time?"

He said, "Perfect, you have time."

I said, "Okay, don't worry, baby." I got so neatly dressed up, you can't believe it. When I arrived, my teacher was walking outside on the lawn.

He said, "You came?"

I said, "Very well dressed up."

He looked at me, and he said, "That's true." Then he sat down and he said, "Whenever you go to get something, be bountiful, beautiful, and look as good, and as perfect as you can. Simple, gracious, and go with a smile."

Well, I was fourteen years old.

One day I was working in the fields, and he looked at me. He said, "Let us go." Now, you know in India, especially when working in the fields, you have on a big underwear, one shirt, and a little turban on your head—that's it. That's how I looked, turning the earth with a hoe in my hand. He said, "Come along." So I started with him. You know, he took me through the main streets of the city, bare-footed.

When I came back, I said, "Thank you, can I go?"

He said, "No, no, I want to tell you something. How was your visit to the city today?"

I said, "Truthfully, or do I just have to tell you what you want to hear?"

He said, "No, truthfully."

I said, "Very embarrassing."

He said, "Thank you. I wanted you to experience embarrassment, that's all. Done. We'll meet again."

So a Teacher is there to teach a person all the facets and faculties of life, and to conquer the mental state in embarrassment, in confrontation. That's the job. You have come here to become Teachers to what, read books, and write stories, teach people how to raise their legs and how to raise their head or stand on their heads? Or just to tell them how good and great you are? No. That will never make you a teacher. That will only make you a book machine. When you become a Teacher, then you become a perfect enlightened creature. It's very easy. You will not be you.

As long as your ego exists, you are not a Teacher. As long as you expect appreciation, you are not a Teacher, you are a beggar. Some are very qualified beggars, some are very rude and crude. I once went to Boulder and there was a Spiritual Teacher there. When the students told me his rules, I had to talk to him. I said, "Hey, what are you doing?"

He said, "I am testing my students."

I said, "I can understand there is a certain code of conduct. But you are exposing them to the laws of the state. "Render unto Caesar the things which are Caesar's, and to God the things that are God's."[1]

As a person you have an authority of contract. But as a Teacher you have no authority—moral, personal, or individual. As a teacher you have no authority of contract. You have only one right—to serve, to serve, to serve; to elevate, to elevate, to elevate; exalt, exalt, exalt.

When a teacher and student meet in a good atmosphere, it creates a spark. Have you heard that?

> *As a Teacher, you cannot be judged by the present time. History will judge you. A Teacher is not judged by his students, nor by his fellow man, nor by anybody. A Teacher is always judged by history. Are you willing to take the risk that in history you shall be known as a bogus idiot who exploited everybody, that you were worthless?*

As long as your ego exists, you are not a Teacher. As long as you expect appreciation, you are not a Teacher, you are a beggar.

Class: Yes, Sir.

YB: It creates a spark. When you take a hammer and chisel, it creates a spark, too. A good Teacher is bad news. A bad Teacher is good news.

We are actually not teachers here in this country. Here in this country there's no standard that you are a teacher. There are so many restrictions—workmen's compensation, insurance for harassment: sensual, sexual, social, personal harassment. The teacher is so heavily insured here. There are hardly any teachers as far as I know in the United States who have not gone through two, three, five, six lawsuits.

The most famous lawsuit I went through is the one we call the "Beet Case." Somebody sued me after I mentioned in a lecture I gave in Boston that beets are good for you. So she ate beets. Under that influence she had a tubalization done, and eight years later she realized she can't have a baby. So she sued. The case went forward, discovery started. But one fine day they withdrew the case, just withdrew it. For two and a half years we stood the torture, and after that she just withdrew it.

They asked me, "What to do?"

I said, "Nothing. It comes with the territory."

Some students you meet are very wise, loving; they serve you. Some like to be with you just to put their hooks somewhere. Some like to come to be insane. This is one of the situations which is very uncommonly insane. You must understand that as a Teacher, you cannot be judged by the present time. History will judge you. A Teacher is not judged by his students, nor by his fellow man, nor by anybody. A Teacher is always judged by history. Are you willing to take the risk that in history you shall be known as a bogus idiot who exploited everybody, that you were worthless?

Class: Yes, Sir.... No, Sir!

YB: My God, what a risk. You didn't understand what I was saying. *(Laughter in the room.)* I forgive you for your affirmation. It's amazing. Don't fall in love with me, because then I'll start testing you and you'll feel miserable. This is the first job of the love of the teacher. When you love a teacher you should become desireless. Not undesirable—desireless.

One day I told somebody, "Become desireless." She came naked to the university, and I said, "What is wrong with you?"

She said, "I have no desire."

I said, "No desire to put clothes on?"

"No, I'm natural, organic. You told me today."

I said, "Holy mother, go put clothes on and come back."

"If you say so." So she came back with clothes.

From that day onwards, I reserved my judgment of what to say and what not to say. You know, most of the time in my classes, I would ask Shakti, "What should I say?" I have twenty-seven years of the funniest experiences.

You don't understand that I am not without pain. I am in humongous pain. It's not that they can't become great teachers. It's not that. They just don't do it.

Some teachers want to be popular. What is this? A popularity contest? Some people want to be very loving. Have you seen one 3HO teacher (I will not name him), who hugs everybody? Do you know him? One day he met me and I said, "Either stop hugging or leave 3HO, because it is not written in the code of conduct. Hug somebody if somebody hugs you. That I can understand. But what are you doing?"

He said, "I just want to hug everybody."

I said, "Action has a reaction equal and opposite. First you hug, then you bug. And this game of hugging and bugging," I said, "It doesn't work."

I was a teacher in India, too. If you came improperly to class or you came one minute late, that's all you needed to raise the Kundalini. The class would sit and watch what that person would go through—you would not believe it. Because without a discipline you can never be a disciple, and without a discipline you cannot be a master, and without a discipline you cannot deliver. And without a discipline you will never know the exalted self. The power to obey is the power to command. Here in the West, to surrender, to be humble, to obey is considered to be a slavery, but actually it is the power of the self. Only a most exalted, most powerful character can surrender. It's a very different culture, different understanding. When I started writing here, "Humbly Yours," people objected to it. "Sir, what does that mean, 'Humbly Yours'?"

I said, "Well, I mean what I say." Because I'm a vehicle, I'm a channel. I'm not the Absolute.

(See page 77 for details of this meditation.)

Let us test out our spirit.

You did well this afternoon. Remember what you did this afternoon? Now you have to do this. Remember? These two fingers have to be open. And you have to do the same thing and hit the seventh rib with full force. Right? Ready? You have done it. Now you must do it, and this time you must experience it, because this is the time to do it. Come on. Ready, set, and go!

(Tape "Gobinday, Mukanday" by Matamandir Singh plays.) Come on now. Remind yourself with every breath that you have to win tonight. Good luck.

Let the breath be the Breath of Fire. Hurry up. Try your best.

Inhale. Stretch your hands up please, and lift up your body to the extent that you stretch your spine. It is one time only. Come on, do it, hard! Lift, tight, tight, tight. Relax.

There cannot be any power which can come to you from outside. There's a dormant power within you which has to be awakened. You must awaken that power and penetrate all the cycles of transmission of your magnetic field energy, in which you have a psyche, which governs your essence to become a greater exalted person, to face everything with grace. That's the beauty.

So we are practicing in one way or the other, trying to be nice to ourselves for the first time. At least we have the desire to become Teachers. Whether we will become or not, act as Teachers or not, it's difficult to say. A Teacher acts in the interest of the higher self of the student. There are three parts of the student—his self, his worldly self, and his higher self. A spiritual Teacher only belongs to the higher self. And when he belongs to the higher self, and the student obeys and reaches his higher self, then the other two lower-grade sides are all taken care of. It is very simple.

You have to elevate to go higher, and then you can't leak downstairs. Here is *shashaaraa (YB puts his hand on top of his head)*. You have to save yourself from your ears, from your eyes, from your mouth, from your hands, and from your legs, and from the other two areas. You have to have a total control of what comes in and what goes out of you, in the interest of you.

This world is our qualification, standard, examination, a place where we must examine our selves in our own interest. We must learn to love ourselves before we love anybody else. We must honor ourselves before we honor anybody else. We must serve ourselves before we serve anybody else. If we do not know how to do things for ourselves, we shall not be in a position to do things for others. Because when we do things for others, that is for a purpose. And purpose will create prejudice. Instead of having friends, you will have enemies. You will have concepts. You have a concept of what is right and what is wrong. You are born and trained and you die in judgment. Things come to you, you feel very honored. Things are taken away from you, you feel very insulted.

ਏਕੁ ਭੀ ਨ ਦੇਇ ਦਸ ਭੀ ਹਿਰਿ ਲੇਇ ॥
ਤਉ ਮੂੜਾ ਕਹੁ ਕਹਾ ਕਰੇਇ ॥
ਜਿਸ ਠਾਕੁਰ ਸਿਉ ਨਾਹੀ ਚਾਰਾ ॥
ਤਾ ਕਉ ਕੀਜੈ ਸਦ ਨਮਸਕਾਰਾ ॥

Ayk bhee na deh, das bhee hir leh.
Ta-o mooraa kaho kahaa karay-eh.
Jis thakur sio naahee chaaraa.
Taakao keejai sad namaskaaraa.
　　-Guru Arjan, *Siri Guru Granth Sahib*, page 268
If God has given you one and takes away ten, what can you do, fool?
You cannot fight with the Master; it is better to bow and accept Him.

If He doesn't give you one and takes away the ten you have, then fool, what can you do? Why fight with that Lord with whom you have no reason to fight? Why not just bow and get the blessings?

I'm not telling you that you should study it, but there is a scripture called *Asa di Var.* It is written in Gurmukhi, and it is translated into English. If you somehow get a chance to read it and understand it, there's not one wisdom in the world you will not be the master of. You don't have to go to a library and search everything out. It tells you exactly what it is, and why it is. And it tells you if you cross it, then *that is.* Pretty good. It tells you about God, soul, and man. It tells you about the Word, the words, and the wonder, the Infinite, the finite. It's a very defined thing. When I was studying I asked one question: "Why do Sikhs sing this every morning? I mean, there should be some reason." Then I studied the words. I discovered that it was a combination of sayings of several of the Gurus put together. There are some *shabads,* and some *slokas,* and there are some *paurees,* like steps. In the end, I said, "My God, it's the science of human behavior in every aspect of life."

I was not a Sikh to begin with. I became a Sikh. I was born in a Sikh family, that's true. But I am a scientist. I do not believe that the God which cannot be explained, needs to be worshipped. I also don't believe that if you do not know who made you, you will make it in this world. I also believe there is a hub, there's a rim, and there are spokes. Every word spoken is like a spoke. It supports you and stops you. I believe every statement of yours affects forever. I also believe that everything which God has done is so open, that every human has to be absolutely open.

So you don't have to follow my religious beliefs. They are very simple, but they will look very weird to you. I don't believe anything is complicated. I think when we hide and seek, and we want to hunt and harm, then we create complicated things. I don't believe anybody loves anybody. I think we use this word to blind another person. Or sometimes we blind ourselves. I believe you cannot love anybody—it happens.

It's very funny. Over the last twenty-five years when I say to somebody, "I love you," I mean it. And when they say they love me, they don't understand what it means to love me. Love me or what? How can you love me? Neither can you see me nor can you hear me, nor can you speak my language, nor understand my strength. Neither do you know my altitude, my longitude and latitude, nor my width. What do you know of me? Am I a statue? There are so many statues at the ranch. Love them. I love them, too. That's why they are there.

Love is something which is a power that makes you know the Unknown. And if you do not know the Unknown of a person, what is this love? Which part do you love? Do you love my nose and my ears? Do you love my fingers? What do you love? What is this love, love, love, love, you talk about? What is it? What is it when you call someone beautiful? You are the ugliest creature on the Earth. Ask the animals. Ask the dog. The moment the dog sees you, he hates you. "What is this two-legged person? I'm at least balanced on four legs."

When an animal gets really injured and in trouble, it is put to sleep. But when you are injured and you are in trouble, there's no law to put you to sleep. The law is you must suffer to the end. You have absolutely no rights.

It's the funniest thing. You can teach a parrot to fire a cannon. You can teach a cat, which cannot be taught. You teach a dog everything. I know one dog who skates. They put him in skating boots and the guy is just having a fun. But you cannot teach your mind, which is your first servant. You cannot potty-train your mind, and you throw slander and garbage everywhere. You're the ugliest born mammal on the Earth. The ugliest. There's nothing uglier beyond you, because you have never potty-trained your mind and it shh, shh, shh, shh... everywhere. It's funny. Have you noticed sometimes you say things which are so ugly. What for? I have heard it. You carry the bacteria of the ugliness from person to person. You gossip, you slander, you do all that kind of stuff. Because you have never potty-trained your mind. You have no power against this thing of yours called "mind."

We'll talk tomorrow. Will that be all right?

Class: Yes, Sir.

There are three parts of the student—his self, his worldly self, and his higher self. A spiritual Teacher only belongs to the higher self. And when he belongs to the higher self, and the student obeys and reaches his higher self, then the other two lower-grade sides are all taken care of. It is very simple.

YB: We'll explore the mind and its perception, its conception, its projections in progressiveness in the sense of how the mind works.

I'll come tomorrow sometime, whenever I will feel like it. I think we finished the business today. All the meetings have been done, orders have been passed. I work also, you know? I'm not that free. I have fourteen corporations. I have to work. I'm a pretty good slave.

Yesterday I came here and I looked so good and nice to you. You should have seen me just before coming, in the guest house yelling and screaming. The neighbors came out to see what happened. One young boy said, "Your blood pressure must be very high."

I said, "No, I was calm. I was a very good actor." I scared everybody to death.

The idea is to project the mental force into the faculty of, in the facility, where another person can understand quickly and things get done. What frequency you use, and what caliber and gauge you use, that is your ability. You never talk like that. You don't speak like that. You don't know anything. So we'll talk tomorrow, we'll start the subject. We'll be here at sometime in the forenoon. Good night.

Meditation to Awaken
the Dormant Power Within

This meditation is similar to Ashtang Agni Kriya which was taught during Class #6.

 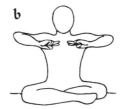 

Mudra: Sit in Easy Pose, with a straight spine.

(a) Basic starting position: bend the elbows down into the sides. Extend the forearms straight up, so the hands are in front of each shoulder, the palms facing one another, with about an 18 inch space in between the two hands. The fingers point towards the ceiling. Bend the ring and mercury finger into the palm, and hold them down with the thumb. The index and middle fingers are spread wide to form a 'V'. Make sure you keep these two fingers spread wide the entire time.

Movement: **(b)** Extend bent elbows up and out to the sides, so they are parallel to the ground.

(c) With a forceful motion, bring elbows down and into the body, to slap against the 7th rib with full force. This movement will cause the shoulders and body to vibrate. Do it in a rhythmic, dancing motion, to the beat of the tape. Let head and shoulders move with the music. Move at a fairly rapid pace, about one time a second.

Eyes: Unspecified.

Breath: Should come to a breath of fire.

Tape: *Gobinday Mukanday* by Matamandir Singh.

Time: Done in class for about 23-1/2 minutes.
End: Inhale deeply, stretch your arms up tightly, and lift your body to the extent you stretch your spine. Hold tightly for 15 seconds. Relax.

Comments/Effects: The sound of the breath must touch the Heavens and it must be hot. It will become like breath of fire.

*You must awaken the dormant power within you
and penetrate all the cycles of transmission of your magnetic field energy,
which governs your essence to become a greater exalted person,
to face everything with grace. That's the beauty.*

Living Above Cause & Effect

*There is one concept you have to have or
you can't be a Teacher:
You don't work, God works for you.*

There is some difficulty in explaining what I have to tell you today. It is important for you to understand it, because without that basic understanding, you'll be gambling with life. First of all, you want to become Teachers. That's what this course is all about. The difficulty is, suppose you become a Teacher, what will happen? Suppose you don't become a teacher, then there's no problem. As a human, you have the right to cause and effect. You cause any cause, you have the effect. You do something wrong, you pay for it. You do right, you gain from it. But as a teacher, you have no cause to cause, and no effect to take. The sense of causation has to go.

Whatever you cause, you create a cause, and effect you will reap. Not only will you reap the effect this time, it will give you the next lifetime to reap the cause. If you do not cause a cause, that's your will, that's your choice. But once you cause a cause, you shall pay for it. So, as a Teacher you shall not cause a cause. So what will you do? What do you do as a Teacher?

Student: Teach?

YB: Elevate. What do they call that thing which goes in, and under, and puts things up?

S: A forklift.

YB: One day somebody gave me a beautiful miniature forklift as a present. I have kept it. That's what you are—not more, not less. Don't worry if you are constipated. If somebody comes and says, "I am constipated," tell him to take Isabgul (an Indian plant fiber) and get rid of it. Your job at that time is to forklift. At that time you cannot say, "Oh, my God I am constipated. How can I help him?" No. the person has done his best. The person has come to you as a teacher and you have to relieve his problem. It doesn't matter what your problems are. Should I give you an example to help you to understad better?

There is a very great man now in Japan. He is an archbishop who has the biggest temple in Japan. But when he was not very big, he came to me in San Francisco and said, "Master, raise my Kundalini." I had bronchial pneumonia, and a 104-degree temperature. I had three quilts and two blankets on me. They gave me a morphine injection so that I could breathe, the pain was so humongous. I had come from India a few days before. They told me that the man had come, that the appointment had been made. So, he came into my room, and you know the Japanese, he bowed and he brought gifts and everything, and he said, "Master, please help me."

The job of a Teacher is to elevate. You are a forklift. The person has come to you as a Teacher, and you have to relieve his problem. It doesn't matter what your problems are.

I said, "Archbishop Kiriyama put your hand under my quilt, find my right hand, put it on your forehead, and then go." It worked. Then one day he brought me so many presents—pearls and dolls and this and that; and in the corner of my room there was a spoon. It's my walking spoon. It's about three feet tall, and in the spoon there is a carved Adi Shakti. I looked at the presents, the money, whatever was there, and I said, "Kiriyama, pick up that spoon in the corner of the room, take it. As long as it shall be with you, in the whole Japan there'll be none who can match you. You'll be the highest, you'll be the richest, and you'll be the best." He still has it.

I sent another person, my Sikh man, as a teacher. I gave him a stick. I said, "Walk with it, all of Japan will follow you." On the third day he lost his stick.

He came back, he said, "I want another stick."

I said, "That was the stick. Figure it out, and that's it."

There are different aspects of you. One aspect of you is that you want what you want, you want to have your cake and eat it, too. Then there is an aspect of you which can make things happen. There are three aspects, but your biggest fault is sex. It doesn't matter what you are, and what jurisdictions you have, your failure is sex. Once the sexual sense, because it is a sensory thing, is aroused, you are bewitched. When you act in that bewitchment, you lose everything. I'm not telling you to stop screwing and romancing and loving. God, do what you want to do. But I just want to tell you, that's one karma from which you cannot escape, and within which you shall never ever be you.

You may look at it this way: "We are human, we have emotions, we have feelings." I understand all that what you are talking about. But look at it this way—you are acting from the second chakra instead of from the sixth. I understand you have a penis and she has a vagina, and you can act and paddle the boat as you want. It's your nonsense, it's not mine. But I want to tell you that if, as a teacher, you have no control to stay at the sixth center, you are in the wrong profession. Because the *Prakirti*, the universe, the surroundings, all have to come and serve you through this, the Command Center *(YB points to the Third Eye, the sixth center)*. You can't do it from here *(YB points to the second chakra)*.

So what are we talking about? We are talking about being a teacher. You can study all the books and you can become the greatest Teacher, like, "I am the greatest of the greatest of the great," or whatever, like that boxer, what is his name, who shakes now?

Class: Mohammed Ali.

YB: Mohammed Ali, the greatest. But, what is the greatest? I'm just telling you about the mental situation. With all my greatness, all my blessings, and all my situations, I have studied, and I have understood my own teacher—I am very grateful. As I feel greatness, I feel grateful, but when I feel extremely grateful, that is to Guru Ram Das. I washed the floors of the Golden Temple for four and a half years, every day. I was the officer in charge of the entire northern area. But I would come back at exactly five o'clock, take off my uniform, wear my simple clothes, go down on my knees, and wash the *perkarma* of the Golden Temple. People asked me, "Why?"

I said, "I have been to every place, I have all the occult powers, but I can't get rid of them."

It was so simple. I had all the occult powers, not just one. Then one day I realized that it was totally ridiculous. "I'm a most ridiculous man. I am performing miracles in the universe of the Almighty, which I know is the miracle of miracles. What am I doing? I'm stupid." But I couldn't get rid of them. If I would say to someone: "This will happen to you," it happened all the time. I didn't know what to do. A chance came to choose a posting out of three places; all three started with "A" —Ajmir, Amballa, Amritsar. They said, "Choose."

I said, "Amritsar."

I said to the Guru, "You are the Guru of miracles, Guru Ram Das. I understand. I am a man of miracles. I want to drop here what I have. I don't want to do a thing. I have come as a human to watch the play of God in His universe, which is beautiful. I want to enjoy it, and now I'm doing these little funky things, and I look like an idiot." It took four and a half years to get rid of those powers.

When we started working in Los Angeles, we were teaching in all the YMCAs. Then one stupid student of mine one day went to replace me, and the lady said, "Hey, you are a Negro. How can you represent the Yogi?"

And he said, "I am a Yogi."

She said, "No, you are not."

He said, "Rise, rise." And he lifted her from the ground about three feet into the air. Then he forgot the other formula, so she fell. All of our classes in the YMCA's got cancelled overnight. We were considered demons. And I told him, I said, "What is wrong with you?"

He said, "She told me I am a Negro."

I said, "So what?"

"Well, I told her 'I'm a Yogi.' I wanted to prove it to her."

I said, "Prove what? You have nothing to prove. God approves and proves for a teacher. We don't do a thing." There is one concept you have to have or you can't be a Teacher: You don't work. God works for you. A human works, men and women work, an earthling works. These are the categories. Earthlings who are not conscious, who are not intuitive people, we call them "egomaniacs"—those who live by ego only. Teachers don't work.

I'll tell you a funny story. I used to teach in a center. One day I went there and taught a class in the morning. I looked at the Director, he was there to receive me. I said, "Where is the chief mother?"

He said, "Oh, Sir, she left and I'm supposed to serve you today."

I said, "Oh, fine." At noontime I said, "Hey, what about the food?"

He said, "Oh, the refrigerator is full, everything that you eat is there, don't worry."

I said, "Fine. Is there something to drink? I want to drink something."

He said, "Okay, I'll go and bring it." He went, and he returned empty-handed.

I said, "Where is the drink?"

He said, "We can't have it."

I said, "Why not?"

He said, "The refrigerator is locked, and I don't have the key. Unless you have the key, you can't open it."

I said, "That is the best way if you are dieting."

It was a huge refrigerator, but there was no way to break it open.

So I said, "Mario, I will not go hungry, but I am going to go have a nap. If food comes, wake me up."

He said, "What food will come? Today is George Washington's birthday. All the markets are closed. We are not going to get even a raw vegetable. Food? What food will come?"

I said, "It will. But don't wake me up before that."

He said, "Okay, Maestro." So I lay down and put a blanket over me. I slept. I was awakened by the sound of the doorbell.

I said, "Mario, what is it?"

He said, "Maestro, come and help me. There is a lot of food."

I said, "Well, receive it. What is wrong with it?" And this student of ours brought Spanish food, very well done. I told him, "How did you think to bring us food?"

He said, "Well, I defrosted my refrigerator and forgot to fill it, and when I got up this morning I didn't have a thing to eat. So I went to these Mexican people who have a restaurant. I went to their house and they served me a beautiful meal. While eating I thought of you. I said, 'I should take this food to the Master.' Then I thought, 'He never eats alone.' So I told them, 'Give me enough for six, seven people.' I thought you would enjoy it."

I said, "Sure we will enjoy it. We were eagerly waiting for it. Come on. Join us."

He said, "But Master, I have brought enough to serve ten people."

I said, "Don't worry about it. Put it on the table. At the moment we are three."

He said, "No, no, I have eaten. You are only two."

Sooner or later seven people showed up. I said, "What are you doing here?"

They said, "We wanted to see you. You didn't come back home, so we thought we would join you for lunch."

I said, "Oh, it is on the table." I said, "Mario, count. And now serve." It was a hot meal.

ਨਕਿ ਨਥ ਖਸਮ ਹਥ ਕਿਰਤੁ ਧਕੇ ਦੇ ॥
ਜਹਾ ਦਾਣੇ ਤਹਾਂ ਖਾਣੇ ਨਾਨਕਾ ਸਚੁ ਹੇ ॥

Nak nath khasam hath kirat dhakay day.
Jahaa daanay tahaa(n) khaanay, Nanak sach hay.

  -Guru Angad, *Siri Guru Granth Sahib*, page 653

The string through the nose is in the Hands of the Lord Master; the mortal's own
actions drive him on. Wherever his food is, there he eats it; O Nanak, this is the Truth.

Like a camel, there's a nail in our nose, and the string is in the Hand of the Lord. And the *karma*, action and reaction, moves us. *Kirat dhakay day:* action and reaction moves us. *Jahaa daanay tahaa(n) khaanay:* there is a food for us and it is where it is, and there we have to eat it. Nanak, that's the truth.

Do you know why we suffer? Because we manipulate things. We are manipulators. But if we manipulate just one thing, if we just make a simple manipulating effort that we shall elevate everybody, then we all shall be elevated ourselves. That is how the law of vacuum works. There is no vacuum. You can't suffer. A teacher shall not suffer, even in the worst of calamity, through the worst torture. Jesus was a teacher. What did he say? "Father forgive them, they know not what they do." He was conscious. Guru Arjan was a Teacher. He said to Mian Mir, "No, those who will follow me, if they have to sit on the hot plate and bake like a potato, they have to learn it from me. I'm just the example."

A teacher has a primary responsibility to be a conscious leader, to be ahead of the times. Why are we here? There's an understanding that we want to be Teachers, and we want to become learned. Well, it doesn't matter who you are, whether you are very low or very high, or great or small. That doesn't matter. There are certain set principles. One of the greatest principles is that the Heavens do not live in the Heavens, the Heavens live at the right toe of the Teacher.

In Kundalini Yoga, God bless us, we never initiate each other. In the olden times, it was traditional to be initiated by having the Master put his right toe into the water, and that water you would drink—that's the initiation. They say the total heavens are on the nail of the right toe of the Teacher. That's why they say, "Look at the Lotus Feet of the Master." If you look at the Lotus Feet of the Master, the heavens will look at you. It's a balance. It's not to humiliate you. What would humiliate you is when you want something and you get it, and it becomes your tragedy.

I want to tell you that if, as a teacher, you have no control to stay at the sixth center, you are in the wrong profession. Because the Prakirti, the universe, the surroundings, all have to come and serve you through this, the Command Center.
(YB points to the Third Eye, the sixth center.)
You can't do it from here
(YB points to the second chakra.)

Once I was going to meet this saint, and there was a man sitting with him. The saint said to him, "He has come."

I said, "What is the matter?"

He said, "Well, I am not getting the car that I am supposed to be given. I need my car."

That saint said, "Can you help him to get that car?"

I turned around and said, "Do you really want a car? Really?"

He said, "Why not?"

I said, "Well, then I'll get you the car, but I wash my hands of it. You really want a car? The car is being delayed."

He said, "No, no, I want a car."

I said, "Okay, tomorrow come at ten o'clock, and I'll get you a car."

So he called me at ten o'clock and I said, "Go to such and such a place and tell them who you are, and they will give you a car out of the President's quota. I have arranged it."

So he went there and they give him the key, the car, fine.

A couple of months later, I went to see this saint just for the fun of it, and he said, "Oh, thank God you have come. Let's go to the hospital."

I said, "For what?"

He said, "Let's go, let's go, let's go."

So we went to the hospital. What I saw was funny. One leg plastered up there, the other leg there, one hand there; of the face, you could only see the two eyes. And I said, "Who's this?"

I had all the occult powers, not just one. Then one day I realized, "I am a most ridiculous man. I am performing miracles in the universe of the Almighty, which I know is the miracle of miracles. What am I doing? I'm stupid." But I couldn't get rid of them.

He said, "The guy who you got the car for."

I said, "I got him the car? You got him the car. You told me to work out a way to get him a car. I told you I washed my hands of it, I am not interested in this."

He said, "You got him a car, so he has become a car himself now." And that was fun to watch.

And I said, "What happened to the car?"

He said, "Totalled."

"Well, how did you survive?" You know, in India when you have an accident, it's *Wahe Guru* —you're gone.

He said, "I don't know. The car busted and I jumped out. I was on the side of the road."

I said, "How did the car look ?"

He said, "I didn't look, but I don't think it looked good. It didn't look like a car. It looked like some pressed metal thing."

There was a head-on impact with a truck and somehow the door flung open, and he was thrown out. The car went right under the truck. I even went to see that car, and I couldn't recognize that a car could be that damaged. It looked like something had sat on it. He should have been juiced, but he was alive.

After a long time I met him again. I said, "Do you want another car?"

He said, "No. I'm cycling these days."

I said, "If you want a car, you can get a car. I can get you another car."

He said, "No way. I'll cycle. You were right, I was wrong."

Sometimes you get what you want, but you never asked God, "Is it right?" You never asked your consciousness, "Is it right?" You never asked your soul, "Is it right?" And you never asked your intelligence, "Is it right?" Well, how the hell is it going to work out for you? Do you understand what I'm saying?

Class: Yes, Sir.

YB: You have your consciousness, you have your intelligence, you have your soul. You have these friends living within you. You are an "in-house society." You have intuition, you have intelligence, you have your spirit, your soul. But you never consult them.

If you work to work, if you are a slave to work, you can't become a Master. If nature works for you, then you are the Master. A Teacher is a slave to be the Master. Only a slave can become a Master. You are already a slave. But either you are a slave of time, or you are a slave of a Teacher. You must be a slave of one or the other. Understood?

Class: Yes, sir.

YB: This does not mean a Master in a physical body. As Sikhs we are slaves of the *Siri Guru Granth*. We take Its Word. "In the beginning there was the Word, Word was with God, and Word was God." Christianity goofed. Jews lost it. Muslims totally defied it. To them the words are just because they got it. They never lived by it. Hindus created so much scripture, you can get lost in it. But in all traditions, you worship the man.

In Kundalini Yoga neither do we initiate the man nor do we worship the man. We follow the Golden Chain—the teachings. We are grateful to the Teacher—he gave us the teachings. That doesn't mean we worship him. It is very difficult to change this. If I am your Teacher, you will like to love me and respect me and honor me. That's not good. But there is a way to show that you really love me, and really exalt me, and really honor me: you will be perfect in the teachings.

Do you know what I mean? There's a little switch we have to make. We just love people. What is in me? A pound of garbage which comes out every morning, and five, six times a day the holy water comes out? Is that what a man is all about?

Class: No, Sir.

YB: America has to become a spiritual leader of the Age of Aquarius. That's why I hang in here. Yes. I want to go home but I am stuck. That's not right. I fought with God this morning, but it didn't work out. So every morning I say, "When?" And He says, "Shut up."

So you are here, I am here, we are here. When "I" and "you" shall become "we," then we'll become the Masters. As long as "I" remains "I" and "you" remains "you," you can just read a book about it.

(See pages 88-89 for details of these meditations.)

Put on that instrumental tape, *Dhuni.* I was very grateful it was found. Now, this is a single stringed instrument in a single melody of a three and a half cycle. I just want to let you know what music can do. Watch this now, he's going to play it.

It is just a simple melody. What it is singing is, *Sat Naam, Sat Naam, Sat Naam Ji. Waa-hay Guroo, Waa-hay Guroo, Waa-hay Guroo Ji.* And it elevates the notes. That's what I wanted to let you know. And once this music can sit in your head, then you don't have to do a thing. Then things will start doing for you, because this note will play and you will play with it, and, within the time, you will become complete.

Now sit down in your meditative mood, as well as you can, and just sing with it. Now you have to dance like this. *(YB demonstrates the movement.)* This *(YB points to his upper arm, from the elbow up to the shoulder)* has to become still, so stiff that if somebody takes a sword and cuts it, the sword breaks, this does not. Muscles have to be complete. This is your digestive system. *(YB points to the lower arm, just below the bend in the elbow.)* This is your mental system. *(YB points to the lower arm right above the wrist area.)* This is your power energy. *(YB indicates the back of the hand and fingers.)* This is your stomach *(YB points to the upper arm, below the shoulder, and the underarm area, as well.)* This is your brain outlet. *(YB places his hand under his armpit.)* Play it. It'll play in three movements. Switch the brain accordingly, and then chant. You will chant with the tip of your tongue. You will move the hands with the movement, and you will enjoy it, too. Whether you like it or not, that doesn't matter. Okay, go.

The hands have to go above the head. Fast or slow, same thing. It's called *"Puja."* This will start opening up. *(YB points to his heart center area.)* Correct. Above the head is essential. Very good. It's called "tuning in."

Keep the tape going—stop. Now sense your body. Sense that your sensory system is playing and your aura is dancing, without your physical body. Your auric body is dancing exactly

Basically there is a greed.
The idea is, "God is impotent,
He will do nothing, I have to
do everything." The fight is
between "I" and "Thou."
But the Teacher belongs to
"Thou," not "I."

as you were dancing. Close your eyes and feel it. It's the start of feeling the aura.

Join it. Stop! Start! Stop! Start then stop. Learn one thing—Obey! Start. Bravo. Get into it. Stop.

Now play that tape, *Laa-Haa-Yaa-Vaar-Yaa.* The whole thing. Every religion has one word, *Jaa-ho-vaah—Yaah, Haa-le-lu-ja—Haa, Laa-ay-laa—Laa, Raa-maa—Raa, Saa-taa-naa-maa—Saa.* They don't have more than one sound. Look at them, they are fighting with each other, killing. For what? Jews, *Ay-yaa-waa-saa—Yaa.* The Christian has *Haa-le-lu-ja—Haa.* The Muslim has *Laa-ay-laa—Laa,* and Hindu has *Raa-maa—Raa.* The combination of all is *Saa—Saa-taa-naa-maa,* which means "Your identity is true." But why are we fighting over one word? You don't have more than one. What are we killing each other for? Ethnic cleansing? Tribal cleansing? And for this Earth, which is not ours, which is a gift, given to just place our foot on, we are putting our foot in our mouths. We have become quarrelsome, obnoxious kids.

Sometimes God feels, "Why the hell did I make it?" Then He brings in "Brrr," Ice Age—wipes it out; like a kid who starts the castle of sand on the beach, then a wave comes and swish.

You might be asking, "Why did the Holocaust happen?" Somebody asked this question. Why not? The Holocaust was not a cause of a cause. The Holocaust was a cause of that sacrifice which brought Israel in. Without the Holocaust there would not have been Israel. The cause may be most dangerous and most terrible. But cause has an effect. First the Jews were living *with* the Muslims, the Arabs, and now they are living *in* the Arabs. They're all around. Do you understand? When they were living together, in between, one to one, they were fine. But now Jews are in the middle and the Arabs are all around, for thousands of miles. And it's happening in America, too. You see in New York, there is a section of Jews and it's all surrounded by Arab and Spanish peoples. Sometimes I find that karma is so good. Even in America they are not out of it.

Somebody once asked, "Why are we Sikhs?"

I said, "They are all Muslims. It's a combined force."

The Jews have one father, Hazarat Abraham. He is the Father of the Jews, of the Christians, of the Muslims, and of the Sufis. Aryan, Dravers, Moorians, Guptas, then finally in the end it came to Sanatan Dharm. You put Sanatan Dharm and Sufism together, and pull out of it Sikhism, if you really want to know. It is amazing. One, two, three, four. Put them together. Well, what is a Sikh? It's a religion? Naa-aa.

Forgive me for this. Man and God are fighting over a beard. There are two things we fight over: beard and bread. I'm not joking. It's true. God gives the beard. Have you seen that ad by the shaving company? It says, "It shaves really close!" How close? It grows out again. You can't get rid of it. It will get rid of you, but you can't get rid of it. There's not one man who wants a beard on his face. Ask them why. Or, don't be a Sikh. Be a Jew. Be a Muslim. Be a Christian. But be a man. I'm not asking you to change your religion. I'm asking you, "What is wrong with your beard?" We people have created a new man, and that is not God's man.

In your idea of sex, the female is like a boat, and the man is like a paddler; it does not invoke the sixth sense. Sex actually comes from the pituitary. *(YB points to his Third Eye point, in the middle of his forehead.)* So, what are we doing? We have created a new man and "our" world. God is saying, "What happened to the man I created?" He's really on a search. He is really looking at woman and man and saying, "Wow."

I went to Barcelona one night and these people came to honor me. They were two thousand-plus transvestites. Oh God, the "pretty women" I have seen, you can't believe. Two thousand of them in one bunch. Not one, not two, not ten, not twenty—two thousand plus! They said, "Grand Maestro, we welcome you to Barcelona. Nothing is wrong with us. We simply like God. God made us all men, we became women—and pretty ones."

I said, "Who are you?"

They said, "We are models in the Kingdom of God. We have come to meet the Grand Maestro to let him know, we can change to be men, we can change to be women. We are unique."

I said, "Bless you, bless you." I said, "Let us go."

In man's world, in his kingdom, men are dividing each other: "I am black, I am yellow, I am pink, I am gold, I am white, I am this." Still they fight with each other. White fights with white. Black fights with black. The fighting has never stopped. Neither religion has stopped it, nor geography has stopped it, nothing, because basically there is a greed. The idea is, "God is impotent, He will do nothing, I have to do everything." The fight is between "I" and "Thou." But the teacher belongs to "Thou," not "I."

The one whose Third Eye opens is that one whose "I" belongs to "Thou."

(The line spoken on the tape is: "As you sow, so shall you reap, Oh Nanak." YB elaborates.)

As you sow, so shall you reap, otherwise you will be a creep. That is common to all.

Have you understood? It's not a big deal. We have practiced religion for thousands of years, but we have never practiced reality. The reality is: We are spirit. We are always spirit. When we are not spirit, we are called "Dead." And when we are alive and we do not recognize spirit, we are "super dead." You know supermarket where you can get every junk on the Earth? See how shameful it is? Jehovah is fighting with Hallelujah, and Hallelujah is fighting with La-ay-lah. What is it? Why to fight? Is there anything to fight about? They are fighting. There's nothing to fight about.

Man always fights for beard and bread. You know, when the beard grows, then his sensory system grows. And with the sensory system working, if his intuition doesn't grow, he will become an attacker, a hunter. Because then he only has one choice, to live with his ego. Either you live by intuition or you live by your ego. You cannot live by both. Where there's "I," there's no "Thou." Where there's "Thou," there's no "I." Simple rule of thumb, it will never change.

Meditation for Tuning into Your Aura

Mudra: Sit in a meditative mood in Easy Pose, with a straight spine. To begin: Place the hands in front of the heart center, fingers point straight ahead. Palms are flat and face one another, separated by about 18 inches (a). During the entire meditation keep the upper arm area, from the elbow to the shoulder, very stiff.

Movement: Move the hands straight up, until they come to a stop when the wrists are level with the top of the head. As the hands glide up, the fingers will begin to angle up, until they are pointing towards the ceiling (b). Begin to glide the hands back down again, and when they are at the level of the heart center, the hands begin to angle down—the palms begin to come parallel to the ground as the hands start to separate, and then glide out to either side. As they move out to the sides, when they are each 12 inches from center, they curve up a little bit (c). Continue to smoothly glide the hands up and down in an arc, in this fashion.

Music: The instrumental tape, *Dhuni*.

Mantra: Chant the mantra *Sat Naam, Sat Naam, Sat Naam Ji, Waa-hay Guroo, Waa-hay Guroo, Waa-hay Guroo Ji,* using only the tip of the tongue. Pull in from the navel as you chant. One complete cycle of the mantra will be approximately 8 seconds.

Eyes: Unspecified.

Time: Yogi Bhajan led the meditation in class in the following fashion:
   Do the exercise for 4 minutes, then stop, sitting very still, and feel the movement of the *prana* in your aura for 1 minute. Resume the exercise for 10 seconds, stop for 5 seconds as you assess the movement in your aura. Continue 12 seconds, then stop and again feel your aura for 10 seconds. Then continue the exercise for 1-1/2 minutes, and then stop to end the exercise.

Comments/Effects: Yogi Bhajan refers to this meditation/exercise as Tuning In. Normally it takes at least 3 minutes to tune in.
   It is essential in the movement that you have your hands go above the level of the head on the up-swing. It is also very important to keep the stiffness in the upper arm area, since this in combination with the movement forces the heart center to start opening up.
   After the allotted time, keep the tape going, but close your eyes and stop the physical body movement. Sense that your sensory system is playing and your aura is dancing, without your physical body. Your auric body is dancing exactly as if you were dancing. Close your eyes and feel it. It's the start of feeling the aura.

Meditating on the Different Names of God

Mudra: No posture is indicated. Just close the eyes, and meditate on the words of the various religions calling God's Name.

Tape: Matamandir Singh's *Jehovaah*, from a tape called *Baria Hath*.

Time: 2 minutes.

End: Inhale and relax.

Comments: Every religion has one word:

Jaa-ho-vaah—Yaah
Haa-le-lu-ja—Haa
Laa-ay-laa—Laa
Raa--maa—Raa
Saa-taa Naa-maa—Saa

They don't have more than one sound, yet still man fights with each other. Man and his world, and his kingdom, and man dividing each other, "I am black, I am yellow, I am pink, I am gold, I am white, I am this." The fighting has never stopped. Neither religion has stopped it, nor geography has stopped it, nothing, because basically there is a greed. The idea is, "God is impotent, He will do nothing, I have to do everything." The fight is between "I" and "Thou." But the Teacher belongs to "Thou," not "I."

We have practiced religion for thousands of years, we have never practiced reality. Reality is: We are spirit. We are always spirit. When we are not spirit, we are called "Dead." And when we are alive and we do not recognize spirit, we are "Super Dead"' The one whose Third Eye opens is that one whose "I" belongs to "Thou."

Don't Find the Master— BE the Master!

We are part of the Golden Link. We come from the Lord of the Lords, Guru Ram Das, the Lord of the Throne of the Miracle, the Master of the Raaj Yog. So in our actions, there will always be reality and royalty. If there's no royalty in us, our reality will never be with us. If there's reality, there has to be royalty. This is our school of thought.

What we are talking about tonight is the most serious thing in life. You don't have to take it seriously, but you must understand it seriously. I'm not saying you should agree with it, but there are two ways to look at it—you can agree, you live; you don't agree, you live and suffer. Normal organic living, the way God laid it out, is always fulfilling and happy, because of a principle that you must understand. When you were born, your mother took care of you, nurtured you, even turned her blood into milk for you. She nursed you, cleaned you, protected you from weather, circumstances, from enemies, even from bad relatives. It's amazing how a child is born and protected, saved, and nurtured. The father is always out there to hang you up on the hand and play with you. Do you remember? If you don't remember your childhood, just remember the childhood of somebody you know, or any child you know. That's the law of nature.

If you live naturally, organically, then Mother Nature will serve you like your mother served you, and the Heavenly Father will serve you as your father did, protecting you to the last breath. I'm not saying that you won't have a cut, or you won't trip or fall. As children you did a lot of things, and you suffered a lot of things. Oh, that you will do, but it will not be an ultimate danger or ultimate disaster. That is a natural law.

How prosperous and how great you can become depends on what opportunities come to you, and the ability of your intuition to bring the intelligence. Intelligence will give you substance, so that you have character, and you have Dharma. Then there's no action and reaction—you are a victor, you are winning; there's no way you can lose. Not at all. You don't have to sell your consciousness, you don't have to come down onto your knees, you don't have to beg for peace and tranquility. No, everything from A to Z, whatever your needs are, shall be yours.

The example is there. When you were born, you were not a graduate, were you? Did you have a degree? When you came out of your Mom, did you need a mate the next day to have intercourse? When you decided you were hungry, and you were not fed, you just let out a little cry, and didn't you get the best milk from the very breast of your Mom? And now you seek that all of your life. You are never satisfied. Why do you grow up and become suckers? Shame

Just become a royal being, and then you'll become a real being. If your personality, your identity, and your mental self does not represent royalty, you will never know the reality.

on you, as humans. Aren't we ridiculous? What is given to us naturally to start with, later on we do everything criminal to get it. Isn't it a stupid way to live? Then you wear wirecut bras, and have the back open and the front open to attract, but nobody sucks. You don't get the feeling that the child needed; instead you get an arrogant, passionate man who's hungry, dissatisfied. There's nothing organic, nothing natural, because you have left behind being natural.

A human is provided all faculties and facets to grow happily. I was talking to a girl. She said, "Oh, am I wrong?"

I said, "No. You are not wrong. You are rotten."

"Why?"

I said, "God made you super intelligent, a very aggressively intelligent person." When a person is aggressively intelligent, no boy will become a friend. They all know that she can see through them. She has X-ray eyes. She created a fantasy, and once she created that fantasy, it didn't work out. The second time she created it, again it didn't work out. It was too far away from reality. When you are far away from reality, your fantasy won't work.

I will tell you a story from my own life. We were twelve people walking through the desert, and we were hungry. We got stuck. I asked my inspector, I said, "Hey, how many miles do we have to walk?"

He said, "About eighteen."

I said, "In this desert where nobody knows us, we are stuck. Who is going to walk eighteen more miles? You look around. Everybody's dragging their feet, and our water is coming to an end. It's a situation we can't even get into."

He said, "Sir, I just want to tell you, we picked up a wrong map."

I said, "Wow. That's very nice, 'I'm sorry to tell you'."

Technically speaking, we had to walk the distance. There was no other way. Both of our vehicles gave up on us. We grabbed whatever we could.

We were getting to a point of exhaustion. We were helping each other out. If I was very healthy, I was giving help to another person to make it easier. So, after a while the possiblity was coming into our minds that we might have to go to drastic measures, like saving our urine and giving it to those who were almost on a verge of collapse, to keep them alive. That whole strategy was working in the minds of everybody.

All of a sudden I had an idea. In the dead, dry desert, why were there a bunch of bushes? So I said, "Forget this, let's move over to that side, and see if we can make some sense. If we have to die, we can at least lie down in those bushes." As weak as we were, we dragged ourselves there. It looked like somebody had been there before, because there was a pot of water left and two pieces of bread. Now it could have been a man, it could have been a bird, or it could have been a saint. We didn't know.

I said, "All right, don't rush. Just take a little water and wet your mouth, and see how it tastes." It tasted good. And then we divided the bread between all of us. It is amazing, how a man in distress acts. When you are in wealth you are insane. When you are in comfort you are absolutely neurotic. You don't understand. Your measurements are off, always. In your life you have never understood that measurement in life is a way of enjoying life. That's why you don't enjoy life. You just live, die. That's all you are. You have no sensitivity of measurement, and you have no sensitivity of figures, what is two, what is three.

I was shocked that this man cut the bread with his hands into twelve equal parts. I was shocked. And he was the dumbest person in my whole contingent. He was the one who picked up the wrong map, and he was the one who never checked the gasoline in the cars, and never had the reserve order. When I saw him do this I said, *"Wahe Guru, Wahe Guru, Wahe Guru."* I must have said it from my entire being. So he gave each of the twelve hungry men their little piece, and a little water. We walked all the way, came to the camp. We had one piece of bread saved. Neither were we thirsty, nor were we hungry, nor were we weak.

When we came to civilization, we were very happy. We were thanking God. Then everybody started fighting, who should have the other piece of bread, who was the hero? I mean, we became animals in civilization, and we were fighting for that bread. I understood what they were thinking, but because I was the commanding officer, they couldn't say anything. They were looking at me, thinking, "Give it to me, give it to me, give it to me, give it to me." I gave the piece of bread to that man again and I said, "Divide it." And this time he was the most incorrect person I have ever seen.

So basically you must understand, you have an infinite capacity for reality. All you have to do is figure it out. All this learning and learning, and loving and living and all that, is not right. You invite your misery, and you cook yourself in a horrible blunder of life. Basically, just as when you were born and your mother and father protected you absolutely, now that you have grown up, Mother Nature and Heavenly Father must protect you. That's your birthright.

But you become obnoxious, commotional, neurotic, psychotic; you lie—you always lie. I said, "Oh God, everybody lies so much. I don't know why. Do you have any idea?" You lie to your friends, you lie to your relatives, you lie to yourself. And you are so insecure. The classic insecure mammal with two legs is a human. You are very insecure. And you hoard things. You have refrigerators, you have cellars, you have banks, you have money, and you show it off. You show off your richness. You live by your richness which is outside of you. You don't live by your inner richness. If the richness inside you is balanced by the richness outside, then you are okay. But if the richness outside is more, and inside is less, you are corrupt. You are way away from your Creator.

You are Teachers. You have to learn something which you will teach. What you have to teach is, "To be, to be." You cannot live and practice, "To be, not to be." Your mood and mind are your servants; they are not your masters. If you want to be a teacher, you have to be a master. Then mood and mind are your servants, and you and your being serve the spirit. If your spirit is here in a common sense for all, then you only see soul.

Religion has not taught you reality. You know why religion wants you? For that basket money. What do they call it? An offering. When I was working with Pope John Paul, I went to Rome and I discussed with him, I said, "You are the Papa, the only living Father. But why can't you have a Peace Prayer Day or something like that?" Ten years later they held a Peace Prayer Day in Assisi, and all the world religions prayed for one week. Do you remember that?

In this whole essence I have found out one thing: There's nothing you want to do for peace, neither for your internal, nor for your external. All you have are moods. Have you remembered this statement that you make: "I don't know, I don't feel good." Physically you are okay. Mentally you are not okay. If a rich person comes, you will serve him. If a poor person comes, you say, "What do you want? What have you come for?"

Imagine now.

Close your eyes. Imagine a very ugly, deformed, dirty-looking, stinking man walking up your driveway. He is terribly bad, wow, you can't stand it. Imagine that you are sitting in your house, meditating, praying happily, and you're getting ready to eat. Imagine you come to the dining table, with your whole family; you do a prayer, and ask for the blessing of Almighty God. Then you hear a knock at the door. You go and you see that man. The man says, "I am very hungry."

Out of great courtesy and desirability you go in, you take some food, put it on a napkin and hand it over to him. And you say to him, "God bless you."

He says, "Thank you," and he leaves. Imagine the next day you are again praying to God and you say, "You blessed me, Almighty. You are my wonderful God. You have given me a home, family, food, money, wealth, health, happiness. I'm so grateful, I do not know how to thank You."

And God appears and He says, "I came yesterday, I thanked you, and you blessed me."

And you say, "No."

And God says, "What do you mean 'No'? It was me. Look at me." And at the same moment, you are looking at that ugly, dirty, stinking man, and that beautiful, charming, angelic self.

Now open your eyes. Wherever there is a spirit or a soul, there is God. And those who do not see God in all, they do not see God at all. So you have complexes, prejudices, premeditative impulses, and you have a wonderful, beautiful knowledge. You are most marvelous people, but you live like a dog, you die like a dog. You raise your own tail and you bark. You never listened to your Teacher in the previous life, you never listened as a Teacher to what was said. That is why when I go for my walk in the morning, all these dogs bark at me. I say to them, "You never listened last time. At least now shut up. Now listen." They were very sincere students; they never listened. Now they even listen to the high frequency, and still they don't listen. Nanak said:

ਸੁਣਿਐ ਸਿਧ ਪੀਰ ਸੁਰਿ ਨਾਥ॥
Suni-ai sidh peer sur naath.
    -Guru Nanak, *Siri Guru Granth Sahib*, page 2 (from 8th *pauree* of *Japji Sahib*)
A mortal becomes a perfect saint, a religious guide, a spiritual leader,
and a great yogi by hearing the Name of God.

By listening, by developing the power to listen, you become a *siddha,* so all occult powers serve you. *Sidh peer*—you become the perfect one, so all nature serves you in perfection. *Sur naath*—you become the entire nucleus of the entire balance of the universe.

ਸੁਣਿਐ ਧਰਤਿ ਧਵਲ ਆਕਾਸ ॥

Sunni-ai dharat dhaval aakaas.

-Guru Nanak, *Siri Guru Granth Sahib*, page 2 (from 8th *pauree* of *Japji Sahib*)
*The reality of Earth and of the bull supporting it and of heaven
becomes known by hearing the Name of God.*

If you have the power to listen, you'll become the whole universe and the entire Heavens.
Do you not feel the joy of that completion? Just listening, just developing a power to listen?
Those who have listened to their teacher, their Master, they became the Masters. Do you think
you are going to get happiness? You can get any happiness, worldly or unworldly, self-related or
unself-related, at the right foot of the Master. Where his nail is, that is the space where Heavens
and Earth meet for you. You cannot conquer that space because your ego has blinded you.

Do you know what obedience is? I will tell you my personal story. One day I was called by my
teacher. A man came, and he said, "You are invited. You are asked to come fully dressed up."

So I dressed up, because I wanted to dress up, and I went in, I sat down, I gave my salutation, and he looked at me. He said, "Glad you have come."

"Yes, Sir."

"Do you know why I have called you?"

I said, "Your will."

"Are you listening?"

I said, "Yes."

He said, "You are the Master."

Automatically, because it was my habit to obey, I said, "Yes, Sir." Then I thought, "What
have I said?" And then I bowed.

He said, "Bless you. Go."

I came back out and all my colleagues asked, "What happened? What happened?" You
know, curiosity.

And I said, "The Master told me I am the Master."

"Heh, heh, heh, heh. You are the Master, what Master?"

I said, "You, all, sit down. Bow!" The next minute everybody's head was on the ground.
And I said, "Ah ha ha ha, I am the Master, don't you believe it?" And I said, "What happened?
Why did you bow?"

They said, "I don't know. You said so."

I said, "He said so, so I said so, so you said so. And that's it."

I was just curious. I started watching left and right. I didn't have to speak a word—the
thoughts started creating things.

One day I came into the room, I'm a Virgo, and I like a good bed. But my bed was a mess.
I looked at it and I said, "I'm not going to sleep in it." I walked out. I started doing my *Kirtan
Sohila,* and I just wanted to pass the time. It was not something I was very curious about. When
I walked in again, the bed was perfectly made. I was in a bachelor hostel. I don't think this is
a practical thing. No fairy came, but the bed was very well made. I just took my chances and
slept and got up in the morning for my *sadhana,* as a routine. Then I asked everybody, "Did
anybody come into my room yesterday and make my bed?"

Everybody said, "No."

I went to my teacher, straight. He said, "Well, you are asking me who made your bed?"

I said, "Yes."

He said, "I did it."

I said, "You made my bed?"

He said, "Well, you didn't want to sleep in a wrong bed, right? You wished it, I heard it, I obeyed."

I said, "Can you make it every day now?" And we laughed.

He said, "Well, I'm not punishing you for not making your own bed, although you are supposed to. And secondly, it was a good bed, right?"

I said, "Yes, it was great. I had a great sleep."

And he said, "Be careful, because all that you wish shall be done."

We are part of the Golden Link. We come from the Lord of the Lords, Guru Ram Das, the Lord of the Throne of the Miracle, the Master of the Raaj Yog. So in our actions, there will always be reality and royalty. If there's no royalty in us, our reality will never be with us. If there's reality, there has to be royalty. This is our school of thought.

So, if you come for study, remember, don't try to become a great master or a great teacher—become a royal being. Just become a royal being, and then you'll become a real being. If your personality, your identity, and your mental self do not represent royalty, you will never know the reality.

It is Raaj Yog, it is a throne. We have a throne of Raaj Yog. We are Raja, we are emperors, it's called "Imperial Destiny of a Yogi." There's only one Golden Temple in the world; it doesn't belong to the Sikhs. It's not anybody's property. It's a crown of the universe. It's the House of the Lord of Miracles, and the Imperial Self, Imperial Divine Self of Raaj Yog. That's what you are.

About Guru Ram Das it's said:

ਕੁੰਡਲਨੀ ਸੁਰਝੀ ਸਤ ਸੰਗਤਿ ਪਰਮਾਨੰਦ ਗੁਰੂ ਮੁਖਿ ਮਚਾ ॥
Kundalini surjhee sat sangat, param aanand guroo mukh machaa.
-Swayas *in Praise of Guru Ram Das,* Siri Guru Granth Sahib*, page 1402*
Associating with the saints, the Kundalini rises and through the Supreme Guru,
they enjoy the Lord of supreme bliss.

"When the Kundalini awakened on the face of the Guru, the greatest bliss burst out of the very face of the Guru."

You don't have to beautify yourself and make yourself up. No. Just stand before a mirror and look as if you are a royal sage, and you'll become a real sage. But if you take the process of a real sage, it will take a very very very very long time, and many many many lifetimes. If you want to go through the cycle of birth and death, and up and down, and idiot and wise, and all that stuff, and window shop and want to be just American, German, or want to be this—I don't know what you want to be—with your petty, little complexes, then nothing will work for you. Then you're wasting time.

Don't love God, for God's sake. Give Him a chance to love you. Give God a chance. A chance! You are so arrogantly cruel, obnoxious, and damn negative. He created you like parents. He nurtures you, loves you. You don't give Him a chance to give you a hug. You don't.

What is this religion you are practicing? It's a hoax. It tells you, "You are born in sin." Sin of what? In me, around me, over me, under me—all this is me. Can't you accept God? No, you can't.

You have not accepted the Owner of this world, therefore you have not accepted your own self. You are fighting over beard and bread. For centuries you have wanted territories. Finally you have come to the lowest of the lowliest of the lowly. Then you have become just a complex yourself. That's not fair. Alice doesn't live here anymore. You are not within yourself. You are out searching. This Piscean religion has taught you, "Go and search God. Go, and leave your home to the thieves." God shows up, and you are not there.

You are born to be a Teacher, and shall teach, but in His Name, and to all, big and small.

Even the Sikhs, who are told to live organically as *akaal moorat*, as God made you, have such trouble with the beard, you can't believe it! Just imagine, an eighty-year-old man with a perfect black beard. Wow, don't you like it? He can't even get up: "Ohh, ooh, ooh." Everybody knows you are eighty years old. But you are so obnoxious and so unreal, you do not want to develop to be a graceful, sage, divine, eighty year old. You want to be eighteen forever. You want to look beautiful to each other because you are hookers. You don't care about looking beautiful to the One who made you.

You know, in my life there was a time when everybody left me. Now they love me because I'm very rich, worldly, wise, you know what I mean? I could buy them in a second. If everything were to be put on auction, my bid would stand. Now they love me. What is the use of loving me now? I knew then that they were obnoxiously negative. They were so stupid, they used to say, "Well, he was an officer, he was so powerful, he was so wonderful, he was so marvelous. Now he's a yogi." Thank you for being abusive and obnoxious. My Master, my Lord adopted me. I don't need them now. They need me. I found my Maker, I found my Lord, I found my Being.

Why do I go to India? Do you know why we go ? To clean the same *perkarma*, the same floors. We don't do anything else there. Nothing. We just take the rags and wipe the floors. One, two days, we go in the morning when the doors open, we sit there, listen to the music. That's all we do. People say, "What is this?" It costs about three thousand dollars. "What are we doing here?"

I said, "We are doing great. We are thieves. We are very qualified thieves. We have come to steal the dust of the feet of the one who is one with the One. And if one has walked, and our rag can touch that place, it's all done. We've had it. One touch, nothing much, just one touch."

That's why Guru Nanak said:

ਆਦਿ ਸਚੁ ਜੁਗਾਦਿ ਸਚੁ ॥ ਹੈ ਭੀ ਸਚੁ ਨਾਨਕ ਹੋਸੀ ਭੀ ਸਚੁ ॥
Aad sach, jugaad sach, hei bhee sach, Naanak hosee bhee sach.
-Guru Nanak, *Siri Guru Granth Sahib*, page 1 (from *Mul Mantra* of *Japji Sahib*)
True in the beginning, True through all time, True even now, Nanak, forever True.

That's what you are. You are true in the beginning, true through time, true now, and you shall be true. If you remain so, but you don't remain so. You want to be something else. Be what God made you to be. Actually, you are wonderful beauty competitors. You compete with each other. You forget who made you, and what God said. Here are the words Nanak said:

ਅਕਾਲਮੁਰਤਿਅਜੂਨੀਸੈਭੰਗੁਰਪ੍ਰਸਾਦਿ॥

Akaal moorat ajoonee saibhang gurprasaad

-Guru Nanak, *Siri Guru Granth Sahib*, page 1 (from *Mul Mantra* of *Japji Sahib*)

He is undying, unborn, self-illumined. This is realized by the Grace of the True Guru.

With the Grace of the Guru, you will get this as a benefit. You'll be *ajoonee*. You'll be free from any action and reaction. You will never come in any cycle. *Saibhang* —and you will realize your Infinite Self. That, He says, is a gift to those who live organically, as God made them to be. Hey, are we bribing here? Are we doing public relations? No. This is the truth.

You'll find people very irritated about the beard—it doesn't matter how rich or poor he is—and about his food, his bread.

Today someone made garlic bread. The smell attracted everybody. On one side they were looking at their fatness, how many calories it had. On the other side they were smelling it and they wanted to eat it. I saw that duality and I laughed. Just to lead the gang, I ate two pieces of bread. Perhaps they will learn. No, no, they smelled it. They wanted it so eagerly, their stomachs wanted to come out on the table and grab the whole thing. But they were saying, "Nain, nain, nain. I'm on a diet. Nain, nain, nain, no, no, no, no." They couldn't say, "Nanak." They said, "No, no, no." You know when a person says, "No," he's anti-Nanak. "Nanak" means where there's no, "no." "No say 'no' when you have to say 'no', that is Nanak." If you want the Infinity of personality and richness and prosperity, beauty, and blessing, then just don't say no. Eliminate that one word. Those who say "no" will never have the Naam, the identity. Then you do not live in reality.

What do you want? Do you want nature to serve you, or do you want to run around like a chicken without a head? What do you want? What do you desire? It's a very funny thing. You will desire, you will collect, you will create, you will go, you'll have children and everything. Then at a certain age, everything will slowly, gradually drift away, lose you, gone. Then in the end, sixty percent of humans pray for a peaceful death and they never get it. Rather, it's a miserable bone-by-bone, molecule-by-molecule, atom-by-atom crushing death.

Just imagine a person who was so powerful, beautiful, he had six wives, nine girlfriends, and sixty-two concubines, a big yacht, and all that. Think of this guy who left behind a lot of wealth, that guy, Howard Hughes. Do you know where he lived? He lived on the top floor of a hotel. He never came out. He was so afraid, and he used to disinfect himself and everybody else.

Insanity is a bewitchment. You don't make any sense, because you compete, compare, and you are confused. You forgot that God is watching over you. You look at this watch. *(YB points to the watch on his wrist.)* There's a watch up there. *(YB points up to the heavens.)* And He knows. He knows you. I wish you could know Him—matter would end. There's no fight. You are born to be a Teacher, and you shall teach, but in His Name, and to all, big and small. That's the reality.

Money is a medium. Wealth is called Lakshmi; she is the wife of Narayan. So everybody is after the wife of God. Nobody cares for Him. And when somebody comes after your wife, what do you do to him? So the same happens to you. Don't blame Him. You go after maya. Maya's a myth. He watches and sees.

In my life there was an experience. A man came and he said, "I want you to be my Teacher."

I said, "I can't initiate. What is a Teacher?"

He said, "I want you as my Teacher."

I said, "I'm not for sale."

"I want you as my Teacher."

I said, "I'm not a Teacher. Not for you."

He said, "Well, I want to have a Teacher."

I said, "It's not written on your forehead. You shall never have a Teacher. You have to take many lifetimes."

He said, "No. I'll have you as a Teacher. You can't refuse me."

I said, "That I know. I'm not going to refuse."

So he served me. He became a Sikh. He became this, he became that. He was very intimate, very popular, very wonderful. One day he said, "How am I doing?"

I said, "Nothing."

"Are you not, now, my Teacher?"

I said, "No."

"You are not happy with me?"

I said, "Very happy. I love you."

"Well, why aren't you my Teacher?"

I said, "It is not written. You shall not have a Teacher."

"Well, I can have any other Teacher."

I said, "Have as many as you like. I am the only Teacher at this time. And I can't be your Teacher. I'm very sorry. I regret. You have served day, night, afternoon, up, down, but I can't accept you as my student. You come to every class, you are everywhere when I want you. But I am not your Teacher."

He said, "I have read in the Siri Guru Granth Sahib, 'By service, one can win.'"

I said, "That's true. I have read it, too. Don't feel disheartened, try."

Six years later he called. He said, "Master, I want to meet you."

I said, " I can meet you as a man, but I can't meet you as a Teacher."

"Master, I am leaving."

I said, "It will be fine. Don't worry about it. Go in good faith. And whenever you finish this life you will die, you will be reborn, and then find your Teacher if you can."

On the other hand, do you know a man called Jim Baker? (Editor's note: This is not the Jim Baker who is an evangelist minister.) I was his Teacher, too. And one day we had a fight. I told him, "Jim, you can't do this."

He said, "Master, it is in my genes. You know me. I cannot live with you telling me not to."

I said, "Then live away from me."

So he moved to Hawaii. Every time he would call, he would say, "You gotta come here. You have to be with me."

I would reply, "No. You live there. You're fine."

One day I was in the middle of traveling and they found me at the Albuquerque airport. It was an emergency telephone call. I went to the phone booth, and he said, "Master, it's time to go. I can't hold on anymore. I'm almost dead for the past seventy-two hours. I can't leave

We are not asking you to find the Master. BE the Master. That's your chance. You are a Hu-Man-Being— you are Light Now.

Man is just a pipe, a vehicle.
The Teacher is a vehicle of
divinity, without duality.
That's why you can uplift.

my *prana* until you bless me." *(Editor's note: Jim had been hang-gliding and fell. He was nearly dead but urgently had people call Yogi Bhajan.)*

I said, "Jim, say 'Sat Naam.'"

He said, "*Sat Naam.*" And that was it. That's called "*Gurprasaad.*" You get it by the Will of God, and by the Will of God you have the mind which you fix on the Lotus Feet of the Master. That Master is the Shabd Guru, not a man. Man is just a pipe, a vehicle. The Teacher is a vehicle of divinity, without duality; that's why you can uplift.

You think I am a Teacher? It is His problem. If I have to teach, He has to come through. If He stops coming through, I have nothing to do with it. He can find somebody else better than me, I'll be very happy to go home. There's nothing left here to do. The Age of Aquarius has set in; I've done my job. What am I hanging here for?

Earth is a hotel—for some it is a five star hotel, for some just a shack. But when you are tired, sleep is good. When you are hungry, food is good, and when you know you are a Master, you are good. What type of Teachers do you want to be? Commercial? Write a billboard, and say, "I am your Teacher?" First learn the meaning of a Spiritual Teacher. A Spiritual Teacher is the spirit of the Infinite Lord.

In our Dharma, for example, there are Singh Sahibs and Mukhia Singh Sahibs. Do you know that? Some of them are such egomaniac idiots, that they don't even understand what it means. They earned this status, but then they don't maintain it. Have you seen that very popular ad for the Jeep Cherokee? It goes through the ups and downs, the stones, and then, da, da, da, da, into the mud it goes. But in the end it comes up. You know? These guys, with that status of Singh Sahib and Mukhia Singh Sahib, are stuck in their own mud. They can't move.

Many people in this world are stuck as "Saints." I go to India, I meet these saints. They are saints. Saints! Saints of what? They screw around at night, and in the morning they pose perfectly and they say they are saints. What saints? They have five gunmen behind them.

One day I went to a saint and he started showing me his wealth. And you know me, my habits are very obnoxious. I'm a very obnoxious man. I thought, "Well, now, he has done his forty-five minutes." And I said to him, "Santji, how much is this whole thing worth? The whole thing."

"Ahh," he said, "maybe that much."

I took the ring from my hand. I said, "Sell it. It is three times its price."

He said, "I don't understand, Yogiji. Have I offended you?"

I said, "No, you have raped me. You are the most obnoxious son of a bitch. You are an old, dirty dog. I came to you just to be with a saint. I came to you with my humility. I came to have a good time. All you are telling me is your achievement, as if you are a construction engineer. What are you talking about? Do you know what you are talking about?"

You are a Sikh. Look what Nanak said:

ਜੇ ਜੁਗ ਚਾਰੇ ਆਰਜਾ ਹੋਰ ਦਸੂਣੀ ਹੋਇ ॥
ਨਵਾ ਖੰਡਾ ਵਿਚਿ ਜਾਣੀਐ ਨਾਲਿ ਚਲੈ ਸਭੁ ਕੋਇ ॥
ਚੰਗਾ ਨਾਉ ਰਖਾਇ ਕੈ ਜਸੁ ਕੀਰਤਿ ਜਗਿ ਲੇਇ ॥
ਜੇ ਤਿਸੁ ਨਦਰਿ ਨ ਆਵਈ ਤ ਵਾਤ ਨ ਪੁਛੈ ਕੇ ॥
ਕੀਟਾ ਅੰਦਰਿ ਕੀਟੁ ਕਰਿ ਦੋਸੀ ਦੋਸੁ ਧਰੇ ॥

Jay jug chaaray aarajaa, hor dasoonee hoeh.
Navaa khandaa vich jaan-ee-ai, naal chalai sabh ko-eh.
Changaa naa-oh rakhaa-eh-kai, jas keerat jag lay-eh.
Jay tis nadar naa(n) aavaee, taa(n) vaat naa(n) puchhai kay.
Keeta(n) andar keet kar dosee(n) dos dhar-eh

     -Guru Nanak, *Siri Guru Granth Sahib*, page 2 (from 7th *pauree* of *Japji Sahib*)

If one were to live for ages four, or for tens of ages more, with fame spread
across the nine continents, followed, honored, and sought by all, yet if he
were to fall from His Grace, he would be counted as a worm among worms,
and even sinners would blame him.

If you have all the life, all the wealth, all the ecstasy, everything, if you have not found your Master, you have lost it. We are not asking you to find the Master. BE the Master. That's your chance. You are a Hu-Man-Being—you are Light Now. Is that clear?

Class: Yes, Sir.

YB: It is difficult to say, "Yes, Sir." Right? Oh my God, you are Americans. Only in boot camp have you learned. Do you know who's responsible for the United States being a superpower? The drill sergeant. Have you seen that sergeant? Very tedious. They become a sergeant, they remain a sergeant, and they die a sergeant. But they teach us how to say, "Yes, sir." God, you can't believe it. To that "Yes, Sir," Heaven listens.

Have some of you been to a training camp?

Class: Yes, Sir.

YB: *(Laughs at one very aggressive "Yes, Sir.")* Very true. That "yes, sir," is so real.

There are three phrases that are good enough: "Yes, sir." "Thank you, sir." "Aye, aye, sir." "Aye, aye, sir" is our way of life. Do you know what "Aye, aye, sir" means? Imperial impact of the Lord. One who recognizes it, knows it.

Put on the *Dhuni* tape. Now let me see how correctly you can copy it. That is the purpose of this evening class. Hurry up! Ready?

Class: Yes, Sir.

(Students do the Meditation from the morning class, Class #8. See page 88.)

Make the mental connection. Let the breath give you the base. Now utter. Pull it from the navel. You are good, thank you. Relax. Good night. You are good, you are good. That's all I wanted to see. You are really good, you tuned in exactly in one minute and a half. Normally it takes three minutes to tune in. You made it today.

Self-Reverence

*Your faculty of projection with your
personal reverence will win all for you.
That is the path of victory.*

Today we'll discuss projection. Is it all right with you?

Class: Yes, Sir.

YB: Were you born? Were you dropped or were you born?

Class: We were born.

YB: You have a nervous system, you have a muscular system, you have a structure, you have features. Did you organize that?

Class: No, Sir.

YB: Did you desire what you got? Were you aware of where you were going to be born? Did you decide who should be your parents? You were told, "These are your parents." Is that true?

Class: Yes, sir.

YB: You were told, "This is your mother." You immediately were nurtured by her, therefore, she became a mother. Then she told you, "This is the father." It's called, "reference by action." There were actions with which you were trained. You were told, "Sit, poop, up, dup, dee, doo, daa." That became your classical reference. So you are human by reference.

YB: What subject are we talking about today?

Class: Projection.

YB: I thought you forgot. So you are human by....?

Class: ...reference.

YB: Not by reverence. Over the years, every religion has lied, lied, and lied, and made a fool out of you as humans. You don't have a chance to be human, because you have never been taught to be human by reverence. Reverence means "self-reverence," not somebody else's reference. You have always been taught by reference: "That's my mother, that's my father, that's my religion, that's my Kabbalah; and that's my synagogue, that's my church, that's my temple, that's my husband, that's my child. That is, that is, that is...."

When somebody does good for you, you have a good reference to that person. When somebody does bad for you, it is a bad reference. You are the most unlearned, unlearnable mammals; you are egomaniac, arrogant individuals—and extremely stupid. You suffer so much. Oh, God, help them!

Animals eat their grass, birds fly with their rhythm, poop where they want, and sit where

If you remember this line, you will project correctly.
Your genetic self contains the Infinite Self.

they want. But you have no place. You are the most misfit category of life. You have no projection, therefore, you are trendy. If everybody's screwing, you are screwing. If nobody's screwing, you are not screwing. There was a time when everybody became celibate. The world population became one third. And now everybody's screwing; the world population is unlimited. There's no room. A boy has a girl, a girl has a boy. A screws B, B screws C, C screws D. What a drama!

Do you know, the word intercourse really refers to when you and I talk. Intercourse doesn't mean a sexual relationship. When *you* say, "He sleeps with he," or, "He sleeps with she," you mean sex. Sleep really means you sleep—with a pillow, you know? Sleeping means sleeping with your pillow. Sleeping does not mean what *you* mean by sleeping. And when you say, "I love him," or, "He loves me," you are insane, because neither do you have your reference to reverence, nor do you have reference to reverence to another person. That's why your relationships never project right.

What subject are we talking about today?

Class: Projection.

YB: I just want to make you understand the meaning of projection.

If a bow and arrow, and its string, and its strength, and the pressure of the air are not measured, you will never hit the bull's-eye. You can't. Even with a rifle, the holding of the breath, the shoulder, the pressure, and the trigger, and the wind pressure have to be measured. It's called "zeroing the rifle" before you fire. Do you do that in life? No.

You have not been taught to have reverence. You have been taught to have reference. But with reference you are prostitutes. You live by reputation, and your reputation goes ahead of you, so you are already known and set. That's not living. That's a low-grade mammal existence. LGME. In high sociology, they call it LGME: Low-Grade Mammal Existence.

And what do you think of yourself? You have landed on the moon. Then what? The moon was already there, he wanted you to come, so you went. What have you gotten from science? If you read the *Mahabharata*, you find that over three thousand years ago they had individual planes in India. They called them *vimaan*, airplane, and they were powered by mercury vapor. That was the energy they used—crystal mercury vapor power. They used to fly from India to visit their second home for the holidays called "America." They called it *pataal desh*, the underworld. You are the underworld. When I was small they used to tell me that under India—India is called *bharat* —there is an underworld—*pataal desh.*

ਭਾਰਤ ਦੇਸ਼ ਕੇ ਨੀਚੇ ਇਕ ਪਤਾਲ ਦੇਸ਼ ਹੈ ॥ ਵਹਾਰਾਕਸ਼ਵਸਤੇ ਹੈ ॥
ਗਊ ਕਾ ਮਾਸ ਖਾਤੇ ਹੈ ॥ ਮਦਰਾ ਪੀਤੇ ਹੈ ॥ ਵਿਸ਼ੇ ਵਿਕਾਰ ਭੋਗਤੇ ਹੈ ॥
Bhaarat desh kay neechay ik pataal desh hai. Wahaa raakshas bastay hai.
Gha-oo kaa maas khaatay hai. Madraa peetay hai, vishay vikaar bhogtey hai.
    - Punjabi saying

"Under India exists an underworld where *raakshas* —demons—live. They eat beef, they drink wine, they have sex with each other," and they die. This is what I was told at three years old.

Leave the other underworld in what you eat and what you do. *Vishay vikaar.* The world is known as *vish. Vishva* means the universe. *Vishay* means the complex. *Vishaa* means a heading, a label. *Vikaar* means wrong heading, corruption.

So all your headings of life are by reference, not by reverence. You don't project that you are born to *be.* You are born, and you are divine, and you are you. You don't have to become a human. You *are* human. Being a human is better than being an angel, and better than a sage, and better than any power of God that there is. You are human, therefore, you are in the image of God. You want to look like your own image, therefore, you are stupid. You are not being like the one who made you. Do you understand?

Nobody wants to tell you this. They want you to be easy, have fun. Fun for what? Folks, what fun? You have "x" amount of prana, and "x" amount of energy called "youth," and in "x" amount of time you can make the best of it, and that's all it is. It's as if there is a bank, and you have ten thousand dollars or one million dollars, whatever your expense account is, and you have a sixty-five year visit in which to spend it. How you'll live, which motel you'll live in, which hotel you'll live in, what you do with life, that's your problem, not God's.

Yes, with your reverence, you can increase yourself. With reference, you can decrease yourself. Now do you understand projection?

Class: Yes, Sir.

YB: You do not love anybody. Absolutely not. You hook people. You project your sensuality, not your sensitivity. What do you need friends for? For personal satisfaction and exploitation? That's why in your relationships you are here, there, everywhere, because you are not within yourself. Your self is empty of you. Forget about becoming a Teacher and then getting into the heart of another person, and understanding the head of another person, and forklifting—that's the job of a Teacher.

I have seen it over and over again in marriages. They fall apart. You counsel them, they fall apart. You tell them, they fall apart. You don't tell them, they fall apart. Why do they fall apart? Because the marriage was based on reference; it was not based on reverence. It was not reverence, greatness, shine, beauty, power of the spirit, the soul. It was sexual—the penis and vagina met. And you expect victory? No. You can't get it. You can't! Any relationship which is based on the second chakra shall never have the quality of the sixth chakra. Anything which is not based on the sixth chakra will not command the universe. "Not command the universe" means that the universe will not come and serve you, although it is your birthright. Happiness is your birthright. You can't get your birthright, so you start fantasizing and you start romancing. Romance and fantasy take you away from reality. That's why you have no endurance, you have no courage to have endurance, and you fall apart. One opposition, two oppositions, ten oppositions, twenty oppositions: You go down as if you don't exist. Jack and Jill went down the hill. Wooshh. Not right, folks. What is not right is left.

You know how simple I am? Things are very simple. There is no complication for us. Life is not a complicated thing. You complicate it to become prostitutes and pimps of the very life which is supposed to be divine and reverent and gracious and absolute for you. And it's given. The tragedy is you don't even have to earn it. It is given.

ਗੁਰ ਸੇਵਾ ਤੇ ਭਗਤਿ ਕਮਾਈ ॥ ਤਬ ਇਹ ਮਾਨਸ ਦੇਹੀ ਪਾਈ ॥
ਇਸ ਦੇਹੀ ਕਉ ਸਿਮਰਹਿ ਦੇਵ ॥ ਸੋ ਦੇਹੀ ਭਜੁ ਹਰਿ ਕੀ ਸੇਵ ॥

Gur sevaa tay bhagat kamaa-ee. Tab eh maanas dayhee paa-ee.
Is dehee ka-ho simareh dev. So dayhee bhaj har kee sayv.
   -Bhagat Kabir, *Siri Guru Granth Sahib*, page 1159
Through the Guru's service the Lord's loving adoration is practiced.
Then alone is the fruit of this human body obtained.
Even the gods long for this body.
So through this body of yours, think of rendering service unto God.

With the Guru's blessing you earned this life, and you have earned this human body which is worshipped by angels, not only by you. And through this body you can understand infinity, and with reverence, worship, and understanding, you can understand the totality of God. You know how blissful it is? *You* see one little thing and you say, "Wow!" "Oh, I met a very beautiful girl today. Wow. Wow." Have you seen these kids? "Wow!" Do you understand these stupids, when they take all that.... *(YB demonstrates a person taking drugs by sniffing some substance through his nose.)* Do you know what I mean? "Oh, I'm in ecstasy." Well, you have three hundred dollars less and you are stupid forever. Yes, you are in ecstasy. Other than that foolishness, you will never do it.

And under the influence of these drugs you do things. You have wet dreams. You have cold sweats. Sometimes you get the shakes. What is this? It's not you. It is good to get sick and fall apart once in a while. A car does it, why not you? But the problem is, *your* parts are not replaceable. They don't have a Jiffy Lube to lube you up. Do you know what I'm saying?

Class: Yes, Sir.

YB: Once you lose a part of you, folks, you are gone. One part that you are losing these days with drugs is called Impactuous Sensitivity. This generation, the Sixties generation, has lost it. Drugs may do good to you for a while, it's your money. I'm not asking you not to use them, but you shall never be you again.

That's why I started Kundalini Yoga here. I wasn't interested in gaining my leadership or membership. I saw the tragedy of mankind. I saw how damaged they were. We picked up young bodies left on trails, eaten by animals, unrecognizable, and sometimes their identification led us to their homes. You can't believe it.

But what is a drug? When you take any drug which makes you hallucinate, it means your brain cells are stretched to the area and extent beyond what they should be. So the chances of developing sensitivity and experiencing infinity are lost.

I remember somebody ate a brownie. For six days he was saying, "I am Yogiji, and I am with Guru Ram Das, and I am having all there is. And I know what it is. Understand me? *(YB says all this in a sing-song voice.)* They are all my friends, I am in Heavens. I'm seeing angels. Lord Shiva came yesterday to massage me." For seven days I had to sit by his bed. And this is what I was hearing: "Oh, oh, Yogiji. I am Yogi Bahan, I'm here. He has gone into my whole body. And my legs are his legs. My hands are...." And I was sitting on the chair, by his side. Seven long days! Finally I got tired of sitting, my buttocks started hurting; I just took care of his temples and he woke up.

I said, "Hi, Yogiji."

He said, "No, you are Yogiji."

I said, "Oh yes? I just wanted you to come back to yourself." There was no self. The self, whether it was great or it was bad, right or wrong, it got stretched. And sometimes when you stretch something, it doesn't come back.

So people have acid and cocaine and all these drugs, but the worst of all is marijuana. That's the worst. Every drug has a limited feature and flushes out through the urine. Marijuana does not get out through the urine. Actually marijuana is an herb which is used for stomach ailments. It numbs the internal wound of the digestive system. That's what it was used for. But the moment you smoke it, it hits your pituitary and that's it, you're gone. It freezes the serum in the spine, and you will never have gray matter of the quality that you had, doesn't matter how you think you may be.

You don't want to project you. You want to project somebody else. You are the power. You don't need the power. You are the beauty. You don't need the beauty. You are the success. You don't need the success. You are the sex. You don't need to sex yourself.

You are human by reference, not by reverence. Over the years, every religion has lied, and made a fool out of you as humans. You don't have a chance to be human, because you have never been taught to be human by reverence. Reverence means "self-reverence," not somebody else's reference. You have always been taught by reference: "That's my mother, that's my father, that's my religion, that's my Kabbalah; and that's my synagogue, that's my church, that's my temple, that's my husband, that's my child. That is, that is, that is...."

The Christians, the Jews, the Hindus, the Muslims, the Sikhs—you name it, the whole humanity has no self-reference to reverence.

Somebody once said, "What can you do?"

I said, "I can give you a face and grace, or I can condemn you."

"What do you mean by 'condemn me?'"

I said, "I'll write down that I met so and so, and he was a living idiot, and that's it. That'll become record. In five hundred years when the world will be different, you will be a living idiot. You will be referred to as an idiot. That I can do."

"Why would you do that?"

I said, "I'm not doing it. You asked me, so I'm telling you what I can do."

"Why?"

I said, "I'm a Mahan Tantric, I'm a Lord of Longitude, Latitude, Altitude, Attitude. I can do what I want. You are not going to tell me what to do. You asked me, 'What can you do?' I'm telling you what I can do. Is there any question?"

He said, "Well, what does it matter if you write me off as an idiot?"

I said, "It shall matter. It shall become a universal energy. You think I am a person. I'm an institution. I am the mansion which has many rooms. Look at the way I am, not the

Any relationship which is based on the second chakra shall never have the quality of the sixth chakra. Anything which is not based on the sixth chakra will not command the universe—the universe will not come and serve you, although it is your birthright.

way you look at it."

He said, "I'm looking at it."

I said, "Look again."

He said, "Wow!"

I said, "What did you see?"

He said, "You disappeared into light."

I said, "No, I was sitting here. I never left the room."

"Well, what was that?"

I said, "I just made you see me. I didn't do anything." I said, "This is the power of a Master of Kundalini Yoga. One who practices in a pure form can become the living light, can become the living awareness, can become the living beings of all beings, and time and space shall serve such an individual." I said, "I just showed you. I'm not showing you anything more or less."

"Well, man, I want to study with you."

I said, "No."

Now watch this. This is called Super Insanity.

"Ten thousand dollars a lesson."

"No."

"This lifetime."

"No."

"Ever?"

"No."

"Why no?"

I said, "You are no. Because you tried to measure with maya a man who is a Master. You missed the chance. You tried to measure it."

Infinity cannot be measured. Reverence cannot be explained, because reverence is Infinity. Reverence has such a power that it becomes Infinity, and for you to become Infinity, you have to have self-reverence, not reference.

What do you do? You prostitute yourself. "I am this, I am beautiful, I have boobs, I have this...." Everybody has. You think others don't have what you have? Some have less, some are right, some are wrong. There's a white gringo student of mine, he married a black girl, and I said, "Will the family accept this marriage?"

He said, "That's why I married her. I don't want to be accepted."

I said, "Wow. Why?"

He said, "I want to get even with my family. This is the only way. But Yogiji, please bless me."

I said, "Why?"

He said, "Just bless me. That'll give me satisfaction."

I said, "I bless you a hundred times. I have nothing to lose. To me it's neither black nor white, nor yellow, nor pink. To me it is all human. But you are not marrying for the purposes of marrying. You are marrying for the purposes of getting even with your family. That's what you are doing."

The majority of young kids get even with their parents, and they lose from the start. Do you know what they say? "I want to do what I want to do. I don't want to hear you tell me what to do." That's called "the first act of disobedience," and nobody has ever recovered from that, because that becomes a mantra.

You live in the world of pushers—sexual pushers, not sensual pushers. You are sexual pushers, like prostitutes with a reference. You are not human with a reverence. Your beauty and your power and your universe guarantee you all happiness if you have self-reference to your reverence. That's the first projection.

You want to look beautiful? What you're seeing in the mirror is the trend and the tendency of the time. You never look in the mirror of your mind and into your soul.

Because you live by reference you have patterns. Five marriages, same pattern; sixteen friends, same pattern; action reaction, same pattern. And sometimes you patent it; it becomes permanent, you are predictable.

I know of a girl who every two and a half years has to have a major shift in her life. I was telling her one day: "Hey," I said, "'Two-and-a-half-years is closing in. "What's next?"

She said, "Well, I know it is coming. I'll try to stop it."

I said, "The last several times in the past you didn't."

Once somebody asked a guy, he said, "Why are you swimming when you can go by boat?"

He said, "I want to swim. I don't want to go by boat."

"Why not?"

He said, "I want to be a fish."

The guy said, "You never forgot your previous incarnation when you were a fish."

You become human but you don't forget your previous incarnation. Have you seen some people who frown like this at everybody? "Heeeee." They were dogs. Have you seen people who hiss at you? They were snakes. Have you seen people who say, "Wonk, wonk, wonk?" They were frogs.

Anyway, you already have nicknames for your friends, don't you? You all have, don't lie. I know. You have their real names, not their legal names. You say, "Hey, save you from this guy. He's a fox."

How many words do we use for naming people? One is fox, that's very common. What else? There's a weasel, and so forth. There's a long list. Once I was given a list that had the real names of the humans. It was the theory of reincarnation. Somebody just sat down and figured it out. From a common focal behavior you can totally study and understand what the previous life of that person was. Absolutely. You don't have to spend five hundred dollars or five thousand dollars to know previous incarnations.

Somebody once brought me about a hundred tapes. "Yogiji, will you listen to this?"

I said, "What for?"

"These are my previous incarnations."

I said, "Then what?"

"Oh, it's very important."

I said, "What did you eat the day before yesterday at lunch?" She couldn't tell me. I said, "If you cannot tell me what you ate two days back, what is the idea of going through these hundreds of tapes? You were something. Why do I have to deal with that?"

"Well, I want to know what I was and what I can do."

I said, "You can do doo-doo, or you do to be. But do me a favor. I'll help you as much as you want, but there's one condition."

She said, "What?"

I said, "Don't become a Sikh. Promise me."

"Why?"

I said, "Then it becomes a headache, and I have a lot of headaches. Please. One less. That's all I want."

"Why?"

I said, "You are nuts. I have so many nuts to deal with, so please, do not become a Sikh. You promise me this and I'll do everything for you."

So we agreed. But she became a Sikh, anyway. That is the tragedy now. And I said, "You broke the promise."

She said, "I broke my promise with you. I now have everything with the Guru. Don't tell me anything. I know." And she is very smart. But what can you do?

She said, "God is infinite. Guru is infinite wisdom. I don't need you."

I said, "That's true. You don't." And every third day I am on the phone. This is how she starts. It is a very typical idea. She says, "I was reading *Siri Guru Granth*. At page such and such, line such and such, now Guru says, 'da, da, da, da, da.' But what does he mean by this?"

I said, "What do you mean? The Guru spoke, you heard it, this is a direct relationship."

She said, "No, you explain to me what it means."

She knows I cannot say "No." So I start saying, "Well, Guru said such and such, it is in Rag such and such. This is what the story is...."

After forty five minutes she says, "Well, what I mean to say is, why did I read that line today?"

I answered, "Now you are behaving nuts."

"Well, I want to talk to you."

I said, "No, as far as the Guru's explanation goes, it's over. I'm going to hang up the phone."

"No, no, no, one more minute. One more question."

I said, "What?"

"Why did the Guru say so?"

I said, "You ask Him directly. We have no relationship, do you remember?" Can you find a more qualified nut than that person? It's fun to watch people.

It is very difficult for people to admit they are wrong, because once you admit you are wrong, then you have a chance that you will be right. And it's not as though I can be your judge, and judge you right or wrong. You know you are right or wrong.

ਬੀਜ ਮੰਤ੍ਰੁ ਸਰਬ ਕੋ ਗਿਆਨੁ ॥
Beej mantar sarb ko giaan.
    -Guru Arjan, from *Sukhmani Sahib, Siri Suru Granth Sahib*, page 274
The comprehension of the seed of God's Name is available to everyone.

Every spermatozoa of yours knows how to go around the egg eight times and penetrate. That spermatozoa never went to a university, did it? Did it go to the university and study and come out a graduate, and then go into the human and ejaculate through the penis, and go in with the other millions of them, and then finally reach the egg? And did the egg know how to form itself? When the egg wants to accept the spermatozoa, it takes its shape, to facilitate this little thing to go eight times, and penetrate. So your seed has all knowledge, like a little seed contains the whole tree. So your genetic self contains the entire Infinite Self.

If you remember this line, you'll project correctly: Your genetic self contains the Infinite Self. Life is like that. A car says, "Seven years guaranteed. Five years guaranteed." You know what I mean? So your genetic guarantee can be very predetermined. "This man is going to live this much and that much."

You need fifteen breaths a minute; that's what you normally take. And when you are excited, emotional, drugged, sexual, sensual, excited, whatever, you go up to twenty-four. Sometimes you go to thirty-one, something like that. It's very simple mathematics. Suppose you have enough breath of life at the rate of one breath for one year, so you take one breath a minute, you can live fifteen years. Suppose you have breath of life for one hundred years. At fifteen breaths a minute, at that rate, you can live 1500 years. That's how yogis extend their life—by practicing one breath a minute. When you practice one breath a minute, then you become *Pavan Guru*— you become the light and knowledge of the *prana*, and then you know the universe, the universe knows you. That's why Nanak, the Guru, said:

ਪਵਣੁ ਗੁਰੂ ਪਾਣੀ ਪਿਤਾ ਮਾਤਾ ਧਰਤਿ ਮਹਤੁ ॥
ਦਿਵਸੁ ਰਾਤਿ ਦੁਇ ਦਾਈ ਦਾਇਆ ਖੇਲੈ ਸਗਲ ਜਗਤੁ ॥
ਚੰਗਿਆਈਆ ਬੁਰਿਆਈਆ ਵਾਚੈ ਧਰਮੁ ਹਦੂਰਿ ॥
ਕਰਮੀ ਆਪੋ ਆਪਣੀ ਕੇ ਨੇੜੈ ਕੇ ਦੂਰਿ ॥
ਜਿਨੀ ਨਾਮੁ ਧਿਆਇਆ ਗਏ ਮਸਕਤਿ ਘਾਲਿ ॥
ਨਾਨਕ ਤੇ ਮੁਖ ਉਜਲੇ ਕੇਤੀ ਛੁਟੀ ਨਾਲਿ ॥

Pavan Guroo paanee pitaa, maataa dharat mahat.
Divas raat du-eh daa-ee daa-i-aa, khay-lai sagal jagat.
Changi-aa-ee-aa buri-aa-ee-aa, vaachai dharam hadoor.
Karamee aapo aapanee, kay nayrai kay dhoor.
Jinee naam dhi-aa-i-aa, ga-ay masakat ghaal.
Naanak tay mukh ujalay, kaytee chhutee naal.
    -Guru Nanak, *Siri Guru Granth Sahib*, page 7 (from *Slok* of *Japji Sahib*)
Air is the Guru, water the father, and Earth the great mother.
Day and night are two male and female nurses in whose lap the entire world plays.
All of our deeds shall be judged by the Lord of Law,
By our own actions we draw Him near or far.
Those who have meditated on God's Name will leave this world
    after putting toil in the right direction.
Shining are their faces and they save many others.

In this Slok, he totally completes the human anatomy, excellence, process, projection in the most clear words which one can understand. He says it with absolute clarity, sparing nothing.

Guru Nanak salutes God as a yogi, by using the yogi's salute: *Aades*. *Aades* means, "I salute Thou."

ਆਦੇਸੁ ਤਿਸੈ ਆਦੇਸੁ ॥
Aades tisai aades...
I salute Thou. I salute Thou, again and again.
ਆਦਿ ਅਨੀਲੁ ਅਨਾਦਿ ਅਨਾਹਤਿ
Aad aneel anaad anaahat...
Aad . You are the beginning. Aad. He describes all dimension of limitlessness...
ਜੁਗੁ ਜੁਗੁ ਏਕੋ ਵੇਸੁ ॥
Jug, jug ayko ves.
Remains True through all Ages, through all time.
    -Guru Nanak, *Siri Guru Granth Sahib*, page 7 (from 30th *pauree* of *Japji Sahib*)

God is primal and pure with unknown beginning, Who cannot be destroyed, and Who remains the same in all Ages. Through all time You will remain.

Because he wanted to let everybody know the nature of God and this universe.

When I said, "The Aquarian Age has come, the axle of the Earth changed," everybody laughed at me. I said, "Fine." Now they say the axle of the Earth has changed, and the Earth is moving slower. They say it is because we have made dams, and the weight of those consolidated waters has slowed down the movement of the Earth. Can you believe that man can now slow down the Earth? First ask him, "When will you start rotating it?"

I asked one of the same scientists, I said, "Well, do you remember in which year you started rotating the Earth, and what type of gasoline you used?"

He said, "You are joking with me."

I said, "You are stupid. I'm not joking, I'm telling you." I said, "I didn't call you, You called me, because you read my note."

He said, "That's true. I want to know, how do you know?"

I said, "The axle of the Earth changes, the momentum of the magnetic field changes. In the Earth, what you call "lava," or "ferrum" exists, and that changes. And the flare of the sun in relevancy changes."

Look at your ability to communicate with a walkie-talkie. Sometimes you can get through at a long distance easily, sometimes you can't. Or with a cell phone, when you go through mountains, you lose communication, then you have communication. Or sometimes on the telephone, you have interference. What are you using? You are using electromagnetic force. Instead of mentally projecting this, you do it through the telephone.

The telephone is nothing but you. The television is nothing but you. People used to have vision, now you have television. But the difference between television and vision is, in your vision you can see what you want to see or not see, with concern for your psyche. In television it is what you are being shown.

(See page 114 for details of this meditation.)

Your faculty of projection with your personal reverence will win all for you. That is the path of victory. Play that tape *Reality, Prosperity, Ecstasy* by Nirinjan. It's a prayer of prosperity. This is the sound and the word of a most religious woman. Her name is Nirinjan Kaur. Just listen carefully to these lyrics which she sings and go into prayer. This is the prayer of the lotus. Do it. Let us see what happens.

(When it comes to an end, YB asks for the tape Dhuni, *and the meditation continues.)*

Stop, I want to tell you something.

Do you know what the word *"Sat Nam,"* actually means? It's a code number for the *Prakirti*, the Creation. If you call New Mexico, you have to dial the 505 area code. Do you understand?

Class: Yes, Sir.

YB: It's an area code number. Mantra is a code projection to decode the mystery of divinity. And when your mantra is perfect, connection is perfect, you get what it is.

"Wahe Guru" is the code mantra of the *Purkha*. There are two things, *Purkha* or *Purshaa* means Creative God, and all of creative Creation which stimulates itself in existence is called *Prakirti*. So there are two area code numbers for the human. One is *"Sat Nam,"* and one is *"Wahe Guru."* And there's a common number, which in Christianity and other religions is used as, *"A-men."* Actually it is *"Om."* It is not *Amen*. And *Om* is not a sound which verbally means anything. It's called "Common Code."

You know when you stay in a hotel and you have your own key? And sometimes you lose the key so you call the floor service and they bring the master key to open the door? And *Om* is chanted like this. *(YB demonstrates how to chant "Om.")* It's chanted in the conch of the human. It's not verbal. *"Om,"* is in *"Ek Ong Kaar,"* which is what you call an "effective code" of the Om. That's why Nanak did a wonderful, scientific job, when he added to this Om, *"Ek Onnnng Kaar."* He did a fantastic job for the human, so that you may not be debauched about things. He gave you a sense of mastery by giving you this *Ek Ong Kaar*, because when you chant it, you revitalize the entire brain matter. There are so many things in the skull. It's not a cantaloupe, and it needs service. These mantras are called "entry codes."

We'll talk about it. We've done enough for today. Thank you.

Lotus Prayer for Prosperity
& Projection unto Victory

 **Mudra:** Sit in Easy Pose with a straight spine. Bend the elbows down into the sides of the body. Bring the hands in front of the heart center, palms facing one another, with the fingers pointing up towards the ceiling. Spread the fingers wide apart. Make your hands into a lotus in front of your heart center by bringing together and touching the tips of the pinkies, the sides of the pads of the thumbs, and the base of the palms. The other fingers will be kept spread apart, and curved slightly to form the lotus petals.

Movement: Keeping the mudra with fingers pointing straight up, begin gliding your arms up in a straight line, until the hands are a little above, and a little in front of your head. Then in a continuous movement, without any abrupt stop, glide them back down to the starting position. Continue.

Eyes: Unspecified.

Tape: *Reality, Prosperity and Ecstasy,* by Nirinjan Kaur. *(Refer to page 246 for lyrics.)* Then the instrumental *Dhuni.*

Time: The meditation was done for 21 minutes in class; 15 minutes with the *Prosperity* tape, and 6 minutes with the *Dhuni* tape.

End: Inhale, exhale. Relax.

Comments/Effects: This is a prayer for prosperity. It is the prayer of the lotus. Just listen to the lyrics of the *Prosperity* tape, and go into a deep prayer.

Your faculty of projection with your personal reverence will win all for you. That's the path of victory.

The Grace of Kundalini Yoga

*The first qualification of a Kundalini Yoga
Teacher is: Let God fail, let His servants not.
If you do not have this concept, you can
never teach Kundalini Yoga.*

would like to be forgiven in advance for whatever I'm going to speak about today. Therefore, I'm going on record, if anybody has an objection to today's lecture, he can leave the class. Today I have to teach as a Teacher, and not as a public relations person. Is it acceptable?

Class: Yes, Sir.

YB: Thank you. I fully understand that you are Western. What we call Western is anything from Istanbul to the western United States. It's not a civilization, it's a geographical location. So, technically speaking, you are Western. But I also understand you have no concept of a Teacher.

You are Western, I understand. I like you because you are aggressive, and I also like you because you are a mental case. No, no, listen to me, it's very clear. Because what you know, you know, and whether it is your fantasy or reality, you do not have hypocrisy. That's what I like about you. Orientals, on the other hand, have the worst hypocrisy in the world. They will never never say what they feel, they will never say what they are. They will say, "yes, yes, yes."

I went to Japan, and I asked the guy to bring my food, and he brought me meat. And I said, "I am vegetarian."

He said, "Yes, yes." And he took away the plate. He brought another dish. And it was a little different meat than the other meat.

I said, "I am a vegetarian, and I don't eat meat." He returned with a dish of a very chopped up snake. And I said, "What is this?"

He said, "This is a special dish—snake."

I said, "Still it is meat."

"Yes sir, yes sir."

The sixth time I asked him to call the manager. He came and said, "All these dishes are made for a special guest, and you are the special guest."

I said, "Get me fruit." He brought me an orange. That was my lunch. But they didn't say one word. All they said was, "Yes, sir. Yes, sir."

The second time I went to Japan I knew what to do, so I stayed at the Ginza Hotel and I told them, "I'm vegetarian, and pre-handling arrangements should be made." So they put before me a dish made up of an orange, a banana, an apple, and very well sautéed green peas, rice,

> *Kundalini Yoga is not a commercial nonsense. It's not public relations. Either a practitioner practices purely or should not practice it. The system has a power not to pollute itself. The system itself does not allow anybody to pollute the system.*

this and that. Thank God, whatever it was, we ate. The bill came to eighty dollars U.S. per person. So I asked this guy, I said, "What is this eighty dollars for? This is about one dollar's worth of food."

He said, "It was specially flown from California, where you came from." And he said, "The bill includes the cost of bringing it here, telephone costs and everything. We have lost twenty dollars on this one dish."

And I said, "For what?"

He said, "This is what you eat. You come from Los Angeles?"

I said, "Yes."

He said, "So we brought the food from there."

I paid the bill. I didn't mind.

I know you are Western, and you think I have come here for religion. That's not true. That's not even true today. They made me a religious leader because they thought I was too dangerous to be left out. Oh yes, that's true. They put this shackle around my neck, and in my environments and circumstances it was not easy for me to say "no," so I accepted it.

But practically speaking, when I worked at the airport in customs, I saw you westerners coming to India with a lot of money to find Swamijis and Yogijis and Mahatmajis, God knows what. The rule in those days was that when you came to India, you had to declare your money, and you had to fill in the customs form to state what you were bringing in and bringing out. There was no restriction. I saw people bringing thousands and thousands of dollars and going back with just ten bucks. And whenever they sat down, I asked them a question about yoga. They were worse than when they came in. So I thought to myself, if ever I get a chance to go to the West to teach, I'll stay there in the West and teach, and I'll produce Teachers. I'll never require students.

On the fifth of January, some twenty-seven years ago, I declared my purpose. They asked me, "What have you come for?"

I said, "I have not come here to collect students. I have come here to create Teachers."

That's why I'm sticking with the teachings, and I'm sticking with the dialogue that I have been speaking, though I know that you are not yet ready to be Teachers. Your ego is too much. You do not have reverence. You are like plastic. You know those credit cards? You put it in, you swipe it, and that's it. For you that's it. But if it doesn't go through, no matter who you are, you have to show a driver's license.

So your personal presence in the West has no identity and your personal presence in the West as a Teacher has no identity, either. You are full of full. (I don't want to use that word which I am willing to say. I think you understand my sentiments.) You are full of that super full. You are neither a woman, nor a man, nor even a mammal. You are just a bubbly little ego, jumping around. You have no width, you have no tolerance. You do not even have patience to listen. It's so amazing. And still you are very beautiful people. It's a classic blunder God made. It's a fact. The most perfect Almighty God went berserk and created you all.

Do you understand that in your life there is no other principle prevalent but to be neutral? Negative is as good as positive. It's the filament which creates the light, and it's the vacuum which brightens it. Do you understand the law of light? That's why when you had a candle, you put the glass around it to create a lamp. That's why you have a bulb, you have a tube. And the law of vacuum is, there's no vacuum.

So the most insane person has some sanity somewhere, and the most sane person has the equivalent insanity somewhere. But the sanity or insanity doesn't matter. The question is: Do you have the width to open up, to accommodate, to listen, to understand, from another point of view, so you may not end up screwing up the whole thing? Do you have a little one minute of patience?

Today I was speaking with a lady who brought a herbal packet which cost about ninety some dollars. It has some grape seed and other things in it, and it promises you everything; and it gives energy. She was extremely enthusiastic: "It energizes me, bah, bah, bah, bah."

I said, "Yes, but here, take just some of our herbs. They are cheap and you can be fine."

"What's the difference?"

I said, "All of our formulas are anti-fatigue. We don't stimulate, we don't stretch the human energy. We minus the fatigue and the human is left with his energy. Simple thing." Because the body is a very dedicated, delicate, decent machine. It cannot be overcharged, over-rushed into anything. People hallucinate with drugs; I have nothing to do with it. All I said when I came to the United States was, "Drugs are a drag. Let's have an organic method to be." That's why people started following me.

I said, "There's an organic, natural way to be high." And when I used to attend these pop festivals, I used to see sixty, seventy thousand people running around naked. I was the main featured speaker. I have seen you naked.

My first experience at one of these festivals was, I went to take a bath, and when I returned to the teepee, two couples were doing what the birds and bees do. And I said, "Shakti. Look what is happening in the teepee."

She as the Mother Superior was with me. She saw it, and it was worth a laugh.

In the first yoga class I taught in a New Mexico meadow, I was teaching cow and cat pose. A girl was underneath and the boy went in and did the whole thing, by the time I got up and came over and asked him, "What are you doing?"

He said, "I've enjoyed it."

What I'm saying is, I know you. You are not foreign to me. And you are not that great a hero just because of those two hanging testicles which make you think you are the biggest macho on the Earth. And if that six-inch thing is your main object, what about your six foot, six inch whole being? After all, you are a full person.

So, what it comes down to is from which chakra you dwell, from which chakra you live, and with which chakra you project. Aren't we talking about projection today?

Class: Yes, Sir.

YB: It's not whether your chakra is open or closed. It is where you are at. Is your projection from here (YB points to his 3rd Eye point), from there (YB points to his 2nd chakra), or from there (YB points to his 1st chakra)? Why do you call each other, "Assholes?" It's a chakra thing. The wrong chakra for a wrong subject.

You must understand. Ten percent of you is projection and ten percent of you is object and subject. You can't be more than that. There's no way. Eighty percent is unknown. The idea of intuition is not to not know. The idea of the development of intuition is that you have to know that eighty percent. You are missing eighty percent.

And don't misunderstand that people have put a turban on and they have become Sikhs and all that. I tell you. When I came one day to the ashram and I saw Guru Singh[1] with a turban on, and he was polishing a chair. I said, "Who are you? Oh, Guru Singh. What have you done to your head?"

He said, "I have put a turban on."

I said, "Oh? What do you mean by putting a turban on?"

"Don't we have to look like Teachers?"

I said, "Looking like a teacher and being a teacher are two different things."

He said, "Well somebody had to start."

I didn't ask you to put a turban on. It's a yarmulke which you have been wearing for centuries, as Jews, as Christians, as Muslims. Because there are twenty-six bones in the head which need a cranial adjustment, and that self-crowning and that adjustment are your right. Your skull has exactly twenty-six parts, as you have twenty-six vertebrae, as your foot has twenty-six bones. One bone off, and the corresponding muscle and nerve will give you a relevant sickness. One vertebrae loose only one thousandth of a millimeter will give you disease. One part of the cranium off will give you absolute depression so much so that you cannot take it.

What's wrong with you when you are depressed? Your cranium is off. And your pattern is your neurological system cannot recuperate. I am not, folks, tying a turban because I'm a Sikh, and I'm not tying a turban because I'm running a boutique business. Not at all. I'm not teaching a religion, minus reality. I'm a scientist. I came to these United States to be in the United States. I am not seeking students. I don't initiate. But I am obligated. Somebody touched me and taught me. I'm willing to touch somebody.

A lot of my students greatly misunderstand me. They think I'm going to take something away from them. It's not true. Because I'm very qualified regarding the Law of Vacuum, sometimes I make a student—if I am in a good mood, not otherwise—and create a vacuum. Because when I say something and they do something, it's a high command, and then all the low areas walk in. This is how the weather works.

What I'm trying to explain to you is that this Teacher's course which we are teaching for the first time as a certified course has a purpose. Your student can sue you in a court of law. One student sued me because I gave a lecture in Boston that beets are good for health. Forget about suing for something else, I'm telling you to what extent they can go to sue. We are trying to certify you with the point of view, that if you stand in a court of law, you can stand honorably and stand tall. Every legitimate court of law which is supposed to do justice, must understand that the basic elementary knowledge has been given, and a person is made to understand and is real.

When we certify somebody as a minister, it goes through the system, through the Chancellor's Office, our legal office, and when one qualifies in writing, then it is issued. We didn't make Singh Sahibs and Mukhia Singh Sahibs to add to anybody's ego. We gave it because we thought people will become humble and give width and grace of leadership. It was not a test of performance, honesty, and knowledge. It was a test of grace, width, and service. People have been misunderstanding things.

And I have gone through a lot of pain. I always say that if you want to make my physical portrait, use a peanut shell—that would accurately portray how many stabs and scabs I have. You know, you feel very hurt, really, as a human when you raise a person like your child, you teach him, and you start seeing the promise. Or, let us put it this way. If I see somebody has a destiny and some promise, and then he starts barking and bitching at me, can you imagine how painful it is? I have seen in these last twenty-seven years, people leaving and rotting. I am not upset with that, either. Coming and going is not under my control. When you control somebody, you carry the weight. But if you have an ego, you shall not be a Teacher, my amigo. You'll just be an actor.

That's why we call it "Golden Chain of Royal Linkage." It's a Raaj Yog — empowering your royalty and your reality at the same time, in a most graceful way.

Kundalini Yoga is not a yoga for everybody or anybody. The one who practices Kundalini Yoga commands the five *tattvas,* the three *gunas,* the seven chakras, and all 108 elements in the universe, including a conscious creation of the Creator. Let's be clear about it. Kundalini Yoga is not a religion. Religions came out of it. Kundalini Yoga is not a fad, and it's not a cult. It's a practice of experience of a person's own excellence which is dormant and which is awakened.

I hope you fully understand. If you see you are rich, you are rich. If you see you are poor, you are poor. If you see you are great, you are great. If you see you are not, you are not. If you are a pimp and a prostitute, bless you. And if you are very saintly and divine and humble and great, fine. Whatever you are, you're a piece of garbage if you have not awakened your own dormant power to become totally excellent. By rowing a boat you can reach the ocean, but you will never know the power of swimming through it. That is what it is.

Kundalini Yoga is dangerous for those who want to use it as a hook, because it is pure energy. Whosoever misuses it, it destroys that person.

So I'll just explain to you what it is. Everything has benefits and losses. Everything is a balance. Life is a balance. I came here to teach yoga, and I was teaching as a yogi, and I lost all my friends. Does anybody remember, when you start teaching Kundalini Yoga, what three things happen?

Person: Your eating habits change, the way you dress changes, the way you communicate changes, and your friends and family change.

YB: These changes are a must. Are you willing to accept these changes?

Class: Yes, Sir.

YB: Kundalini Yoga is not a commercial nonsense. It's not public relations. Either a practitioner practices purely or should not practice it. The system has a power in itself not to pollute itself. The system itself does not allow anybody to pollute the system. That's why we call it Golden Chain of Royal Linkage. It's a Raaj Yog — empowering your royalty and your reality at the same time, in a most graceful way.

A king is a human, an emperor is a human, but he rules the human. A beggar is a human, and he begs in order to stay as a human. That's the difference. And this difference shall continue. It is not my duty to have to explain to you. It's my duty to state it as it is. It's not Judaism, it is not Christianity, it is not Islam, it is not Hinduism, it's not Sikhism, it's not Shintoism, or Taoism, it's not this, it is not that. It is Kundalini Yoga. It is a science, and it can be explained. And it can be experienced, like in a lab where you find your total potential awakened to experience your own excellence. That's why the Teacher who has perfected Kundalini Yoga becomes the Lord of Time, Space, Longitude, Latitude, Altitude, and Attitude. It's not self-grabbing or self-praising or boasting. These are the facts.

When the Master, Guru Arjan, was tortured, the orders were he had to be put on a hot plate—a red-hot, burning iron plate—and burning red sand poured on him to cook him. For five days he sat solid. And Mian Mir, the Sufi Pir, came and he said, "Lord, this is just nothing. You give me the orders. I can stop all this."

He said, "No. I'm a Teacher. I have to go through it to let people know how to go through the calamity with a radiant smile."

That is the first sign, the first qualification of a Kundalini Yoga Teacher, that he goes through calamity with a radiant smile. He deals with another person with a most humble understanding, and he lives in the core relationship of Imperial Majesty. He appears as he appears, in utmost grace, with a bright and beautiful face, and he doesn't look like he belongs to this Earth. He belongs to the Lord, because he *is* the Lord. So if you have any spiritual nonsense that God is your Lord, and you are just a piece of nothing, and guilt, and you are born in sin—that is out. That's outdated.

A Teacher of Kundalini Yoga is a Lord living on the Earth as a viceroy of the Lord in the Heavens. Less than that is not acceptable. I just wanted to give this news to you so that you may not feel that, "Well, you know, it's just a course." It's not an intercourse, it's not a course. It is just to experience. You all have come, you are most welcome. If none of you would have come, we would still have taught it. Let God fail, let His servants not. That's the first qualification of a Kundalini Yoga Teacher. If you do not have this concept, you can never teach Kundalini Yoga, it doesn't matter how fakely, pretentiously, or correctly you can copy me. I know it. We started as 275 people. In the end we were only two left. You have to understand, just repeat after me:

YB: God is Lord.
Class: God is Lord.
YB: I am the representing Lord.
Class: I am the representing Lord.
YB: This is your affirmation. Can you do it?
Class: Yes, Sir.
YB: God is Lord.
Class: God is Lord.
YB: And I am the...?
Class: representing Lord.
YB: With this, how much misbehaving can you do? What is the margin in this?
CLASS: Zero.
YB: It's called zero tolerance. Between you and God there is zero tolerance. But between you and God there's a little rod which hangs in between your legs and that you have to conquer. In the words of Nanak:[2]

ਇੰਦ੍ਰੀ ਜਿਤ ਪੰਚ ਦੋਖ ਤੇ ਰਹਤ ॥

Indree jit panch dokh tay rehet.

-Guru Arjan, *Siri Guru Granth Sahib*, page 274, (from *Sukhmani Sahib*)

One who conquers his lust is free from the five deadly sins.

A male urinates through his penis. This is your ejaculation artery. Combined with your gonads, it makes up your male system. But its command center is not down in the second chakra. Its command center is in the pituitary. *(YB points to the middle of his forehead.)* So there is almost a three-foot distance that you have to travel. Thirty-six inches in your whole life you have to control, from the first chakra to the sixth chakra. (Normally around thirty-six inches.) Is that understood?

Class: Yes, Sir.

YB: This is an important thing. I'm surprised that there are books and books, and libraries and libraries, and I am teaching Kundalini Yoga for twenty-seven years, yet we have not written even one book. We have written manuals to practically practice. But now I'm very grateful to Shakti, the Mother Divine of this whole thing, that she came out with a most wonderful book.[3] When I went through it, I had tears in my eyes. It's a very good book. You know the beauty in this book, what I like is, Shakti has put her humor in it. That was fantastic. She represented Kundalini Yoga better than anything else I have ever seen. I have seen some books, for instance like a book written by two psychologists on Kundalini Yoga. One Swami produced books and he didn't know what a chakra even is. It's funny.

There are saints and there are great people, and there are marvelous saintly people, incarnations of God, and there are *avtaars*—they are not human. God made you human. Be human. I knew when they put all the "Siri Singh Sahib Bhai Sahib Harbhajan Singh Khalsa Yogiji, Ph.D.," it didn't mean a thing. It's just to survive among the insanity.

There's no nonsense about one thing. Just remember, all objectives are yours, and every objective will subject you. Now, as Siri Singh Sahib, I'm head of the religion, I can't say many things. This is our Teacher's course, so I'm using human language. Normally you see how sophisticatedly I speak in Gurdwara? Every word has to be measured. Do you understand that? When you are in the Court of the Guru, you have to speak very nicely, you have to be very polished. All nice things.

Have you ever met two friends, those who are buddies? Have you seen them talking nicely? You know how they speak? You know how President Bill Clinton was addressed by our governor, Bruce King? He said, "Hello kid, you are winning. I wish to see you winning." It was the meeting of a big uncle governor, and a young governor from Arkansas. He was senior, and Clinton was a junior governor. He didn't say, "Mr. President." Not at all. He said, "Hey kid." I was standing there. He said, "Oh, by the way, I want to introduce you to Yogiji." And he said, "Yes, I know him."

And I gave Hillary a bracelet. I said, "Have it today. Tomorrow, as a president's wife, you shall never have the chance to have it, neither can you accept it, because its value is more than

Kundalini Yoga is not a religion. Religions come out of it. Kundalini Yoga is not a fad, and it's not a cult. It's a practice of experience of a person's own excellence which is dormant and which is awakened.

twenty-five dollars." And she looked at me and laughed.

So just understand, with the grace of being a Kundalini Yoga teacher, there's a vastness of your heart which must go with it. Not exploitation or breaking somebody's heart. And learn to live straight. There are three things, if you can do, it will come to you automatically. Be straight, talk straight, and live straight.

Sometimes people get very upset with me, because it doesn't matter what you say, I have to say what I have to say. They feel very frustrated, really angry sometimes. They feel they can't change me. Fools. If I have to be changed, then how will you be changed? Whose job is it to change? It is my job to change you, and your job to get changed. The hammer and chisel have to carve the stone. If the stone can carve the chisel, there's no need of a chisel. Then the stone is the chisel. If a teacher depends upon the student, he's not a teacher to begin with. Then it's a commercial situation.

That's why it has taken twenty-seven years to start this teacher's course. We used to teach White Tantric Yoga Courses for five days, for thirty-five bucks. And then we had to collect money to pay the bills. It was funny. You know why? At that time we wanted to give people the experience that there is more of God which man can enjoy.

Even though I myself wrote: "God, save me from the psychics, they pollute and dilute my faith," sometimes I go to the psychics. That's my entertainment. What should I do? I have no peer group, so what should I do? I go to these psychics, and I end up psychic-ing them. I go for a reading of the tarot cards, and I end up reading for myself. You get frustrated after a while, you know? When I went to Cancun, one of the healers who was working on me was giving me such a powerful massage, and I could feel that there was a defect in him. I ended up fixing his spine. I told him, "Could you lie down on the table where I'm lying down?" I saw on the lower spine, where the lumbar meets the thoracic, there was a hook.

I said, "Do you sometimes feel absolutely energy-less?"

He said, "Yes, Master." Oh, they were calling me Master. And they were beating me up with sticks and all those things they do. It was an experience. But I wanted to go through it, I wanted to see what it was all about. They were very sincere, and really marvelous people. They would tie all the tree leaves around me, wrap me up at night and say, "Go to sleep." How much can you sleep with tons of leaves tied around you? But one thing they appreciated: I was a very good student. Only a good student can become a great master. It's the goodness of the heart.

It was fun. Then they took me into a little tent and baked me, really. It was an old old ancient method like that fire ceremony. They bring herbs so that everybody can smell them and purify, and get healthy. Great experience. It was a combination of everything. It was just like living in 20th century B.C. It was fun.

It was not what they were doing. It was that their sincerity was humongous. That lady who was the healer, oh God, when she went into prayer, I told her, "Whatever you do to me is fine, but keep on in this aura. You are more bright than the sun itself." The funny part in this whole thing was, they were reading from the book of Christ, saying their prayers in Spanish and chanting *Sat Naam* at the same time. There was no indignity or disqualification of anything. So technically speaking, a Teacher has to have width of heart, and a deep understanding to know. If you don't know to know, how can you know the Unknown? Do you hear me?

Class: Yes, Sir.

YB: You're trying to understand. Things are very simple the way I put it, and that's the way they are. Nothing is complicated. Please understand.

You have come from the Perfect to be perfect. It is not that you have come from the Perfect and you have been put here as imperfect, and you have to become perfect. This damn religion, whatever it is, has put God outside of you, and that's the most sickening thing that we have practiced for thousands of years. We cannot recuperate from it. "We are we, and God is outside of us." But if you have put God outside of you, there's nothing in you, and that's why you're suffering. You don't need a religion. You need a reality that *Ang Sang Wahe Guru*, with every limb, with thirty trillion cells of you which change themselves every seventy-two hours, God is in you. When Nanak said that, they threw stones at him.

They said, "What are you talking about?"

He said, "It's the truth."

Ang means every limb. *Sang* means with yourself, where that Lord, Infinite God, the High One, is. There's no denial. Religion has to teach you a denial. They have to. Because you teach denial, you accept denial, and denial becomes your faith. Then you have guilt, and then you have sin, and then you pay for it. That's how we can build temples and churches. Don't you understand that?

Class: Yes, Sir.

YB: That's needed; money is needed; the Priest has to be paid; money has to be paid. Fools do not know that where there's God, there's no dearth on this Earth.

By the Grace of God, that day shall never come when I'll have to do this. *(YB holds his palm out as if he is begging for money.)* I shall always do this. *(YB makes a gesture with his hand. He turns the palm facing down, then brings the fingers into a point, pointing down.)* I believed that even when I had no money, no clothes, no shoes to wear, no relatives. All these relatives of mine respect me now that I'm very rich, and very powerful, and well-respected in the world. But I remember twenty-seven years ago, they used to treat me like I was worse than a rabbit. They used to think I'd gone insane. Now they don't think so. But it's too late. The Akashic record is never wiped out.

ਨਰ ਅਚੇਤ ਪਾਪ ਤੇ ਡਰੁ ਰੇ ॥

Nar achayt paap tay dhar ray
-Guru Tegbahadur, *Siri Guru Granth Sahib*, page 220
You are so unconsious. You should be afraid of the unconscious sin.

Oh my mind, be scared of the unthinkable. *Paa-aap* is what you earn with your ego. Whatever you received for yourself with your ego is a sin. The English translation of *paap* is —*paa* means get, *aap* means yourself; what you get by yourself, and for yourself. That which God doesn't give to you. When you create imbalance, you earn with the wrong means; then when you

***Kundalini Yoga is dangerous for those who want to use it as a hook,
because it is pure energy. Whosoever misuses it, it destroys that person.***

become pure, what you earned by wrong means is not going to make you happy. There'll be no *barkat*, no blessing in it.

That's why you see that all rich people are very unhappy. The money is not wrong; the collection is wrong, the process is wrong. You are not straight. When you do not feel secure, the moment you are insecure, you are unhappy. Then your projection is handicapped. Don't we look at somebody's face and say, "Hey, what is the matter?" We do not say, "What happened to your spirit?" We don't. Some material thing goes wrong, and we disturb our spirit. What a bargain. Do you know what I'm saying?

Class: Yes, Sir.

YB: So, when you waste your energy on the senses, you shall never have a sixth sense, and the sixth sense is called the Power of Self-Intuition." When you use English words, I would like you to open up the dictionary and figure it out, because each word has four or five meanings. They are called applied meanings. But in your mind there's always one meaning.

Some people ask me, "Can a Hatha Yogi practice Kundalini Yoga?"

I said, "What? What are you talking about?"

"I mean, I practice Hatha Yoga."

I said, "Do it. The purpose of all branches of yoga is to raise the Kundalini, to raise the dormant power of the being so that he can have excellence."

The idea is not what wiring is and what electricity is running through it, or what the light bulbs are. The idea is to switch it on. You switch it on with Hatha Yoga, so switch it on with any yoga, go ahead. We are not asking you to practice Kundalini Yoga. But Kundalini Yoga is for householders, people who are married, and have a life with family, children. It's a scientific, time-saving device. In just a few minutes you can be whatever you want to be.

Life is a lie if you do not find the internal truth. Life is a tragedy if you only find the external truth. Life is an absolute loss if you do not live to your status as a human, or your reality status or your religious status, whatever you want to call it. You can get a status, but you have to live it, and you have to experience it. That's where most Teachers fall. They become a Teacher, all right. They earn the right to be Teachers. But then they can't maintain it. They become something else.

When people say, "Oh, I can't teach. I do business," I laugh. Do you think I *don't* do business? It's fun to watch these people. You have one business. I have fourteen corporations. You do not even earn in one year what I pay as my quarterly income tax. And still I'm a *darvesh*, I'm a *fakir*. Some people make my robes, and some people bring my shoes, and some people bring me things. So be it.

It's great to have and not to have—that's the principle. Poverty is a curse. You *have* to have. But *have* to have, and then *not* to have, is *tiaagaa*, renunciation, abandonment. To have the body and not to have the body, and become humble into *shuniaa*, zero, to become nobody, is the highest body. You become the highest being. So the rules are very simple.

When you use your neuroses in life, you'll never be natural. Mother Nature will never serve you. I'm not saying don't have emotions and feelings and neuroses. All the psychiatrists and psychologists will go home. How will they make money, poor guys? I mean, they need money, they need patients, they need you. Every nut cracker needs nuts. So you are very much needed, I'm not denying you that. But God, what is it?

Action has a reaction equal and opposite. It's Newton's third law. In the spiritual science it's called Law of Aavagan—cause and effect. If you want to avoid an effect, don't cause a cause. So if you cause a cause, you *have* to have an effect. You can't escape it. Maybe not this lifetime, but the next, even the tenth lifetime. Once cause is caused, effect shall be faced, and Almighty God, which you think is the Ultimate of all, cannot change His rule, because this is His rule. Rule rules. Cause must have an effect. Now or later. Time doesn't mean anything.

So, you are not who you are. You are what your projection is, and your projection will have a reaction. You may be a good person, but your face is like this. *(YB makes a really weird face, eyes bugging out, long face).* How would you feel if I came to the class and said, "Hello my students, ha ha ha. How are you?" *(YB talks in a very strange voice.)* The next day only five people will be left. Or you do like this. *(YB makes a very angry-looking face).* Have you seen these people, these stone faces, glaring, like a dry sand? Have you seen these faces? You have to pay them fifty dollars to smile. God, you call them human? When God was making them, He took a bathroom break, and the machine produced so many. When He returned, there were so many things missing, and He didn't recall them.

That's why, once in a while, a disaster comes. God goes into a limbo and says, "Forget it. Wipe it out. Let us start again." He did it many times. He did it once and for forty-two years there was not a drop of rain. The entire humanity was wiped out. He did it in Noah's time, and brought such a flood, everything was drowned, when the North cap melted. He's going to do something soon. Very soon. This is the Age of Aquarius. Every person shall have four mega billion information units on the tip of their finger, so that humongous amount of information will create a nervous breakdown in every human who is not in his excellence with his mental condition. That's going to take the biggest toll.

Tomorrow Gurucharan will teach you my lecture on the *Shabad Guru*, which he compiled. Tomorrow's Saturday.

Class: Yes, Sir.

YB: You are off?

Class: No, Sir.

YB: You are not off. You will come here. This is my course. Are we subject to time?

Class: No, Sir.

YB: Have we come here to remain normal human beings or absolutely excellently abnormal?

Class: Excellently abnormal.

YB: We have come all this distance; we have wasted money, and every minute is costly, paid for. Don't be stupid. You have come in faith, you have come with grace, you have come with trust. You have come here to learn. If we don't deliver we'll have caused a cause, and we'll pay for it. You have already paid for it. It's not a commercial system here. It's a contract of the soul, and there should be no hole. It's a chance which we must capture at one glance. There's no way out. There's no other route. You have come here to become teachers. Make up your mind you will not leave until you become perfect teachers. A perfect teacher is one who's ten times better than me, including my handicaps, with no handicap. Make no mistake. Mistake is, miss the take which you are supposed to take. As long as you serve the time, you will serve the time. Those who serve the time shall never be the master of time. Is that understood?

Class: Yes, Sir.

YB: You have not come here to learn. You have just come to open yourself up with your faculty, with your facility, which is God-given to you. What you have done wrong yesterday, it is gone. What you do today, that will cause the effect. But if somehow the Hand of God has guided you here and brought you here in His Mercy, His blessing, He's guiding you through any channel, it doesn't matter. It's the time to be. Do not juggle with time and space. Time and space is of the Earth, it doesn't belong to the Heavens.

It's good to see you. At least it's very loving to me that you have decided to become teachers. I have a very humble prayer to Almighty God. I said to Him this morning, "God, you have brought them here. I'm not enough. Please help them. Get into them and awaken Yourself in them. Give them a chance. Don't look at their misery, but look at their sense of mastery. They have made it. Give them what they need."

And He said, "Work it out."

I said, "That's a bad idea."

God is a funny damn thing. We fight every morning. We had fun with each other. That's the concept of my family. *(YB refers to a drawing on the board.)* I draw it all the time when I'm in a good mood. Three roly-polies: male, female, and the child. Be a family. We are God's family. The goats, the sheep, the chickens, the lambs. They are all God's family; we are all spirit. Don't be so blind looking at the physical body. Don't forget there is a spirit in it, there's a soul in it. Even the stone has a soul in it.

Some gold is coined, some gold is made into ornaments, some gold is made into jewelry, and some gold makes the dome of the temple shine. All is gold. Some reach the heights, they become beautiful and bright, and they see the light. That's what your mission should be here. You should have that privilege. You came.

All your soul is promised by God is one chance. When the soul took the body and saw the karma and the domain, and it was coming to the planet Earth for practice, the soul resisted. He said, "No, I'm not going."

God said, "Why? What's the problem? It's a test. Don't you want to pass it?"

He said, "I want to pass it, but I don't have the tools." So God gave the mind. She said, "What is this damn thing?"

He said, "Well, this is something. Like a swing, it can take you towards me or away from me 180 degrees. Take it, but be its master."

That's why Nanak said:

ਮਨਿ ਜੀਤੈ ਜਗੁ ਜੀਤੁ ॥
Man jeetai jag jeet.

-Guru Nanak, *Siri Guru Granth Sahib*, page 6 (from the 28th *pauree* of *Japji Sahib*)
By conquering your mind, you can conquer the world.

Those who master their mind, master the universe, and the Lord of the universe.

So you were given the mind. And you were given the body according to *paralabhad*—your past actions—according to cause and effect. You were all born on a longitude and latitude. You are not here by your will. Your will only brought you here, under God's Will. Our will, which is our free will, makes us see God's Will. So you have come here in a very pure resolution, and very powerful self-domain. Please make it happen.

Do not keep God outside of you. Keep God inside you. He's not your guide. He seeks your guidance, because God prevailed through a human. Religiously they have wrongly told you that you are sinners, you are evil, you are born in sin, just to collect your money. Ridiculous. If you are born in sin, why do they want your dollars? Why? You're not supposed to touch the untouchable. If you are so wrong, why do they want you in a church, in a temple, or a synagogue? What are you needed for? To be reminded, and exploited, and used?

Just understand, with the grace of being a Kundalini Yoga Teacher, there is a vastness of your heart which must go with it. Not exploitation, or breaking somebody's heart.

Nobody will give you anything. You have to learn the art and science of giving yourself your own excellence. That's the purpose of life. Life is a lie if the truth is not found. Prayer is the power for which you must reach your excellence. The teacher shall, when being merciful, be very cruel. When he's kind, it's your misfortune. I know you are in the West, therefore you cannot have that hardship. You don't have that training. I understand. You have workers compensation, you have insurance, you have laws. Those laws are not the laws of spirit, they are the laws of the body. They are not even the laws of the mind, forget about spirit. So you live in a very handicapped universe. Let us see what we can achieve.

You have come here to achieve—that's your prayer, and that's your power, both together. You have spared your time, you have spared your energy, you have spent money, you have come here in the most odd circumstances. But get even with it.

I'm the head of a religion. That's fine. But I have over a million students whom I have touched. I thought that some day they would like to come and see how I lived. So I took a headstone, like a grave stone, to the Ranch. It's six feet, two inches long, exactly my height. It says "Harbhajan Singh Khalsa Yogiji, born at...?"

Class: ...zero.

YB: Died at...?

Class: ...One.

YB: Then I wrote on it the line by which I live. I don't know much. I know only this one line.

ਕੇਤਿਆ ਦੂਖ ਭੂਖ ਸਦ ਮਾਰ ॥ ਏਹਿ ਭਿ ਦਾਤਿ ਤੇਰੀ ਦਾਤਾਰ ॥
Kaytiaa dukh bukh sad maar, Eh bhe daat teree daataar.
   -Guru Nanak, *Siri Guru Granth Sahib*, page 5 (25th pauree of *Japji Sahib*)
Many suffer privation and pain and are continuously beaten. Even these are God's gifts.

Kaytiaa means many, many, many, many, many. One woman understands it. She has gone through tragedy after tragedy, after tragedy. Treachery after treachery after treachery. And she is the one woman who sang the Guru's words more and more and more than anybody can. So she took 192 lifetimes and paid it in one to end the whole thing. What a bank clearance. Sometimes I wonder if she even understands what she is doing. Once in a while she asks a question. In the morning, when I meditate and I am in the universe, I look at her and she says, "Why me?" Why not? You are walking very fast. You are clearing it all.

That's how it is sometimes. *Kaytiaa*. Many, many, many, many, many. Unlimited.

Dukh. Discomfort, disease, tragedy, calamity, torture. All are included in that *dukh*.

Bukh: hunger. Nothing to eat, nothing to drink, nothing to be.

Sad maar: If it multiplies to a hundred thousand times.

Eh bhe daat teree daataar: Oh Lord, that's your gift. At least. You thought me a deserving candidate for all that torture, sickness, insult, and spitting. At least I deserved it. At least He remembers me. Don't misunderstand that all those who have wealth are the only ones blessed by the Lord. Not true. Those who are like me, are also loved by God.

Hazarat Abraham, the father of this Judeo-Christian nation, one day was meditating. He saw a vision that told him: "You go into your hut, and meditate on light." So he went there alone, and meditated on light. But he was lazy. He slept. He woke up, he saw the Israel sitting there and writing names and names and names and names. He said, "What are you writing?"

He said, " I make an annual list of those who love God."

He said, "Oh, I slept through it. Is my name there?"

He said, "No."

"All right, what do I care?"

The next day he again got up and he saw him writing the names. But he was sitting and dozing himself. He said, "What is wrong with you? You are dozing."

He said, "List is complete. I have no work. You were sleeping, so we couldn't talk."

He said, "What is this list?"

He said, "Those whom God loves."

He said, "Forget it. My name is not on the list of those who love God. How could it be on this list?"

He said, "Damn it, you are the only name. That's why I have no work. Look at it. God loves Abraham."

He said, "I am not worthy." That's where the guilt started. Jews produced guilt and Catholics spread it. That's how it happened.

And he said, "Look at it."

He said, "No, no. I can't look at it." He denied.

Do you know why Moses did not go to the Holy Land? He gave the Ten Commandments, but did not show people the Ten Promises God gave. Moses only told fifty percent. Do you know that?

Class: No, Sir.

YB: I wrote it. God gave Ten Commandments and Ten Promises. Everybody knows it.

I once gave a lecture in which I gave the scientific explanation of why to tie a turban. In the olden days, that is what the yarmulke was like. That's a fact.

If you want your turbines to work and change, to keep the electromagnetic charge in the field, either cycle in a macro co-reaction so that under the influence of theta you have the alpha consciousness with the beta excellence, you have to put a turban on properly. That is the science. I don't want barbers to go out of business, cut your hair as you want. It's your pure protein, heavy protein. Your body will end up replacing it. You can't get a chance to grow out of it.

There was one girl working for me. I said, "Go and get a hair cut."

She said, "Why?"

"You are just not right."

Cut them as you want. Who's stopping you? But just remember, it is the purest protein of your body. Just like heavy wet water is responsible for giving us control on atomic energy, it's a heavy protein you have on your head. Do you think God is an idiot, giving you that much long hair? Did He have some extra grass sitting somewhere, and put it on a man's head, and gave the male a beard? What, is it a bib? Now what are you talking about? You talk about God and Almighty and this whole nonsense, all these thousands of years. Do you understand you have not yet even come to terms with the fact of why you are the way you are? I say, "How can you tie a turban? You do not know how your turbine works." This head is not a cantaloupe. It is an electromagnetic creative field in the shield of the pattern to the correlative essence of the micro and macro existence, with the absolute power of the stars into the projection where the human body absolutely correlates congenially together in an absolute harmony. Harmony. And it must recuperate within one thirty-trillionth of a second.

It is true. It is true. This machine must recuperate. That's why it is above your shoulders. Your whole sensory system and control center is in the sixth chakra, *ajna*, which is your command center. It's above the shoulders. And your brain has its own blood supply. And own elementary mixture.

Did you tell them all that, Gurucharan? Oh yeah? They know it? They must have heard. They are like a herd. Sometimes the herd doesn't hear. Make them hear. They are here. They are here, therefore they must hear. And they must have heard, because they are a herd. Understand that?

Class: Yes, Sir.

YB: Is it a fun? That's why I did my Ph.D. in psychology of communication. Well, don't worry, you'll get cookies today.

See Things as God Sees Them

You are born a gem, you are born innocent. What happened is you lost your innocence, so you became arrogant. When you were born, you survived. You only have to make the shift from your mother and father as your security, to the Heavens and the Earth as your security. That shift has been promised to you.

1 know about the academic world. I did my Ph.D. When it came time to defend my Ph.D. thesis, I came before three professors. I said, "Well, come on. Let us defend ourselves."

And they said, "Just let us know what you wrote. That's all we want."

So I said, "Okay." Normally when you do your Ph.D. the internal professors really blast you, and they can fail you. But these guys just wanted to know what it was about. I started to explain to them what it was about, and by that time I saw them signing the paper, and that was it. No fun. Gurucharan, can you get my Ph.D. thesis printed and give it to them[1]? Without this, these people cannot be Teachers. They have to have that fundamental elementary human projection.

Poke, provoke, confront, and elevate. That is how your life must be. If one aspect of these four is missing, you are handicapped. That's the gist of my Ph.D. on the psychology of communication. Regardless of what we understand or do not understand, we are what we speak. That's how we are known. We are always afraid, "Oh, if I put a turban on, what will happen? If I put a coat on, what will happen? If I put knickers on, what will happen? If I do not dress this way, this will not happen. If my hair is not that way, I am not this." We are actually subject to trends and tendencies, not to our originality and reality. If we do not have originality and reality, we don't have royalty. And if we don't have royalty, we can't elevate.

You're talking of religion. It is all damn lies. There's no religion. What is a religion? Suppose your religion gives you God. What are you going to do? Eat it—like a pizza? What will you do with God? They give you false promises: "You'll get God, you'll go to the Heavens." Well, what about here? How will you deal with here? Who wants to go to the Heavens? It's an ice cold, meditating place. Nothing happens there. Hell is more exciting, you know, with crying, and everybody will be there.

Class: (*Laughter.*)

YB: Honest to God, it's true. Look how corrupt religion is. I'm a simple Yogi. I came here with no intention to do anything. I was secretly being forced to go to the Soviet Union, and I didn't want to go. They wanted me to teach parapsychology, not in the form of miracles, but in a sensory form. So I ran to Canada for shelter, period. That's all.

I understand why this whole religion thing got onto me. I told you the story of how we became a Sikh religion here in the West? This young guy had very long hair, and he didn't want the sheriff to cut it. So he claimed to be a Sikh. *(See full story on page 271.)* One thing led to another. What God wants is His problem, not mine.

The fact is they made me the head of the religion. They thought that when I would become head of the religion, I would just become like the Pope, that I would not say anything. You know what I mean? They will give me a paper, and I will read it. Right? My staff will tell me things, and I will say, "Very good, very good. Very good, oh yes. Very good." I would agree to everything. Agree to what? What can I agree with, with these stupid earthlings? What do they have to do with me, or I have to do with them? There's no bargain. We have no relationship. What is my relationship? In adversity I enjoy, while in the best happiness you are just adverse. What's the relationship? You are looking for things, idiotic things. But things must come to you—that's a law. The law of birth is that your berth is reserved, like on a train the way they give you a seat called a berth. Berth has two meanings. Your berth is reserved, therefore you get birth, and you get all the comfort. You have a conductor, you have a service car, and it's all paid for.

Your values shall come to you when you live originally, organically as divine. You are made in God. Everything is a process. It's called a support system. So Mother Nature should support you and Heavenly Father should guide you, and time and space should not goad you—that's the agreement. Religion has to explain to you your reality, not their philosophy. If you feel bad, they have to explain to you why you feel bad, and how from feeling bad you can feel good. That's a religion. Religion is the relationship between a man and his reality, guided by the technique or technology of the Master, so you can be the Master, so that you can never be slaves for the rest of your life; because if you don't make it, then the Golden Chain breaks. You have to grow. Your growth has to be perpetual. You are entitled to perpetual growth. Your progression must keep your honor, your respect, your trust, your faith, your charm. You are born to be revered, worshipped.

You are holy—you have nine holes, and this *(points to top of head)* is the Tenth Gate or tenth hole. If you watch what comes in and out of them; if you can control in that way, you are great. Your greatness is because you are born. The very fact that you are born and God willed it that way is the best thing that has ever happened. Everybody needs you. The thief needs you, the policeman needs you, the attorney needs you, the court needs you, the doctor needs you, the cheat needs you, the liar needs you, the truthful one needs you, the holy one needs you, the unholy one needs you, the restaurant needs you, and the shelter needs you. Everything around needs you. They are sucking your blood. They are taking your energy. You have nothing, you are old.

When in your life have you ever just sat down for one hour and said, "I am going to be me, I am going to be me, I am going to be me, I'm going to be me. I'm not this. I'm not that. I am me." When was the last time that you did your *prathyahar,* synchronizing yourself to zero in experience? Did you? *(YB shakes his head "no.")* I know. I know. I know your pain. I know what causes it. I'm not saying that I don't know. I never spoke all these years, because I said, "Well, let us see."

There was one Christian minister who told me, "Well man, we spent lots of money, we sent our preachers to India to turn them into Christians. You came from India and stole our children."

I said, "What did I steal? I stole nobody. You can take them. Have them all. Pickle them. Keep them. I am not asking for anybody."

Once I went to the School of Chaplains in New Jersey. It is an army school where the officers are uniformed. There are Jewish and Christian Chaplains there who serve the army as ministers. I was there to address them on religion. The commanding officer was great. When he introduced me he said, "Today I have a surprise for you officers. We had gems, pearls, rubies, diamonds, emeralds, and precious stones, and we didn't take care of them. We threw them in the mud and they got lost. Then came a man from India and he picked them from the mud, he cleaned them off, he polished them, he shaped them. And now he wears them around his neck in a necklace. Now he looks beautiful, bright in his own self, and now we are jealous of him. They were ours, now they are his. I introduce you to His Holiness, Siri Singh Sahib Bhai Sahib Harbhajan Singh Khalsa Yogiji, head of the Sikh religion in the Western Hemisphere."

Religion has to explain to you your reality, not their philosophy. If you feel bad, they have to explain to you why you feel bad, and how from feeling bad you can feel good. That's a religion. Religion is the relationship between a man and his reality, guided by the technique or technology of the Master, so you can be the Master, so that you can never be slaves for the rest of your life.

I looked at him. I said, "What is he talking about?"

I felt, "Yes, everybody is a gem." Otherwise you cannot be born. You are not born in sin. You are born innocent. You are told you are insane and you accept it. "You're wrong. Don't do this, don't do that. Don't, don't, don't, don't, don't, don't, don't, don't." After that you start saying, "Don't, don't, don't, don't, don't, don't, don't, don't." You're crazy. Everything you are told is, "Don't." "Don't answer the door. Don't answer the phone. Don't speak to this. Don't, don't, don't, don't, don't." You become a living "don't."

Or you are told, "Say 'yes.'" So sometimes when you are supposed to answer "no," you say "yes." All you are told in your life is to say 'no' or to say 'yes.' That's your training. So what are you to say? Either you can say "yes" or you can say "no." Why don't you wear a billboard, with one side saying 'yes,' the other 'no.' "Yes, no, yes, yes, yes, no, no, no, yes, no, yes, no." Are we human? Agree with me, disagree with me. What is there to agree with, to disagree with, yes or no, or right and wrong? There's nothing right or wrong, thinking makes it so. It's your judgment against another judgment.

You are not wrong. You are born a gem; you are born innocent. What happened is you lost your innocence, so you became arrogant. When you were born, you survived. Why will you not survive? You only have to make the shift from your mother and father as your security, to the Heavens and the Earth as your security. That shift has been promised to you. "Oh come to me, my children. I'll teach you that." But it's the blind leading the blind. Teach you what? Nobody teaches anybody anything. You tell people what to do, and how not to do doo-doo, and you watch them. That's the real system.

But normally in these days we play games. We want our personal life to be respected. We do not impersonally see that another's life is respected. I want my students to be rich, so that when I go to their home, we can have a good breakfast. Really. That's what it is. If somebody is rich, good, powerful, that can help you. You are a Teacher. You're not a person, not yourself. The first oath you take is, "I am not a woman, I am not a man, I am not a person, I am not myself, I am a Teacher." That's your oath. So why are you attached?

Man and his manners are a very basic situation which we must understand. We must look at things the way God is looking at things. Our purity lies in our originality. Our intuition lies in our innocence. Somebody is telling you, or you are telling yourself (mostly you are telling yourself), that you are wrong—this is your mantra. But if you are not right, you would not have been born. You are a fully matured soul, sent on the Earth for the test of facing the Heavens and the Earth and returning back home victorious. Fateh (Victory). "*Wahe Guru Ji Ki Fateh*" — "Victory unto God that I come back home." "*Wahe Guru Ji Ka Khalsa*" means "My purity belongs to God." You don't belong to God, your body doesn't belong to God, your mind doesn't belong to God—your spirit belongs to God only in the essence of its purity. It is your purity, the piety of the spirit which belongs to God. The rest is all yours. That's your free will. Do whatever you do, nobody cares. But the moment you understand that there is an essence of purity in you, you will realize reality. The moment you realize reality, you will have royalty, and then you don't have to say or do a thing. When your presence will work, then you will emit wisdom. When you walk into a room of fifty people, everybody will feel calmness; everybody will feel reverence; everybody will think that he is going to get something. You are like God. Either God gives or you give. You are not takers.

And remember, don't make yourself shallow. Don't take—ever. You fool, you are thinking you are getting something, but you are missing what God has for you. So you are substituting a little stone for a gold coin. That's not a good deal.

Are you ready for a heavy thing today, or do you just want to do something light and go home?

Class: The real thing.

YB: No, I am discussing with you. How do you want to deal with yourself? Do you have energy? We are going to meet on Monday, anyway, it doesn't matter. It's not such a rushed situation.

(See page 143 for details of the following warm-ups to the meditation.)

Sit straight. Spread your hands, balance yourself, and stretch your shoulders out. These are essential warm-ups. Without this you will have muscle pain. Don't take that risk. Move like this. See all the faculty. You have to do this because you have to free the nerves, because the nerves, with the muscles and bones can get in rock hard place, and it can cause trouble.

(YB demonstrates the posture.) This is what you have to do now. This is your starting position—it is your "*Sat Naam,*" your original Oriental self. Just see that the center of the head is here. It has to meet in the back here. It's painful. You wanted a warrior position. Do you want to do something else?

Class: No, Sir!

YB: Try it. It is something very good. The angle is very important in Kundalini Yoga. Kundalini Yoga is angles, triangles, and cutting the square. The square doesn't exist in Kundalini

Yoga. They even say in astrology that when you have a square in your horoscope it is a bad sign. "The Sun is squaring this and that is squaring this." Diagonally cut it.

How do you feel? If you correctly hold it in balance, you will start feeling energy and tingling. It's a very very simple rule of your being, of your body. It is not that you are an idiot, or that you are not worthy, or that you are wrong. You have *become* unworthy or wrong. Originally your system is absolutely God-given and correct. You see? Now you see that "*Sat Naam, Sat Naam,*" with that tune we had with one string? "*Dhuni.*" *Dhuni* is that which accelerates the excellence in us. It's simple music, played on one wire string.

You are a fully matured soul, sent on the Earth for the test of facing the Heavens and the Earth and returning back home victorious. Fateh! "Wahe Guru Ji Ki Fateh"— "Victory unto God that I come back home." "Wahe Guru Ji Ka Khalsa"— "My purity belongs to God."

Okay, put it on. Hold on. Stretch out like this. Stretch out. Go!

Go a little faster with the hands.

After 70 seconds: Okay, stop, stop, stop, stop. Hey, hey, hey. Can we do it?

Class: Yes, Sir.

YB: I'm just asking, I'm not willing to let you misunderstand this. If we start doing it, we're going to reach a stage called "The Twilight Zone," and then there'll be humongous pain; pain so much that you do not know. But that is a facade, that there will be no pain, but you will feel you are hurt, because the hemispheres have to adjust. If the hemispheres do not project their endorphins, pain will be humongous. Ooh, it's ugly. Then when the endorphins start coming, then you don't want to stop. That's how it will be if we keep on doing it.

Question: Can we bend our elbows?

YB: No. There are only two things on this planet: *Sat Naam* is your back, your Earth, your spine. *Wahe Guru* is your face, God is your front. The Sikhs stole it. They say, "This is our religious thing." What damn religious thing? Patanjali Rishi wrote about *Wahe Guru* 3,000 years ago. The Sikhs took it. They don't know what they're talking about. It's Patanjali's mantra. God spoke to him. He wrote the future of the world, and it's exactly true what he wrote. Word for word it is true what he said. And he said there'll be Nanak, and he said his mantra will be that of God's creation, God's organization, and God's deliverance. And that's what you sing in Sanskrit:

ਵਾਹਯੰਤੀ ਕਰ ਯੰਤੀ ਜਗ ਦੂਤ ਪਤੀ ਆਦਕ ਇਤਿ ਵਾਹਾ ॥
ਬ੍ਰਹਮਾਦੇ ਤ੍ਰੇਸ਼ਾਂ ਗੁਰੂ ਇਤਿ ਵਾਹਿਗੁਰੂ ॥

Waah yantee, kaar yantee, Jag dut patee, aadik it waahaa
Brahmaaday treyshaa guru, it wahe guru.
-Rishi Patanjali, *Push Puran*
Great Macro-self, creative Self, all that is, Creative through time, all that is the Great One. Three aspects of God: Brahma, Vishnu, Mahesh (Shiva). That is Wahe Guru.

Who was this Sikh? It was Guru Gobind Singh, who had that knowledge, wisdom, and equation. He took *Wahe Guru* as the Guru Mantra and gave it to the Sikhs. They should be grateful. It is Patanjali's mantra. Nanak gave *Sat Naam*.

ਸਤਿਨਾਮੁ ਤੇਰਾ ਪਰਾ ਪੂਰਬਲਾ ॥
Satinaam teraa paraa poorbalaa.
-Guru Arjan, *Siri Guru Granth Sahib,* page 1083
Sat Naam is Thy primal and ancient Name.

It's the buddy name of the elementary equation of God. When you say *Sat Naam*, purity exists. It's not "will exist, shall exist, may exist." With mantra there's no "will, shall, or maybe." No. It *is*. When I say, "*Sat Naam Ji,*" to you, I am saying, "Truth is your soul". That is exactly what it means. That's why I told people, when they call each other, instead of giving them hell, "Hello," just say "*Sat Naam*". Just like how Jews say, "*Shalom.*" They stopped saying it, though. We all stop saying certain things.

The elementary self of God is "*Sat Satya Satiaam.*" "*Sat*"—my true essence is *Sat*. "*Satya*" —the power of my true essence. "*Satiaam*" —in true essence, I am. "*Sat Naam*" —*Naam* means a noun. Noun is the name of a person, place, or thing. So, *Sat Nam* means "Truth is my identity." That's my *Naam*, that's my name. When I ask for a spiritual name, that name describes my distance, my destiny, and my guiding word.

In the Beginning was the Word, the Word was with God, and the Word was God.
-The Bible, The Gospel According to St. John

It has to be calculated. I don't know what's so difficult.

The purpose of life is to cover a distance. If it doesn't cover the distance, you'll keep on going through the cycle of birth and death. Then people have to create something like rebirthing, and for six thousand dollars you cry. *(YB makes a sound of a crying person.)* It's insanity to live in fantasy and pay seven thousand bucks. You had pain when you were born, right? Yesterday you had a pain, right? That was yesterday. You faced it. It's gone. It's over. You are a winner. Why are you carrying it on to today in your memory? Why? Don't you know the simple formula? What was yesterday was yesterday. It's gone. You faced it. Now you are afraid of tomorrow?

Class: No, Sir.

YB: Good. Because tomorrow will become today and only then can you face it. If tomorrow remains tomorrow, there's nothing to worry about. Every tomorrow has to become today in order to face it. And remember, you have already faced today, today, and you have already faced yesterday. So what are you losing? However you faced yesterday, good or bad, it's a matter of feeling. However you're facing today, good or bad, it's a matter of feeling. How you face tomorrow, good or bad, that's also a matter of feeling. Because when tomorrow will become today and face you, God shall give you the energy to face it. God made you to face it tomorrow. That's your relationship. You may not know it. When God gave you birth, God gave you existence, and God gave you time and space to conquer it. "Come home victorious, my children," He said.

Today someone brought me the Alphabets, the first Ten Commandments of the Bible, and the Ten Promises, followed by the Alphabets of Love and the Alphabets of Business. *(See the Resources section for these "Alphabets.")* You've got so many papers.

You know, the only thing that goes wrong with us is that we forget. Look at the word "forget." "For-get. What do you mean by "get"? And what do you mean by "for"? "For" means "to." "To get." So you forget that Giveth is Giveth, and has been given. So, "to get" you "forget" you are divine. I'm not joking. Do you understand why you forget? What for? To get what? What happens when you are "to get?" You forget that you are getting that which *you* are getting, not what God is giving you. When *God* gives you something, you won't forget.

One day I was sitting with somebody, and I said, "Where is my present?"

He said, "I didn't bring a present." Then he said, "Oh, wait a minute, it's in the trunk of my car."

I said, "That's my present, you thief. Bring it. Give me my present. How come you brought a present and put it in the trunk of the car and forgot it?"

He said, "Well, I was just thinking and I want to talk to you."

I said, "First bring my present, then we'll talk." So he brought it. It was a good present.

Forget, for what? You forget to get. What *you* get is not given by God. What's given by God, you will not forget. That will stay for your good will and prosperity. What *you* get will bring your downfall. So do not live a manipulative life. Don't manipulate and twist with an itch. Be natural; as humans we have to be natural. We can't forget. We can't forget to get.

Get it together and get together what you want to get together. To-gather. To-gather. Get it together, to gather. When you're together, then you have to be diplomatic, nice, kind, smiling. Otherwise you are not together. To-gather—get it together, to gather. Same word. If you do not get it together, whatever you gather is not going to be good.

Oh, you got my thesis? They printed it? Come on, show me. *Communication: Liberation or Condemnation*, by Harbhajan Singh Khalsa Yogiji, Ph.D. *"Submitted in partial fulfillment of the requirement of the Degree of the Doctor of Philosophy and Psychology. The University of Humanistic Studies, San Francisco, 1980."* Wow. *"For more copies of this publication, yoga manual, audio or video tape, plus ayurvedic herbs, teas, oils, vegetarian cookbooks, holistic health books, and more of the ancient healing...."* Oh, they put it in their catalogue. They are good. Somebody must be doing a good job.

It's fun. Why not? Everybody's a Ph.D. Why should I not be? What's wrong with that? I was fifty years old. It is a good work. It has good chapters: Statement of the Problem; Importance of the Problem; Limitation and Delineations; A Review of Literature; Communication: What Is It; and What It Is Not; Communication with The Self; Kundalini Meditation for Communication with Self; Kundalini Meditation for Positive Communication; Kundalini Meditation for Effective Communication; Alternate Nostril Breathing; Communication with Others; Frequency of Communication; Who's On the Other End; Summary. Well. Pretty good.

Then we have *The Teachings of Yogi Bhajan*. Here is a chapter on Mind. Do you want to know what it says about the mind?

"Meditation is the creative control of self where the Infinite can talk to you."

"All talking, all thinking, all thoughts must be pure."

"Conquer your mind and you will conquer the world."

"Which mind? The conscious mind? No. The supreme conscious mind? No. Which mind? The subconscious mind. If you conquer your subconscious mind, then you win the world."

The subconscious mind is a storehouse of garbage. Every thought of your mind is contained there.

"A relaxed mind is a creative mind, and a creative mind is a relaxed mind; and only a relaxed mind can become a one-pointed mind; and a one-pointed mind is the most wonderful mind. It is most powerful; it can do anything."

"Purity of mind is a necessity for man to have supreme, spiritual power."

I learned the hard way. You must not be interested in the mind. It's a boring subject.

"Realization: You have to realize that you are the center of your own mental psyche."

Have we taught them about psyche?

Class: Yes, Sir.

YB: What is it? What is the psyche?

Student: Mind plus body.

Second Student: Total creative power of the mind.

YB: The psyche is what does not allow you to goof, but it makes you goof. Psyche is your Creative Mother, very beautiful, but if you go on the wrong side of it, it spanks you so badly.

(YB continues reading.)

"Understanding and humility lead to the perfection of love, and God is love."

"Male and female make a union and this complete union is the greatest yoga."

"Marriage is when there are two bodies, but one soul."

"The moment you can love the being of an individual, then you love the God of an individual. The moment that experience happens, then you become a Universal soul yourself."

"Love is the experience of sacrifice within One's self."

Pretty good. The man who wrote it at that time was called "Yogi Bahaan." Look how many chapters are covered: Introduction to "Sa-Ta-Na-Ma Meditation," "Word, Love, Woman, Happiness, Self, Wisdom, God, Mind, Realization, Polarity, Devotion, Relationship and Techniques. There's no chapter on "Man." Can you believe that? Hawthorne books. Quite a fun.

All right, ready now? Set yourself, folks. You asked for it. I forgive myself and wash my hands of it.

(See pages 142-143 for details of this meditation.)

Balance your wrists and your open fingers. The muscles must hold the weight. The first time you go up, you have to go in the back of your head. The second time you go up, you must go in front. All right. Thank you. Put on the tape, *Dhuni.*

It is your honesty, your strength. Not mine. Keep the hand in balance, because it's going to move the central nerve, we call it *shushmanaa,* in the inner spinal chord.

(After just a few minutes) Okay, okay, okay, okay. You are getting into it. Stop, stop. This is enough initiation into this. We'll do it on Monday. Otherwise, you'll get into it, and then your whole afternoon will be wasted. You'll sit here like zombies. You are getting good. You are getting way better than I thought. You are into it now. Let's give ourselves a chance and a time. It's not good to become holy overnight. It's not that important; take your time.

***When I ask for a spiritual name, that name describes my distance,
my destiny, and my guiding word.***

A Sikh means a seeker, and when you become a Teacher, then you are nothing else. A seeker is a Sikh. The one who has taught himself to seek is the Master. So please don't misunderstand your situation. For three thousand years you have been told you are born in sin, and that Eve and Adam did something, you know which we do, but these days we don't talk about. Birds do it, bees do it, they did it. They ate that apple. That was juicy stuff which made him horny, and she seduced him. Now what is wrong with that? We seduce every day. So our ancestors seduced each other, and for that they were thrown out of the boredom of Eden. That was a totally boring place. All that was there was an apple tree and a snake. Now who wants that? It was a bad neighborhood. So they were thrown out to the Earth. Then they thought, "Wow!" But they forgot that sex is the sixth sense. When sex does not invoke the sixth sense, it is called "fucking." And that messes up the psyche forever. It is very clear.

Actually, sex used to be described with a very beautiful word. Not the way you use it now. It was "cohabitation." "Oh, they are cohabiting together." It's original English. But later on we became like machines in the machine age, and then it actually became an abuse. Now when you talk about sex you have to hide yourself. It's not nice. It's not graceful. Right? Gentlemen do it, but they don't talk about it. Did Adam tell Eve that he's going to have sex? Is there something written like that? Even in the Bible they are silent. They said, "they have 'sinned,' and they were thrown out of the Garden of Eden." Actually they enjoyed it, and they didn't want to live in that boring place, with that apple tree and one little snake. So they got out. They didn't want any part of it. And still man doesn't want any part of the Garden of Eden.

What are you going to do with long life? Live sixty-two-hundred-thousand years? As what? A skeleton hanging? You don't want to live long. You want to live young, you want to live alert, you want to live happily, you want to live fulfilled, you want to live achieved, you want to live purposefully, you want to live powerfully. Don't lie. I know what you want. I can give it to you. I got it, therefore, I can give it to you.

Don't misunderstand me. I have been stabbed and spit at and shadowed and insulted. You do not yet even know what I went through. But I achieved the power to laugh at it. Do you know why? It didn't mean a thing.

That's why you chant that mantra, "God and me, me and God, are One." See what an affirmation it is? "God and me, me and God, are One. God and me, me and God, are One." We made Him plural, not single. "God and me, me and God, *may* be One. God and me, me and God, *can* be One. God and me, me and God, *should* be One. God and me, me and God, *have to* be One." Nonsense. That would be ugly teachings. That's what they call religion. These are all conditions. No, there's no condition. The truth is: "God and me, me and God, *are* One." *Humeh Hum, Brahm Hum. Ek Ong Kaar, Satgur Prasaad, Satgur Prasaad, Ek Ong Kaar.* These are very powerful things, very real things, total things.

One Creator created the creation, and that creation is a blessing of the Creator. The blessing of the Creator is that He created because He was bored, too. Ask God why He created us.

Did we apply? Did I apply, "Please create me as Yogiji. I want to go to Earth. Here are ten dollars as my deposit fee?" Nobody applied. He wanted us to go and when we came here, we forgot Him. God got bored in the Heavens; Adam got bored in the Garden of Eden, so out of boredom he wanted to talk to something. He got in touch with this damn snake. That was the only thing available. Snake is called "Naa-gaa." Naga means where nothing can go. So, where nothing can go, a snake can go. That's why it's a snake. By the way, it was not an apple tree, it was a fig tree. I know it. I was watching. After intercourse, she enjoyed it so much, she wanted to cover it for him. She put the fig leaf on it. I know. They don't talk about it. They think this is not spiritual. What is not spiritual about it? You are a product of that path, you created that path, and every day you do it, but it's not spiritual? What is spiritual then?

⌖

(The class is read "The Ten Commandments and the Ten Promises" from a lecture by Siri Singh Sahib, August 6, 1991." This can be found in the Resources section.)

Do you remember that Moses was not allowed to enter the Promised Land? Because he only told the Commandments, he never told the Promises God made. So I covered the guy, and here it is. Somebody has to do the job. He forgot and the Jews do not want to talk about it. They know it. They even found it in the Dead Sea Scrolls, and still they didn't want to talk about it.

If you are a good Jew, just remember that with every Commandment there shall be a Promise. There cannot be any Commandment without obedience. And Moses was not that foolish. He was the Law Giver. So he gave the Commandments and held back the Promises. I think he was in a hurry, and he forgot.

You know, when he came back down from the mountain, they were having intercourse with each other, they were dancing, they had put a gold bull as an idol. It was not a good scene. He was greatly annoyed. So he said, "Get your scene together." He got angry, and threw the tablets. You know all that drama you see? He really was in pain. In spite of the fact that it took forty years to take the idiots to strength. Otherwise, the whole journey from there to there by walking is two and a half years, with absolute rest. Well, he took them around and had fights and went through all that. But when he came to the Promised Land, he said, "I can't go. You go now." That was fun.

You know, the Jews sacrificed six million Jews to create Israel. It didn't happen in one day. Should they condemn Hitler for that, or should they be grateful? That's a question to ponder. Did the Holocaust create a Holy Land? Was it worth it or not? This is the question of debate.

Hey, what is that?

S: The Alphabet of Self Esteem.

YB: The Alphabet of Self Esteem. What else?

S: The Alphabet of Marriage.

YB: Oh, that's important. The Alphabet of Marriage. Here are the various categories of people and how they function in life, alphabetically.

Ten Sacred Secrets of Success, and The Alphabet of Marriage, The Alphabet of Self Esteem, the Alphabet of a Woman. Where is the The Alphabet of a Man?

S: You usually don't do Man.

(These Alphabets can be found in the Resources section.)

YB: I don't. *(Reading the Alphabet of a Woman.)* "Able, blessed, compassionate, dharma, exercise, fulfilled, graceful, honest, intellectual, joyful, Khalsa, learned, meditate, noble, organize, patient, queenly, radiant, smiling, thoughtful, understanding, vital, Wahe Guru, excellence, yoga, zestful." Very good.

There's a tape of old songs. Can you find it? It begins with a tune that I like. These are our old songs. *(Tape by Ragu Rai Kaur is played, with the song "All For You.")*

The line in it is, "So that I can prove to Mukanday." All that exists about the body shall fall. The soul has to leave in the subtle body; the subtle body has to leave in the essence of divinity. And the essence of divinity cannot exist without royalty. We'll prove how one can be spiritually divine, gorgeously rich, and rule this Earth, with the rule of life. Life has no other rule. So the song says, "So that I can prove to *Mukanday*," "The Lord of Dimension who gives absolute *Mukhti*. What do the Jews call that? Atonement? Hindus call it *nirvana*. Everybody has a word for it. There are eight aspects of God:

Gobinday:	*Sustainer.*
Mukanday:	*Liberator.*
Udaaray:	*Enlightener.* One who takes us across, uplifts us.
Apaaray:	*Infinite.*
Hareeang:	*Destroyer.*
Kareeang:	*Creator.* Through whose Grace everything is done.
Nirnaamay:	*Nameless.* He is not bound down. He is without the identity of the Name.
Akaamay:	*Desireless.* It is by Itself.

These are the eight aspects, known, found. And we remember God by His action. But the most powerful word used in this song is *"Mukunday."* "So I can prove to *Mukunday.*" Look at the essence of the power. I can go and stand before God, the One who will redeem my life. "...that I was pure." But when it came to the body, everything fell apart. Because the body is the combination of five *tattwas* put together by the spirit, guided by the mind, and subject to time and space. So as it grows, it must diminish. When you hold this body and the personality by the power of the ego, then you must be bewitched by insanity, not by love. And you shall not recognize the man, the spirit, the soul, the self.

Oh, Lord of Lords, Giver of the breath of life, Giver of birth, and Giver of the opportunity in time and space, by Thy Will we have come here presuming, and we consume Thy Wisdom. Give us forgiveness forever. Give us the altitude and attitude of that feeling of fulfillment. Give us the power to serve, and give us grace and face, in Thy Name. Give us a chance. We ask Thee in Your Own Self, we have come here to become Teachers. Give us the purity, piety, and let the self be dropped, and the Teacher rise out of the ashes of it, so we can be what Thy Will is to be.

Sat Naam.

Warrior's Exercise
for Opening the Energy into the Shushmanaa & Balancing the Hemispheres of the Brain

Mudra: Stretch arms out to the sides, parallel to the ground. Make palms flat, facing forward, and the fingers spread wide apart. The muscles of the body should hold the weight of the arms, to perform the exercise. This position is your base.

Movement: Keeping the palms flat, fingers spread apart the whole time, begin the following movement:

a

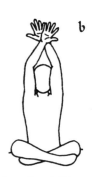 b

(a) Raise your arms up directly over your head, criss-crossing them at the wrists, left palm in front, right behind. They actually should cross a few inches behind the area directly over your head. Then bring the arms back down to the starting position.

(b) Raise your arms up and criss-cross them with the right palm in front of the left, but angle the arms forward a bit, so they are crossing about 12 inches in front of the area directly above the head. Then bring the arms back down to the starting position.

Continue alternating in this fashion.

Music: The musical tape, *Dhuni*, is played during the exercise. One repetition of the mantra is approximately 8 seconds.

Mantra: Mentally recite *Sat Naam, Sat Naam, Sat Naam Ji, Waa-hay Guroo, Waa-hay Guroo, Waa-hay Guroo Ji.*

Eyes: Unspecified. Although for maximum strength, keep the eyes closed.

Time: Done for 2-1/2 minutes in class. Yogi Bhajan said this was enough to initiate. the students into this meditation and not space them out too much.

Comments/Effects: This is a warrior's exercise, and can call upon inner strength and determination.

In the starting position, keep the arms in balance, letting the weight of the arms be held up by the muscles of the body (as opposed to the muscles of the arms doing all the work). This will cause a movement in the central nerve, the *shushmanaa*, in the inner spinal chord. If held in the proper position, you will begin to feel a tingling of energy. Yogi Bhajan refers to position (a) as your *Sat Naam*, and he calls it your original Oriental Self, your Earth, your spine. He refers to position (b) as your *Wahe Guru*, your God, your front face. "There are only two things on this planet—*Sat Naam* is your back; *Wahe Guru* is your front."

Remember, angle is very important in Kundalini Yoga. Kundalini Yoga is a series of angles and triangles, which cut the squares. After a few minutes of practice, you'll reach a stage called The Twilight Zone, and then there'll be huge pain. You will feel you are hurting, because the hemispheres of the brain have to adjust; but soon the endorphins will be released, and you won't want to stop.

Warm-ups

The warm-ups are an essential part of this meditation and will help loosen the nerves, muscles and bones. Without that, you may experience muscle pain the next day.

Sit with a straight spine, and extend your arms out to the sides, parallel to the ground. Begin wiggling the fingers, twisting the hands, bending the arms, stretching the elbows, moving the head, for a few minutes before you begin. This is an important part of this exercise. Time for warm-ups: 1-2 minutes.

The Teacher & the Student

A Teacher is a process to make saints, sages, givers, who are godly and graceful. A Teacher is a factory to manifest all this. A Teacher is not an egomaniac playboy.

When you teach, you must teach with confrontation, not by stimulation. When you teach by stimulation, doubts keep floating. But when you teach by confrontation, it is an either/or situation. In that situation at least doubt is dispelled. That's the advantage of confrontation.

You must be aware of the fact that the intellect releases one thousand thoughts per wink of the eye. You can calculate how many winks of the eye are in a second. The effect is that all these thoughts come, whether you want them or you don't want them. And when a thought comes, it can only do two things: either the thought can become a feeling or the thought can go into the subconscious. The feeling can become an emotion, or the feeling can go into the subconscious. The emotion can become a desire or it can go into the subconscious. The desire can be fulfilled or it can go into the subconscious.

So you have a four-cycle pressure filling your subconscious. If you do not meditate, do not consolidate, do not bring yourself to *pratyahaar*, then you are inviting danger. The danger is that when your subconscious gets overloaded, it starts unloading into the unconscious, and your capacity to think, to work, to be smart, is gone. Then you are an emotional zombie. People in this state become sexually very active, socially very active, and personally very active. The outcome of these habits is masturbation, too much talking, too much partying and drinking, too much sexual activity, and undesirable perversions. I'm telling you where those things come from.

So at some point, this loading becomes unbearable, and it starts going into the unconscious. The tragedy is that the unconscious is a very small sphere of mind, and when that cannot take it, it starts putting it back into the conscious. And once the conscious is polluted by the unconscious, then all you have are nightmares or daydreams. We call them fantasies.

When you fantasize about something, it seems to you that you are doing a great job. Actually, you are killing your precious *prana*, and your life is becoming empty. It goes like this: "I will have an egg, the egg will have a chicken, the chicken will have a hen, the hen will have a rooster, the hen will have another egg, and we'll make a dairy farm. Then we will sell all the eggs in the marketplace. After the marketplace, I'll build a plaza. After the plaza, I'll have a franchise over the whole state, and from the state it will grow to the whole country...." You go on and on, and on, and on, and on. Actually this fantasizing is very comfortable, because

A Teacher is a different character with different characteristics, because he is not a person. He is a pure extended self of the student, therefore he has no boundary, no jurisdiction but to be straight.

you spend nothing, you do nothing, you sweat nothing, yet you feel the feeling of having a big plaza, of big power. That's what drugs do—they give you a feeling of non-reality.

But the tragedy is, in sociology, sexology, and sensology, when you have extended yourself to a dimension which is non-reality, you come back to reality but not in an original way, and then there is a gap. That gap is where your caliber is deficient. And that's why people are poor and rich, happy, unhappy, great, not great. That's a fact.

[handwritten margin note: Cleansing the subconscious]

So the idea is, sit up and meditate. Thoughts come, they hit the floor, and you say, "*Waa-hay Guroo, Waa-hay Guroo, Waa-hay Guroo, Waa-hay Guroo.*" They hit you, you hit them. They come this way, you hit them this way. You clean it out. You get up in the ambrosial hours, when the sun is hitting at a sixty-degree angle, exercise and stimulate yourself, then sit and meditate for hours just to clean the subconscious. You do this so there may be some space left where more garbage can be dumped. It's a very personal thing. It's not a big religious thing, "Oh, I'm going to become spiritual. I'm going to find God, and He's going to to give me a banana; and if I don't do it, He won't give me a banana." That not true.

I want to share this tragedy with you. In Los Angeles I have a friend. One day he said, "Yogiji, you must understand."

"What do I have to understand?"

And he said, "Ummm, that girl, you know?"

I said, "Don't touch it."

"No, Yogiji, yes, Yogiji, umm, umm."

One day I got fed up. I said, "To hell with it, do whatever you want."

He did it. He came back complaining. "Now you want to complain to me?"

"Oh Yogiji, you didn't stop me. Your heart is not with me."

I said, "I told you thirty thousand times, 'Don't do it. Just don't do it.'" Because when a Teacher does not care for one's own status, and thinks he can hide behind the hide of his own ego, respect in the heart of the other is gone. It's not a matter of whether it is a reality, or a non-reality, it is a matter of moral consciousness.

It's not that I have not been accused of bad conduct. I'm very grateful to the United States. They are very nice. If they want something, and they can't get it, they accuse you. That's fine. But there's a moral sense. There's a moral essence. At least you in yourself as a Teacher must feel that you yourself are clean. I read that, "Thou Shalt Not Covet Thy Neighbor's Wife." I'm not saying you should not covet thy neighbor's wife, and not go after anybody you want, or take away their money. I'm not worried about it. All I'm saying is, go ahead and do it, and see what it does to you. It will put a shadow on you which you can't get out of.

You must understand that there is a faculty of a Teacher, and it has no facility. All you are judging as a Teacher is how popular you are. You must understand how unpopular I am. I have to be unpopular. Do you understand, if I would be catering and caring and dramatizing, how powerful and popular I could be? It takes five acres of grass to feed three Jersey cows, and it takes one month of their milk to take the cream and bring out the butter. But that butter is not going to keep until you put it through the test of fire and make clarified butter, *ghee*, out of it. That can keep.

A Teacher is not judged by his popularity, his richness, his money, his knowledge, his essence. A Teacher is judged by his character. If under all temptations he can fly through, then he knows how to fly. But what is happening? You fall apart in relation to money, you fall apart in relation to sex, you fall apart in relation to status.

You may be a very popular Teacher who can write books, and everybody may know you. But you shall not create another Teacher, because you never took the responsibility of taking the chisel and hammer and shaping it. Therefore, as a Teacher you have to shape your own destiny and experience it, before you shape somebody else's destiny. It's your responsibility. I'm not saying don't become popular or don't become rich. I'm saying, do whatever you want to do. Just understand one thing.

ਕਰਮੀ ਆਪੋ ਆਪਣੀ ਕੇ ਨੇੜੈ ਕੇ ਦੂਰਿ ॥

Karmee aapo aapanee, kay nayrai kay door.

-Guru Nanak, *Siri Guru Granth Sahib*, page 8 (from the *Slok* of *Japji Sahib*)
Some will be called in, and others will be pushed away in accordance with their actions.

Nanak said, your actions will prove how near you are, or how far away you are.

It is very funny. In my personal case, when I was a Teacher in Hollywood, and I had all those Hollywood people in my class, it was a very comfortable situation. There were people with me and I just walked away. Ask me why?

Class: Why?

YB: Because I found in them nothing. Their ego was all-consuming. And a man who has an all-consuming ego will never become a Teacher because he will never become a student.

There is one man who is in a very respectable, honorable position. I asked, "What do these people go and do there with him?"

"Well, they say he pretends from dawn to dusk to be very holy. At night it's all drinking, smoking, and etcetera." What is that?

You can read in books what a great Teacher once said: "If you have a desire you must fulfill it by letting it go." Desire is like a fire. How many times when you keep on putting wood on the fire does it go away? Normally when a Teacher discusses desire, he says to deny the desire. That's not correct. That's cheating. Desire cannot be denied, but desire can be elevated. Do not deny the desire, and do not fulfill the desire if it does not fit your excellence and honor. No desire is desirable if it does not add to your character and grace. What is your strength? Your personal strength as a Teacher is your character. What is your power as a Teacher? The power of a Teacher is grace.

One person said, "Hi Yogiji, I teach a class."

I said, "How many students come to your class?"

She said, "One or two."

I said, "Can you expand?"

The person said, "I'm trying everything. I'm putting out leaflets, I'm putting this, I'm putting that."

I said, "How do you survive?"

And the person said, "Barely. Barely." She said that these two students come every day, and donation is on an honor basis, so they leave sometimes fifty bucks, sometimes twenty bucks. "Money-wise, I don't think I'm hurting, but..."

Just today, before I came here, somebody gave me one thousand dollars, as a gift to me, as a Teacher. Somehow I felt uncomfortable. I looked, I counted it, and I said, "Hundred dollars more." And I said, "The job you are asking for is too big for it. You can't give me just a thousand dollars and get away with it, because it's not correct. It's your money, it's not mine. I'm going to spend it for you, but the question is, there should be one hundred more, just not stuck on a zero, man. Just one more hundred." They both were laughing because the wife was saying, "I knew you were going to say that. I even told him, and he said, 'No, no, it's all right.'"

I'm giving you an example. What will you do if somebody gives you a thousand dollars?

Student: Ask for a hundred more.

YB: No, that I did—you are not going to ask, I know. What will you do?

S: Put it on the altar.

YB: Put it on the altar. You never put anything on the altar on a zero number, remember this. It has to be zero plus. The word for it is *Savaaiyaa*. One and a quarter. One is to the One, and quarter is the continuity. That's why I asked for the extra.

A Teacher is a different character with different characteristics, because it's not a person. It's a pure, extended self of the student, therefore, it has no boundary, no jurisdiction but to be straight. Asking for one hundred dollars more brought joy and love and understanding, in the sense that they knew it.

All these faculties as a Teacher will come to you, because you will also understand what the desire is, what the prayer is, and what the fulfillment is. They're asking you to augment. Money is not a situation. Money is a medium.

At Summer Solstice I said, "I have a noble work for which I need money. Give to me from your heart." I had no right to ask, but I knew, if I ask, they will give to me. It came to almost exactly what was needed. So now some beautiful people for beautiful reasons will go and get educated in their life.

You are participating in life, but it's not a matter of temptation. Your glory is not temptation. Your grace is not temptation. It's not achievement either. You have to create in your lifetime somebody ten times better than you. That's the first and the last job of a Teacher.

You'll find great Teachers with great egos, and you will also find great Teachers with a lot of knowledge. You'll find great Teachers who will talk and convince you of their divinity—you can find anybody. But nobody is going to kick your ass. You will never meet a Teacher who'll face you from the neck and put two fingers in your nose and say, "You son of so and so, how come yesterday at five o'clock you were doing this?" It's a practical effect, it's no joke.

You do not understand the relationship. The relationship between a Teacher and student is that the Teacher is in pain if the student is not progressing. The Teacher feels terrible. It's as if he is going to go impotent, become an orphan, be without any child. And the only child he's looking at is that student who is going to be greater than him to cover his shortcomings, and expand his teachings. It's not how many come to your classes, how many you screw, or how many you kiss and hug. It's not how much influence you have, how many V.I.P.'s you know, how many times you are invited to places, or how much you are circulated. That has nothing to do with it, damn it. It has nothing to do with you. As a Teacher you are a Teacher, not a creature, not a preacher.

I will tell you the story of a Teacher. There was a man sitting with a loin cloth on a hill, and he was exercising like this. *(YB demonstrates a person sitting in easy pose, hands on his knees, rocking back and forth.)* He was too old and he couldn't move and he was just jerking around. The king of the state brought horses, men, wealth, food, and touched his feet. He continued doing his exercise.

The king said, "Oh Master, I am the imperial self of this area."

He said, "I know you are my king, thank you."

He said, "I have brought you this offering."

He said, "Thank you."

The king said, "Bless me."

He said, "You are blessed. Thank you."

He said, "Give me some orders."

He said, "Pack it up and go."

The king implored, "No, no, no, master. No, master. No."

He said, "What did you come for? I have blessed you. Take it and go. Take it. I'm fine. Don't interfere with my exercises."

He said, "No, Master. Please bless me, please bless me."

He said, "You are blessed, blessed, blessed, blessed, as many times as blessed means anything, you are blessed."

So he said, "Well, give me something to do."

He said, "Pack up all your gifts and go home. Leave me alone. I don't want to have guards and all that stuff."

He said, "I can provide it. I'll build it up, whatever you want."

He said, "I don't need it. I want a place to move, and you are stopping me from my joy of being nothing."

And he said, "No, no, Master, you are the greatest Master. It is a tragedy that I have never served you. I am very guilty, obligated, and I am the great giver."

The teacher laughed. He said, "I am the greatest denial, if you want to know. You're not going to give me anything."

And he asked (remember this question), "Master, why?"

The Teacher said, "All the wealth is loaded in the sky. It comes down through the drops of rain and nurtures the Earth. The One who loves me can pick up the water from the ocean, through the clouds, through the mountains, and make the rain run through the brooks and the rivers. The One who creates that cycle knows me. I'm not going to ask somebody else."

The king said, "Lord master, I have brought this. Do you know what we can do? We can build here a place where people can come, worship, for religious purposes."

Do not deny the desire, and do not fulfill the desire if it does not fit your excellence and honor. No desire is desirable if it does not add to your character and grace. What is your strength? Your personal strength as a Teacher is your character. What is your power as a Teacher? The power of a Teacher is grace.

He said, "The greatest religious job you have already done, which was to come through this hilly tract, seventeen miles. My calculations were wrong—I thought you could never reach me here. But you made it, and you just faced me. Wasn't that something very pure in your life?"

He said, "That's true."

Calamity sometimes brings in you spiritual climax. Challenge is not bad. Actually, telling you frankly, a teacher must have moral, ethical, personal authority to do what he has to do.

When I started in Hollywood, we used to have lots of these celebrities. Even now some of the overflow of Guru Singh's classes come through my classes. But I don't know them. I just think they are artificial blond girls who come for yoga class. What should I do with them? Who are they? Sometimes I go home and they say, "Look at the magazine, look at the front page. This was the girl who was sitting on the left side of you, and this one was sitting on the right side of you."

They came to the class, God bless them, bless them, bless them, bless them. I don't know whether they are on the front of a magazine. As long as they don't sit on my head, I am okay. I go into a class to teach, not to count how many celebrities, stars, or models are there. I am naive in a certain way. I go to teach the class and finish with it. I'm not looking at all these alphabets. All I know is that it doesn't matter what I teach, once the arcline and aura coincide to be blue with a golden tinge, the job is done. Then it's time to go home. It means that day the purification has happened.

I don't care whether people say I am a good Teacher or a bad Teacher, I'm a right Teacher or a wrong Teacher, as long as I know there are teachings, and I am carrying and sharing them as they are. In the purity of the teachings lies the purity of the Teacher. There's no other rule. You have the right to joke. You can add astrology, astronomy, whatever you want to talk about. But you know, at the time that you say, "Ong Namo Guru Dev Namo," you are not an astrologer.

I read an ad which I should have brought to read to you. I don't believe it. The ad was for Kundalini Yoga classes and everything else with it. No subject was left out. The thing which I liked most was, that it said you can also be taught how to select your soul mate. And I said to myself, "God, do they know what a soul mate is?"

You have soul mates: your intellect, consciousness, subconscious, unconscious, you have your ten bodies. They are the mates of your soul; they come with the soul. So in your soul-mate system, you have bodies and you have aspects of your mind all together. Then you have a soul-mate which is called time and space and longitude and latitude. It's a mating season of you and your self. Then you take the altitude and attitude to keep all these sixteen horses going, so you can carry your carriage.

So actually, the soul mate is not another person; there's nothing outside of you. If you as a teacher say there is something outside of you, then you must believe that outside of you there's a positive. So then you remember there must also be a negative. If there's positive, there's negative. You can't be neutral. You'll be churned like a churning wheel, and you shall never find contentment, stability and self-happiness as a Teacher. You will be a Teacher, I'm not saying you will not be a Teacher. But you will deny yourself.

There's no good and bad. There's no right and wrong. There's no high and low. A yogi is a person whom the opposite polarities do not affect—he recognizes there are polarities.

(See page 152 for details of this meditation.)

Do you want to do Moon Kriya?

Class: Yes, sir.

YB: Ready? All right. Come on. Put on those European drums. This is the moon area. *(YB points to the area on the palms, the fleshy area along the side, under the pinkie finger. He makes his hands into light fists, and bangs the sides of the hands together.)* It hurts, but please don't make them black and blue. With those drum beats, chant "*Har, Har, Har, Har, Har, Har, Har.*" Twist it. That way you'll beat less. Otherwise you'll go insane and beat hard. It's terrible. Don't do that. All right, go ahead.

(European Drum Tape begins playing.)

Hold the navel in also. Experience is a good thing. *(After several minutes):* You have a last minute to try your luck.

Inhale. And please, even if you have not, during the whole exercise, touched your moon point here, hit it now. Hit and exhale. Inhale deep, do it again. Exhale. Inhale, and relax.

You're pretty good. You had a couple of good minutes. This is the Moon center *(fleshy area under pinkie)* and with the navel and the tip of the tongue, you hit this nerve center, it sometimes gives you clarity and reality faster than anything else.

The question in life is not how strong and energetic you are. There is all this dialogue going on about, "Be energetic, be strong, must have energy." People talk to me, "Energy, energy." What about eliminating fatigue?

You never say, "I don't want fatigue, I don't want tension." No, no, no. A *sattvic* life is without fatigue, tension. It's called calm and cool.

You always feel you are great when you are very energetic, right? There's a feeling about it. Actually you are great when you are a sober, calm, sustained, saintly self.

A teacher is a process to make saints, sages, givers, who are godly and graceful. A teacher is a factory to manifest all this. A Teacher is not an egomaniac playboy.

One thing you must understand, it doesn't matter whether somebody hears you or not, but as a Teacher when you speak from the command center and say, "You've got to stop it," it stops. But when you have never stopped and never obeyed, how can you command? My first thing is to stop your mind. People say, "What is *japa,* what is mantra?" Mantra is to stop your thoughts and say, "*Wahe Guru.*" That's a mantra. If there's a temptation and you can really grab it, instead, stop it and see what comes to you. Don't grab what you can get; get what is going to be given, what God is going to give you. It will be mega-multi-times more than what you're going to ask for.

You may ask for a pizza, and end up with a factory. Yes. Somebody once said, "God bless, I like biscuits." She ended up working in a biscuit factory. God, she's still working in biscuits.

You know, sometimes you feel, "I can divorce my husband, I can marry this person." You know? In some cases you feel it works. It doesn't work. Because you have not finished the karma. You jumped the boat. So union and departure are not the achievement. You are at play in the hand of time, and a Teacher doesn't play in the hand of time. If you are to suffer, suffer. If you are to be happy, be happy. If you are having a good time, have a good time. If it's a horrible time, then enjoy it. Enjoy your day.

Moon Kriya

a   b

Mudra: Sitting in Easy Pose with a straight spine, bend the elbows down by the sides. Extend the forearms out in front, so they are parallel to the ground, palms facing up. Make the palms into loose fists, with the thumbs on the outside.

Movement: (a) Bring the sides of the hands together with a force, and hit the fleshy area of the hand below the pinkie fingers together very forcefully. This is the area of the hand known as the Moon center. Chant *Har* as you strike.
(b) Move the hands apart, separating them by 12 inches, twisting the hands on the wrists until they are palm down when they get to the area above the knees.
    Continue this movement in a steady motion.

Eyes: Unspecified.

Mantra: Chant *Har, Har, Har,* continuously in a monotone, by striking the tongue against the upper palate each time you chant the word. Pull in slightly on the navel with each recitation. Every time you chant one *Har,* you will also strike the hands together at the same time.

Tape: *Rhythms of Gatka* by Matamandir Singh. Rhythm is 1 movement per second.

Time: Practiced for 9 minutes in class.

End: Inhale deeply, and hold about 6-10 seconds as you hit the Moon centers together forcefully. Exhale. Repeat 3 times total.

Comments/Effects: When the Moon centers hit (along with the navel point being pulled in and the tip of the tongue striking the upper palate), it brings a clarity and reality.
    People are always striving to be energetic. What about eliminating fatigue? It's important to live *sattvic*— in a state of purity which allows you to be calm and cool. *Sattvic* is life without fatigue, without tension. You always feel you are great when you are very energetic. Actually you are great when you are sober, calm, and living in your sustained saintly self.

Descending God & Ascending Human

Out of existence a non-existence arises, which is ascended. That is the Teacher. Not this idot who has a defect in the brain, who has sensuality and sexuality and thus creates greed, attachment and charisma to suck in, and develops pride.

The subject of tonight's talk is: "Man and His Handicaps, Teacher and His Downfall, Descending God, and Ascending Human."

You cannot, will not, and shall not, love another human. Thou shall love no one. Even though everybody wants to love, needs to love, is in love, and there's nothing but love. The question is, why is this statement so flatly true? Does anybody have the answer?

Student: No attachments?

YB: No, no, we're not talking philosophy here. We're saying something very simple. The statement is very heavy. You should hear it. "You cannot, will not, shall not love another human." My God, it's disastrous. And then the statement is, "Everything without Love is nothing." So you will not love. Thou shall not love. It is a statement in a very probable and direct form. It's very heavy, and you can't admit it. You can't even accept it, because everything in you, intuitively and in a fantasy mood, wants love.

S: People don't love, they love their idea of you.

YB: People don't love you, they love their idea of you.

S: God in us loves the God in the other.

YB: God in us loves the God in the other. Good.

S: Love is the unknown of another person.

YB: Love is the unknown of another person. All right.

S: You should love God. God is in me, in you, in everyone.

YB: God we should love, God is in me, you.

S: Not one person. God is not just in one person.

YB: God is in everybody. Yeah, yeah, yeah, yeah. I wish I had studied this subject before I started it.

S: We should not search for anything outside of us.

YB: We are stupid. What are we talking about? Do you understand the statement that has been made, "You cannot, will not, shall not love another human?" Even though love is everything, you want to love, and love is all that there is, this very heavy statement has been made, and you are being asked to answer the question, "Why?"

A Teacher is sharp enough to cut the hardness of the heart, the rudeness of the mind, the falsehood of the head, and the shakiness of the feet.
A Teacher challenges you with an absolute definitive graceful power of projection and leaves you no alternative but to submit, surrender, and come in obedience. You are going to become Teachers. Are you going to be that powerful, with that caliber?

S: We don't know how to love ourselves.

YB: We *know* how to love ourselves. That's not a statement. What do you mean by, "don't you know?"

S: Love is a vibration we pull through.

YB: Love is a vibration we pull through. We need something to pull us through, right?

S: We can't love another because we're too self-centered and too selfish.

YB: Well, that is a pretty heavy statement. "We cannot love"—that is a statement. "We need to love"—that's a statement. "We shall not love"—that's a very heavy statement. The fact is, if a person has not experienced love of his or her soul, within one's self, there is no chance that that person can go out and love, even though it is the faculty of love that you most powerfully need.

So when I make such a flat statement as I made, it makes you understand the handicap. There is a handicap in us, that as we develop, we have not been taught to experience our own spiritual soul, our self-love. The word "spiritual" is foreign to us. Spiritual means good, spiritual means right, spiritual means high, spiritual means a lot of things to us. But spiritual only means *me within me is infinite*. Spiritual means me within me is infinite, and me within me as infinite shall relate, experience, express, and project Infinity.

So where are you coming from? You are all coming from the flea market. You have all your sexual, sensual, sensitive shops open, and you sell yourself in the name of love. Do you know what love is? It is the most beautiful, comprehensive, divine *pranic* energy given to you by God, which you should have experienced. But what did you do? You turned it into mucous and saliva, and you call it kisses and hugs and sex.

You have no sensitivity that your soul shall leave in the subtle body, and that your subtle body is as sophisticated as anything in the universe can be. So unless you produce in yourself elegance, grace, sophisticatedness in your mind, manners, and attitude, and unless you come from that Infinite altitude, and ascend to that altitude, you cannot descend in love. The higher is your being, the deeper is the love.

I understand what kind of love you understand in English. It is that kind of love which consumes you. It is that which is a natural biological essence of the human mind, body, and spirit in which you are consumed. That's a way to die, and you must die, and therefore you must practice that. But you waste time in emotion, feeling, and commotions.

There are five things which are bad. One is lust, another is anger, the third is greed, then there is attachment and pride. They come from Ether, Air, Fire, Water, and Earth. You can't get rid of those five things, because those five things come from the five elements, and you are the product of those five elements.

Now try to understand as Teachers. You are of the five elements and you are not the five elements. You have a spirit and a soul, but you have no spirit and soul. You have the body, but you don't have the body. You have the mind, and you don't have the mind. Now what are we talking about here? You have and you don't have? What is this? Because what you have is the existence. What you are is the non-existence. Because out of existence a non-existence arises, which is ascended. That is the Teacher. Not this idiot who has a defect in the brain, who has sensuality and sexuality, and thus creates greed, attachment, and charisma to suck in, and develops the pride of being a teacher.

You're not a Teacher, you're a sucker. You're an idiot sucker who is wasting your life. This life has been gifted to you by God, in the body of a human, with a mind which is a part of Infinity, and a soul which is absolute purity. You are not a Teacher, because you don't project your nothingness into Oneness. A Teacher projects his or her nothingness, *shuniaa*, into *prana*. It is a very simple, human living thing which looks very elevated, but which is just a must. So, what do you do? You substitute yourself with emotions, commotions, feelings, fantasies, dramas, dreams—God knows what—there are thousands of things. The tragedy is, you have not met a Teacher.

When the soul was told that it had to come to the Earth, it said, "I'm not gonna go."

God said, "You have to go because you asked for the test and challenge, and you challenged the Infinity of Divinity. I have to create Infinity and Divinity, and I'm going to send you to this planet. Go!"

So you said, "No. I first agreed, now I don't agree." So like a kid you just started playing games.

And God said, "You've got to go."

You said, "No, I am afraid. I don't have courage. I don't want to go. I'm too cozy here. I don't want to be tested."

So God gave you the mind. And you said, "What is this?"

"It's a tool which can take you to Infinity. Beyond Infinity is Me. It takes you to *shuniaa* , and beyond *shuniaa* is Me. So both sides is Me. In between is a swing. Play, baby, play, swing. But you have to leap, both sides to Infinity, and you have to remember it. If you ever want to come to Me, yes, you can."

And you said, "What is the guarantee?" You know, you are pretty American. You said, "No, what is the guarantee? Give me the guarantee; at least a warranty. How do I know that this mind will work? How do you know I will work? How do you know I'll come back? I want to be sure. I want to come back."

God said, "You shall meet a Teacher, *ustaad*, one who teaches you *ustatee*. *Ustaad* is that institute, that being which will teach you *ustatee*. *Ustatee* means "praise." But it will be for only a moment. If you recognize and organize, you shall be liberated, you shall come."

You said, "Okay, that's worthwhile. Okay, I'm going. Give me the *tattvas*."

So all these *tattvas* , these five elements, have some essence. *Kaam* is desire. *Kaamanaa* is the reference to the self-reverence. So you learn through the experience of a yogi that *kaam* should be converted into *kaamanaa*. You can't get rid of it. Don't misunderstand that you can blame and say it is bad. What is bad about it? It is what it is. Without that desire, you cannot reach. But you can desire desirelessness. To be desireless, is a desire. So you can convert desire into desirelessness. What are the benefits? Catch-22. If you desire the desirelessness and you perfect it, you don't have to desire; desirability will be yours. Your ability to get all desirability, and produce it in your environments, is granted. Very good deal.

Krodh is what you have from fire. You have anger. Mostly you get angry. If you do not get angry, people make you angry. The only times that you become truthful are when you are absolutely insensitively and sensitively in a passionate love, when you are in utmost fear, or when you are angry. These are the times that you come out without reservation, because when you are practicing anger, you are practicing insanity. At that time you have no sense of metabolism, you have no sense of self-protection, you have no sense of anything.

So anger is very consuming. Anger makes you less than a human, and more of a beast. But on the other hand, if you divert this anger toward your weaknesses, you'll be perfect. In essence you get angry if you do not do what is correct. So anger was meant for self-purification. It was not meant to burn others.

Then third was greed: *Lobh.* You want. You want beautiful things, you want sex, you want a partner, you want a soul mate, God knows how many stories you have made about yourself. But you want. It's very uncomfortable that you keep on wanting everything. But if you get diverted into one want, use your greed to live extremely greedily with the goal that you will not be greedy, then all of nature will serve you. You will have all. Nature will give you all that you need.

Now comes attachment: *Moh.* Well, you can be attached to me, you, us, all, none. And you can be attached to your neuroses, which normally 99.9 percent of us are. People are very neurotic. They circulate their life like a wheel, with the hub as self-neurosis. But out of the self neurosis, if you become insane enough, neurotic enough, in love enough to attach yourself to Infinity, you can, from that mental swing, reach God on both sides. It's very simple.

Ahangkaar: pride. You will boast, you will be prideful. You will feel others as inferior, yourself as superior. So you'll play the game of inferiority and superiority complex. You live a life of complexes and everything you do has a complex. So you are very divided into pigeonholes. You do not know how to get out of it. But what is there which you cannot get out of? Let us be very sensitive about it.

You can be very proud and grateful and gracious that you have this chance of time and space. "I should be very grateful that I have time with you, and I have space with you. I can be very proud that my name is spiritual, guiding, reminding, going." So many things your self-pride can give you. But if you do not compete and compare yourself with others, and confuse yourself, you can be marvelous. So all that there is, is self realization. But basically your fulfillment is not because of your insecurity. Because with that insecurity you are handicapped, and people see it.

As I was telling you this morning, a Teacher is not one who is very popular, who's very wise, who's all knowing, who has all the powers. That's not a Teacher. A Teacher is an artist, with a hammer and a chisel. Whenever you meet a Teacher, God, there will be a spark. At the first introduction of you and your Teacher, you are going to find what is wrong with you. Mostly you will not like to hear that. You'll skip that person. You are most welcome to skip it, but you do not know that you have lost that one chance which the soul was promised.

A Teacher is not a public relations package—very charming, very beautiful, very marvelous, very gracious, very kind, very sweet. That's an angel, not a Teacher. Very passionate, very loving, very darling, very attractive, very knowing—that may be a professor, not a Teacher. Very knowledgeable, very sharing, very high-grade knowing, absolutely, amazingly all the best there is. That may be a sage, a wise sage, a saint—not a Teacher.

So, you have all come here to become teachers and you must understand the faculty of teacher. A Teacher is sharp enough to cut the hardness of the heart, the rudeness of the mind, the falsehood of the head, and the shakiness of the feet. A Teacher challenges you with an absolute definitive graceful power of projection and leaves you no alternative but to submit, surrender, and come in obedience. You are going to become Teachers. Are you going to be that powerful, with that caliber?

It is not that the Teacher is a super human being. The Teacher gives you a chance to become a super human being.

A Teacher is not a fast-food lane, call-in, drive-in situation. When you meet your Teacher you will wish and pray you would not have met that person. *(Laughter.)* The first encounter will be, "Why are you such an idiot?" That was my first encounter with my teacher. I went with my servants and my this and that, and when I came in the evening, everything was gone. There was absolutely nothing. And he told me, he said, "Who do you think you are? Why are you here?"

I said, "I came to study with you."

He said, "What? Your horses will study with me? Your servants will study with me? Your clothes will study with me? Hey, you! You're going to stay here bare-naked, and you have a job to do."

I said, "I saw a bucket with lime."

He said, "There are outhouses. See that they don't smell. Keep them clean. That's it for today. That's the first lesson."

I looked at the guy, and I thought, "How many of this kind can I buy? Thirty thousand? Sixty thousand? Who is he? What is he telling me? I am going to sleep tonight on this bunk bed? Somebody's going to sleep over me and pass wind? Is this teaching? What am I going to learn here? To smell someone's wind and look at the guy who's next door to me, while God made me so beautiful and so elegant. I'm born in a good family. I have everything that I need. What do I need these teachings for? And now I have to go and look at the excrement of others, and I'm going to put this lime on it? This is my first job? Who can I hire to do this? I can hire a whole town for it, but what is this? Why did I come? Oh no." That was my exact feeling. I'm telling you.

I was so angry. I said, "This middle-aged puffy fellow, who does he think he is? Why did my grandfather tell me to go? What for? What am I doing here? He's totally rude and ridiculous." And on and on and on and on and on and on.... I was so nervous, so angry, and so mindful, so insulted. Then I touched my forehead, and I felt that I was sweating. I said, "So be it. I'll prove that I can stand all this. God has blessed me. This man is a living challenge, and I am going to win. Victory, *Fateh!*" I said. "Hmmmmmmmmmmm." And you know, when I slept that night, I didn't even take a turn. The next morning I was good. And then there was no unhappy moment. Even when everything was super-unhappy, I was happy. Either I sailed through it, I came out of it, or I came over it. Finally I learned my breath of life is the only thing I know.

What do you want—a boyfriend or a girlfriend as a teacher? Have it. That's fine. How do you treat a boyfriend or a girlfriend? No, I didn't misunderstand it. I knew he was going to create so much anger and reaction and make me feel so dumb and like such a dud, yet I would have to bless him with the fragrance, and with my prayer, with my power, and with my bright-

A Teacher is not a fast-food lane, call-in, drive-in situation. When you meet your Teacher you will wish and pray you would not have met that person. The first encounter will be, "Why are you such an idiot?"

ness to win him over, which is impossible. And when I make it possible, that is the day I'm born for. We had a hassle. I had an eternal hassle, external misery, and it was all horrible, but it was honorable.

You are born like a worm, you die like a worm, you are gone. You came, you did itchy, titchy, witchy, itchy, bitchy, wichy, and then you are gone. You managed, you manipulated, you lied, you were sweet, you put on *bana*, you became a saint, you became a yogi—you fake freak. Pretentiously to be righteous, always telling others what to do, and you are doo-doo yourself. This is what you call a Teacher? You look very elegant, you look very professional, you look very perfect, you are absolutely all right. And you do not know it is very dirty to be a Teacher because you have to clean the dirt, all of which is in the mind:

Many lifetimes this mind became pitch dark, dark black with silt. It had nothing bright and clear. It has to be chiseled out, cleaned. It is all here, the pain is all here, the sensitivity is all here, the relationship is all here. Whatever you are here, you are here. But over there, there's nothing. It's all light. You look to the sky, you look to the sun, and you feel it's very bright. You go in space, it's all dark. Space is all dark, and space creates time, time creates space. When you are in space, you have time. When you are in time, you have space. And when you are in light, you are in "Wow!" Not Guru yet, you have not met. But if you meet the Guru, you enter the *"Waah."* Then you become the *"Hay." "Waa-hay,"* and that is Thou. You become "Thou." Then "I" dissolves. The moment your "I" dissolves, you become Thou, and then your Third Eye opens. Then these two eyes mean nothing.

A disciple was once asked, "How does your teacher look?"

The disciple answered, "My teacher looks as he looks."

He said, "Have you looked at him?"

He said, "Yes, I look all the time."

"What does he look like?"

He said, "As he wants to look. I look and his looks bewitch me so that there's nothing to see."

How many of you can do that? Because *prana* is your base, *shuniaa* is your achievement, *pratyahaar* —zero. From the One you came, the one you are, in zero, into Infinity you have to merge. Or from Infinity you have to come. In that One Infinity you exist, and then you merge into that One which is your Infinity. So you are born from zero, and you are to die at One. That's your exit. If your exit is Oneness, that Infinity, that quality, that quantity, that realm of consciousness which has absolutely all the width you need, finally you will have no dimension; Then you are not measurable, you are not understandable, you are not. You become "not"'

That is just the first step of a Teacher. When he becomes "not," then he or she becomes all. Your beauty, if it does not have infinite bounty, will never enjoy bliss. And that you can get just at the sight, touch, and projection of that which is that horrible thing that you call "Teacher." Just at that moment when you surrender, that's the only moment you excel, you resurrect.

You think surrender is a weakness, cowardice, shallowness. I have seen in my last twenty-seven years, people calling me "Teacher,'" and then arguing. They have logic, reason, arguments, maybe's. What do I lose? I lose nothing, they gain nothing. The relationship is in that balance. They are in the web and the cycle of their own mental neuroses. They have a chance to break through it, to agree. But they are afraid that if they agree, they will disagree with their neuroses, and when they disagree with their neuroses, everything will disagree, because that's the only security they have got. They have a security.

It is not that the Teacher is a super human being. It's not. A Teacher is not a super human being. The Teacher gives you a chance to become a super human being. A hammer and chisel is not infinity, but it can carve you into infinity. It can carve out of you a God, and you can be worshipped, and you will remain stone no more.

I had those two huge stones. Nobody ever said, "This is a stone." I said, "This is Ganesha. That's Ganesha." Stones became Ganeshas. They are not stones anymore. They were stone, and they are stone, but now they project Ganeshas, because somebody carved them into Ganesha. And there's nothing we can do.

Even one of my friends, who is the most fanatic, came, and he said, "Oh, these two Ganeshas are very powerful."

I said, "Why don't you go and shake a hand? It has an elephant face and a trunk. Touch it."

He said, "No, no, no, no, no. I, I, I can't do it, these are, you know, Ganesh, Ganesh, Ganesh."

And I was shocked. I said, "This man's a fanatic. He never believes in anything. But look at his reaction to those stones carved into Ganeshas." The stone became powerful; it has an identity, it has an existence of projection.

Why can't you as a human become God, which you are? If a stone can become Ganesha, you cannot become Infinity? You don't, because you waste all your *prana* into "I" and do not become "Thou." You say you are in love, but you are in non-love. You just want your mucous to pass into something else. You call love kisses and hugs, and exchange of saliva.

What is the matter with your life that you ejaculate through your mouth or you ejaculate through your penis or your vagina? You think you are lovers? What a shallow bargain. Where is your essence? Where is your essence as a Teacher? You have come from the Universal Infinite Teacher and you are just the image of that Infinite Perfect God. Can you not reach it? Can you not understand it? Can you not allow yourself to be it?

In the entire distance of your destiny you have one chance. Don't buy it, but don't let it go.

I was wondering one day, how there must have been so many stones, but these two became Ganeshas. There are tons of stones which must have been carved into tons of configurations, projections. But these two stones became Ganeshas. Somebody bought them and somebody brought them to me, and somebody put them there. Now they are there.

Can you believe a stone can become God and a human can't? Isn't it a mystery? A human which can make a stone into God, cannot become God himself? Why not? Because stone doesn't know how to sell its consciousness. You do know. You are prostitutes. You are prostitutes in time and consciousness. Don't misunderstand the word 'prostitute' to only mean sexual. No. In consciousness you are prostitutes, because you have never admitted or conceived that you are by the will of Infinity, and you are forever.

It's not true that one who's born shall die. Normally it is true. But it's not true. True, not true. Nanak never died. Moses never died. Abraham doesn't die. Mohammed doesn't die.

Rama doesn't die. Krishna doesn't die. They died, but they didn't die. Are you confused with the subject? Do you understand? You forgot to answer.

Class: Yes, Sir. *(Said weakly.)*

YB: I didn't hear it.

Class: Yes, Sir. *(Said strongly.)*

YB: Good. It is not that you are yelling. It shows your spirit, your alertness, and the affirmation of a confirmation that you have heard, deep in your basic navel point, and you answer, "Yes, Sir." You don't say, "Yes, Sir. Yes, Sir" —like a little puppy. *(Said very weakly.)* You're not dogs. You are human. Confirm it with spirit or don't speak! Never utter a word if it's not from your navel point, and it doesn't confirm your regal, highest self. Once you start speaking from your *anhad*, the navel point, in your royalty, you shall live royally. All riches shall come to you, and everybody will feel you. Not all the time. Sometimes they freak out. Who cares, though? Who cares? Who cares for these earthlings? They are like mosquitoes. They're born, they sting, and they die. Like those stones, they are there, they pound, they scatter and turn into sand. But some stones become Ganeshas.

You are fortunate. You have come here to become Teachers. We have been talking since last Saturday about the faculty, the facet, the power, the projection— all that a teacher is. When it came to Nanak, it was so simple. Nanak said, "The Guru is the one who takes you from darkness to light." It is not a person. It's the projection of that person; it is that power which is the Guru, which is the Teacher. There's nothing personal. That stone is stone, but it's the most difficult thing—you can't pass by that stone and not feel Ganesha. Even if you don't know about Ganesha, still that stone reminds you that it is something.

That's the minimum of the human. The human is the light: mental, spiritual, self, and the teacher is the embodiment of it. It delightfully lights everything, and removes the darkness. That's why you came here. You have made your attempt, you have surrendered. And now our prayer is that you shall become that.

There are four or five more days—put in your best. Make an effort. Achieve it. Desire it, and become desirable, become deserving. You can, because you have been promised a chance.

The moment you become a wife, if you have an understanding to ignore "why" and "if," if you leave those two things, you will remain a wife. Otherwise, wives have many names: "bitchy wife," "quarreling wife," "nagging wife." She has a long alphabetical dictionary.

ਇਸੁ ਜਗ ਮਹਿ ਪੁਰਖੁ ਏਕੁ ਹੈ ਹੋਰ ਸਗਲੀ ਨਾਰ ਸਬਾਈ
Is jag meh purakh ek hai, hor sagalee naar sabaaee.
-Guru Amar Das, *Siri Guru Granth Sahib*, page 591
In this world there is One Husband and all others are His wives.

There is One Lord and everybody is His consort. But when a consort does not consent, and becomes "why" and "if," then she becomes "wife." Understand the original word. "*Why* are you saying so? *If* you would have said that, matter would have been all right." Every female questions the male. It's amazing. The man, a half-brained individual, is being questioned by a complete-brained individual—the woman. Can you believe the justice? Where is the justice? There never is going to be justice.

Now people have started saying that because I am in a man's body, I am always justifying men. What am I justifying about men? They have no left brain! I said it twenty-seven years ago. Now everybody has caught up with those words of mine. They are writing books, *Men Are From Mars, Women Are From Venus.* Years ago, I taught in UCLA: "Man is not a woman. Woman is not a man. There's nothing in common. One is the moon, one is the sun. One has to reflect, one has to project. Project and reflect may be a cause and effect, but it's not the same thing." God, why do you all become tomboys and transvestites? You do not identify with your identity. Therefore, you can't find your reality.

Let us see if we can find something tonight. All right?

◉

(See page 162 for the details of this meditation.)

Let us see how we can make the best out of the worst. It's difficult. Take your pinkie, Mercury, communication finger. Put your three antennas up and touch your Id, the Ego, and sit in this roly-poly state. Stretch your spine and stretch it back and stretch it back, and stretch it back, until all the muscles of the chest become unstretchable, and then hold.

Close your eyes and meditate. We are not going to do anything special, no miracle. But it will happen. Remember, all muscles of the chest must reach a point where nothing more can be reached. Do it to your maximum.

Put that *"Dhuni"* tape on. Elevate with that unto Infinity. That sound is the basic one-stringed sound of two words, *"Sat Naam,"* and *"Wahe Guru."* So, it is up to you.

Pressure the muscles. Play, yogi, play, your one string, and God shall dwell in Thee.

Pull back, pull back. If there is a pain, let there be pain. Pull back, pull back, you are losing the muscles! You are losing the pressure, you are losing the height.

Experience. Push, push back, and you will go forward equally and equivalently.

From the navel point, with the tip of the tongue! You have one more minute left. Stand by. Inhale. Inhale deep. Deep. Hold tight. Cannon fire out. Inhale deep again. Deep, deep, deep. Concentrate deeply. Cannon fire out. Inhale deep, deep. Pressurize perfectly to your maximum. Relax.

We'll observe one minute of silence for those who are born as human and couldn't become Teachers. It's one minute of silent prayer unto that God, Who gave all the chance as He promised. And though some or many might have missed it, please be merciful.

◉

Out of Thy mercy, out of Thy grace, out of Thy Infinity, we ask Thee to be kind, compassionate, and bless us, elevate us, take us to Your bosom, and from the heart give us the health we need to be, to be, to be. Sat Naam.

Meditation to Open the Energy Channels & Take You to the Heights

Mudra: Hands are flat, palms facing forward, and fingers point towards the ceiling. Bend the pinkie finger down into the palm, and touch the pinkie tip to the tip of the thumb. The other three fingers are straight and held side by side.

    Place this mudra so that the wrists are at the level of the shoulders, and the hands are a little bit to the sides of, and also in front of, each shoulder. Just hold the mudra still, but press back very hard on your shoulders, the hands and elbows, and bring the chin slightly into the chest. Imagine you are trying to sit up very straight, and are trying to bring the shoulder blades to touch. This will force your chest to expand out. Press as hard as you can, then just hold it.

Music: The instrumental *Dhuni*.

Eyes: Close your eyes and meditate.

Mantra: *Sat Naam, Sat Naam, Sat Naam Ji, Wahe Guru, Wahe Guru, Wahe Guru Ji.* Chant this mantra, pulling in on your navel point on each *"Sat Naam"* and on each *"Wahe Guru."* Chant, using the tip of your tongue to strike the upper palate. This will stimulate the hypothalmus. One repetition of the mantra is 8 seconds; each phrase is 1 second.

Time: Done in class for 10-1/2 minutes.

End: Inhale very deeply, hold for 10 seconds while you press back as hard as you can on the mudra, shoulders, elbows, etc. Cannon fire the breath out. Repeat 3 times total. Relax.

Comments/Effects: At first it may hurt to put as much pressure on the back and chest as is being asked for, but just hold it still, and it will begin to work itself out. The pressure is required to open up the chest and the energy channels in the spine. This will allow the energy to ascend to the heights. Do not allow yourself to relax the pressure as the meditation carries on.

Becoming a Sage in the Aquarian Age

If you take what I have said, and say to yourself, "I'm going to follow it," you will be a sage of the Aquarian Age.

The tragedy is that you don't understand life. You believe that you are born, you grow up, and that you are going to die. You want to be healthy, you want to live. But you don't understand that there is an action and reaction in this life, and there is an action and performance because of your previous life. The tragic thing which you don't understand is that there will be an action and reaction to the life you choose. The majority of people have come as a human just to choose their next animal life. Some of you are not going to be human again. It's the way it is.

So, you are not human. You cannot bisect or dissect or disengage yourself from the entanglement of impulse and passion. As long as a person is entangled with this passion and impulse, he is an animal. Whether you look human or not doesn't make any difference. It has to be understood, but the whole humanity is not willing to understand.

If you tell a person, "Well, let's sit down and understand." You can sit with that person for two hours, three hours, and five minutes later he'll be doing the same damn thing he was doing three hours ago. That is a person of impulse.

You may tell a person, "Don't do it." He will agree with everything, fine. Not only will he not do what you tell him, he will do the opposite. Why? There's no understanding. When in a human the understanding is impulse, you are a beast. There are three parts of you: beast, human, and angel.

So what we are talking about with all this *pad* business *(YB is referring to saram pad, shakti pad, etc.).* These are steps in understanding. But the question is, "Are you a human?" That's the first question. Have you conquered your urge to act from impulse, or are you going to act from intuition? It's very important that you simply divide it. The majority of the time you act in a very high-grade angelic way. Sometimes you are very compassionately human. But sometimes you are a brute, like an animal. This varies depending on which chakra you are coming from; from which chakra are you shooting the strength out, to achieve what goal? I am just asking you one thing: What is your goal in life? Can we dialogue about it? What do you think is your goal in life? You are all educated, you are mature, you are full-fledged, and we are just friends. Let's talk simply. Yes?

Student: To realize the Divine.

YB: If you say this again, Divine will come down and punch your face. He sent you on Earth not to realize Him. This is spiritual nonsense. Everybody here is insane, absolutely. You should go to a mental hospital. "You have come to realize the Divine." Who told you that? There's no Divine—you are divine. But you are realizing the Divine somewhere else. There's no divine but you. So don't try to realize anything but you. Yes?

S: Teach.

YB: That's easy.

S: To produce a Teacher ten times better than yourself.

YB: Yes, well that you will do. That I'm asking of you. What is the purpose you want?

S: To be, to be.

S: To live my destiny.

S: To learn how to be a friend.

S: To replace karma with dharma.

YB: Hmm. These are procedures. All you have said is procedure. What is the motive, what do you want to be?

S: Nothing.

S: Liberated.

YB: That's the worst of all, this "liberated" business. When I gave the concept of a liberated man, I never said, "get liberated." It's beautiful to be here in all this suffering and misery, and people, and lies, and tragedies. Without all this drama there's no life. It's fun; this whole thing is a fun. It's people's insanity. You know how enjoyable it is to see somebody insane and thanking God it's not you? You know what I mean?

There was a girl, I asked her, "What do you want to do?"

She said, "What do you think I'm gonna do?"

I said, "In three months you are going to be sexed. In four, five months you are going to be sick."

She said, "No. I'm a good girl."

I said, "Well, let's write it down." Later on they brought her to me and she was absolutely distraught. I had to say, "Wahe Guru."

"Why did it happen to me?" she said.

I said, "You were inviting it. I told you that you were projecting a wrong purpose of life."

If you do not have the purpose of your life, all purposes of life will not fit in. You don't understand that there is a problem in us. We are not born to suffer. We suffer because we don't have motivation, we don't have purpose. We think if we are making "x" amount of money, we are fine, if we have "x" amount of sex, we are fine, if we have "x" amount of security, we are fine. We have a judgment on everything. That's what our measurement is, but this measurement is ridiculous.

You want to be happy. You think you are happy if a girl gets a boy. But when she gets the boy, then she suffers. What did you get? Do you know what should be your motive? I know— I have counseled too much, and I know how rudely inferior you are as humans. Rudely inferior. It's not on a small scale. I don't want to use abusive language, but you are rude to yourself, you are low grade in your thinking, and you are poor in your imagination. And religion has made it worse. What religion has taught is to create a mental coercive stage of slaves. Religion didn't do anything to free you. Go ahead and be.

When I came to the United States and we became Sikh Dharma, religion was forced on us. You have to understand, I am very anti-religion. I know all the loopholes, I studied every religion. And I said, "Why do we have to be Sikhs? What nonsense is this? Forget it."

Then I thought, "Wait a minute. There is one way to do it. Give them *bana*, give them *bani*, give them *seva*, give them *simran*, put them out in the market, and if by self-consciousness they will survive, they will automatically become intuitive."

What is the power in life?
With all the ungraceful dirt,
nonsense,
you remain graceful.

I took a very calculated risk. I said, "What do I want to have Sikhs for?" I said, "If they can stand amongst 250 million Americans, looking totally different, dealing differently, not saying "hello," but saying "*Sat Naam*," then let us see what happens."

Well, some people came out really great. If you get into yourself in totality, you have reality. I don't study books and I don't do this, I don't do that. I'm fine. You see, I have a purpose in my life. I know I am hypoglycemic, and I know that my days are full of grief, I have to hear everybody's dirt, and that I'm an easy target. I'm the most dishonored man. What I came from and what I live through is inhuman. There is no human who has those conditions, and nobody has tragedy like me. I have to hear everybody's tragedy. But I know that I am just a vehicle for dirt, and that's what I am. I understand it, though I do not like it. But this is the job I have to do. So I say to myself, "Okay."

I am sick. I am very seriously ill. Try to understand. I am very seriously ill, and I am absolutely in the greatest tragedy of life. I can't trust anybody. I love everybody. It's not that I didn't make money. I made money and I made people. But I was also betrayed, I was lied to. I went through a hell that you can't go through. You can't even spell it. But what does it matter? I'm a garbage cleaner of the United States. I got the first title, "The greatest garbage cleaner of the United States." I still have that robe with the "U.S. Garbage Collector" label sewn in it.

So there has always been a purpose. The purpose did not include taking care of myself, and I flew left, I flew right, I went in, I went out—worked eighteen-twenty hours a day. I took a calculated risk because I thought, "I have to build people, I have to build a nation, I have to leave these teachings, I want to give something to America, because America gave me shelter." I came to America to ruin Russia. I'm not denying it. It was my simple thing. I didn't like the Soviet Union, and I single-handedly had to fight it. I had to. So I came to the West to seek help. To me, Communism is nothing but capitalism for a few people. That's all. I have a Master's in Economics, I understand. I'm not a fool. Communism is nothing. It's a tragedy. They said that in Russia everybody had a house. What house? A one room apartment and nine people living there with two dogs? You call that a house? "Oh, no, everybody has shelter. Everybody has food." What food? Now, when their economy fell, the people realized, "Oh, my God, we have been lying to ourselves."

What is a country and who are the people? Do you know that atomic reactor accident at Chernobyl was nothing but an insanity of two engineers who tried to test how much it can stand? Do you know how many hundreds and thousands of people just went, "Woosh?" And nobody talks about it.

What is the purpose of life?
To elevate all, big or small.

So what is the purpose of life? Have you decided what? Do you know?

S: The purpose is to do something in time that will last forever.

YB: Try it. Good luck.

S: To merge into the *Naam*.

YB: That's what Guru Nanak said. Forget Guru Nanak at the moment. Look, can we just be ourselves?

S: To get our popcorn and coke and to enjoy the show.

YB: *(YB points at that girl and smiles.)* The purpose of life is to watch and experience living. That is the purpose of life. To enjoy living, every moment of it. Because the priceless breath of life will never come back again. And to live in environments which are calm, quiet, slow, sophisticated, elegant. Just to be. Whether you are naked or you have a golden robe on you, that doesn't make any difference. The ideal purpose of your life is that you are grateful—great and full—that you are alive, and you enjoy it.

What is the best in life, folks? Come on. What is the best in life? Humor. Enjoy living, have a sense of humor. Correct?

Class: Yes, Sir.

YB: And what is the power in life?

S: Strength to sacrifice.

YB: Un uh. *(YB shakes his head "no.")*

S: Love?

YB: Grace. With all ungraceful dirt, nonsense, you remain graceful.

What is the faith of life?

S: *Sat Naam.*

YB: *Sat Naam* is the faith of life. Your true identity and you are God. "God and me, me and God are One." That's the faith of life.

What is the purpose of life? To elevate all, big or small.

What is the reality of life? Incur no more karma. If you incur more karma, the cycle of birth and death will continue. You can't afford it. You want to be free. You want to go Home.

If you take what I have said, and say to yourself, "I'm going to follow it," you will be a sage of the Aquarian Age.

What can you do which God cannot do? Let me put it directly: You all talk of sex and potency and impotency. How potent are you and how impotent is God? If you are more potent than God, what can you do which God cannot do? It's a question. Don't you know the answer?

S: Create another human being.

YB: You can create another being like youself. God cannot create another God better than Him. It's a male energy. It is surrounded by the female, *Prakirti*. *Purkha* cannot create another *Purkha*, whereas the human body—*Purkha* with *Prakirti*—can create another *Purkha*.

You have many faculties. You can act like God, you can be God, and you can create like God. But God can't. God can only create you in His Image. You cannot be created until you do not have karma, and you cannot get rid of karma until you have absolute dharma to guide you. God is very clever. He doesn't want everybody to come back. You know what I mean? I see His business. He is like a mother who gets tired of the kids, He says, "Go and play in the karma, and come back three days later. I need a rest." So God has given you to Mother Nature, and gives you birth. "Go, go, go, go, and play your play." He created maya in that play, so:

ਪਲਚਿ ਪਲਚਿ ਸਗਲੀ ਮੁਈ ਝੂਠੈ ਧੰਧੈ ਮੋਹੁ ॥

Palach palach sagalee mu-ee jhootai dhandhai mo-ho.
>-Guru Arjan, *Siri Guru Granth Sahib*, page 133
Everybody dies suffering in false entanglements with worldly things.

In your love of all these entanglements, you get involved and your karma increases and increases, and keeps you going.

Once somebody had a great aura, a great arcline. I used to enjoy it. But it went totally out of the window. Out of curiosity, one day I looked at it, and I said to the person, "What happened?"

"I don't know."

It is like losing a diamond and putting a cubic zirconia in its place and calling it a diamond. Where have you learned this ridiculous behavior? You have a diamond-like life, and priceless *prana,* and you just play these little games here, there? What for? What do you want to get out of it? Nothing. You miss a chance.

Once a girl said to me, "I am in love with this man."

I said, "Okay, thank you." Well, what should I say?

Then a minute later she said, "I am in love with you, too."

I said, "It can't happen."

"Well, why not?"

I said, "If you would have loved me, you would have come to where I am. If you are in love with somebody, that's your level; you are stuck. It's a long staircase. I wish you should love me, come to where I am. I want you to love me. I need somebody to love me. Love me, but come to where I am. Don't love me and bring me down to where you are. That's not love."

Love you? Love you for what? You have a golden chance which God gave to you, and which you can enjoy and use. It is my sincere prayer that everybody should use this chance, become a teacher, serve others, elevate others, cut down the shackles of the karma of others. Don't incur more karma. Balance it out. Go home with a smile, and what Nanak says may come true:

ਜਿਨੀ ਨਾਮੁ ਧਿਆਇਆ ਗਏ ਮਸਕਤਿ ਘਾਲਿ ॥
ਨਾਨਕ ਤੇ ਮੁਖ ਉਜਲੇ ਕੇਤੀ ਛੁਟੀ ਨਾਲਿ ॥

Jinee naam dhi-aa-i-aa, ga-ay masakat ghaal.
Naanak tay mukh ujalay, kaytee chhutee naal.
>-Guru Nanak, *Siri Guru Granth Sahib*, page 8, (Slok of *Japji Sahib*)
Those who dwell on the Name, and depart after putting in their efforts in the
right direction. Shining are their faces and they save many others.

Let me translate for the Age of Aquarius, not the literal translation you have: "Nanak, those who have purified their identity—*Jinee naam dhi-aa-iaa*: Those who have micro- and macro-consciously looked at their identity of Self. *Ga-ay masakat ghaal*: those who have done this great, hard job, this very difficult task. *Naanak tay mukh ujalay*: Nanak, they have beautiful, bright, and bountiful faces. *Ketee chhutee naal*: They left their karma here, forever."

The purpose of visiting Earth and being a human is to unload your karma here, not to carry it to the next life. That's the purpose. That's why you serve the Master. You don't love the Master, you don't learn from the Master. Learn what you can learn. You have everything in you. You can learn from books from the library, but you learn from the Master how to surrender. You do not understand that there is a catch-22. When you surrender, the karma surrenders, too. You rise like a phoenix rises from the ashes, and the karma remains behind. Then it's the Master's headache. That's a fact. You don't understand. Nobody has taught you. I understand you are all spiritual, and God bless you. But you are all blind. So the blind leads the blind into the pit. Actually, when a human consciousness surrenders to the Master, and along with that the karma surrenders and is left behind, the man rises. That's how you break the shackle of karma.

ਜੇ ਸਉ ਚੰਦਾ ਉਗਵਹਿ ਸੂਰਜ ਚੜਹਿ ਹਜਾਰ ॥
ਏਤੇ ਚਾਨਣ ਹੋਦਿਆਂ ਗੁਰ ਬਿਨ ਘੋਰ ਅੰਧਾਰ ॥

Je sa-o chandaa ogav-eh sooraj char-eh hazaar.
Aytay chaanan hoodiaa(n), gur bin ghor andhaar
-Guru Nanak, *Siri Guru Granth Sahib*, page 463
If a hundred moons arise and a thousand suns appear,
even with such light, there would be pitch darkness without the Guru.

"If there are a hundred thousand moons, and there are a hundred thousand suns, without the Guru there's no light. There's darkness."

Why was this said? Why? Because it's a fact. Somebody asked me, "Why should I surrender?"

I said, "Wait a minute. If your consciousness has not become that Infinite, that you in nothing can see and experience that Oneness, why do you think the shackle of karma will go away?"

"So that's another way of interpretation."

I said, "No, it's not an interpretation. It's a fact."

Who can tell you about surrender, about marriage, and love, and relationship?

ਧਨ ਪਿਰੁ ਏਹਿ ਨ ਆਖੀਅਨਿ ਬਹਨਿ ਇਕਠੇ ਹੋਇ ॥
ਏਕ ਜੋਤਿ ਦੁਇ ਮੂਰਤੀ ਧਨ ਪਿਰੁ ਕਹੀਐ ਸੋਇ ॥

Dhan pir ay-eh na aakhee-an bahen ikathay ho-eh.
Ayk jot du-eh mooratee dhan pir kehee-ai so-eh
-Guru Amar Das, *Siri Guru Granth Sahib*, page 788
They are not said to be husband and wife, who merely sit together.
They alone are called husband and wife, who have one light in two bodies.

"Don't call them great, those who sit together, love together, be together, enjoy together. *Ayk jot du-eh mooratee*: One soul in two bodies, they are great." That means a merger. You merge. You have the surge of life, and urge of life to merge in the Oneness of the Self.

Some people waste their entire life showing off that they are somebody. Some people waste their entire life rebelling. Some people are egomaniac neurotics; they will build themselves into a millionaire, and then destroy it. What a drama! What is this? Have you seen some people? With all that God has given to them, they are very ungrateful. They will plead poor, they will plead miserable.

People ask me, "How is your health?"

I say, "Fine. Better than yesterday." Because yesterday I was very sick, and today I am alive. So it's better than yesterday. Anyway, why are sickness and disease so bad? What is wrong with them? After all, this is the most athletic body, it was built like steel. It's a body of a Mahan Tantric, a Yogi. It was given for forty-eight years, and the poor thing has extended itself to sixty-seven or something. What do you want with this body, to live forever? I'm not supposed to be sick and die? After all, there has to be a reason to kill it. This body is just like a shirt. How long do you wear a shirt, sweaty and torn—what do you want to do with it? I don't want a new shirt. I want to go to the land of the absolute nude—that's called God. You know the other name of God? "The Land of the Absolute Nude." And you can enter it through the Valley of Death.

What is the reality of life? Incur no more karma. If you incur more karma, the cycle of birth and death will continue. You can't afford it. You want to be free. You want to go Home.

You have not heard me speak on death. I'm fantastic, because I know it. Do you know what your real name is? "Living Trouble." We are funny. We are really funnies, like those funnies that appear in the newspaper everyday. And sometimes we are very funny. For sympathy we create empathy, we create loneliness. These people are lying.

One day a girl told me, "This man is telling me this, this, this, this."

I said, "He just wants to have sex with you, and you believe in free sex. One day have the sex, see what he does."

"Oh no, he's serious."

I said, "You wanna bet? Ten dollars to a hundred. How much?"

She said, "One hundred."

I said, "Okay." I won the bet. They had sex for three, four, five days. Later on he said, "I'll call you, don't call me." She was very desperate when she called me.

She said, "God. It was another blunder."

I said, "Well, what about my bet? I want my money. I want to see green notes. I want my money. A bet is a bet."

She said, "Why did I do it?"

I said, "That's a separate session. Why you did it, why you do it, why you're doing it all the time. What's wrong with you is that it's a fantasy. But that has nothing to do with the bet. Please, first pay me, and then I'll talk to you."

You know, sometimes in counseling I say to people, "I will charge another fifty bucks," because in Kundalini Yoga you don't teach without payment. You do not take personal obligation. You are paid up-front. The principle is: *If you ever come empty-handed, you shall go empty-handed.* It's a law which should never be broken. If somebody comes empty-handed, send him back empty-handed. Not that we are greedy and we have to have money. Not that. But there's a principle involved in it. You earn to learn.

(See page 170 for details of this meditation.)

You feel very relaxed today. You will do this meditation for sixty-two minutes, because tonight we have to do a most powerful *kriya*. So I need you to have the faculty to deal with it, otherwise we'll not be right. I'm just pre-preparing you.

Dancing Hand Meditation

Mudra: Sit in Easy Pose, with a straight spine. Bend the elbows down into the sides of the body. Bring the hands up in front of each shoulder, palms facing forward. Make a loose fist, with the thumb on the outside of the fingers, and extend the Jupiter (index) fingers straight up towards the ceiling.

Movement: Start to rotate the hands and the arms from the wrist to the elbow, in a half circle. This is not just a movement of the wrists, but involves the forearms, also. Begin with the hands held in front of the shoulders, backs of the hands facing the body (**a**). Then rotate around (right hand moves counter-clockwise, and left hand moves clockwise) until you end up with the palms facing the body (**b**). Then immediately return to the beginning position. Move very fast; it is almost as if you are "dancing" your hands, forearms and fingers. Flow with it, enjoy it, and get into it. This is a very relaxed movement. There should be no tension in the hands, wrists, elbows or forearms.

Music: *Dhuni* is played.

Mantra: *Sat Naam, Sat Naam, Sat Naam Ji, Waa-hay Guroo, Waa-hay Guroo, Waa-hay Guroo Ji*, is the mantra which goes along with this tape, but does not indicate to sing aloud. Rhythm is one complete repetition of the mantra in 8 seconds; 1 complete movement (**a & b**) per second.

Eyes: Yogi Bhajan closed his eyes while demonstrating the exercise.

Time: 62 minutes.

End: Inhale deep, and relax.

Comments/Effects: Let there be absolutely no tension in the forearm and elbow area. Let the movement be very loose, relaxed and lively. Feel there is no weight at all from the elbow to the wrist area.

This meditation was done as a preparation for the meditation that was to be done that evening. The Dancing Hand Meditation opens and relaxes the heart meridian, (one of the meridians in the forearm area), thus allowing for a deeper experience in that evening's class.

Emotional Compensation

Emotional compensation is your biggest enemy. When you start emotionally compensating yourself, then your intelligence, your growth, your width, your height, your altitude are all gone. It is like living drunk.

We are now talking about emotional compensation. Have you heard that term before?

Class: Yes, Sir.

YB: Emotional compensation is a factual state of mind of a person through which his faculty is subconsciously guided. We put everything into the subconscious. Is that understandable?

Class: Yes, Sir.

YB: So when you put everything into the subconscious, the subconscious picks up certain areas and then starts guiding you. Those who are guided by their subconscious are never intelligent. Period. As they say, "Intellectuals are great, but intellectuals are never intelligent." It is because the intellect wraps you up, and once you are wrapped up by the intellect, you will never be in a position to perform. You will see a lot of intellectuals in coffeehouses. That's where they hang out. They drink coffee, keep on talking, drink coffee, keep on talking, drink coffee, keep on talking. That's what they do. Intellectuals are among those who, if you give them any practical job, will not do it. A physical intellectual will often end up as a masseuse. They love to massage other people because they can't massage themselves. These are sicknesses which you practically can't even discuss, because the attitude of a person is that the person is lonely. And a lonely person wants to make a connection, but, in that connection, you have a problem.

Emotional compensation is your biggest enemy. When you start emotionally compensating yourself, then your intelligence, your growth, your width, your height, your altitude are all gone. It's like living drunk. In emotional compensation you do a most foolish thing. You want to have your cake and eat it, too. Then you want to do what you want. Emotional compensation is one thing which will keep you lonely, because emotional compensation feeds the ego. It does not enhance your spirit. That's the worst part of it. You are in conflict: "I want to be me, and on the other hand I want to be that, I want to be this, I want...." Have you seen that with some people you can't even talk? You can't be with them.

The tragedy of a person is not what you think. The tragedy of a person is that if you are foolish, if you are emotional, if you are not honorable, then you are exploitable. If you are not spiritual, not strong, not morally high, then you are exploitable, and why should you not be exploitable? Everybody has to exploit something to live. You are exploited in eight ways: sexually, sensually, physically, personally, mentally, monetarily, socially, and psychically exploited. These are the exploitations. Everybody wants you and you want everybody. That's the war. It is a psychic war.

But there is a price for everything. Some people want to become healers without spiritually uplifting themselves. Without knowledge of anatomy and the proper experience, they want to become a masseuse. Some people want to be Teachers, but where is the character? Where are the characteristics?

What is psychology? You lie down on a sofa, you tell your story, "Uh huh, ooh, aah haa." Actually, you vomit it out, and you feel relieved. Then he tells you: "Well, you know, take a middle line."

What is love? It's a compensatory bewitchment in which you do not know yourself. Unawareness is your love bewitchment. If you love yourself, if you are in ecstasy, who can you love, who can you know, what can you do?

So there is a price for everything, and we all pay the price. I have seen people who have millions and millions of dollars. They are young, they are successful, and they are in great pain. There is no fulfillment in the mind of a person who does not know how to surrender. That's your problem. Instead of surrendering, you do a very powerful compensatory process. Once you surrender, the karma surrenders with it; and once the karma surrenders with it, you are free. Then you can adopt Dharma. The moment you are in Dharma, and Dharma is your priority, you will never be subject to karma—you are free, you are liberated, you are fine. You are yourself. And then you enjoy yourself. You say what you feel, you do what you feel, you are an elevated self. It's very fine, it's very neat.

But then you can't use this emotional compensation. With it comes mental compensation, social compensation, personal compensation, creative compensation, God, it takes you through hell. Is there any chance you can be you?

The beauty of the whole thing is it's not necessary. We are not fools when we tell you, "Get up in the morning and have a cold shower." All we want is the blood to circulate through the capillaries, and there's no way to open the capillaries but to take a cold shower. There's no other way. In the West it is called "hydrotherapy." In the East it's called "ishnaan." It's a most beautiful thing. When you take a cold shower, the blood from inside hits the outside to cover the attack. In that fast movement, it opens the capillaries. When the capillaries are open, they feed your glands, and when a glandular system is well-fed, it secretes. The chemistry of your blood becomes perfect. That gives you a capacity to act, think, know; and it gives you grit, stamina. What is so bad about that? But people cannot take cold showers, because it costs nothing. You want to do something special which you can talk about.

I was talking to a lady in Los Angeles. She said, "Oh, I have to go to my shrink. I have an appointment."

And I said, "Go ahead, then we'll speak later."

She went to the shrink, and he said, "Where were you, you are a little late?"

She said, "Well, on the way, I saw Yogi Bahan."

"Oh," he said, "my teacher?" He said, "I used to study with him."

So a week later she came to me and said, "I want an appointment with you."

I said, "I don't do that work."

"Oh, you were talking to me that day."

I said, "That was my compassion. I was kind to you."

"Well, I really want you as my counselor."

I said, "Five thousand dollars a minute. Write a check. We'll talk."

"You are mad at me."

I said, "No, I'm not mad at you. I know how sick you are, and I know how much you should pay to get hurt, so what could I say that you will hear? You don't value free counseling."

With emotional compensation comes mental compensation, social compensation, personal compensation, and creative compensation. God, it takes you through hell. Is there any chance you can be you?

Because in our concept of life, we have a conception. We have all these conceptions, and we are all compensations. Then when are we going to be we? You are not emotional compensation, and you are not this, you are not that. You are you.

Now look in yourself for a few minutes; and see how you do it to everybody but God. Come on. Close your eyes and watch, and see. Admit it.

(Silence for about 30 seconds.)

Now open your eyes and look at me, and see how many times in your life you have done wrong, and found that the root cause of all of it is emotional compensation?

"Now this is my son, this is my daughter. Oh, this is my friend. Oh, this is my this, this is my that." Then you want to control, guide, counsel—so many things. Why? What do you do? Emotional compensation. But you cannot confront and cannot correct. You deal with it with emotional compensation.

The Teacher's first job is to confront. Hey, there is something better than all that you have—that is human fulfillment. It's very high, it's priceless. It's very wonderful. It's elegant. Fulfillment is not a small thing. Achievement—what is it your achievement? You can't achieve anything. Because you are doing...?

Class: ...emotional compensation.

YB: Everything is so important to you emotionally. Is there anything important to you, really? A child comes and starts laying a tantrum, you start giving him money. Money, honey, bunny—you wrap everything around it. Or you don't want to fight. You are scared.

Then there is a split personality problem, where you create an alternative personality. A normal person has sixteen personalities. So technically you do not know if you are talking with "A," or you are talking with "D," or you are talking with "G," or you are talking with "F." You have no idea. That's why we are the way we are. Let's get out of it, should we?

Class: Yes, Sir.

(See pages 176-177 for the details of this meditation.)

YB: This is a kriya which you have to do sitting on your heels. Do you have that tape of...

ਆਦੇਸੁ ਤਿਸੈ ਆਦੇਸੁ ॥ ਆਦਿ ਅਨੀਲੁ ਅਨਾਦਿ ਅਨਾਹਤਿ ਜੁਗੁ ਜੁਗੁ ਏਕੋ ਵੇਸੁ ॥

Aadays tisai aadays. Aad aneel anaad anaahat jug jug ayko vays.

-Guru Nanak, *Siri Guru Granth Sahib*, page 7, (30th pauri of *Japji Sahib*)

I salute God again and again. God is primal and pure, with unknown beginning, Who cannot be destroyed, and Who remains the same through all the ages.

I don't think we have that tape. All right, put your hands up, let's do it—we'll make the tape later, or this will become a tape.

(Class begins chanting in a spoken monotone. Every word is spoken very distinctly with a slight pause between each word, except "jug-jug" is run together as one word.)

YB: Very good. From the navel. Eyes at the tip of the nose. Keep on. Today you either win or you lose. It's up to you.

YB: Don't give up! Steady, steady. Cross the pain, cross the pain! Steady and sturdy.

Stretch your arms, get sturdy. Come on. Stretch, stretch!

From the navel! From the navel!

Thirty seconds.

Inhale. Hold the breath. Squeeze the spine. Exhale. Inhale deep. Hold tight. Squeeze the spine from base to top. Relax.

You've done a good job. Sit down at peace. How was it?

It's not a small exercise. You have to sit on the heels, so you will never have a digestive problem. And when you do this, you will never have *any* problem.

These are the words of Nanak who was such a great Teacher. He went to the *siddhas*, the perfect ones, and corrected them. You know, things don't come easily. You have to pay for them. This is a salutation to the Infinite—to the God beyond the Infinite God. *Aadays tisai ades. Aad aneel anaad anaahat, jug jug ayko vays.* It means: "I salute Thee, and I salute Thee who is in the beginning: *Aad aneel.* Through all the specifics: *Anaad anaahat.* Through all self and selfless, and throughout all time you will remain the same: *Jug jug ayko vays.*" If you just learn this *Pauree* of *Japji*, make it as a routine, the entire knowledge of the entire universe and beyond the universe will come to you without reading a book. In this *sutra* is initiation of that knowledge which is in all of you.

ਏਕਾ ਮਾਈ ਜੁਗਤਿ ਵਿਆਈ ਤਿਨਿ ਚੇਲੇ ਪਰਵਾਣੁ

Ayk maa-eh jugat viaa-ee, tin chalay parvaan.

There's One mother, who is married to time and she has accepted the trinity, the three chelas, the three disciples.

ਇਕੁ ਸੰਸਾਰੀ ਇਕੁ ਭੰਡਾਰੀ ਇਕੁ ਲਾਏ ਦੀਬਾਣੁ

Ik sansaaree, ik bhandhaaree, ik laa-ay deebaan.

One creates, one sustains, one assesses, so he Destroys or Delivers.

ਜਿਵ ਤਿਸੁ ਭਾਵੈ ਤਿਵੈ ਚਲਾਵੈ ਜਿਵ ਹੋਵੈ ਫੁਰਮਾਣੁ

Jiv tis bhaavai, tivai chalaavai, jiv hovai furmaan.

As God wishes and pleases Him, that's how everything runs, and that's how He commands. Then there's a very beautiful line:

ਓਹੁ ਵੇਖੈ ਓਨਾ ਨਦਰਿ ਨ ਆਵੈ ਬਹੁਤਾ ਏਹੁ ਵਿਡਾਣੁ

Oh vekhai ohnaa nadar na(n) aavai bahotaa ayho vidaan.

God sees everything, but we can't see Him. That's the biggest surprise for us.

ਆਦੇਸੁ ਤਿਸੈ ਆਦੇਸੁ

Aadays tisai aadays.

Aadays means the message from the Infinite. This is the salutation of the yogi.

ਆਦਿ ਅਨੀਲੁ ਅਨਾਦਿ ਅਨਾਹਤਿ

Aadays tisai aadays. Aad aneel anaad anaahat.

From the beginning, now, through the time and ever He's Infinite.

ਜੁਗੁ ਜੁਗੁ ਏਕੋ ਵੇਸੁ

Jug jug ayko vays.

From all times He has that, that form. That is His appearance.

Feel good?

Class: Yes, Sir.

YB: A little spaced out, though. If we would have pulled it another ten minutes, we would have a very different experience. So proceed with it slowly. It is not that you have to become a *siddha yogi* in one day. This meditation gives the *siddhis*, the occult powers we talk about?

There are two most powerful things. One we are going to do tomorrow; one we have done today. And we are going to be fine. We are going for the gold. Come on, this is Planet Earth, we are in Espanola, it's nice. We are the same people. I will tell you how we used to do it. Sit on the heels. *Aadays tisai aadays. Aad aneel anaad anaahat, jug jug ayko vays. Aadays tisai aadays.* See my hands? They are old, trained hands. You will not find a bend in the elbow. They are trained. Oh God, sometimes you feel such a fire in the spine! You enjoy it. And for the love of that, you want to do it. Good night.

Meditation to Get Rid of
Fear & Split Personalities

Mudra: Sit on your heels with a straight spine. Stretch the arms straight out in front, parallel to the ground. The palms are flat and facing the ground, fingers pointing straight forward. The arms will be shoulder-width apart.

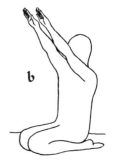

Movement: Alternate between (a) and (b) in the following way:

Begin in position (a)

Aadays	(b) Raise the arms up to 60 degrees
Tisai	(a) Bring the arms parallel to the ground in front
Aadays	(b) Arms up to 60 degrees
Aad	(a) Arms straight in front
Aneel	(b) Arms up to 60 degrees
Anaad	(a) Arms straight in front
Anaahat	(b) Arms up to 60 degrees
Jug-jug	(a) Arms straight in front
Ayko	(b) Arms up to 60 degrees
Vays	(a) Arms straight in front

Continue, keeping the hands and elbows held straight out firmly, and with no bend, fingers pointing straight forward, chin pulled slightly in, and spine straight. This is done in a precise beat, done with a projection of strength.

Mantra: *Aadays tisai aadays, aad aneel anaad anaahat, jug jug ayko vays.* This mantra is spoken in a continuous monotone. Each word is spoken individually, with a slight pause between each word, except *"jug jug"* —which is run together as one word. Speak from the navel point.

Eyes: Tip of the nose.

Time: Done in class for about 23-1/2 minutes

End: Inhale deeply, stretch the spine, and hold for 10 seconds. Exhale. Repeat one more time. Relax.

Comments/Effects: This mudra will help you get rid of fear. Fear is the cause of all emotional compensation—which is the cause of many personality imbalances and behavioral problems.

A normal person has anywhere from sixteen to twenty split personalities. These are personalities we have created to deal with life. When you are speaking with a person, you don't know just who you are really talking to. This meditation will help to correct this problem.

This mantra is a salutation to the Infinite God. Its meaning is:

ਆਦੇਸੁ ਤਿਸੈ ਆਦੇਸੁ ॥
ਆਦਿ ਅਨੀਲੁ ਅਨਾਦਿ ਅਨਾਹਤਿ ਜੁਗੁ ਜੁਗੁ ਏਕੋ ਵੇਸੁ ॥

Aades tisai aadays. Aad aneel anaad anaahat jug jug ayko vays.

  -Guru Nanak, *Siri Guru Granth Sahib*, page 7, (30th *pauree* of *Japji Sahib*)
*I salute God again and again. God is primal and pure, with unknown
beginning, Who cannot be destroyed, and Who remains the same
through all the ages.*

With practice, this mantra can give you *siddhis*, spiritual powers. A secondary effect of this meditation is that by sitting on your heels, you can help to clear away any digestive problems.

Proceed with the practice of this meditation slowly. Do not over do it at first, as it can space you out too much.

Projecting as a Teacher

How are you going to fit in? How are you going to come out of
your shell? How are you going to come out of your cocoon?
How are you going to deal with everybody with openness of self?
How can you open so much that you can embrace everything?
How can you close yourself so that you can be.

Y ou have been here for a week. How much have you learned so far? What do you think you have learned?

Student: To surrender.

YB: No. Who wants it? There's nobody to accept the surrender. People have the most non-sense idea on the planet, that you surrender and somebody's going to accept it. Forget it. Nobody wants it.

You have come here to be teachers. You should understand something about life. Life is not what you think. Life is not what you want. Life is not in surrender. Life is not in revolt. Life is not in disobedience. Life is not in obedience. Life is in life, which must be accepted, must be lived, must be recognized, must be organized. It must be mutual in essence. There are three stages. If there is a truth, it will be universal and mutual to all. If it is an ego, it will be mutual only to a few. If it is a neurosis, then it will be mutual only to you.

You know, when I came here, I had thirty-five dollars in my pocket; I still have that same thirty-five dollars, and I still have nothing, and I still have everything. It's a faculty of life. Nobody made me Siri Singh Sahib, nobody made me Yogi Bhajan. Nobody made me a Teacher. Your life has to accept *you* and your acceptance has to be projected out so everybody else can accept it.

You are willing to go out and project out, but if somebody does not accept it, what are you going to do? What do you think?

Student: It depends.

YB: See? "Depends." The idea in this life is not to depend. Never depend. That's what I wanted you to say: "It depends." We fluctuate. We are never exact. We don't know.

Take this as an example. I came from India. I was an officer. I used to wear a uniform. I had a five-point star on my shoulder. I only taught yoga in the embassies, to the ambassadors and that kind of thing. There was a Vishvayatna Yoga Ashram; it was one of the finest. I used to direct that, telling them what to do, what not to do. But all of a sudden, from a most uni-formed officer, I became a yogi. I never knew anybody, I never made all the arrangements, everything failed. But I didn't say, "I don't know." You know what I said?

One day the day shall come
When all the glory shall be Thine.
People will say , "It is yours,"
I shall deny: "Not mine!"
   -From a poem by the same name, by Yogi Bhajan[1]

This came out of those most painful, most treacherous, most troubled circumstances.

When you tell me you love me, I know you don't know what love is. Love is an Infinite sustenance. Love is not a relationship which can be wavered or challenged, or inferior or superior. There's no such thing. Love is forever. Love is a power. It is the love of the mission which carried me through, I understand that. You are gringos, you are Western, you do not know the dedication of love.

Oh yes, you are love makers, that's fine. That's okay. But what we are creating here is for the Age of Aquarius. We are not teaching here for the Piscean Age. You all have to die, one way or the other. The next twenty-one years is the cusp period—it will be difficult to survive. There'll be different diseases, viruses. Out! The whole thing is going to change. What are you going to do? "Maybe." What is "maybe" in life? You must have a command of the intuitive self to know exactly what you are, and you must fit in with everybody. That is your surrender—to bring mutuality to any non-reality, reality, lies, and truth—without judgment.

Can you understand my position? I can't see—all I see is the aura. The aura never lies. I can read the aura like a blind person reads braille. A person sits in my presence, he or she lies, and I say, "Yeah, yeah, yeah, you are right, you are right." What a lie I am telling. Why don't I get up and slap them across the face, take all the thirty-two teeth, put them in their hand and say, "Get out, you liar." Shouldn't I do that? No. Life is mutual.

Once in my life I started doing a foolish thing. I started reading people's minds. I scared everybody, so I stopped it. I said, "Never again." If people know you know everything or you know too much, they hate you. Nobody wants to know, nobody wants to be directed. Nobody wants to deal.

I know you, and I know myself. When my teacher said, "You are a Master," I accepted it. You all want to be Masters. Forget it. Surrender to being a Master within yourself—opportunity will come, reality will be at your door. But you can't play the way you play. One day you are correct, the next day you are so-so, the third day you are wrong, the fourth day you are right again. You are not willing to change yourself, how can you change anybody else? The first job of a teacher is to change. You don't want to change, how can you change others? You don't want to obey, how will people obey you? You don't want to excel, how can other people excel with you? Your P.R. is wrong.

A Teacher is not a human. A human is not a Teacher. It's a vehicle. It's a medium. Man is a medium, like money. Money is a medium. It does what you make it to do. So a human is a medium of the Teacher. A human is not a Teacher. Please don't misunderstand that. When a human is a Teacher, then we have human problems.

The first faculty of a Teacher is to identify to one's self that one is a Teacher. Then one must identify to the whole world that one is a Teacher. Third, one should know there's nothing else but a teacher. Those three things are essential. Let yourself know once and for all that you are a Teacher. Let the whole world know once and for all that you are Teacher. Less than this you are phony, you are a ruthless liar, you are good for nothing, you are a fake, and you have no reality whatsoever. I don't want to be more abusive than this, but if you can add something, it's fine.

As a Teacher you have to be real, you have to deliver. Similarly, if a woman cannot reflect the man, she's not a woman for that man. Period. If a man cannot grow and glow, he's not a man. What is it then? Living in a mess. There's no depth, no roots. Where will the nurturing come from?

The first faculty of a Teacher is to identify to one's self that one is a Teacher, and then identify to the whole world that one is a Teacher, and third, one should know there is nothing else but a Teacher.

Have you seen this Whole Life Expo? It's a very good business. One day I was given a pamphlet for it. There were hundreds and hundreds of therapies and hundreds and hundreds of ideas, and hundreds and hundreds of Teachers. They bifurcated almost every fiber of human existence and humanology. And I laughed. We were the only ones who were offering to teach something: "There will be a class taught in humanology by Yogi Bhajan." That's all. There were three lines. We are humans without humanology.

You have a life. How are you going to fit in? How are you going to come out of your shell? How are you going to come out of your cocoon? How are you going to deal with everybody with openness of self? How can you open so much that you can embrace everything? How can you close yourself so that you can be?

Student: Practice.

YB: Yes, discipline and practice, fine. But how are you going to do it fast? If you're a Teacher, you must be aware. If you want everybody's faults to be cured, don't be at fault yourself.

It doesn't matter how much you hide. Whatever you say, it will show up in the projection of your energy. Do you know what makes you corrupt? What makes you corrupt is the weakness of your habit, the weakness of your discipline, the weakness of your courage, the weakness of your strength. There are so many things. But nobody wants to be corrupt.

Once I interviewed a group of criminals who were all sentenced to death I said, "Let me see what they say." Not one person admitted that they had committed a crime. They each had a perfect story. Basically they all said that they had not been heard, and they were being unjustly punished.

So you have stories. But learn one story—excuse is a personal abuse. It's a self-abuse. It doesn't make sense.

Somebody once said, "I love God. I love God. I love God."

And God appeared and said, "Oh yes, I love you, too." Matter settled.

Six months later, God said, "Six months have gone by and you have never called on me."

"Now I love Shiva."

He said, "Oh? Well, okay." So God went and took Shiva by the hair, and threw him at her feet, and said, "You love this idiot?"

A Teacher is not a human. A human is not a teacher. It's vehicle. It's a medium. Man is a medium, like money. Money is a medium. It does what you make it to do. So a human is a medium of the Teacher. A human is not a Teacher. Please don't misunderstand that. When a human is a Teacher, then we have human problems.

"Oh, my Lord Shiva. Oh, my God, I actually love You."

And He said, "I don't know, you are confused." God disappeared, and so did Shiva.

The oneness of a person, or a teacher, or a human, is tested by the One God—it doesn't matter who you are. And when you cannot maintain the standard of your oneness, you shall never find the One which is ultimately the One.

Those who try to swim in two boats are torn at the crotch. Have you heard that slang? It is a very simple phrase. These are the ones who have "maybe's" and "may not be's." Think of split personalities, those who swim in nine boats, fifteen boats. What will happen? It looks good to spread out, but it won't come out right.

Your life has one authentic personality. You have one authentic projection. You have one pure self. Do not allow it to be polluted by maya—you will lose. What is the idea to get the one who is just one here and now, and lose the One who's in all, the One who is here, now and forever?

It is like the difference between taking a little oar and paddling with it or going another way: Why not go through life in a luxury liner, in the love boat? Life which is run by your neurosis shall always end up in the middle of a shark-infested ocean. You won't land on the other side of the port of entry.

Five and a half billion people live on this Earth, but you can count on your fingers the people who are internationally known by their spirit. You may have people internationally known by political office, by status. The American President is known internationally because of that office. Nobody knows Clinton. Clinton became known when he became President. It's not that Clinton was internationally known.

But the Dalai Lama is internationally known for his spirit. Pope John Paul II is internationally known for his spirit. "Yogi Bahan"[2] is internationally known for his spirit. They are known as they are—good and bad, right and wrong, up and down: whatever you call it, still they are known. It is called "The Essence of the Psyche Prevails with all Psyches." That has to be the level of a teacher who says what is right, not what is pleasing, wanting, or needing. Those three things you must avoid. Don't speak what is pleasing, wanting, or needing. You will never realize the truth. Speak what it is. And please avoid in your life "maybe," "I don't know," "perhaps." There's no affirmation in your life. Life is an affirmation.

I was counseling a teenage girl and I suggested something to her. She was beautiful. I said, "Come out of this duality and then we'll work it out."

She said, "No, no, no. I have to do this. I have to do that."

How much can you discuss? Let it go. What is there? Because maya creates the passion in a woman and a man. Like I was telling you, life is eighteen years. After eighteen years you just want to be united. Either you can unite your spirit, your soul, your discipline, your higher self, or you can just be choosing a physical partner. Well, remember when you choose a physical partner, that the Earth is not the Heavens. And then one thing leads to another.

All these girls who are going to be married never talk to somebody who is divorced, and ask, "Why?" They don't even feel their passion. That's what I saw when I came to America. Everybody was on drugs. Everybody. The Indians stopped sending smoke signals, but these humans were all living smoke signals. There was no party without drugs. And some people were pushing all the paraphernalia for it. It made it all very easy. Everybody slept with everybody. "I'll just have sex with everybody, I'll do everything." There was nothing. Nothing. And when I came, I started saying, "Drugs are a drag. There's a natural way to be high. Stop this. This is going to kill us." A lot of people did not listen. Finally they did.

Now I am saying "There's no religion without reality and royalty." Many people don't listen. But they will.

A teacher is a holy omen with a grace as an aspect, and excellence as a projection. I hope against hope by tonight you must have decided that you want to be a Teacher and nothing else. Tomorrow you can take the Teacher's Oath. You can take it ceremoniously that: "I am not a man, I am not a woman, I am not a person, I am not myself...."

Class: "...I am a Teacher."

YB: That's the purpose of this course. Then we'll see how many of you survive.

There's a catch-22: One who's a Teacher will never go hungry, will never go without. Prosperity, maya, *Prakirti*, serves the Teacher. That's a law. Everybody else is a hustler.

There are two ways to live. Either you be here, and let everything come to you; or you go after everything, and find what you want. Don't feel upset. I'm just telling you what is; you are hearing what you want to. But if you want to become a Teacher, become one now. It's useless when all the teeth are gone and the wolf says, "I am a vegetarian." It doesn't sound right.

When you will be my age and all kinds of things happen and don't happen, if you try to become very holy, it will be too late.

Gar jaavanee tobaa kardam, shevaa-e paigambar eest.
Vakte peeree, gurag-e jaalam
Me shavad parhez gaar.
          -Persian saying
If you prohibit yourself from negative and wrong things, do it when you are young.
That's the act of a Godly prophet. If the wolf becomes old, loses all his teeth, goes into
the jungle, and declares himself a vegetarian, who is going to believe him?

Gar jaavanee tobaa kardam: "If you want to say "no" and be pious, deny wrong things, do so when you are young." *Shevaa-e paigambar eest.* "This is the act of the prophet." *Vakte peeree, gurag-e jaalam:* "In the old days the bloody wolf, *Me shavad parhez gaar:* says 'Now I have become vegetarian.' Not right, not correct."

Kundalini. When that youthful energy of Infinity is vibrating in the impulse of a human, if it is not harnessed, it can never be harnessed. Is that understood?

Class: Yes, Sir.

YB: So God has brought you here for a purpose. Unfortunately, that's the chance. Do not deny it, do not let it go. Make it. "To be, not to be," is not the way. "To be, to be," is the only way. There's One God, One Path, One Discipline, One Achievement—that is to Be God.

(See page 186 for details of this meditation.)

Close your eyes and meditate. Show me how you like to look like a yogi.

Meditate on your being a yogi, on your purity, your honesty, your higher self.

(Class meditates silently for a few minutes.)

Please open your eyes. How many times a day do you meditate on yourself as a yogi? Since you have come here, how many days have you meditated on yourself as a yogi? How many times in your whole life have you meditated on yourself as an angel? How many times have you understood in your life that you are extremely and absolutely pure? How many times have you meditated and understood in your life that you are here at the Will of God, not by your will? I'm just suggesting these ways to meditate. I'm not asking you anything.

Kundalini Yoga says:

"All in self is the Self. Oh yogi, meditate and then find that precious, priceless gem of Self, and the whole world is yours."

We can't extend the course. Perhaps we will come sometime, next year, and learn.

In this life, the man who is not learned shall not enjoy. The purpose of life is happiness, and happiness is only for the learned. Even Almighty God cannot interfere. God is very Infinite. There's no punishment. But *Prakirti*, Mother Nature, spares nothing, spanks everything. That's the rule of thumb. Mama, Mama, mama-mia. Hurts. Because *Prakirti*, Mother of Time and Space, will never spare a human. No chance. No choice. Nothing. Good and bad is all the same. That's okay.

A Muslim friend of mine once said, "*Rabbul Raheem*: God is merciful. He'll forgive." What are you talking about?

I said, "But you have to go through the mama, and by the time you have gone through the mama, what will be left of you to go to God?"

He thought, "Well, I never thought of it that way."

I said, "You just blind people by telling them 'God is merciful, therefore, do whatever you want to do in the name of religion. Kill everybody.' Are you stupid? Don't you know, even God has to come through the *Prakirti*, has to take birth through the woman? How can you justify yourself that God is merciful, therefore kill everybody? That's why the Christians had their Crusades, that's why you did Jihad." I said, "What is this? What are you preaching? Religion which promises and promises and promises is not a religion. Religion is a reality which must be experienced by a human."

We had a good discussion. In the end he said, "Where did you learn from?"

I said, "Within myself."

From where do you learn? You don't learn from anybody. You learn within yourself. Everything you learn, you learn from your self-discipline. Anything you learn, you learn from self-ecstasy. Anything you want to learn, you learn from self-honor. The Self within one's self is a great teacher.

I hope tomorrow morning some of you, or all of you, would like to be honorable and self-pure, and find themselves fit in that experience to take an oath of discipline. We are going to write on your diploma, "So-and-so has taken the Oath of a Kundalini Yoga Teacher." It is an oath taken consciously to be a Teacher. On the other side we'll write, "This person has attended this Teachers Course with excellence." We'll praise you.

Meditation on Your Self as a Yogi

Mudra: Sit in a meditative posture of your choice. Close your eyes, and meditate on your being a yogi, on your purity, your honesty, your higher self. Meditate in complete silence.

Time: 7 minutes.

Comments/Effects: How many times a day do you meditate on yourself as a yogi? How many times in your whole life have you meditated upon yourself as an angel, that your being is absolutely pure, and that you are here by the Will of God and not by your own individual will?

All in self is the Self.
Oh yogi, meditate
and then find that precious,
priceless gem of Self,
and the whole world
is yours.

The Caliber of a Teacher

Caliber is the total capacity of an individual to communicate and to project one's identity. It is a combination of the total personality.

aliber. The main power of a male and a female is caliber. Caliber with endurance, courage, patience, manners, and communication—with a rhythm. Caliber is not an idealistic situation. Caliber is a combination of the total personality. The concept of caliber is very well known. Unfortunately, we do not develop caliber in ourselves. Instead, we develop personality, we develop identity, we develop knowledge, we have certifications. You may be certified as a Teacher, but you may not have the caliber of a Teacher. You can be a full-fledged, charming male, but you may not have the caliber of a male. You may be a very wonderful woman, but if your caliber is not that of a woman, then you are not a woman at all. In a woman's case, it is very unfortunate. When a woman does not have the caliber of a woman, she cannot have the character of a woman. Then she cannot have the characteristics of a woman, because of the balanced brain. It's a painless situation and an endless pain in a situation.

If he does not have caliber, a male shall have no roots. It's shocking. Every male and female are absolutely afraid to identify themselves, because they don't have caliber. They have organization, they have sense, they have knowledge. They are very intelligent people, very clear. But they don't have caliber. And you'll find sometimes men and women who will rise rapidly like a star, and then they come tumbling down. They fall apart, because they don't have the caliber to maintain their dignity, integrity, and their reality.

You know, it's not a question of who you are, and what you are, and how you are. There has to be a caliber to even have a day.

Human caliber is like the caliber of a gun. There's a gun called a twenty-two (a .22 caliber rifle or pistol), or there is a BB gun (a small air rifle that shoots .18 caliber lead shot), that is the smallest. Then there are high-caliber rifles. Now, take a pigeon and hit it with a .22, it'll be dead. With a BB gun, you can injure it. But if you use the high-caliber rifle, you'll end up with a bunch of feathers. That's all you will get. On the other hand, if you hit an elephant, it'll be dead in seconds with the high-caliber gun. But if you take a twenty-two or a BB gun to an elephant, he will just shrug and move on.

Caliber is the total capacity of an individual to project one's identity. You do not miss, you do not fail, you do not go wrong, you do not go under. Your caliber does not fail you. Caliber is a basic, consistent power in which a person can project, communicate, and lodge oneself, like a bullet. You fire; the bullet goes into the person, it sits there. Human caliber is all that comes into

A Teacher is not a god, but he is a God-giver. A Teacher is impersonal, like Infinity, and has integrity, self-awareness, and personality, with absolute grace.

the memory of every person whom you meet.

So a Teacher has a caliber. How do you define the Teacher's caliber? The Teacher is not a god, but he is a God-giver. Can you believe this definition? And you have come here to become Teachers. A Teacher is not a god, the Teacher is a God-giver.

If God and the Teacher are standing together, and the question is to whom to pay respect first, pay respect to the Teacher, because he gave you God and he can give you God again. That is the faculty of a Teacher, described in everything.

Caliber is a unique capacity. When a person deals with a person of caliber, and he takes the hit of the caliber, when the caliber lodges in that person, the identity of the person—it is forever. But you forget people, you use people, you abuse people, you manipulate people. You can do everything to anybody, but when you meet a person of caliber, you will automatically fall apart. Have you seen when someone has a knife, and the other person pulls out a revolver and says, "You...?" The knife just drops.

You are very successful when you are young, when you are in a sexual, sensual situation. You get hot at the age of seventeen. Normally you start getting hot at the age of eleven. But eleven and seven is eighteen. That is the cycle of years, and you have a cycle of consciousness and a cycle of intelligence. And what do you do? You have humongous *pranic* energy. It is automatic. Humongous. What do you waste it on? Sex, fantasies, dreams, imaginations. Let's say you start, if there's a chance, as late as seventeen, which is very rare. So seventeen, ten years. Twenty-seven. Then you have another twenty-seven years in which to develop caliber. It doesn't matter who you are, if your caliber is not standardized with grace, dignity, and it doesn't have the character of a sage, even with all the money and all the other privileges, for the rest of your life you shall be empty and in pain. There's no way out.

When the marrow in the blood does not have the faculty to change itself, then it cannot be changed. The only last chance is that you can transplant it. That's why people who do not take cold showers have arthritis and bone problems, marrow problems, and artery problems. Every problem in the body is a result of your capillaries not opening and not getting flushed every day. Your glandular system is the guardian of your whole system.

And what do you do over and above that? You have a sex life faster than you can handle it. Sex is not only the actual physical intercourse. Sex is also mental. Sex is also spiritual. And worst of all, you go into a fantasy of sex. A wet dream is equal to eleven physical intercourses. It causes that much nervous destruction. It's like a twister going through you.

After all, God gave you power, energy, strength, and youth, so that you can be forever. If you have a hundred dollars, you can spend it in one day or you can spend a dollar a day and take a hundred days. In the science of physics, what leaks downstairs has nothing upstairs. *(YB points to his head.)* It's a very simple law. I am not going to explain. You think you are having sex, but when you activate the first or second chakra it goes downhill. Take your first chakra. When it is imbalanced—you have diarrhea. How do you feel after two, three hours? "Oh!" *(YB grabs his navel point and stomach.)* Isn't it? When you do not use your youth or your youthfulness to preserve it, or use it for your higher stimulation of increasing your caliber, you live without caliber. And what is the sign of a person whose physical caliber is not developed? Headaches, itchiness, mood changes, mood swings. All social shortcomings come to those who do not have a developed caliber.

When does your caliber start developing? The 120th day in the womb of the mother.[1] Whatever she goes through is imprinted. Then, throughout your life, whatever you go through is imprinted, and it becomes your body language.

Once I was counseling a young girl. She was twenty-one, and she said, "So far I have lived a very graceful life, and I'm going to continue to live a graceful life."

I said, "Nope. You will not live gracefully. You have a well-definition of a graceful life, but you do not have the caliber which it takes to be graceful."

Three years later, at the age of twenty-four, one month she got confused, and four months later she found herself pregnant. And it was very difficult. She decided to go for abortion, and it defected her body to the point that even today she's not herself.

You cannot sustain your character, you cannot sustain yourself, you cannot sustain your relationship, if you do not have a normal character and the caliber of being you. Your love is false, your relationship is false, everything about you is false. The tragedy of you is that when you are a Teacher and people trust you and come to you, open their heart to you, and open their selves to you, you'll end up exploiting them because you don't have the caliber of a Teacher. You are not impersonal. A Teacher is impersonal, like Infinity, and has integrity, self-awareness, and personality with absolute grace. It doesn't matter what you give him, what you say to him, or how you deal with him. His faculty is only one. He or she must have the caliber to make another person best within the time and space, and happy within life's race, and continue to uplift.

I'll give you an example in Sikh Dharma. People came, they became ministers, they didn't care. They became Singh Sahibs and Mukhia Singh Sahibs, they didn't care. All they want is to become Siri Singh Sahib. That's what they all want. They're most welcome to come tomorrow and say, "I'm capable. I have the caliber." Take it, and sit there.

One who will call himself Siri Singh Sahib shall take care of everybody's neuroses, psychoses, fears, identities. With their trans-implant personality conflict, their split-personality conflict, they will do 150 things. How can this man do it, who himself has all the miseries to himself?

If I were a person, I would not touch a million things which I touch every day. I would not tolerate things which I tolerate. I would not become an easy target of any idiot who I pay or who I raise. It's just like getting slapped by your son or by your daughter every morning and every afternoon. I say, "Hello." But you need that caliber, with that tolerance and that daring intelligence, because a Teacher is not interested in the person. A Teacher always knows what he can do to a person to make the best out of it. It is not the wood, it is what you carve out of it. Sometimes you have to give it time, sometimes you have tolerance, but ultimately sometimes you yell and scream, sometimes you chisel it out, sometime this, sometimes that. But in the end you have to polish it to be something.

A Teacher has the infinite capacity of sacrifice. Normally all Teachers face accusation, because a Teacher becomes the fantasy of the student, and to accomplish that fantasy, it becomes a reality. When a fantasy becomes reality, the person's life is very unrealistic, and the Teacher has to bear the burden of bringing that person into reality. Sometimes it takes many many lifetimes. The Teacher and student relationship is not every day, every month, every year, or one lifetime. The Teacher-student relationship is from Infinity to Infinity. It is the consistency of caliber.

(See pages 191-192 for details of this meditation.)

Let us see if we have a caliber or we don't have caliber. Let us measure it. This is a very common thing you see in Kundalini Yoga. Your thumb is totally out, with your all fingers touching, and your hand is flat. Very straight. Put your hands just straight, tight. Correct. Now very kindly look at the tip of your nose.

There are six sounds in this world. The six sounds are *Har Haray Haree Waa-Hay Guru.*

ਛਿਅ ਘਰ ਛਿਅ ਗੁਰ ਛਿਅ ਉਪਦੇਸ ॥

Che ghar, che gur, che upadaysh.

-Guru Nanak, *Siri Guru Granth Sahib*, page 12 (from *Kirtan Sohila*)

There are six systems (schools of Hindu thought), six teachers, and six methods of teaching.

There are six houses of knowledge, six gurus of that knowledge, and six systems to reach it. Some systems are long, short, medium, whatever, but there are six recognized houses. One can achieve mastery of those six areas, and you can qualify to be an extreme Master of Self, of the Seventh Self. They call it the Seventh Ray of the Master.

With every pump of the navel you will chant: *Har Haray Haree, Waa-Hay Guroo. (Class continues to chant in a spoken monotone, pausing after every word for a split second.)* In harmony.

Spine straight. Posture perfect.

Get it somewhere. Get it. Perfect the posture. Open up the navel.

Stick with the rhythm. It will give you caliber. Get into the sound current.

Bravo. We are getting there.

Stop. Put on the instrumental version of *Ardaas Bhayee, Amar Daas Guroo.* Hold your posture. You have reached a stage, you only need a little more of a push, and this time you will make it happen. You have done so good that we achieved five minutes ahead of time. Hold your position tight, posture perfect. Indulge mentally in this prayer, and whistle from the navel. Power of the breath must speak. Hold! Start Breath of Fire.

Now Breath of fire, from the navel point. Powerful. At the end you are going to lose? What is this? Powerful!

Sing. Loud from the navel. Don't lose it. Don't use the upper area. Only from the lower area. From the guts!

Inhale deep. Inhale deep. Inhale deep. Hold. Cannon fire, all the way out. Inhale deep again. Deep. Inhale again. Hold tight. Bring the lower areas up and in again. Cannon fire. Inhale deep. Fill up the upper area, inhale deep. Pull the lower area. Pull. Pull the navel in. Cannon fire. Relax.

You did it. I just helped. It was nice. Keep the music side of that tape playing.

Oh, there is one little request. We need volunteers to transcribe these lectures in the next two days. We can take the transcription and make it into a book for all teachers or those who come behind you and after you. It's a good, noble act.

Meditation to Develop the Mature, Elevated Caliber of a Spiritual Teacher

Part I:

Mudra: Sit in Easy Pose with a straight spine. Bend the elbows near the sides, and bring the flattened hands to either side of the shoulders. The palms are facing forward, fingers straight and side by side, pointing towards the ceiling. Extend the thumbs out away from the hands so they are parallel to the ground and point back towards the body. Hands are flat and tight. Continue to keep the spine straight throughout the exercise.

Eyes: Look at the tip of the nose.

Mantra: *Har Haray Haree Waa-Hay Guroo.* Chanted in very distinct syllables, in a spoken monotone, with a brief pause after each syllable.

Movement: Pull in on the navel point as you recite each syllable.

Time: 31 minutes.

End: Inhale, and move directly to Part II.

Comments/Effects: This meditation will develop in you a mature, elevated caliber—a caliber with endurance, courage, patience, manners, rhythm, and communication. Caliber is the main power of the person.

Every person is afraid to identify himself or herself because they don't have caliber. So caliber is the capacity of an individual to identify the inner self, and project one's identity. Caliber is the total capacity of an individual to communicate and to project one's identity. With a well-developed caliber, you can project and lodge yourself into the memory of every person you come across. A Teacher has a caliber standardized with grace, dignity, and the character of a sage—full of tolerance, daring intelligence, and the power to sacrifice.

There are six houses of knowledge, six gurus of that knowledge, and six systems to reach that knowledge. And a mastery of those six areas can qualify you to be a Master of Self, which is called the Seventh Self or the Seventh Ray of the Master. The six sounds which represent the six houses of knowledge, are: *Har Haray Haree Waa-Hay Guroo.*"

This meditation also helps to open up the navel. Powerfully get into the rhythm and the sound current to make it most effective.

continued next page

Part II:

Mudra: Continue to hold the same position as Part I.

Music: The instrumental version of *Ardas Bhaee:*
Ardaas Bhayee, Amar Daas Guroo, Amar Daas Guroo, Ardaas Bhayee,
Raam Daas Guroo, Raam Daas Guroo, Raam Daas Guroo, Sachee Sahee.
The rhythm of the music is slow.

Time: Total, 8 minutes, in the following fashion, with no break between sections:
- 4 minutes: Whistle along with the tape from the navel, very powerfully.
- 1-1/2 minutes: Do Breath of Fire powerfully from the navel.
- 2-1/2 minutes: Sing powerfully from the navel. Sing from the navel and *not* from the chest or throat area.

End: Inhale, inhale, inhale, deep, deeper, deepest. Hold 10-15 seconds. Cannon fire out very powerfully. Repeat 3 times total. Relax.

Comments/Effects: With this mantra, project out your prayer with the help of the strength of the navel. This mantra calls upon the Third Sikh Guru, Guru Amar Das, and the Fourth Sikh *Guru, Guru Ram Das,* to answer one's prayers. The literal meaning of this mantra, in the words of Yogi Bhajan, is:

> *The prayer has gone out. Guru Amar Das hears the prayer, and*
> *Guru Ram Das confirms it, and is the true guarantee that it is accepted.*

End: Listen to the music for a while, then talk to someone before you get up and try to drive or go out.

The Golden Chain of Teachers

Scripturally, they call it the Golden Chain of Teachers, passing it on from one to another, to another, to another. They keep the standard, they keep the identity, they keep the personality, they keep the teachings.

There are many great teachers who work in the Golden Chain of Action. Gold represents purity. When you mix it with any metal, and you heat it, in the end gold will come out as gold. Other than platinum, it's the heaviest metal. Gold has the capacity of purity. When it's 24 karat, it's 24 karat. Therefore, scripturally they call it the Golden Chain of Teachers, passing it on from one to another, to another, to another. They keep the standard, they keep the identity, they keep the personality, they keep the teachings. In this Raaj Yog, or what you commonly call Kundalini Yoga, in this Shakti Yoga, any teacher who changes the teachings for any reason, self-destroys himself or herself. There is no force required. It's not that we have to propagate it or do anything. So the teachings are pure; they have to be kept pure, they have to be taught pure, and they act purely. They do their set scientific thing.

There is a very popular saying amongst these teachers, which I would like to repeat. This is what a teacher said to his students: "If you love me, God shall love you. If you don't, you don't count." Do you understand this statement?

Class: Yes, Sir.

YB: "If you don't, you don't count." But this is how it is. This is a Teacher. You take the teachings and you flow. When you become the Teacher, you take the teachings and it flows. It's one link. So let us not have any misunderstanding that if I am teaching or she is teaching, there are two different people teaching. That's why on a stage you have seen, when somebody else comes on the stage, I get out. Because there has to be one Teacher at that time. There's no duplication of it. If you love me, the return is, God shall love you. If you don't, you don't count.

So technically speaking, the Teacher has something to sacrifice. The Teacher has to look like and has to be a teacher. It's a very personal determination.

To teach is a faculty, it's a facility. It's not a facade. The satisfaction of a Teacher is that he's immortal. From mortal to immortal. You are mortals. You will die. The Teacher will never die. The Teacher will live. The Teacher lives forever.

It's a different story. Sometimes you call yourself Oshu, or Bhagwan. Some people go after titles. But a Teacher has no title. A Teacher has only one title: "Teacher." He's neither an angel,

Your relationship is based on service, and your trust with people is based on your purity. Your impact is in your identity, and your happiness is in your royalty and reality, mixed together. These are the principal factors you have to deal with.

nor a human, nor a person, nor God. Nothing. He's a giver of God. Why does he need to be God? He can give God to anybody. He can kindle the light in anybody and everybody. You can disagree with me. I know you have been bastardized by 3,000 years of religious writings and teachings. But the faculty and beauty of a Teacher is he's the giver of God to anybody and everybody. His joy is that he lives forever. All that joy is there. This link of the Golden Chain continues. But for that, there's a price: the ego doesn't work.

It is like an army. You are in uniform, you are exact. There's no variance. "Uno Form"—one form. One God, one form, one teaching. Everything becomes standardized. Because once you are not shaky, you are not wavering, then you are standardized. Once you teach with a firm self, surprisingly, the entire Mother Nature and God's Will come to uplift you. You cannot fall.

Man always seeks to be immortal. He wants to live forever. But there's only one way to live forever—that is to teach, and teach the teachings purely, keep the teachings pure, and be pure. Then everything will come, there's no dearth, and there's no need for a power play.

If you would have asked me ten years or twenty years ago to teach a Teacher's Course, I would have refused. Rather, I would have said, "We'll teach a class and Teachers will come out of it." Now we are certifying Teachers and doing all that. But in the old days, I used to pick people in the class and say, "Okay, you two, go to Alaska. You two, go to such and such a place." And they became Teachers. They took their faith and trust, and they took the understanding that "He has said, 'Be the Teacher', so we are the Teacher."

Once a couple said to me, "We have no money, no means."

I said, "Money and means will be provided. Start proceeding." So they met with one of their friends the next day for lunch, and he said, "What are you doing?"

He said, "We don't have any money. We can't go. And Yogiji has said we should go to such and such a place."

He said, "I have three thousand dollars. I can give it to you."

Look at the Nirvairs,[1] who went all the way to Alaska by road in a little Volkswagen Love Bug, which was impossible. When they reached Anchorage, and they were hungry, they went to a restaurant and health food store. When he saw them, the owner said, "Oh, you are Yogi Bhajan's students. We wanted to give the restaurant as a home to somebody. You have come. Would you like to take it?" The money was decided, and they had a home, they had a business, they had everything. They are still there today.

Most of the time you do not have the capacity to obey. Therefore, most of the time you do not have the capacity to command. There are six things which are your downfall: emotion, commotion, feeling, fantasy, sexuality, and sensuality. You waste energy in those shakes. They don't give you any strength, they don't give you any depth. You must understand, you are so badly misguided.

In making our herbs and products, we have a very different philosophy than anybody else.

Most people say about their products, "If you take these vitamins you will have tons of energy. If you take this thing, you will be very well off. If you take this thing...."

But you know what I say? "If you take this, it will take away your fatigue, and you'll be real. The real you is very beautiful. The real you is very healthy. The real you is very fulfilled. The real you is God." Why do you need all this extra?

Somebody was kidding me. "Oh, this vitamin is so good. You take it and everything becomes all right."

I said, "Well, leave me two or three." I took them. I couldn't sleep the whole night—the whole night! I was very energetic. Oh, it felt so wonderful. The next day I couldn't get out of the bed. Forget it. I took the pill again. I took it the third day. I was a walking zombie. It accelerated me so much that the day after I could not recalculate myself. Luckily I know hydrotherapy, so I sat in water for hours and hours and hours.

Any stimulation which is outside, abnormal, and unnatural will totally tear you apart and you'll pay for it moon to moon. At the full moon you are naturally accelerated, and you are naturally brought down during a new moon. Your biofeedback moves from full moon to new moon, and then new moon to full moon. That's natural. But if on the eleventh day of the moon, you just live on water and melon, your health will be perfect.

If you want to take care of your mind, eat nothing on these three days of the moon: a new moon, a full moon, and the eleventh day of the moon. At the new moon you are at the lowest. On the full moon your glandular system is at the highest. On the eleventh day of the moon you are in balance, in twilight. So if on these three days in the month you can fast on lemon and water, it will help you out. If you feel very cold, then add ginger to it.

Each morning these days I take two ounces of ginger, two ounces of lemon, with one spoonful of flaxseed oil. But, when I was in Cancun, I couldn't get flaxseed oil, so I used olive oil.

There was something ailing a woman who was there in Mexico, and it was worrying me. She said that she had tried everything. So we flew in red chili oil. That's the most powerful oil. You know, Heaven is Heaven, and Earth is Earth. But one drop of it can make you feel like, "Earth is a Heaven...la...la...la."

Do you know how powerful that little red thing, Tabasco sauce, is? Well, this is a pure oil, squeezed out of the red chilies. And if it touches you, it's a Master's Touch.

Class: *Laughter.*

YB: The most powerful thing that a teacher can rely on is his own diet. Try Trinity Milk—ginger, garlic, and onion boiled in goat's milk, and taken as a first drink in the morning They call it "Trinity Milk." The formula is available.

The second most powerful thing you can use to straighten out your life is called *tabbouleh*. Normally it is made from cracked wheat. Instead, make this *tabbouleh* with black *cholé*, which are black garbanzo beans. This is because cracked wheat can give you something which you don't need. Therefore, you should substitute black garbanzos. Black garbanzos control the electromagnetic field of the body. It's the most powerful food in the world.

Once in a while in your life you need something called Yogi Tea. You think it's just a tea. No. If you drink a really good amount of Yogi Tea, it will keep your liver in good shape. It is actually for the liver. When we started out in the Sixties, people who had a drug habit, who couldn't even move, we put on Yogi Tea. We took them out of every trouble. Drugs do damage. The only thing that can counteract that is Yogi Tea. That's why we started promoting it.

Something good for ladies is to cut a banana in the center, put mango powder on it, put lemon juice on it, and just eat it for potassium, vitamin C, and for more energy. That is enough.

We have a new formula which we have not marketed yet, but we are going to market it now. It's an herbal formula like 7-R, 3-R, 2-R, and 1-R. 1-R is for night elimination. 2-R is for purifying your blood and keeping your stomach in good shape, as well as the blood cells. 3-R is for your structural balance, like the bone marrow structure. 7-R is to take away your fatigue. For balance. So we have this new formula—it is very good.

Then we have Young Blood Powder. We also have GRD Oil. We don't want people to take it and O.D. We want things to proceed responsibly. There's no hurry. We want these gringos (Westerners) to learn to live in a very Oriental way.

You have your mind, and you torture your mind. You work it like an idiot, and it becomes an idiot. Then it's not handy, it's not fresh. So technically speaking, the best vitamin you have is your breath, the *prana.* If you can deep-breathe, one breath per minute—twenty seconds to breathe in, twenty seconds to hold, and twenty seconds to exhale—it's very powerful, it is very perfect, and it will not give you any trouble whatsoever.

Your life is, and should be, very simple. Food is part of a healthy life. Take one part of garbanzo flour, one part of whole wheat flour, and mix it together. Then make the dough and use ginger, garlic, and onion juice, instead of water. When the dough is made you put to pulp into it like a stuffed *parantha.* To ghee, add a little bit of red chili oil, and if black pepper oil is available, use it. But if you can't get it, you can get black peppercorns. And if you have them, use *ajwan* (oregano seeds) and turmeric. Put these in the *ghee,* it makes a very good ghee. Then put that ghee on that *parantha.* Don't worry that it's fat. You might be afraid of it. But ghee is not fat. Ghee is not oil, ghee is not butter. Ghee is protein. And it's a protein which dissolves the fat in the body. In India, if somebody gets obese, they start living on ghee. In Tibet and all these areas, they put ghee in their tea, and drink it. They live on it. They don't care. That's their protein. You see all those lamas? They take a cup of tea, put the ghee in, and drink it. You call it butter, yak butter. But actually yak butter is clarified ghee.

If you are not into hot things, then you should not listen to what I am going to tell you next. Anyway, I'm not suggesting it, because my insurance won't cover it. However, if you can, take three or five jalapenos, depending on how much you hate or love them, take eight to ten ounces of milk, and blend them together for twenty-thirty minutes. People don't understand how long you have to blend it. And then sip it. Don't drink it. Sip it. Ummmm. (*YB makes his arms into muscles like a strong man demonstrating his strength.*) The spirit will go through.

Once I went to Mexico and I asked the teacher, "Where is your wife?"

He said, "She's very sick."

And I said, "How sick?"

He said, "She was in the hospital. Now they have sent her back home."

Oh, I understood what that meant in the Mexican language. So I went straight into the kitchen, I took jalapenos and milk, blended it right, and put tons of honey in, because I knew she would react. I started feeding it to her with a spoon. It was very difficult for her to get it down. But on the fifth or sixth spoon she opened up her eyes. And by the time the glass was empty, she got up. She said, "What was that?"

I said, "Nothing, nothing, nothing." I said, "I have come all the way and you are not there to serve me. I hate it. So you be up."

Next day we secretly made it again and told her, "Bottoms up. Sip it slowly, spoon by spoon."

She said, "It is sweet and bitter."

I said, "Yeah, yeah, yeah, yeah, yeah." She still takes it every day.

Once in a while, when you really want to have a trouble-free life, hallelujah and jalapenos are the same. You need that drink.

We have some very simple herbs to use. We have 108-R. God bless us, it's great.

You know, the best fruit in the world is guava. Guava is the most powerful fruit for your mental balance. And if you eat pears, you will never have stones in your body, you will never have fibroids in your body. Pears are called *amarpal*—the food of longevity.

Apples are great, pears are great, and the best friend of yours in this life is the plum. And the beauty of the nectarine is so good, you can't believe it. It is sensory. Eat a nectarine any time. Don't question this. Just eat a nectarine sometime, and you'll feel fresh.

Sometime take cherries and blend them. Take the pulp out, and then mix it with pear and apple, and blend it again. Then put vanilla ice cream in it. Figure it out. You talk of energy? You will have to put weights on your legs to keep yourself on the ground.

What are those little things called? Blackberries? Mix them with milk sometime and blend it really hard. It will become a kind of dark bluish milk. Wow.

Or, make a *masala*—you can ask my kitchen manager for a list of all those ten, fifteen things that you put in it, including onion, ginger, all that stuff, and cook them in ghee. Then take a full head of lettuce, and put it in the pressure cooker—really cook it, like a turkey, like Peking duck. Cut the lettuce into four pieces or two, however you want to present it, take that beautiful *masala* with everything in it, and fill the leafs all around. You will have energy to work through the day, as well as relaxation.

Lettuce juice at night can help put you to sleep. Provided the lettuce soup is made with milk, then you can't get up. You don't even hit the pillow, you are gone. Very powerful. It is relaxing.

The joy of relaxation is better than drugs and sex, and it does not allow you to destroy a relationship. You only destroy a relationship when you are not relaxed, when you are tense. Once your mind gets caught in a frequency, divorce is inevitable. And after divorce, the tragedy is that you have to relive your life. There are two things which do not exist in the world—there is no woman who is a lesbian, and there is no divorce which is practical. It's all in the memory. When you divorce somebody, you remember that person more than when you were with that person.

I have seen a gentleman who had just gone through a divorce. He was standing by the side of the road on a Saturday with a big limousine. I said, "Son of a gun, what are you doing here?"

He said, "I'm picking up my children."

I said, "When you were married, did you ever pick your children up like this?"

He said, "No. If I would have done it, we would never have been divorced."

So every Saturday morning at eight o'clock he picks them up. It is up to her whether she lets them go Friday or Saturday. For a while she was letting them go Saturday morning, then she became a little free, and she said, "You can take them on Friday afternoon. Carry them, baby, Friday, Saturday, Sunday."

Now this guy is very social. He never used to come home, he never used to think of anything. Now, if you ask him for anything Friday afternoon, Saturday, Sunday, he'll say, "I have no time." He's a baby-sitter. If he would have done this when he was married, this would not have happened.

Men become arrogant and ignore things. Women become frigid and destroy things. Frigid, frigid, frigid. Cold. When a woman is over-sexual for the first twenty-seven years, then for the next twenty-seven years she'll be cold like dead ice.

(Reading from The Oath of a Kundalini Yoga Teacher:)

"I am not a woman, I am not a man, I'm not a person, I'm not myself. I'm a Teacher. Ong Namo Guru Dev Namo. I hereby affirm that I am a Teacher of Kundalini Yoga as taught by Yogi Bhajan. I commit to fulfill the highest standard of excellence in maintaining the Teachers Oath." Signature, date, legal name (please print), witness, state, country, etc.

So this is all made very legal, notarized, and all that. The idea is to make you so good and perfect that you can stand tall in a court of law.

So, you are what you eat. And your power is what you speak. Your strength is what your manners are. And your prosperity is based on mutuality. That's how you will spell it. Your relationship is based on service. And your trust with people is based on your purity. Your impact is in your identity. And your happiness is in your royalty and reality, mixed together. These are the principal factors you have to deal with.

Now I would like to leave you because you will now take the Oath. If you don't want to take it, you don't have to. It's not compulsory. You should not go from this course: "To be, not to be"—forget it. Go from this course: "To be, to be," and then let the world follow you.

That's my word for the day. Thank you.

Healing Breath Formula

20 seconds to inhale · 20 seconds to hold · 20 seconds to exhale

Practice for 11 minutes a day for maximum health and healing, energy and vitality.

A Self-Surrender to the Higher Self

A Teacher is a self-surrender to his higher self. After that surrender, the first sign comes—you don't do wrong things, you don't get mad at people, and you don't talk about them. You do not relate to any weakness in anyone. That's the first faculty of the teacher. He relates to the strength and tries to make the best of it.

You are a Teacher. A Teacher is supposed to *teach*. A teacher teaches people—the matter ends. On the other hand, a person goes to the library, acquires the knowledge, understands it, grasps it—the matter ends. What is the difference between gaining knowledge from books and the knowledge which a Teacher gives? I'm not talking of a preacher here, I'm talking about a real Teacher.

A Teacher penetrates. But understand that the Teacher fails. Again he penetrates, and again he fails. Rejection is not a matter of action for the Teacher. The Teacher's job is to keep on acting, and the student's job is to keep on reacting, and not accepting. But once a student starts accepting, he's not a student anymore—he then becomes a Teacher. It is human faculty not to listen. Listen, don't listen; speak, don't mean anything; hear, don't hear. The whole thing is based on "To be, not to be." But if you want to be a Teacher, then your purity and piety are your power.

It's not that there's any dearth of Teachers here; everybody wants to be a Teacher, everybody is a Teacher. But actually a Teacher is a self-surrender to his higher self. After that surrender, the first sign comes—you don't do wrong things, even in your remotest thoughts. You don't get mad at people, and you don't talk about them. You do not relate to any weakness in anyone. That's the first faculty of the Teacher. He doesn't relate to weakness. He relates to the strength and tries to make the best of it. That is the Teacher's pride, that is the Teacher's orientation, that is the Teacher's job. Know this first: a person has a strength, and then a person has a weakness. None of us are saints. That's why there are so many rules and regulations, like drivers licenses, building permits.

Life is not a very polite thing. Most of you are competing and comparing, and the result of that is that you are confused. A confused person is a confused person. You will be very glad to see that most Teachers are very confused. The first wrong thing they do is that they cater to their students. Second, they want to run an election and be very popular. Third, they want to be controlling. Fourth, they want everybody to relate to them with utmost respect, while they do whatever they want.

Don't worry about the obnoxiousness, narrowness, abusiveness, negativity of a student. Had he not been all that, why should he come to you? So please, when you become a Teacher, serve with light and warmth for all, like sunshine.

I will tell you what an easy target a Teacher is. I was discussing something with someone today, and the person said, "We freaked out."

I said, "Why?

"Oh, you wanted my business."

I said, "Your business? What do I need your business for? I said, "If you cannot do a business, let me help you with your business. Don't freak out." That's all I said."

"No, we thought you were going to take over our business."

I said, "How?"

There are a lot of people here who have forgotten who they were and what their financial statements looked like when I met them, and what their financial statements look like today. I would be very glad to let you know how much you have paid back. As far as I'm concerned, not a penny. What you earn, belongs to you. Whatever I earn, belongs to you. You can't see that grace, because you don't have that grace.

What is this? How can a Teacher with teachings measure things with money? If a student measures with it, it's okay; a student is an obnoxious, crazy, undisciplined raw material. Don't misunderstand, a student is not a god, not a human. A student is just one bulk of obnoxiousness and ignorance, with arrogance about their status: "I'm an attorney, I am a doctor, I am this, I am that." They are very earthly.

The Spiritual Teacher actually has no relevance to that earthliness—absolutely none. He can't relate to it. The Spiritual Teacher is a very easy target of this madness and insanity. It happens all the time to him. But without you, who else will do it? Think about it. You took an oath, you took a job to serve the deep spirit of humanity. And if you took an oath to do that job, that you will serve humanity, who else will do it? There is nothing the student will not try to do to bring you down to his or her level, and there's nothing in you which will come down. Every student will judge you as a man or a woman. To everyone you are supposed to look like a God-giver. Don't *be* God—*give* God. If you cannot accept this condition, don't become a Teacher.

The tragedy of this whole thing is that once a student comes to you, that's all the student can do. So if you are expecting the student to be very moral, mannerful, ethical, nice, sweet, obedient, I think you are nuts. You are not a teacher. If there were no insanity, no garbage, no nonsense, no tragedy, no whatever, why would you be needed to begin with? The more idiots there are, the more you are needed. More work.

So it comes with the territory, it's a part of your job. You might be feeling sometimes that you are being respected, people bow to you and all that. That is equal compensation for all the obnoxiousness and abusiveness. It's just a little compensation, no big deal. It's not something to be very proud of.

Let me tell you how things happen. I lived for thirty-nine years in India. I was a total misfit there. I came here, and I am also a misfit here. A Teacher cannot fit with the obnoxiousness and the insanity. So you are a misfit. You have come here to make things relevant. You do not understand your job. You are not running an election, you are not winning wealth. You are being taken care of.

But, you cannot pocket anything. Whatever comes to you: "Unto Thee, unto Thee, Oh Lord, unto Thee."

Another thing as a Teacher which is most painful is that you love a student with heart and head—you admire them. But because of their obnoxiousness and their neurosis they hit you so hard under the belt that, as a human, you can't even take it, but as a Teacher it's okay. The student shall keep on insulting you. The student doesn't want to respect you, because the student doesn't respect himself or herself. It's not the student's fault. The student has come, that's his job. Beyond that, you can't expect from a student. Either you compete, compare, and you are confused, or you are contained, content, and continuous.

In the *Ardas*, the prayer of the Sikhs, they count all sacrifices: Those who were burned alive, those who were cut up piece by piece, broiled, tied with the trees and burned. It's a long history of torture. And for all of them, and for their resolution, we say: "Say '*Wahe Guru.*'" And there's one most beautiful line:

ਜਿਨ੍ਹਾ ਵੇਖ ਕੇ ਅਣਡਿੱਠ ਕੀਤਾ
Jinnaa vekh kay andith keetaa...
　　-From the *Ardas,* the daily prayer of the Sikhs
Those who saw the faults of others and chose to unsee them.

Those who saw and made it unseen. Those who saw others' weakness, and took it as unseen. For their graciousness and forgiveness, say "*Wahe Guru.*" It's an amazing line. You cannot give anybody anything other than trouble, you enjoy trouble, and you want trouble. That is how you pass your time. You can't give anybody anything other than trouble, or you can give somebody forgiveness. You cannot give forgiveness to anybody if you do not give forgiveness to yourself. If you have not learned to forgive yourself, you cannot forgive anybody. If you cannot forgive anybody, you have to react, and when you react, you bring action into your life.

Somebody filed a lawsuit against me, and it was very heavy for two and a half years. Then finally the case fell apart and the charges were dropped. I had the choice of filing a counter-suit for malicious prosecution. I said, "Why? It's over. Finished." It is not that you are right or wrong, and somebody else will judge you. But you should not judge if you are a conscious person. Because the crown of spirituality is always bestowed. It is not something you can conquer in a court of law.

There is a story of Guru Hargobind, the sixth Guru. He announced, "If somebody can read to me the *Japji* of Nanak, I'll be very grateful."

One very old Sikh came, and he said, "I can correctly read it."

The Guru sat down and the Sikh started reading it. During the entire reading, the Guru was slowly shifting from his place. When the *Japji* came to an end, the Guru just came back to his position. One Sikh said, "My Lord, we have not seen you do this before. As the *Japji* was being recited, you started shifting, and when it ended, you just jumped back to your place. Then you gave this man a beautiful horse and a bag full of gold and other things. Can you explain why you were moving like that?"

He said, "When he was reading the *Japji* of Nanak, he was like Nanak, and I thought, 'What can I give him as a reward?' To my mind it came, 'I'll give him Guru Nanak's seat on which I am sitting. So I'll retire and make him the Guru.' I was having that in my mind and I was slowly moving. In the end it came into his mind, 'If the Guru is real and he likes me as I'm reciting, he should give me such and such a horse, and a bag of gold, and I'll be very satisfied.' He decided it. I jumped back. Why should I give him this place? This place has no price. He asked for the price, so I gave him the price."

Those who put Jesus Christ on the cross must have been very happy that day because they were asked to compete and compare. They compared him with a thief and a murderer, and they let the murderer and the thief go; and they asked him to be put on the cross. They thrashed him, and to mock him they put a crown of thorns and mockingly called him the "King of the Jews." Can you understand the humiliation? But today he is the Son of God, and those who were, are not, and never shall be.

You do not understand; you judge things by pain and pleasure. Things are actually judged by time and beyond time. Jesu, Fatima's son, was born. To cover him there was no cloth. To put him to rest there was no place. So in a manger they made a little place and covered him with straw. That's exactly a fact. If you were there, you must have seen it. If you were not, still it is true. He was an orphan, and the boys beat him and called him "bastard." One day he came home from school, and they said, "You are a bastard. You have no father." He asked his mother. "Mother, Madre, where's my father?"

She said, "Your father lives in Heaven, with many mansions."

That boy never forgot those words. And he asked her, "How can you say this?"

She said, "Israel, the Angel, told me. And if you don't believe me, you can go and ask your aunt."

So that was his belief. That boy was a bastard; now he's the Son of God. That man who didn't have a place other than a manger. Today property is held all over the world in his name—beautiful buildings with steeples and all—and no government can tax it. He has homes everywhere. At that time the manager of the Inn said, "Hey, you can go into the barnyard." And that is where he was born.

Who knows on whose destiny the blessing of the Hand of God will shine Its light? That's not your relationship. Your relationship is in gain and loss, in popularity and understanding, in fulfillment of emotions and feelings, in vengeance and revenge, in complaints and in cries. Your relationships are measured by money, and marred by emotions. You are not comprehensive. You are always apprehensive. You are happy when you gain, you are unhappy when you lose. Judgment is yours. When you gain you should not be happy, because your gain is somebody's loss. When you lose you should not be unhappy, because it is somebody's gain. Who cares? Matter can neither be created nor destroyed; it can only be converted into energy.

The Teacher has the status of a God-giver, free and clear. He serves tirelessly. He relates with a smile; and yells and screams in order to shape the student. The harder the stone, the heavier is the hammer.

But don't misunderstand that when you will become Teachers, you will not face slander and abuse. This comes with the territory. If you have any obnoxious thought that to be a Teacher is all a bed of roses, and you are going to be worshipped, I think you are very badly mistaken. First of all, if you are a Teacher, your wife is going to be jealous that, "All these women relate to you. What is your relationship with them?" If you are a woman Teacher, you know better what happens. It's all there.

Then why are we becoming Teachers? Because it is the highest status in a human life. It is elegant, it is excellent, and it is very, very, very, very, very fulfilling.

I went to my old school which is in Ludhiana. They have placed a plaque on the wall in my honor, as a student of that school. One of my old professors showed up. He wanted to touch my feet. I held him back, saying, "What are you doing?"

Every student will judge you as a man or a woman. To everyone you are to look like the God-giver. Don't be God—give God. If you cannot accept this condition, don't become a Teacher.

He said, "At one time I taught you worldly things. Today I look at you, I have found God. Let me touch your feet."

I said, "You can't."

He said, "Then I order you."

I took my hands back. I said, "Go ahead. You can have it." And there were tears in his eyes.

He said, "Even God can't say anything to me. I have achieved everything. I am proud of you. I am fulfilled today." He was my professor in college—and a tough one. It reminded me how when I came to America people slandered me, left and right.

What did they do to Jesus? What did they do to Mohammed? What did they do to the Fifth Nanak, Guru Arjan Dev? Believe me or not, they put him on a burning hot plate, and poured burning hot sand on him, for five days and nights. Then they took him to the coldest river and put him in. They wondered what happened—there was nothing there. He disappeared.

The two sons of Guru Gobind Singh were seven and nine years old. They didn't kill them—they bricked them alive. Understand the torture of this. These two little boys stood with a smile. Man's tyranny is man's joy. Causing pain to others is man's greatest pleasure. Man is a ruthless, obnoxious, uncaring brute. Once in a while, with the blessing of a Teacher, he becomes human. And if the merciful Lord comes through his Teacher, he may become an Angel; and in the angelic form, he may serve humanity to bring consideration of the absolute union, oneness with God. That's why I made that statement this afternoon: "If you love me, God shall love you. But if you don't, you don't count."

Then sometimes your students feel you are depending on them—they give you this, they give you that. That's the most rude act of a student. But you are not supposed to react, you are supposed to bless them. Students are like little children. A Teacher is supposed, in spite of it all, to clean all their garbage. I'm just giving you a job description.

It's a very funny situation. Sometimes you have a student who will give you life. They will look to you in awe. They are fine. Then there are others who will try to figure out how they can get you. Actually, to be a Teacher is a test of patience.

Once I wrote in *Beads of Truth*, "God save me. I'm running a hospital. I have no nurses and no doctors—all I have are patients."

Try to understand what this is like: you are eating and you are about to put a mouthful of food to your mouth, and somebody says: "Can I ask you a question?" So you have to decide whether you should say, "Yes," or you should get this into your mouth.

The faculty of a Teacher is a very powerful, dominant, open sacrifice. There's no doubt about it. It takes not only internal courage, it takes external courage also. That's the Teacher. Because either you take care of yourself, or you let God take care of you.

There are two relationships: *nadi* and *bindi*. A *bindi* relationship is one which is created from your semen. A *nadi* relationship is one which is created from your word, from your sound. The difference between a son who is your student, and a son who is your son, is that your son who is a son can say "no," but the son who is your student cannot say "no." The student is an ultimate challenger of all that there is, and his goal is victory.

Guru Arjan was the son of Guru Ram Das, and he became the Guru. Prithi Chand was also the son—and the eldest. He couldn't become the Guru; he only remained a son. By the right of heritage, he wanted to be a Guru. He forgot that the crown of spirituality is bestowed. It cannot be conquered.

The relationship of student and Teacher is that, if the Teacher blesses you, God vouches for it. If he curses you, God vouches for it. That's the relationship.

ਮੇਰੀ ਬਾਂਧੀ ਭਗਤੁ ਛਡਾਵੈ ਬਾਂਧੈ ਭਗਤੁ ਨ ਛੁਟੈ ਮੋਹਿ ॥
Meree baandhee bhagat chadhaavai, baandhai bhagat na chutai mo-heh
  -Bhagat Namdev, page 1252
A devotee can release anyone from My bondage, but I cannot release anyone from his.

"If God gives you a knot, the devotee of God can open it. But when a devotee of God gives a knot, God cannot open it." It's the Law of Divinity, and will hold true until Infinity, because God is known through His disciples, and His first disciple is the Teacher.

A Teacher is not an attorney, or a medical doctor, or an engineer, or a businessman. A Teacher is a Teacher. Guru Nanak was a Teacher, who also acted as a peasant, who also acted as a traveler. He went everywhere. Because one quality of a Teacher is that he will reach out, touch the heart—he is the touch divine. Without his contact and connection, without his grace and blessing, divinity cannot exist. You can deal with it or you can deny it, it doesn't matter. Life is virtue and values. If the virtues and values of a person are fulfilled, then life is worth-while. Let us see how much and how far we go. Ready?

Class: Yes, Sir.

YB: My idea is that if I give you an eleven minute exercise, you may not experience what I want you to experience. I don't expect any change, I don't expect anything. The contract is between you and your God. I am just an avenue that allows the honor of you, I serve that avenue. I have no relationship with you. I can grant your petition or I can reject it. You call on *Ong Namo Guru Dev Namo* —either I'll come through or I won't. I am the Big Guy, on which you have no control. Don't misunderstand. You have tortured me, you have burned me, you have put me on the cross, you have put stakes through me, you have put me through fire, you have insulted me—as humanity, you have done everything . Yet I always come. I am a Teacher. The Teacher never goes away, it only changes body as people change a shirt, or Italy changes its government. It makes no difference. The Teacher is always one. One is God, One is the Teacher. People will die, but the Teacher will continue to live until Eternity.

Even when I am blind, I see. Even when I am dumb, I speak. Even when I am deaf, I hear.

In spite of the fact that you speak, you see and you hear, you are a dud, because you have not awakened in you the essence of your totality. Therefore, reality will never touch your shoulders. So you compensate with ego. That's not a Teacher. A Teacher shall not compensate his identity with ego.

But your happiness or displeasure as a Teacher is all rewarded in the end, when out of you another Teacher is born. Therefore you are better than God. God cannot create another God, but a Teacher can create another Teacher. You belong to a different humanity, you have a different relationship.

So please understand the facts of life. You can't look ordinary and be a Teacher. You have to look special, because you are a special person, you have to do a special job. That's why you see Padres with a collar and with a particular dress. They're not insane. A Teacher without discipline of identity, mind, and spirit is not a Teacher of worth. There is an obligation, there is a command, there is a need. You have to come through.

(See page 208 for details of this meditation.)

This exercise is for your arcline and for the karma which you have stocked up in it. It's just a hand of prayer, no big deal. This is a control of the psyche, and it will elevate you. It looks like a very simple exercise, but it's very powerful. When you say, "*Wahe Guru,*" you make a movement with it. "*Wahe Guru, Wahe Guru, Wahe Guru, Wahe Jeeo.*" It is as if you are picking up something, and you are throwing it over your shoulders. If you do it correctly, you are going to learn in a very simple way what "*Wahe Guru*" actually means. So, let's go.

Inhale, and put your hands behind your head as you were doing in the exercise, and stretch them in a regular cycle. Exhale. You were cheating. Inhale. Hold the breath. Put your hands over your shoulders, backward. Exhale. Inhale deep. Stretch. Relax.

Are you okay?

Class: Yes, Sir.

YB: The power of Infinity is not outside of you. It is inside of you. When "I" and Infinity create the impact, you will become totally divine. Otherwise there's a duality which keeps you away from reality, and the pain is humongous.

It doesn't matter who you belong to, or who you *think* you belong to, or who or what you think you are. It has absolutely nothing to do with your totality. It is as if you have a small amount of food and you think it is so great. But then you go somewhere and you see the whole universe, and you see that there is no comparison. The fulfillment of "I" with the impact of personal Infinity is beyond what can even be uttered.

It's my prayer that you will prepare yourself for the Age of Aquarius, and let your neurosis go, and let yourself be nice to yourself. You are cruel, obnoxious, and negative to yourself. It is your own self you put in danger when you are negative. You don't harm anybody else. Nobody is within your reach. And the pain you cause to another comes back to you a hundred times. You can't escape it. The difficulty is that you cannot measure it, because it comes in many ways and over great distances of time. Therefore, you think you are succeeding momentarily, but in Infinity you lose.

Remember, Teachers, if you do nothing, somebody's destiny is ruined. Just understand that. You may not do anything; you may refuse, it is your right. But if your destiny is to be a Teacher, and you don't become a Teacher, you hurt yourself. But if somebody comes to you and you do nothing, the destiny is ruined.

But when you have a personal impact of your Infinity on yourself, then you find great dignity, great divinity, and great grace. It's a very solid state. It doesn't matter if you live in a palace, or you live in a hut—grace is grace, manners are manners. When your altitude and manners, and your grace, your dignity, and your divinity are all put together, God is in awe of you. But then you bitch, you yell and scream, you are negative, and talk ill of others. I don't know why you do all that.

Chiseling is only allowed between a Teacher and a student. Period. But the purpose is so noble that the pain becomes pleasure, because it's the ecstasy of the enjoyment of the status of Infinity.

So please understand, the Teacher is that unique thing, and there will never be anything like it. Period. You have no price, no temptation, no attempt, no drag. You are free—liberator and liberated. These faculties of you as a Teacher will bring you happiness on a silver platter by the Hand of God. Your worldly ugliness and shallowness, and your narrow-mindedness shall not be with you. You will enjoy the status of ecstasy. Just remember, those who serve the Master, God in masterful ways serves them. That's the promise.

It's not everybody's karma; it's not everybody's dharma.

Lehna served Nanak, and he became Angad, he became part of him. Amar Das served Angad, and he became Guru Amar Das. Jetha served Guru Amar Das, and he became Guru Ram Das. It's not that there were no other children or no other relatives. No, it was the absolute service. It's called the Master's Will. Those who find within themselves the Master's Will, become the Lord Masters of Longitude, Latitude, Altitude, and Attitude. And that is what a Mahan Tantric is. But other people saw this same Nanak like this:

ਕੋਈਆਖੈਭੂਤਨਾਕੋਕਹੈਬੇਤਾਲਾ॥ ਕੋਈਆਖੈਆਦਮੀਨਾਨਕੁਵੇਚਾਰਾ॥
Ko-ee aakhai bhootanaa, ko kahai baytaalaa, Ko-ee aakhai aadmee naanak vay-chaaraa.
   -Guru Nanak, *Siri Guru Granth Sahib*, page 991
Some say poor Nanak is a spirit. Some say that he is a demon, and some call him a man.

Some people said, "He's a ghost." Some said, "He's out of tune." And some said, "Just leave him. He's just a poor little fellow." Unless you have the eye to put in the eyes of your Master and recognize Him, you'll never become a Master. And if you do not have the heart, and the power, and the courage to surrender your head, the phoenix will not rise from the ashes—you will be by-passed.

There's no blame and no claim. The grateful Master shall bestow the totality of Godhood on those who invoke the mercy, the kindness, and the gratitude. Such a crown is earned, not learned. So you all live in the ecstasy and mystery of maya and God.

By the way, whether you are a Sikh, a Muslim, a Jew, or a Hindu, I have nothing to do with it. If you want to learn wisdom, study *Asa di Vaar* in English. You will discover absolute capsulated, practical applied consciousness and wisdom. It's very simple. It will guide you. If you can understand those words, they'll come in handy when you confront life.

If you want to know the science of Infinity, you have to understand *Japji*. There's nothing better than it. So normally, if you know these two things, you'll be satisfied, content.

What is the Shabad Guru? When somebody insults you, and you don't like it, the Shabad comes in handy. That's when it is handy to have the Guru's words in your memory. It is said that "the money which is in your pocket and the Guru's words which you remember by heart, are the most powerful help." That's why you repeat it. *Jap* means "Repeat." We repeat and repeat, so it becomes part of us, we become part of it. We who practice this are not insane. We look insane to those who are insane. Please understand that.

Once somebody asked me, "What can you do?"

I said, "If I do nothing, you will cycle through 8.4 million lifetimes and you shall never be free. If I do something, something may happen."

"What can you do?"

I said, "I can give you face and grace, and you can win life's race. If I do nothing you *are* nothing."

"What do you mean?"

I said, "If I do nothing, you are nothing, you shall be nothing. Is that not enough?"

"What do you mean?"

I said, "I mean, when I am very very mean, I'll do nothing, and you will mean nothing. Don't you understand?"

He said, "I understand. Do something."

I said, "Why? I don't have to do anything. You are the one who is asking, 'What can you do?' If I do nothing, you'll be doo-doo."

"Why is it essential that you do something?"

I said, "That's the way it is, that's the way it was, that's the way it shall be."

Remember, Teachers, if you do nothing, somebody's destiny is ruined. Just understand that. You may not do anything; you may refuse, it is your right. But if your destiny is to be a Teacher, and you don't become a Teacher, you hurt yourself. But if somebody comes to you and you do nothing, the destiny is ruined."

Don't worry about the obnoxiousness, narrowness, abusiveness, negativity, and neurosis of a student. Had he not been all that, why should he come to you? So please, when you become a teacher, serve all, like the sun, which shines on all, with light and warmth.

Thank you very much. Good night.

Meditation for the Arcline
& to Clear the Karmas

Mudra: Sit in Easy Pose with a straight spine. Relax the elbows down by the sides, and bring the forearms straight out in front of your body, palms flat and facing up. Have the palms slightly cupped, and place them a few inches above the knees.

Movement: Bring arms up, back behind head, stretching hands and arms as far back over shoulders as you can. Imagine you are scooping water, and throwing it through your arcline, over your shoulders, with a flick of the wrists. The movement is slow and smooth, and gracefully flows along with the lyrics and rhythm of the music.

Music: *Wahe Guru, Wahe Guru, Wahe Guru, Wahe Jio* by Giani Ji. On each *"Wa-hay Guroo,"* as well as on the *"Wa-hay Jeeo,"* do one complete round—scooping up, throwing over your shoulders, and come back to the starting position. Approximately 2 seconds per "scoop."

Eyes: Closed.

Time: 31 minutes.

End: Inhale, and stretch your hands back as far as possible, hands right behind your head, Posture for the Inhale must be correct.

Hold: 10-15 seconds. Exhale. Repeat 3 times total. Relax.

Comments/Effects: This meditation is for the arcline and to clear the karma that has been stocked up in it. You'll experience what *Wahe Guru* actually means. It's just a hand of prayer. Remember, the power of Infinity is not outside of you—it is inside of you. When "I" and Infinity create Impact, you'll become totally divine. Otherwise there's a duality which keeps you away from reality, and the pain is humongous.

Trouble Comes into Your Life When You Ask For It

The ocean is a very calm thing, but when the winds are heavy and high, then it's very choppy. The wind represents your ego—the higher the ego, the choppier is a person's life.

1 n economics we have the Law of Diminishing Returns. If you start eating bananas, you can eat one, two, three, four. At the fifth or sixth banana, you cannot eat. You may eat the eighth banana but if somebody will say, "I'll give you a thousand dollars if you eat the ninth," you absolutely can't. That's called the Law of Diminishing Returns.

Actually, this is how life is. The process of growth and decay is natural. You shall grow, and then you shall decay. That's natural. But when you are growing, you grow very fast and very extensively. And then you stimulate yourself with drugs and with sex. So the growth which has to go slowly and gradually—diagonally—goes vertically. The unfortunate part is when decay comes, it comes fast. If you have reached a height and you come down, it's a long miserable process. Why miserable? Misery is caused when you confront life at the same rhythm which is natural, but you do not have the energy of the natural. So when you shoot up like this *(YB demonstrates with his hand a line going straight up in the air)*, then you are not natural. When you come down like this *(YB demonstrates with his hand a line going at a very sharp decline downwards)*, you are not natural. And if a person develops himself or herself naturally, and decay comes naturally, life is very harmonious, smooth. Why? Because then it is within the realm of nature. So, any stimulation from outside is not correct. Every meditation inside is right. What is a meditation? With it you take away the fatigue, you clear the subconscious, you clean your being, and you are natural, you are normal.

There is a story I might have told you before. May I tell you? There was a Chinese Emperor. He was eighty-eight years old. He called his Grand Wazir. He said, "How many years old am I?"

He said, "Eighty-eight, my Lord."

He said, "Go to my twelve provinces. Find the most beautiful woman in each province and bring them all here. I want to marry them."

The orders were sent, the girls were marked, a ceremony took place. The Emperor married the twelve women. He called his *Ved*, his doctor. He said, "These are twelve women. I am married. I want to have the energy of an eighteen-year old."

He said, "My lord, you are eighty-eight years old."

Whenever the other person gets the message that you are on sale, or the possibility is there, there's no basic deep relationship. It turns into a hunter's attitude. We are hunting, we get hunted, we get haunted.

The Emperor said, "That I know, but I have you."

The doctor said, "You are taking a risk."

He said, "Doesn't matter. How long do you think I can live?"

He said, "You can live to be about a hundred-twenty years old. Something like that."

The Emperor asked, "Why do you say so?"

He said, "You are eighty-eight years old, you look like thirty-years old."

He said, "That's what I am telling you."

The doctor said, "Well, you are going to live to be one-hundred twenty-years old, and you are going to look only fifty-years old. So I don't guarantee any-thing."

He said, "That is true. But do it."

So the doctor brought some pills and said, "My lord, take these and do whatever you're going to do."

His assistant asked him, "Hey, why are you giving this medicine to him?"

He said, "He's not going to live six to eight days, why bother? But if he lives and I don't give him the medicine, he's going to kill me. So let me give it to him."

On the eighth day the king was found dead in his bed. The Grand Queen said, "How come my husband has died?"

The doctor said, "He asked for it."

Troubles in your life are those which you ask for. Blinded by your passion, insane by your ego, quick with your wrong judgment, you have no mutual aspect of grace, dignity, divinity, and humanity. You are not using your angelic power up front. You are living through your butt instead of the hemispheres of your head. You ask for pain, you ask for tragedy, you ask for death, you ask for difficulties.

It's not true that it is written that you should be in trouble. Troubles are those which you ask for. The ocean is a very calm thing, but when the winds are heavy and high, then it's very choppy. The wind represents your ego. The higher the ego, the choppier is a person's life. I love when the airplane captain says, "Well, the weather is causing a little turbulence, so please fasten your seatbelts and sit nicely 'till we go through it." Meanwhile, you notice that even the attendant who is very expert at carrying the drinks on the tray starts shaking. That's the way your life is.

No human is born to suffer. What he is going to suffer is a challenge through which a human can grow with strength. That's the law. But humans suffer without strength; they come out weak. Any challenge of life or calamity or disturbance through which you come out as weak is your fault. It's not natural.

So technically what we do is we say a prayer to God. Prayer is our power, so that we may not become locked in to deal with our life from ego. Pain is an ego. When you fight life with your truth, you have no pain. It's a challenge, you love it. You get excited. And this is fortu-nate that you live a life in essence. Because you must understand once and for all, you have earned this life. It's prepaid, earned, and it is, it is.

Now, to be in the wrong place, at the wrong time, for the wrong reason, is not required. Somebody went to the bank to cash a check and there was a holdup. Now what was his fault? He was normal, he went there. But he was in the wrong place at the wrong time. So when you are in a wrong mood at a wrong place, you ask for trouble.

And then you have a faculty as a human to look sexy. That's your base root of trouble. When you look sexy, you have to look sensual. When you look sensual, you look like you are for sale—you are never real. If you undertake that you will be original, organic, and you are not for sale, then you shall be social, and your beauty shall be that of a wizard, not of an idiot. Whenever the other person gets the message that you are on sale, or the possibility is there, there's no basic deep relationship. It turns into a hunter's attitude. We get hunted, we are hunting, we get hunted, we get haunted. The majority of us are chased down by haunting thoughts of desire. Haunting thoughts of desire make us totally non-realistic; they take us away from our originality.

Let's talk about something. Jews are Jews, and Jews have a certain robe of appearance. Christians are Christians, and Christians have a certain robe of appearance. Muslims are Muslims, and Muslims have a certain robe of appearance. This uniqueness may be geographical, it may be spiritual, it may be authentic, but there is a code of conduct of dress. Why? Those who have their faith in Christ will do this; those who have their faith in Mohammed will do this. That's how it was. But now the code of conduct is "I am for sale."

Everybody says, "How popular can I be?" Nobody says, "How wise can I be?" Isn't that funny?

So technically speaking, when you speak or hear anything negative, it pollutes your mind. If you do anything negative, it pollutes your body. If you deny anything positive, it weakens your spirit, your soul. So there's a streak of self-destruction in you. There's a streak of death in you. You feed it yourself. If you are born naturally, you live naturally, you grow naturally, you die naturally—it's beautiful. That's the way it is. But you over-stimulate yourself, then your belly underneath is not covered. You need to live a sheltered life which should be organic, natural, covered by the state of nature, by the environments. The tide of time should be with you, space should be right, and you should not be in the wrong place.

We can get all this in a simple way: That is, to be Masters. When mentally you confirm in yourself and take an oath that you are a Master, and that you have to serve the Master, you become the Master. Everything is a thought. God is a thought. It's just a thought. One pure thought can bring you all that you need.

Let's say somebody is abusive, very angry. Just start smiling at that moment. Try it sometime. See how much oil you put on that anger and abuse, on that reaction. There are people who react, and people who talk, and people who want to be known, people who want to be popular, people who want to control, people who are paranoid, people who are scared—take all of these examples—they are not original. These are parts of the destructive streak which you all have. It's amazing.

Nobody wants to be recognized by his performance. Nobody wants to be great by his delivery. Everybody wants to manipulate. People think that if they put their legs in three boats, they'll make the journey faster. Actually, they tear themselves up, and they make no sense.

We are technically corrupt. Righteously we are liars, gracefully we are deceitful, and temperamentally we are thieves. That is our beast side, our impulse side. That's the side we use when we want to go after something. As humans we are sober, we are sage, we are serene, we are serious, we are servants, and we are smiling. As angelic beings we are delightful, beautiful, bountiful, blissful, brave, and we bounce with energy; and that drama of the psyche and energy in us attracts the whole world. So you can choose what you want to be. Nobody wants to stop you.

There's another thing in you. You think that by messing things up you draw attention. It's just crying wolf—after a while nobody cares who you are.

So, technically, let us see if we can understand what we are talking about today and how we can achieve it, because this is your last class with me.

Tonight you are celebrating your completion and you are having fun. I'm just a guest. I have been sharing something with you, as if you are my own. I was sharing with you without any prejudice. I was sharing with you, without any idea even to reach you. I was sharing with you in gratitude. My gratitude was that somebody touched me. I'm grateful that I got touched. It was painful at that time, but I'm grateful to God who gave me the courage and health and help that I could go through it. I am grateful that I got guidance through which I survived through such times that a person of great courage cannot survive.

The only thing which I enjoy in life is trust, dependability. If you are not trustworthy, and you are not dependable, nobody will trust you. If you behave in a shallow manner, you will never be bright and beautiful. You will be just yellow. You'll be gray.

And understand something once and for all, please. Your handicaps travel ahead of you, and your reputation is known before you even reach a place. So it is very beautiful for humans to drop their past, change their attitude, have an altitude, make sense to themselves, so everybody can be sensibly made to understand that you are beautiful, bountiful and blissful, trustworthy, gracious, with divinity and dignity, and you can be a friend unto Infinity.

Make some sense to yourself. First look great, look gracious. Deal with everything from wisdom. Anything you say, say it wisely, and say it well. Say what you are saying to make the other person understand, not to just say what you want. So say it well, say it so that it's understood. Be priceless in dress, be priceless in every dealing; it doesn't matter where and why. In all that, understand that there is no prize which can give you back your honor.

(See page 214 for details to this meditation.)

We are going to put our hands unto the Heavens like this. We are going to look at the tip of our nose. And without the help of breath, we are going to pump our navel very fast. Pump it fast. I didn't say Breath of Fire. I didn't say help of the breath. Do whatever you can do with muscle, or with anything you want to do. Move it fast.

(After several minutes of silence.)

You are entering a twilight zone. Concentrate harder, push better. This time zone is very hard. On some it's harsher, but don't give up.

(Silence for a long while.)

Inhale deep. Hold, and pump as hard as you can. In this moment, it is all there is! Pump hard, hold the breath. Exhale. Inhale deep. Hold. Pump hard. Exhale. Inhale deep. Deep. Pump. Harder. Relax.

Thirty-one minutes. You are very lucky. We used to do this for two and a half hours at a stretch. And if we missed one little thing, the monitor would teach us such a lesson that we dared not make a mistake the next time.

Your caliber, your consciousness is the guarantor of your character and your power. It's my pleasure that I have been with you and to share with you something that I know, which I believe, which I carry. Hopefully as the future of the Age of Aquarius holds, you will also hold many hearts, give people a chance to live healthy, happy, holy.

Thank you, and God bless you.

Meditation for Maturity & Wisdom

Mudra: Bend your elbows down by your sides. Extend the forearms up so the palms are a few inches in front of each shoulder, palms flat and facing the body. Then bend the palms back slightly at the wrists, until the palms are facing up, and are somewhat relaxed and somewhat cupped. Just hold this position.

Movement: Without using the breath in any specific way, begin to pump the navel point powerfully. Pump very hard, and pump very fast. (Not Breath of Fire.)

Eyes: Stare at the tip of the nose.

Mantra: None indicated.

Time: 31 minutes.

End: Inhale, and pump the navel vigorously. Hold 10 seconds. Exhale. Repeat 3 times total. Relax.

Comments/Effects: Your handicaps travel ahead of you, and your reputation is known before you even reach a place. So it is very beautiful for humans to drop their past, change their attitude, have an altitude, and make sense to themselves. Then everybody can be sensibly made to understand that you are beautiful, bountiful and blissful, trustworthy, gracious, with divinity and dignity, and you can be a friend unto Infinity. You must understand: there is no prize which can give you back your honor.

To make sense to yourself:

• First look great, look gracious, look good.

• Deal with everything from a point of wisdom, and say things to the other person so he can understand what you say. Say it so that it's understood.

• Be priceless in all dealings; it doesn't matter where and why.

Living in Reality with Royalty

Your reality must project royalty. If you cannot project royalty with your reality, you don't belong to this Raaj Yog. On the throne of Raaj Yog sits Guru Ram Das, the Lord of Miracles. It means everything will be done for you, provided you have that strength, that association.

Patanjali gave us the system of yoga, and he gave us the human system where one can be a householder:

> *Grisht ashraam mahaa(n) ashraam, Devee dev poojatum.*
> > -Sanskrit saying
> *The institution of the householder is the highest institution.*
> *Even gods and goddesses worship it.*

The householder's life is the highest life of all lives. Angels and demi-gods worship it. So, the fact is that it was given to us. *"Wahe Guru, Guru Mantar hai."* *Wahe Guru* was given to us as the *Gurmantar*. Actually, thousands of years ago Pantanjali said:

> ਵਾਹਯੰਤੀਕਾਰਯੰਤੀਜਗਦੁਤਪਤੀ
> ਆਦਕ ਇਤਿ ਵਾਹਾ ॥
> ਬ੍ਰਹਮਾਦੇ ਤ੍ਰੇਸ਼ਾਂ ਗੁਰੂ ਇਤਿ ਵਾਹਿਗੁਰੂ ॥
> *Waah yantee, kaar yantee*
> *Jag dut patee, aadak it waahaa*
> *Brahmaaday Treyshaa Guru, it Wahe Guru.*
> > -Patanjali, *Push Puran*
> *Great Macro-self, creative Self, all that is,*
> *Creative through time, all that is the Great One.*
> *Three aspects of God: Brahma, Vishnu, Mahesh (Shiva).*
> *That is Wahe Guru.*

This is the personal mantra of the Trinity of God: Father, Son, and Holy Ghost; or Brahma, Vishnu, Mahesh; or the One who Generates, Organizes, Destroys or Delivers (G-O-D); those are the three powers of God. Accepted.

We say, "Kundalini Yoga as taught by Yogi Bhajan," because we don't want to pollute it

As a Teacher, follow these three things:
Don't let yourself down,
don't let anybody down,
and don't participate in
any let down.

with other things. We do not want to denounce anybody, but we also do not want to announce anybody. We just want to say it directly, that the Golden Chain must be kept correct.

That's why we ourselves named it "White Tantric Yoga." White Tantric is for the spirit, for elevation, and it completes everything. That's why we distinguish it from Black Tantric and Red Tantric. Those are temporary nonsenses. We don't even want to associate ourselves with them.

There are three things which are very important to you as a Teacher. One is your respect. You must live a respectful life. Your reality must project royalty. If you cannot project royalty with your reality, you don't belong to this Raaj Yog. On the throne of Raaj Yog sits Guru Ram Das, the Lord of Miracles. It means everything will be done for you, provided you have that strength, that association. So, you must have respectful living, graceful living, honorable living. That's a must.

Secondly, you must not be bought or sold. No temptation, no planning, no scheme, no money, no gain, no loss, no threat can tempt you.

Third, whether you know or not, whether you are competent or not, capable or not, you must undertake to serve. And if you are not competent, not capable, the Law of Vacuum of God will come through. So you shall not be let down. Technically what I am saying, is a Teacher must follow these three things: Don't let yourself down, don't let anybody down, and don't participate in the letdown.

As Teachers you will meet certain things. You will meet an enemy which presents itself in many colors: "I." Forget about *you* saying "I," students all come with their "I." The problem is with the "I." When the Third Eye opens, there's not going to be any problem. Having the Third Eye open means you intuitively know everything. Why should there be a problem? Why to suffer? What is suffering? All suffering is because of the "I." "Thou" never suffers. So when you come from "I," then there is no "Thou." When there is a "Thou" there is no "I." So all you have to do is to turn everybody's "I" into "Thou."

A lot of people love me—I'm not saying they don't. And a lot of people want things the way they want, and they see what they want to see. But the question is "I" has no "eye." I have the "eye" which they don't have. So, how can we meet? Their "I" sees what my "eye" doesn't see. Their "I's" are not my "eyes" and my "eye" is not their "I." Until we have that central "eye" we can't meet. So until then, we'll decide things based on emotions, feelings.

As a Teacher, if you do not stand the tense or sense of altitude and attitude and manners in behavior, in communication and projection, you may succeed for a while, but in the long run you will lose. You must understand that a student is a student is a student. The student's inferiority, his behavior, his negativity, are all that make him a student. He has come to learn excellence, altitude, power, strength, and purity from you. So the relationship is very solid. It's a solid relationship. But for God's sake, don't make it a commercial one. It's not commercial.

So let us have a deep understanding. When we go, let us grow. If we glow, we shall grow. It is automatic. We don't have to do anything. People who don't glow don't make sense. A candle is made of wax. You light the head and immediately darkness will run away. When it's not lit, the candle is a part of the darkness. It's useless. It doesn't make sense.

There's one poem of mine, in which I say, "When my thread of life will pass through you." It is most powerful. You can't understand it, but when you will understand that, you will understand divinity. In *The Man Called Siri Singh Sahib*, there are some poems. You have to remember them by heart.

Then there's a book called *Furmaan Khalsa*. The subjects covered in that collection of poems are those for which there is no answer. You have to search and search, but they are right there, for you to see in one minute.

There's a book called *The Teachings of Yogi Bhajan*, which is just one part of it. Actually, it was to be published in eleven parts, the rest of which we'll publish later.

So there are certain fundamental things you have to know. Why should you know? Because that will give you strength when you will meet up with some intellectual idiot. That's also an "I." There is intelligence impact and there are intellectual idiots. Intellectuals are never intelligent. Intellectuals are those who are overly intelligent; they are more intelligent than we need them to be. They don't make sense. You'll find them in coffee houses and places where they sit and talk, and talk, and talk, till they die. They have answers for everything. When you have answers for everything, when are you going to work? So when I say intellectuals are not intelligent, I'm very very calculatingly correct.

Those who love this world—W-O-R-L-D—will never understand the Word—W-O-R-D. So you have to make up your mind. There are very set rules.

If you are a Teacher, you have no comparison, no comparing, and no confusion. The first sign of a Teacher is that you are contained, you are content, and you are very continuously dependable. Your behavior reflects it. Your identity must have a personality of royalty and reality. Royalty and reality must be in you. This is called Shakti Yoga. This is called Kundalini Yoga. This is called the Yoga of Power, Self, and Stimulation. It is also called the Yoga of Awareness. I hope you will understand.

My prayers are with you. I'm grateful that you came. I'm grateful that you studied. I'm grateful that you will go. I'm grateful to that time and space when I didn't have anything, but I had myself. Just understand, the most priceless thing a person has is one's own self, and I'm grateful to my Teacher who was so harsh, so bitterly strategy wise that I don't think anybody could have survived.

There's a story of a Teacher and his student, a Greek philosopher named Aflatoon. Aflatoon was born into his parent's house, and when he was five-years old, his father said, "I have to take you to your Teacher."

His mother said, "My son, let me love you, let me feed you, let me dress you, because tomorrow you will return dead."

He said, "Why?"

She said, "Six brothers of yours have already died. I give birth to a child, I raise him, I take him to the Master, and the next day we get a dead body. But we have made up our minds that one of our children has to study from him."

He said, "Okay, I'll go. I'll come back tomorrow."

She said, "How are you going to come tomorrow? You're not going to come tomorrow. None of them has come."

He said, "Well, Mom, just make some very good food. I'll be coming tomorrow."

"Okay."

So his father took money, and fruit, and food, and clothes, and went to this Teacher with his son. He said, "Master, here is my son again."

And the Master said, "You are very consistent. Why do you want to give him to me?"

He said, "Well, as long as I live and I can have children, that's what I'm going to do. Every year I have come, because every year God has blessed us with a son. Unfortunately, this is our last son because my wife has not given birth to any children for all these years. So this is my last son. He will be yours."

He said, "Okay, thank you. Go. I'll give him the first lesson."

So when the evening came, he gave him food. He said, "How are you?"

The child said, "I am very fine, Master."

He said, "Come with me."

The child followed him to a huge room with a little hole. The Master said, "Get into this."

The child climbed into it. The Teacher blocked it with a big stone. The child thought, "He's the Master. He has put me here. It's all nothing but snow. I'm going to freeze to death like my other brothers. But," he said, "he's a Teacher. There must be something to it. Because everything has to be in balance. Life and death have to be in balance. I'm going to find it. Oh, that is his first lesson, 'find the balance.'" So he started, with his teeny tiny hands, looking around. He found a grinding wheel, and he found certain stones. He said, "That's it."

So he started putting stones into the grinding wheel and started grinding. In a couple of minutes, instead of shivering and being cold, he started sweating. He had found the answer. The whole night he kept the wheel grinding and kept the stone grinding. The more he ground the stones, the more that grinding wheel became heavy, and the more he sweated. So he was doing it very consistently, consciously, and he said, "This is the Cold Room of Death. This is the source of life. And life is nothing but balance."

When things are out of balance, they are undivine. When you deal with an idiot, you should be balanced with him as an idiot. If two idiots don't balance themselves, wisdom will never have a chance. You're all mistaken fundamentally for one thing. When you meet an idiot, you start giving him wisdom. That's it. You're out of balance. You have no sense of balance. When you meet an idiot, become an equal idiot, and come to that balanced level. Then start lifting. Then your wisdom will prevail. First go down like a fork-lift, and then start bringing things up. The principle of the forklift must be understood by every Teacher.

So, in the morning, when his Teacher, took the stone off, the boy came out. "Hello Master. Good morning. How are you?"

The teacher looked at him. He said, "Fine." And he said, "Okay, go, get ready. Take a bath, and change your clothes and come."

He came up fully dressed. He said, "What is the command, my Master?"

He said, "You are the Master. You have found the biggest law of all laws, the law of balance. Now go home."

So he came home and the mother and father fell over, "Ahh, who is this?"

He said, "Me. Your son."

"How can you come away from the Master? We gave you to him."

He said, "He sent me back. Now I'm the Master."

"You are the Master? In one night you have become the Master?"

He said, "It was too much grinding. I am the Master."

Many years later, Aflatoon had calculated that his death had come. So the Angel of Death got the command order. When he came into his house, there were 108 like him. Now, the Angel of Death has one letter to deliver and one command projection. If he misses it, then the guy will never be able to die—forever. So the Angel came back to God and God said, "Where is he?"

Whether you are competent or not, capable or not, you must undertake to serve. If you are not competent, not capable, the Law of Vacuum of God will come through. So you shall not be let down.

He said, "Impossible. There are 108 elements on this Earth and 108 Aflatoons, each one perfect. I talked to them. They were working perfectly. It's all fantastic."

He said, "Did you use the microscope lens to see?"

The Angel said, "Look God, don't question me. I'm getting tired now. My answer to you is I did everything known and unknown, and I even called upon Your power and all You said is, 'Figure it out.' That's it. So I'm back here. First of all, I will ask you to leave him alone. He will multiply himself. Let him be in this tragedy."

God said, "No. He served humanity. He must die and come back to the Heavens. I don't want him there anymore. He has served well, and it's My gratitude towards him."

The Angel said, "Well, he doesn't understand."

He said, "No, he understands. He's going to grind you, because he learned the law of balance from grinding."

The Angel said, "I have been ground. I couldn't do anything. I am here."

God said, "Well, there is one formula which will work."

He said, "What is that?"

He said, "Go there and start smiling and moving and being, and say, 'Oh, the one who has become 108 is all-perfect. I served God all my life, but now I shall serve thee. But there's one little defect.' And whosoever will say 'What?'—grab him."

So the Angel went there and said, "Oh, now I have come. You, the multiple of the equilibrium are equal self, and who created all this from the One—you are really Lord. I would like to serve thee. I bow, I salute."

ਆਦੇਸੁ ਤਿਸੈ ਆਦੇਸੁ ॥ ਆਦਿ ਅਨੀਲੁ ਅਨਾਦਿ ਅਨਾਹਤਿ ਜੁਗੁ ਜੁਗੁ ਏਕੋ ਵੇਸੁ ॥
Aadays tisai aadays. Aad aneel anaad anaahat jug jug ayko vays.
-Guru Nanak, *Siri Guru Granth Sahib*, page 6 (from the 30th *pauree* of *Japji Sahib*)
I salute God again and again. God is primal and pure with unknown beginning,
Who cannot be destroyed and Who remains the same in all the Ages.

This is the salutation of the yogis.

The angel continued speaking: "But there's a... I should not say it. I mean, who am I to say this? But there is one little thing. If that could be corrected, wow. Then it's all..."

Then somebody said, "What?"

He grabbed him. "Let's go!"

So, never, ever trust your teacher. It is his job to test you. It is your job to not fail. He doesn't want you to fail, but he doesn't want you to fail with others, so he wants to test out whether you will pass or fail. Normally you think, "A Teacher is a father." He's mostly a father figure, he's your love figure, he's your fantasy. He's almost all to you, except one thing. He'll test your garbage and that you normally will not like. You see, your garbage is equally important.

When You Become Soft Like Wax

One day when you will become soft like wax,
Then my thread of life will pass through you, and
Out of the accident of the warmth of my heart
one end will get lit
And you will burn... slowly melting in the heat of the flame.
And when you will reach the end,
You will find God waiting for you
To embrace you into His Infinity.

And one day, when you will become soft like wax,
My thread of life will pass through you, and
Out of the passion and compassion of the time
Your one end will get lit
And the spread of Light through you will bring joy...
But the jealousy will hover on you and the moths will burn alive.
But you will keep on...
Melting and burning and spreading the Light,
Knowing that on the base of you
God is waiting to embrace you and to merge you in Infinity.

When one day you will love me and become known to me
And in that knowledge when I will forget
The meaning of life and your image...
You will exist no more.
And that is the state of experience in consciousness:
Then God wants you and you don't want God.
The face value of every human is mostly not like that of an adult,
Because that inner being has never tried
To merge with the outer being.

In the depth of my heart there is a beat.
Sometimes I hope against hope that there will be common moments of life
When neither you will talk, nor listen
But will enjoy the experience of the voice
Which comes through my heart,
Through my beat.
And when our vibration will merge
We may be in a position to experience
The ecstasy of Undying Self.

Siri Singh Sahib Bhai Sahib Harbhajan Singh Khalsa Yogiji (Yogi Bhajan)

May the long time sun shine upon you
All love surround you
And the pure light within you
Guide Your Way On.

Sat Naam.

The Master's Touch

Excerpts & Meditations
from the
Assisi Lectures
April 1997

The Teachers Oath

I am not a Woman
I am not a Man
I am not a Person
I am not Myself
I am a Teacher.

Love Through Service

We have no consideration whether you are a man or a woman, young or old, pretty or ugly, whether you are French, German, Norwegian, or anything. First of all, I will request you to get rid of your prejudice and remember the Oath of a Kundalini Yoga Teacher.

This is a Teacher's Course. We have no consideration whether you are a man or a woman, young or old, pretty or ugly, whether you are French, German, Norwegian, or anything. First of all, I will request you to get rid of your prejudice and remember the Oath of a Kundalini Yoga Teacher which we take.

It doesn't matter how much I teach you, and how much you learn—the role of the Teacher is to elevate another person. The Teacher works through body language. He works through his sight. He works through his word. A Teacher is not one who covers the distance of destiny—he rewrites the destiny.

This course reflects my second side of the teachings, which I hid for twenty-eight years. I didn't come here to collect students or to start a religion. That was not my idea.

On the Eleventh of November 1991, the Age of Pisces ended, and the Age of Aquarius started. In between we have actually twenty-one years of the cusp, during which time you will find a change. The majority of people will go beserk. Signs and symptoms are as follows: People will become convincingly argumentative and negative. Second, people will feel a lot of unhappiness in their hearts, in spite of the fact that everything is normal. Thirdly, you will feel deep deep loneliness. Fourth, you will feel tired. Tired of what? Tired of eating, tired of living, tired of tired. The fundamental has changed—the Age of Aquarius is different than the Age of Pisces. In the Piscean Age, it was, "I want knowledge. Take me where it is available or I'll go where I can get it." In the Aquarian Age, it is "I want experience, I have knowledge." It is opposite.

This is what is going to happen. I may live or not, it doesn't matter. I have done my job. People will grab you in the street saying, "Help me." You may not know their name, you may not know who they are. They don't know your name, they will not know who you are. But the fact is they have to just see your radiant body, and they will be attracted to you as iron to a magnet. You will not know what to do. Sometimes you will try to say something, sometimes you will try to run away. There's nothing bad you can do, or good you can do. The only thing you should do is what I do. I just hold the hand of the person, and all I say is, "You are the

Lord of the Miracles. I can't do it. Help this person." I don't say that I'm very pure or that I am very saintly—I don't care to be a saint or pure. But it happens on the spot. And that's what you have to do to protect yourself.

🌀 You have been chanting all these years without knowing the meaning of, "God and me, me and God, are One." Now it is the time to understand it. Your purity and piety will work. There's no other miracle. Everybody has longitude and latitude, but at the moment within the time and space, if you can have an altitude and attitude, you win. If you forget this, you lose. There's no other big miracle.

🌀 We should learn to contain our negativity. God gave you the negative mind just to see through where you can be damaged. God didn't give you the negative mind to become negative. There are two powers on this Earth—one is lever, one is lens. The lever of a person is his word, and the lens of a person is his intuition.

I am sitting higher than you because I learned and you are learning. That's the only difference. You'll be as powerful tomorrow as I am today. Rather, the standard is that you should be ten times stronger than me. Then you can hold that flood of students. All these days you will hate me, I know. There's no other way, because some of the exercises are very painful. Because within this time, we have to rebuild your inner channels, rebuild your projection, and attack your ego. The last part you will not like, because you are still playing that, "This Earth belongs to me." It doesn't. Never has. The One who rotates this Earth will take care of your routine. None of you are orphans, none of you are poor, none of you are insane or miserable. Just widen yourself so you can get all that there is. Close yourself and everything will run away.

🌀 You know, this is St. Francis's place. He saw all things as God—particularly the birds. That's what he saw. Think of a butcher who kills every animal, then think of this man whose shoulder was loaded with birds wherever he walked. Those birds understood his innocence. In the same way, when you are innocent, students who want to learn the language of light will come to you, love you, hug you, and adore you. Just like the birds came and sat on top of his head. Do you know what he did? He chopped off his hair from the center. So the birds could have a proper sitting place. With hair, they used to fall left and right. It was his way of saying, "You are better than me. Come on, sit here." Sometimes for hours and hours he used to walk like that. Do you think he was insane? No. He's a saint and you are not. That was his mind.

You have to have that mental power to welcome everybody. When you sit in judgment, you shall sit in insecurity. The moment you are insecure, you are done, you are cooked, you make no sense. Because then you limit yourself, you make yourself small. Our way of life is infinite vastness and love through service.

🌀 This is the body—through its touch, its sight, and its expression you are going to heal the world. If this body does not have unlimited strength to elevate, it won't work. Do not deceive yourself. What you need is the strength of your soul and your determination. Let us see if we are balanced or not.

Meditation for Blessing

Part 1

Mudra: Sit in Easy Pose with a straight spine, chin in, chest out.

Hand position: Bend the ring and pinkie fingers into the palm, and hold them down with the thumb. Extend the index and middle fingers out straight. Extend the arms straight out to the sides, no bend to the elbows, right hand palm up towards the ceiling, and left hand palm down towards the ground. Keep them up at shoulder level, parallel to the ground.

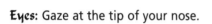

Eyes: Gaze at the tip of your nose.

Music: *Wahe Guru, Wahe Guru, Wahe Guru, Wahe Jio* by Giani ji. (*YB refers to this tape as the "Paris Tape."*)

Time: 11 minutes.

End: Inhale, hold the breath, and concentrate on all the vertebrae of the spine, starting from the base, and going all the way up to the neck, pulling them into the spine, tightening them into place. Hold the breath 20 seconds. Cannon-fire the breath out. Repeat 3 times total, expanding the lungs wider on each inhale, and tightening the spine with all your power each time. Relax.

Comments/Effects: The spine must not move. As you look at the tip of your nose, your forehead will begin to feel like lead. This is a pressure which is helping to develop the frontal lobe, which controls the personality. Just go through it and conquer the pain. The hands must be in balance with the spine because with these hands you will heal. You need that touch, so let the energy flow.

The words you are singing mean, "God, take me from darkness to light." It's an affirmation, a prayer. If the exercise becomes very painful, try singing along with the tape, copying the words. It may help. Keep the arms in balance, the spine straight, and stretch the arms out tightly—it will make it easier. Keep the posture perfect in the final 2 minutes—it is a very critical time.

Part II

Mudra: Extend the arms straight out in front of the body, with no bend in the elbows. Have the hands flat, palms face down, and the thumbs extended out. Touch the tips of the thumbs together. Keeping this position, raise the arms up to a 30-degree angle. Lift from the shoulders. Hold the position as if they were steel bars.

Eyes: Closed.

Music: *Prabh Joo To Keh Laaj Hamaaree* by Master Darshan Singh. It says, "God, come through and come through for me. Oh my God, save my honor."

Time: 9 minutes.

End: Inhale deeply, stretch your arms forward stiffly, and make them as hard as if steel bars are coming through them from your shoulders. Hold 20 seconds. Exhale. Repeat, hold the breath for 13 seconds each time. Relax.

Comments/Effects: In this position, bless the Earth. Bless everything. You must learn to bless. As a Teacher, you are the blessing, and your blessing must work, otherwise your students will not trust you. Bless, and bless gracefully. Feel the healing power flowing through your hands. Keep your concentration steady. Make sure the angle stays up at the proper height, and that there is no bend in the elbow.

Bless the Earth. Bless everything. You must learn to bless. As a Teacher, you are the blessing, and your blessing must work, otherwise your students will not trust you. Bless, and bless gracefully.

Part III

Mudra: Sit straight with your chin in, chest out. Put your left hand flat on your navel, fingers pointing towards the right. Place the right hand next to the right shoulder, palm flat and facing forward, fingers pointing straight up.

Music: Drum tape, called *Rhythms of Gatka* by Matamandir Singh.

Mantra: Begin reciting the mantra *Har* in a continuous spoken monotone, recited about one time per second. Press in on the hand very firmly every time you recite *Har.* Make the recitation very forceful.

Eyes: Stare straight ahead, parallel, with a perfect *Tratika* eye—not looking right or left.

Time: 3-1/2 minutes.

End: Inhale and move immediately into Part IV.

Comments/Effects: Think about what you want to be. Do you want to walk tall, do you want to bless people, do you want to be kind, compassionate, and caring? Can you love an enemy? If you cannot love your enemy, you still hate yourself. If you cannot help somebody who needs you, you are still poor. If you do not reach out with the idea to serve, and you can't serve, you have a fundamental mental problem. You are small. If somebody trusts you, and you betray, lie, or cheat them, you will never escape the wrath of nature.

In this exercise, I'll release the energy from 2.7 mega-cycle to 3 or 3.2. That is the maximum I can do. In layman's language, we are pushing you from one third of your existence to two thirds of your existence.

Part IV *(Done with a partner)*

Mudra: Sit across from a partner, and place the palm of your right hand flat against the flattened right palm of your partner. Both put an equal amount of pressure on the right hands to hold the hands in the middle between the two people. Place the left palm flat against the navel point. Begin pushing in on the navel point on the word *Har,* in the same fashion as done in Part III above. A person without a partner should imagine a partner sitting across from him or her.

Eyes: Look straight into the very small center of the other person's eyes. Feel you are connecting there.

Tape: Drum tape, called *Rhythms of Gatka* by Matamandir Singh

Mantra: Begin to chant'*Har* in a continuous monotone as in Part III. The sound comes from the navel point with each powerful push of the hand. *Har* is pronounced with a short sound,with the tongue, not the lip, with practically no vowel sounded.

Time: 1 minute.

End: Inhale and move immediately into Part V.

Part V *(Done with a partner)*

Mudra: Stay in the position for Part IV, but close your eyes.

Breath: Breathe long and deep.

Focus: Go into a deep meditation. Receive the Heavens in you. Go absolutely thoughtless, and hypnotize yourself into the total energy of God.

Music/Time:
>   20-1/2 minutes with *Nightingale of India* tape, also known as
>   "*Sat Nam Wahe Guru #3,*" by Lata Mangeshkar.
>   7 minutes with *Flowers in the Rain*, played on the guitar
>   by Gurudass Singh of Spain.

End: Relax.

Comments/Effects: After this meditation series you must drink a lot of lemon and water to cleanse out what has been released through this meditation. "The nuclei of the blood cells have burned their negativity. If you take a lot of lemon and water, you will urinate out all the dirt."

Part VI

> *Be open, be honest. It is between you and your God inside.*
> *Awaken your saintliness. It is your inner prayer for yourself.*
> *But remember, don't seek anything negative,*
> *because this energy will conflict.*

Music: *Ardas Bhaee* (The instrumental version was played in class, with the healers chanting aloud while standing, and everyone else sitting down and chanting.)

Ardaas Bhayee, Amar Daas Guru, Amar Daas Guru, Ardaas Bhayee.
Raam Das Guroo, Raam Daas Guroo, Raam Daas Guroo, Sachee Sahee.

Sing loud and clear. (The rhythm is slow.) Concentrate. Meditatively chant for 3 minutes.

End: Sit down and personally meditate what your wish is. Be open, be honest. It is between you and your God inside. Meditate in your honest way what you feel is to feel. What you want to know, to know. What you want to be, to be. Don't seek outside. Just close your eyes, go inside, and seek it. Remember, don't seek the negative, because this energy will conflict. Concentrate. It is your inner prayer for yourself. Rebirth yourself. Awaken your saintliness. (2 minutes.)

Part VII

Every breath of life, we are sending you a message. You must copy that message in the depths of your heart. This meditation is between you and God. And God within, not outside. Concentrate deeply on the words, feel it, know it, and be it.
Music: *Every Heartbeat* by Nirinjan Kaur. Meditate with these words to your inner depth. This song contains the mantra: *Aad Sach, Jugaad Sach, Haibhay Sach, Naanak Hosee Bhay Sach.*
Time: 3-1/2 minutes.

Part VIII *(Done as a group)*

Learn this mantra by heart. The power of this mantra is:
Sometime when you want to help, hold the hand of another person,
and chant that mantra only in your mind.
Shockingly, right there and then, you'll see it working right away!

If you are a husband, help your wife, help your children, help your neighbors, help your students, help your relatives. Become a living help, and the purity of God shall come through you. Lift yourself from the problem, and the problem will be gone. You must understand my practical experience. I get all the negative news, the problems, the miseries. I have one answer. "God, this person has reached out to me in Thy Name. Now You go and solve it." That's the longing of the heart. Once you have this meditative heart, you'll be surprised to see how that Almighty, Omnipresent, Omniscient God works for you without payment. Once you have that one thought, all things will be straightened out.

Hold each other's hands, just as if we are helping each other. Make an endless chain. Cooperate. Now, watch what happens. Don't trust my words, feel it yourself. Just sit meditatively and go through it. Hold the hands and see, for yourself, not for me, not for anybody, but for your experience, so that tomorrow you may know.

Music: *The Mantra of the Age of Aquarius* by Yogi Bhajan. *The Aquarian March* by Nirinjan Kaur.

Sat Siree, Siree Akaal, Siree Akaal Maahaa Akaal.
Maahaa Akaal Sat Nam, Akaal Moorat. Wahe Guru.

Mudra: Class sat holding hands, making a chain of the people in the room.

Time: 3 minutes.

End: Inhale, hold the breath, placing both your hands flat on the chest, left under, right over. Press hard and with the power of the mind, spread the energy to every tissue in your body. Hold between 15-20 seconds. Cannon-fire the breath out. Repeat 3 times total. Relax.

Belong to Yourself—
God Will Belong to You

If you don't believe you belong to yourself, why should God belong to you? That person who does not belong to that person inside, and respect that person inside, will have chaos.

L ife is a gift. A gift is a gift, whether it's a good gift or a bad gift. Life you cannot buy, you cannot sell, you cannot do anything with it—it is a gift. When you put a price on the gift, then your tragedy starts, then your discomfort starts, and from Heaven you shift to Hell. Nobody wants to put a price on a gift. Rather, when people give a gift they take away the price tag. A gift is from the heart, not from the head.

◎

You cannot say, "In God We Trust." That was Piscean. Now you have to say, "In God I Dwell." Now you cannot say this body is for sale, and this body fashion is to attract a sale. You have to say, "This body is the temple of my God within me." The disrespect, discourtesy, insult, and abuse you do to your body is totally, absolutely unwanted, unneeded, and inhuman. The body was given to you as a gift, according to the journey of your soul towards the destiny. A raindrop starts, it has to reach the ocean. It doesn't want to, so what does it do? It gets stuck on ponds and in different places. That's all right, but until the raindrop ends up in the ocean, it will not become rain again. The cycle must be completed.

◎ You want to be Teachers. Then you have to rise above all people. You have to rise above yourself, also, and then everything becomes minor. What becomes major is the answer to the call of duty. Suppose you're going to the office. All that matters to that office is how well you work.

◎ The tragedy in life is that your hidden agenda will surface, one day or the other. And trust me, when the other person will know that you have a hidden agenda, the relationship is off. You try to be clever, you try to hide things. Well, for some days, or for some months, or for some years you can be successful. Therefore, in life the only way you can live is, live straight. Don't let your inside be different from your outside. There is no such thing as neurosis. It is your hidden agenda which you cannot control. Then you find it comes out at different times. That evaporates the happiness of life. But technically speaking, when your flow is all right, you are all right.

As teachers of tomorrow, I don't know whether you understand or not. If you don't understand you will never be teachers. To me, there's no American, no German, no Japanese, no French, no Indian. I am a teacher, the person before me is a student. I am a human, they are human. Somebody touched me; I am supposed to touch them. Somebody taught me; I am supposed to teach them. If it wasn't for that somebody, I would have been an idiot. Therefore I should not tolerate any idiot. Somebody did their best, chiseled me out, and made me such a beautiful man. I am supposed to do the same. It's not always easy. People don't like to be criticized. People don't like to be chiseled. People do not like to be ground down. Neither do they like to be guided and goaded.

☉

Why do we meditate? These thoughts which the subconscious, the id, releases; some we deal with, some we don't deal with. Those we don't deal with go into the unconscious. Meditation is nothing but a self-invoked hypnotic dream. The proper translation of meditation is, "Self-Invoked Hypnotic Dream in which you Clean Your Subconscious."

When somebody says, "I had a dream of this, I had a dream of that," actually what you are dreaming comes from your subconscious. And then you have day-dreaming, you have night-dreaming, you have nightmares. That is when the subconscious starts unloading into the unconsciousness.

If you meditate, you are not doing anybody any favor, and you are not going to grow wings from your armpits. It will only help you to be a self-controlled person. It will only mean people will respect you, trust you, and like you. You will not have a split personality, and your words will mean exactly what you are saying. That's all. It's no big miracle. If you don't meditate, you won't be true to yourself.

☉ When you people say, "I love you," that is really saying to the other person, "Don't move." What matters more than that? "Don't move. I love you." If you say, "I love you," then you don't have to say anything. Love is right, wrong, has no jurisdiction, has no territory, has no domain, has no end—it is Infinite. But if your love is not Infinite, if it is purposeful, or it is for pleasure, or purpose, or projection, then using this word for fishing is not love. That's why today we love, tomorrow we don't. Today we love "A," then we love "B," then we love "C," then we love "D." You do not love yourself, so you do not know what love is. If you love yourself, if you feel yourself, then you can feel the pain and the pleasure of the universe. Then you will not hurt anyone. Then you can be a Jew or a Christian. Otherwise, neither you are a Jew or a Christian. Because the Commandments say, "Thou Shall Not Kill." They didn't say, "Thou Shall Not Kill—but kosher killing is okay."

☉ There are two things you should never do in your life: Don't lie to anybody, and don't have an agenda when you speak. Because when the other person will find out you have lied, your whole teachership is out of the window. When the other person will feel that what you were saying had an agenda behind it, you have not only lost a friend, but you have created an enemy. There are some essential things in life to make it happy. Happiness is your birthright.

⊘ You can't see a human as a human. Either a human is black or brown or heathen or faithful or loyal, or he belongs to Allah or Yallah, or Ballah. God knows. A human is a human. A human belongs to a human in a human. A human doesn't belong to anything or anybody. If you do not belong to a human in you, you do not belong to humanity, and you will not enjoy that brightness which that will give you.

It's just like with parents. Heavenly Father and Mother Earth have given you birth through the Earthly parents. They nurture you, train you, do their best. But in the end it is *you* who are accountable. You cannot live in the parents' house all your life. You cannot hide in a closet. That's life. You don't belong to God—God belongs to you. But God will belong to you when you will belong to yourself. If you don't believe you belong to yourself, why should God belong to you? That person who does not belong to that person inside, and respect that person inside, will have chaos. That low brand of life which is caught in status, is not a real life. Life is when you are free, open to serve, to be, to hug, and love without demarcation. That is saintliness. You are a man first, and a saint very first. Your spirit has taken the body; your body has not taken the spirit. Your spirit may leave; you will drop. You are dependent on spirit, not on body. And my dear fellows, never decide a matter of heart with head. You can be brain dead, and still be living, but you cannot be heart dead and still be living.

So the Age of Aquarius has different teachings, different thought forms, to build a different personality to fit in the new change. Old formulas will not work. That's why, if we don't go out and help people, a lot of people will be destroyed, and it will be your fault. You could have risen yourself and helped others.

Tonight we will just give ourselves a little lift. We'll do a very simple *kriya,* if you are in the mood.

⊘

Meditation for Upliftment

Part I

Every religion has one word, one sound only: *Yaa-ho-vaah—Yaa. Hallelujah—Haa. La-e-laah—Laa. Rama—Raa. Saa-Taa-Naa-Maa—Saa.* What are they talking about? What happened to the rest? All these big philosophies will go. Man will merge as a man, and emerge as a God's man. Nobody will waste time in finding God. Everybody will be there to make God find them. God is everywhere. Let Him find us. Why should we find Him? Be a human and God will find you. All you have to do to become beautiful as a human: See yourself through your spirit, and see what comes to you. You have been taught to go after things. Let things come to you.

Mudra: Bring the hands palm to palm, fingers pointing up. Place the mudra at your forehead, making sure the wrist line meets the eyebrows. Sit straight.

Music: Sounds of the various religions, from a recording by Matamandir Singh, from the musical tape called *Bharia Hath*—the 20th *pauree* of *Japji Sahib*.

Eyes: Closed. Meditate on the tape.

Time: 7 minutes.

End: Immediately move into Part II.

Part II *(Done as a group)*

Mudra: Sit straight, in a meditative posture. Everyone in the room holds hands.

Eyes: Closed.

Music: Same as in Part I. Sing along with the tape. Sing from the navel.

Time: 4 minutes.

End: Inhale and repeat the prayer which Yogi Bhajan recited:

Oh my soul, give me the light. Show me the path.
Give me the excellence and beauty to be
bountiful, blissful, kind, and compassionate,
and true to myself.

The Divine Essence of a Teacher

CLASS THREE ✦ Morning of April 22, 1997

You have come here to become teachers. It is my responsibility to tell you what a Teacher is. We are playing the tape of that shabad of Nanak in which a Teacher is described. If you understand what is written in this shabad, and you understand that is the way you want to be, you are a Teacher.

You have one friend in you—that is your mind. When your mind has duality, it takes you away from your reality. The difference between a Teacher and a human is, the Teacher surrenders his duality. God is in us, therefore we do not say, "In God we Trust." We say, "In God I Dwell." The gap between man and God has to be eliminated. If a human wants to enjoy the Earth: There are many roads and many ways—I am not disagreeing—there are many philosophies and many theories; there are many choices and many therapies. But one thing is always true: There is always one experience.

If you do not have an experience of bliss, you should work for it. Because it is not your teaching, your philosophy, your knowledge which matters. It is your bliss that you share with another person who is unfortunate which is all that matters.

You have ten bodies, but your radiant body solidly affects and acts within a twenty-five mile radius. When the glow of the shield of your radiant body extends to twelve and a half miles, you are just an ordinary human being. When it extends to three miles, you are worse than a bird. Every species created by God has a soul. The difference is how that soul radiates in its surroundings. One bulb is fifty watts, another bulb is a hundred watts, another is a thousand watts. Each light is different. All three are bulbs. All run on electricity. The purpose of all is to spread light, but the glow is different. And there's another thing. The bulb is made out of vacuum. Because the healer isn't, even if it uses 5,000 watts, it can give you heat, but not the glow.

You have three minds: negative, positive and neutral. A person who does not deal with the neutral mind, even with all wealth shall not prosper and can't be happy, because negative and positive cancel each other. It is the neutral mind which becomes the intuitive force in you.

You must know where you have to go. You must know what you have to conquer. With every thought, ask only one question: "Will this thought, if I pursue it, make me noble, or will it make me bitter? Will it make me a stonehead, or will my fragrance be all over the world? Will it give me the strength to make people happy, or will I make other people unhappy?"

What kind of Teacher will you be? Do you want to limit yourself with territory? A Teacher has no territory, a Teacher has no personality, a Teacher has no reality. His only reality is he uplifts, uplifts, uplifts; he keeps up and uplifts, keep ups and uplifts. It's like a philosopher's stone: any metal he touches becomes gold.

You have to start your thoughts like this. "I come from the Heavenly Father, to be on Mother Earth. She will nurture me and nurse me if I only ask."

No. You are taught, "Go, get money. Find a rich woman. Find a rich man. Have good sex." All that kind of stuff which if you go after, is going to give you trouble. When you "go and get it" then you have to carry the weight. There's no difference between you and a slave. You are actually a mental tragedy and a coolie. In your head, you carry all the weight. You make no sense to the Divine.

Do you know what God thinks, sitting in you? He says, "Oh, I'm living in an idiot." God sits inside you, you mess Him up inside you, and He gets very mad. So He tells His wife, *Prakirti*, "Teach this guy a lesson."

Now, you know what God's lesson is? Do you know the vengeance of God? He will give you all wealth, but no satisfaction. That's a "Nerd #1." God is a Nerd. When He starts behaving at your level, He's really very indifferent.

Any person who has no time for God and meditation or yoga, you will find him or her getting rich about middle age. Watch my words. It's true. They become rich. The moment they become rich, they are attached, and they are hooked. They can't let attachment go, and they can't become Infinite. They can't go, grow, and glow. They are finished. This is God's revenge. But if you sit tight, bright, things will come to you.

There's no fault with any student. Sometimes I am criticized for that, but I don't react. Some people I help, some I counsel, some I advise, some I talk to, and some I leave alone. They have made up their minds not to listen, and I have made up my mind not to say anything. If one is not willing to change for himself or herself, they are never going to change for anybody else.

You all must have dated at one time or another. Just remember today how many lies you told while dating. How much you made up to impress? Did you ever tell your man that, "At night I snore. Even my cat and dog leave the house"? Did you ever tell your fiancée, "My menstruation is fifteen days long"? Did you ever tell your fianceé that, "I have been raped six times"? Did you ever tell anything which will concern that man tomorrow? No. Because you are afraid that he will exploit it. That is the quality of a Teacher. If his students tell him anything or everything, and if the Teacher betrays it, exploits it, then it is a natural law, that Teacher either has to elevate that person into the Heavens or go to hell himself or herself.

So this has created students who window-shop, and Teachers who are philosophers. Nobody is willing to take the pain to wake up another person. The majority of the Teachers are themselves asleep.

It is good to be good. It is good to have goods, but the reality is, you are God.

Technically, your mind is your tool. If you do not correctly use it, you will look like a fool. Don't let your mind rule you—rule your mind. You will be prosperous, powerful and princely. It's up to you. As a Teacher, you cannot dress like a commoner. You cannot behave like a commoner. You cannot eat and sleep like a commoner. Because it is the commoner you are going to lead. The only way you can lead is with your own discipline. The effectiveness is your own power. Therefore, you should decide with your mind.

It looks great. People stand up when you come, they touch your feet, they give you presents, they love you very much. All that is great, but there's a consequence to it. You will rebel and revolt from inside if you don't have a discipline. This world is a conscious world, and you have to take charge of every thought consciously.

If your words do not have a smile, if you do not talk heart to heart, and you decide everything with your head, it is better to keep a dog as a friend rather than you. You are a useless, painful drag. The only thing in this world that counts is your smile, your uplifting word, and your kindly body gesture. These are three fundamental requirements of a Teacher.

There are three more:. When you have a student, chisel the student, penetrate into the student, and make a student better than you. Otherwise your tomorrow is dead. Teach your student to become a Teacher. And make him understand again and again and again.

The whole world is your student. Trees are your students, stones are your students, your family is your student—everything is your student. A Teacher cannot think in any other way. If you think anything else, you are not a Teacher.

Today the world has become very literal. Minds have to become very vast. Today's world is the Aquarian world—a small mind will never be happy. In this room there are so many denominations of religions that you can't even count them. But we have only one purpose—to experience, to help, and to serve the future. That is fundamental. It is the basic nature of the human which is born in the image of God, not to let that image be tarnished. Divinity is your reality, and the false side is maya. When "I" and "Thou" fight, "I" always loses. But "Thou" is never happy to win.

Purkha and *Prakirti*, or *Shakta* and *Shakti*, are our parents. Though they are God, the rude stonehead miserable children, the children in duality, are not happy news to the parents. That's why God changes the system after a while. This planet Earth and humanity have been wiped out four times before. What we do here doesn't work right. We need to change for ourselves; nobody can change us, nobody can love us, nobody can take care of us. It is always we in the beginning, we in the middle, and we in the end. As you sow, so shall you reap. If you sow wrong, you will weep, Mr. Creep.

You have come here to become teachers. It is my responsibility to tell you what a teacher is. We are putting the tape of that *shabad* of Nanak in which a Teacher is described. If you understand what is written in this *shabad*, and you understand that is the way you want to be, you are a Teacher. As long as I live, I will keep on hammering you, that's all it is.

Yogi Bhajan translates the lines of the shabad "Gurdev Mata," which appears on page 250 of Siri Guru Granth Sahib, and was written by the 5th Nanak, Guru Arjun.

ਗੁਰਦੇਵ ਮਾਤਾ ਗੁਰਦੇਵ ਪਿਤਾ ਗੁਰਦੇਵ ਸੁਆਮੀ ਪਰਮੇਸੁਰਾ

Gurdev maataa Gurdev pitaa. Gurdev swami parmeysuraa.

The Teacher is Madre and Padre. Transparent Mother, Transparent Father. The Teacher is the Master, like God.

ਗੁਰਦੇਵ ਸਖਾ ਅਗਿਆਨ ਭੰਜਨੁ ਗੁਰਦੇਵ ਬੰਧਿਪ ਸਹੋਦਰਾ

Gurdev sakhaa agiaan bhanjan, Gurdev bandhap sahodaraa

Guru Dev is a friend who dismisses the darkness of ignorance, who removes the ignorance. Such a relative which comes through every time.

ਗੁਰਦੇਵ ਦਾਤਾ ਹਰਿ ਨਾਮੁ ਉਪਦੇਸੈ ਗੁਰਦੇਵ ਮੰਤੁ ਨਿਰੋਧਰਾ

Gurdev daataa har naam updeysai, Gurdev mant nirodharaa

Gurdev is the Giver, the Teacher of the Lord's Name. Gurdev is the Mantra which never fails.

ਗੁਰਦੇਵ ਸਾਂਤਿ ਸਤਿ ਬੁਧਿ ਮੂਰਤਿ ਗੁਰਦੇਵ ਪਾਰਸ ਪਰਸ ਪਰਾ

Gurdev shaant sat budh moorat, Gurdev paaras paras paraa

Gurdev is a saint and wisdom personified. The Teacher is like the Philosopher's stone; whatever it touches, changes. The power of the Teacher is the touch of the Teacher, whether it's through words, body gesture, sight, or presence.

ਗੁਰਦੇਵ ਤੀਰਥੁ ਅੰਮ੍ਰਿਤ ਸਰੋਵਰੁ ਗੁਰ ਗਿਆਨ ਮਜਨੁ ਅਪਰੰਪਰਾ

Gurdev teerath amrit sarovar, Gur giaan majan aparanparaa

The Teacher is like a pilgrimage to a pond of nectar. His uplifting knowledge is beyond, beyond, beyond.

ਗੁਰਦੇਵ ਕਰਤਾ ਸਭਿ ਪਾਪ ਹਰਤਾ ਗੁਰਦੇਵ ਪਤਿਤ ਪਵਿਤ ਕਰਾ

Gurdev kartaa sabh paap hartaa, Gurdev patit pavit karaa

Gurudev does everything and removes all sins, is honorable, and stands with purity.

ਗੁਰਦੇਵ ਆਦਿ ਜੁਗਾਦਿ ਜੁਗੁ ਜੁਗੁ ਗੁਰਦੇਵ ਮੰਤੁ ਹਰਿ ਜਪਿ ਉਧਰਾ

Gurdev aad jugaad jug jug, Gurdev mant har jap udharaa

The Teacher is from the very start, through all time, and always shall be. Guru Dev meditates, repeats the mantra of the Divine, ever, and perfects it.

ਗੁਰਦੇਵ ਸੰਗਤਿ ਪ੍ਰਭ ਮੇਲਿ ਕਰਿ ਕਿਰਪਾ ਹਮ ਮੂੜ ਪਾਪੀ ਜਿਤੁ ਲਗਿ ਤਰਾ

Gurdev sangat prabh mel kar kirpaa. Ham moor paapee jit lag taraa

The Teacher creates the union between the congregation and God. Through blessings, the Teacher removes the arrogance and ignorance and takes the human across.

ਗੁਰਦੇਵ ਸਤਿਗੁਰੁ ਪਾਰਬ੍ਰਹਮੁ ਪਰਮੇਸਰੁ ਗੁਰਦੇਵ ਨਾਨਕ ਹਰਿ ਨਮਸਕਰਾ

Gurdev satgur paarbrahm parmeshar, Gurdev naanak har namskaraa

The Spiritual Teacher is a divinely true Teacher and true guide, like God. Through a Teacher, Nanak salutes God.

Meditation to Experience the Essence of a Teacher

I have given you the words of Nanak, which define the essence of a Spiritual Teacher. It's not a commercial thing, it is real. And the key to that, joining into that, is the mantra, Ong Namo Guru Dev Namo. That is the mantra, that's a key to the essence of that shabad, Gurdev Mata.

Mudra: Place the palms flat together at the heart center in Prayer Pose.

Eyes: Closed.

Music/Time

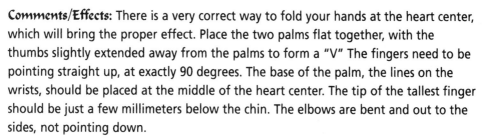

(a) 3-1/2 minutes *Ong Namo Guru Dev Namo* sung by Nirinjan Kaur. Sing along with the tape. Rhythm is slow.

(b) Meditate on one full repetition of the tape for *Gurdev Mata* sung by Guru Jiwan Singh. *(See words page 240.)*

(c) 1 minute *Ong Namo Guru Dev Namo*

End: Inhale deeply. Hold for 12 seconds, while you go deep into your soul, finding the Divine tranquillity within. Exhale. Repeat 3 times. Relax.

Comments/Effects: There is a very correct way to fold your hands at the heart center, which will bring the proper effect. Place the two palms flat together, with the thumbs slightly extended away from the palms to form a "V" The fingers need to be pointing straight up, at exactly 90 degrees. The base of the palm, the lines on the wrists, should be placed at the middle of the heart center. The tip of the tallest finger should be just a few millimeters below the chin. The elbows are bent and out to the sides, not pointing down.

The incorrect way to do this posture, which sometimes is done, is to place your palms flat together at the heart center, and to angle the fingers forward at a 45 degree angle, and some people even angle the fingers down towards the floor. This will not bring the proper effects.

In Kundalini Yoga we do not start without this mantra *Ong Namo Guru Dev Namo*. It's a telephone number of *Shakti*, with its own area code number, and it is a direct line.

This is a simple *kriya* which you all must know. You may read about Kundalini Yoga, you may write about Kundalini Yoga, but you will never be in a position to project Kundalini Yoga with your word, and through your body, if you do not have a mastery of this mantra.

The Power of the Mind

CLASS FOUR ✦ Evening of April 22, 1997

*You are a human being. "Hu" means "halo, light,"
which we all have. "Man" means "mental." "Being"
means "for the time being." For the time being, you
are a mental halo of light.*

What is a mantra? You have the right to ask that question. Mantra is two words—
"*Man*" "*tra*." "*Man*" means mind. "*Tra*" means the heat of life. "*Ra*" means sun.
So, mantra is a powerful combination of words which, if recited, takes the vibratory effect of each of your molecules into the Infinity of the Cosmos. That is called "Mantra."

"*Tantra*" means the "length and breadth" which takes the sun energy and purifies you.
"*Antra*" means your nucleus. "*Bantra*" means your constitution. "*Jantra*" is the faculty and facility of your constitution in combination with the totality of the universe and your individuality.

I have nothing against what you read in books, and what you read in religion. But it is a long, scenic route, and people do not have that long a life. Even if you sincerely like to work, if you do not know the real definition, you do not reach anywhere. If I want you do understand what "*Mantra, jantra, tantra, antra, sotantra, patantra*" is, I'll say it like this: " *Mantra*—the projected combination of my words. *Jantra*—the personality focus of my arcline which projects with my shield. *Tantra*—my length and breadth. *Antra*—the elementary constitution, my inner nucleus. *Sotantra*—my independence. And *Patantra*—is my definite beam projection. I am a Lord and a sovereign of all mind and mental states. One, two, three, four, five, six." You have to remember it that way.

The job of the Teacher is like an elevator—it lifts you up to any floor you want to go. Your existence has only one value—that you can share your values, free and clear, so you can walk with your enemies and your friends, alike. Your value is nothing if you cannot honor your word. If you do not mean what you say, you are the most mean person on the Earth. All this decoration, beauty is nonsense. But when you speak, God speaks through you. You are a water pipe. You are not the water. From one pipe comes the oil, the other pipe brings water. But when you need water, you cannot drink oil. People need from you one thing—to nurse them and nurture them.

Some Teachers do not want to look like a Teacher, because they think they cannot reach students. To become a Teacher is an election? Is it an election? The student will come to you if you are a Teacher. It is fundamentally wrong to go after a student. The second wrong is to depend on a student, and the third wrong is not to be absolutely neutral with a student. These are the first three requirements of your own honor as a Teacher. Because on one hand, as a Teacher, you are going to stretch the student; on the other hand you are dependent on him? How can this oil and water meet? On one hand you have to be in the command center and command the situation. You have to goad and guide the student, on the other hand you are looking for help from him or her? On one side you are teaching about God, on the other side you are dependent on God's creation? Has your God gone on holiday?

All right, a little man, Jesu, got killed on the cross like a million others. But his purity and his piety created a billion and a half Christians on this Earth. That is the power of the mind of a man.

When Nanak traveled around and told the religious people, "You are lying to people; what you are teaching is not divine, and you are teaching duality," they threw stones at him. But in five hundred years there are twenty-two million of those who shape themselves into the form of a Sikh, and who live by his word.

Some people are very ashamed of learning; they are very shy. The majority of people window shop, and many people want to become Kundalini-God-awakened instantly. God has given you that much energy at the time of birth that at one moment, on one instruction, or at the sight of your Teacher, you can become a Teacher—if your discipline is pure. The power in you is not your power, the power in you is your purity and piety.

You are born pure, but you forget to live pure. You put too much commotion and feeling into your love life. I understand spermatozoa mature when you are young. But you must not forget one very important thing: Sex is not in the second chakra. The sixth is the command center, and it's the sixth center which will serve you, not the second. So when you talk to another human being, sort it out.

One way to test something is to say: "Does this make me noble, does this make me Divine, does this elevate me to my Creator?" If the thing does not align with these three things, depart. And make it as a habit.

First ask yourself, are you noble or not? If you are not, do anything you want—drink, eat meat, womanize, become gay, get uppers, downers, run for politics—do anything, it will not matter, because you have decided you are not noble, and your decision must be blessed. But if you care to decide you are noble, honorable, truthful, and pure, then whatever comes to you, filter it with one word which is very personal and selfish. "Does it make me noble, pure, truthful? Is it a love without condition or with condition?" Just do this for forty days, and your life will change. In forty days you will develop a habit.

If I am noble, why should I allow myself to be insulted? Why should I have a result which is nothing but ugly, dirty, good-for-nothing? You are a human being. "Hu" means "halo, light," which we all have. "Man" means "mental." "Being" means "for the time being." For the time being, you are a mental halo of light.

Once you decide to be noble, Mother Nature and Heavenly Father will treat you so. Otherwise your life will be a yo-yo—up, down, up, down, left, right, left, right, left. But you will be marching in place. You won't go anywhere.

Those who have no power to obey shall never have the power to command. Those who have no power to give never take anything in peace. Those who don't honor themselves shall have no honor. Those who have no personal discipline shall be betrayed by their disciples. And those who do not understand with their principles shall stand under nothing—they'll be wasted. These are the laws of nature which cannot be changed.

Our relationship is not what our relationship is here. It comes from many lives, and it'll go on for many lives. As a human you have a breakthrough chance. You have come from Infinity to finite to merge back into Infinity. This is your temporary place. It's a motel. Do not take the pillows from the motel away with you.

Why pollute this beautiful human life with emotion and commotion, and ruin the whole thing? Why? There's a beauty in spiritual grace. That beauty is very attractive, very real. Conscious living is better than God Itself. When you live consciously, you dwell in God. Then you have a very beautiful power. Wherever you cast your gaze, elevation occurs. Wherever you touch, elevation occurs. Wherever you speak, elevation occurs. You uplift even the dead. You not only release a person from bondage, but you free generations from bondage—that's the beauty of a Teacher. A Teacher is not a circus monkey. No, my dear friends, a Teacher is God, and God is the Teacher, and the only difference between the two is that man feels he is not God.

For three thousand years you have been told by every religion, "Find God." Where are you going to find God? God is everywhere—Omnipresent, Omniscient, Omni, Omni, Omni. That is "Om, Om, Om." All-prevalent is "Om." You call it "Omni." And you are nowhere. Why are you looking for something which is everywhere? Why don't you find yourself? Why are you not at peace so God can visit you? Why do you want to run after God? What is wrong with you? And all the time you are praying, "Give me this, give me this, give me this," as if He's deaf, dumb, and cannot speak. He knows what to give you, and what to take away.

I have only one line on which I live. You might misunderstand me. I have never opened a book in my life. I don't read books. This is not my policy. I don't like reading books. I have written forty books, which I did not publish on a commercial basis. We have tons and tons of tape recordings and music, which we have not published publicly, because they belong to the Age of Aquarius, not to the Piscean Cusp. The one line I practice is:

ਕੇਤਿਆ ਦੂਖ ਭੂਖ ਸਦ ਮਾਰ ॥ ਏਹਿ ਭਿ ਦਾਤਿ ਤੇਰੀ ਦਾਤਾਰ ॥
Ketiaa dookh bhookh sad maar. Eh bhee daat teree daataar.
   -Guru Nanak, *Siri Guru Granth Sahib*, page 5 (25th *pauree* of *Japji Sahib*)
Many suffer privation and pain and are continuously beaten. Even these are God's gifts.

So I made a granite headstone, and I had these two lines of mine engraved on it. The translation is: *Ketiaa*—many, many, many. *Dookh* means discomfort. *Bhookh* means hunger. *Sad maar* means it is multiplied a hundred thousand times. "God, if you give me pain, hunger, and displeasure, and multiply it a hundred thousand times, I will take it as Thy gift." If you cannot live this, you cannot be a Teacher. It doesn't matter what comes, at least God thought you are capable, and He trusted you, so you must come through. *Eh* bhee: That is. *Daat:* Gift. *Teree:* Belongs to Thou, Oh Giver.

You know, if just a needle sticks in your butt and you start crying, God knows what happens. If something goes wrong, the Doer of all is God, so why not? Why don't you see Him? If you cannot see God in all, you cannot see God at all. In every action see His play—you'll be Divine. Nothing is wrong, nothing is right. It is His world. He rotates it. And if He can give you a night and day by rotating the Earth, why can't you be sure that He will take care of your routine?

Let us process ourselves.

Reality, Prosperity, and Ecstasy

I know Thou Thee
Wahe Guru Ji
Give my day prosperity.
Prosperity, prosperity.
Wahe Guru Ji
Give my day prosperity.
I know Thou Thee.
Reality, prosperity, and ecstasy.

Blessing

Part I

This posture is called "Blessing." This is how the Popes used to bless the people: "May the Jupiter energy as Guru, and the Saturn energy as Guru, be with you."

Mudra: Sit in Easy Pose with a very straight spine, chin in, chest out. Bend the elbows into the sides, and bring the hands up so they are about six inches away from each ear. The palms are facing forward, fingers pointing towards the ceiling. Make the hands into fists, and extend the index (Jupiter) and middle (Saturn) fingers straight up, holding them side by side.

Eyes: Closed.

Music: *Reality, Prosperity, and Ecstasy* by Nirinjan Kaur. Sing along with the tape.

Time: 8 minutes.

End: Inhale and move immediately into Part II.

Part II

Mudra: Stretch the arms overhead, elbows straight, hands in fists. Extend the index and middle fingers straight, and bring the tips of the index and middle fingers together, so they are touching. No other part of the hands touch. Make a triangle with these fingers.

Music: *Humee Hum Brahm Hum* by Nirinjan Kaur. Sing along with the tape.

Eyes: Unspecified.

Time: 6-1/2 minutes

End: Inhale. Hold for 10 seconds. Exhale. Inhale, and immediately move into Part III.

Comments/Effects: Make a perfect triangle, and let the Almighty descend. Sing with the tape from the navel. We are chanting, "We are we, we are God." The tongue will touch the proper meridian points and create the result if you correctly pronounce it.

Part III

Mudra: Fold the hands in Prayer Pose, palms flat at the heart center.

Music: *Ong Namo Guru Dev Namo* by Nirinjan Kaur. Sing with the tape, from the navel.

Time: 1-1/2 minutes.

End: Inhale and relax.

Blessed Divine within me, around me, and in all living beings.
It is Thy Will I must perform today, tomorrow, and as long as I live and breathe.
To understand Thy vastness, to understand Thy Grace,
and to understand Thy power within me. As Thou dwell in me, give me the
strength to be pure, graceful, radiant that I may deal with the
world with kindness, compassion and care, and make my body as Thy temple.
Be with me as my Presiding Lord.
Walk with me, talk with me, and be with me.
I shall be grateful.
Sat Naam.

Drop Your Limitations

*Drop your prejudice against yourself—Number One. Drop
your limitation against yourself, and drop your insecurities
against yourself. Drop your self unto the Altar of the Creator.
You will never need an alternative. God shall come
through in your case, in person.*

P roblems do not exist in this world because of a man. Medically it is a proven fact that man does not have both parts of the brain working simultaneously. Man has a projected brain; his elementary brain does not work at the same time. Unfortunately woman has both working, and that is the root cause of the problem. Woman wants to know, she wants to talk about it, she wants to understand. Men don't have energy in that way. You know what a man wants? A dumb, deaf, and blind woman who tells him, "You are great, you are great, you are great." Whether he is early or late, whether he is a jerk or a god, he wants her to tell him, "You are great, you are great."

Why does a man need a woman? You think for sex? No. That's not true. Man needs a woman to share his pillow talk. Man does not need a woman for any other purpose. When a man is extremely tired and totally shattered by circumstances, and beaten up, he needs somebody who can say, "My love, don't worry, tomorrow there'll be sunshine." That's all it is. And a woman who fails to do that shall be divorced, shall be prostituted, prosecuted, have every wrong done to her. It doesn't matter who you are, you can never change a man, and you can never change a woman. You have longitude and latitude—you need altitude and attitude. Attitude is to appreciate.

First admit you are married to a nut. Then admit that it's your duty to nurture him. If you can nurture your son, you can nurture your husband. The only difference between the two is the size of the body and the sexual relationship.

All divorces are based on just one thing. A divorce never starts because of environments, poverty, circumstances, the man getting another woman who is very beautiful. The cause of divorce is that a woman starts questioning a man beyond what he can tolerate. That's it. Then the woman says, "What about me?" What about you? You are a woman, he's not.

You know, he is he, and the word, "S-H-E" contains "H-E." "F-E-M-A-L-E" contains the "M-A-L-E," and "W-O-M-A-N" contains the "M-A-N." It is in the spelling. So the process of the moon and sun is very well prescribed. The sun is stationary, warm, bright. The moon is waning and waxing and diplomatic—it reflects the sun. Learn from the heavens, not from anything else. Children are like stars. They must be made to understand the value of being shining, and that what is in the Heavens should be lived on the Earth. But when you just consider you are a male or a female, you have lost a few things.

First of all, you are a human. Then you are a person. Third is your mission. Fourth is your achievement. And then is your steadfastness. When a person gets to steadfastness, his commitment will give him character; character will give him absolute dignity, which will give him divinity. Then divinity will give him grace. Then he will have the power to sacrifice. That will bring him happiness. These are the seven steps to happiness.

Let us look at it this way: A person who has a Teacher is corrected each time. A person who doesn't have a Teacher has nobody to correct him. It is not that I am asking you to have a Teacher; but if you don't have it, you don't have yourself. Because if you are not corrected, and you don't have a tolerance to be corrected, then your neurosis will eat you up like termites. You'll be totally eaten inside and you cannot carry on.

What is a middle-age crisis? The energy in "bio-feed" starts slowing down, so inside secretion of the glandular system is less. If there's no proportionate maturity, you will fall apart. Every husband falls apart in the hands of his own wife. Every husband, out of frustration, seeks another woman. The problem is, she wants security, and the man wants relaxation. They never meet. I don't know why people marry. I think they are young, they are hot, they think the grass is greener on the other side. But when they walk in it and their feet step in the cow turds, then they understand what they are into. That is why man is so cruel by nature.

In 1867, woman was sold in the marketplace. That is the plight of humanity which can never, ever be forgiven. Four million children in this world—most of whom are women—are taken away, and they have never been found. The brutal habit of a man has never changed, even today, with all the civilization we talk about. Woman is nothing but a sex object, not an object of grace. You want to sell cigarettes, you want to sell purses, you want to sell dresses—you put a woman naked, half-naked, whatever attracts. In other words, man knows she is attractive. But the tragedy is, woman doesn't know she's attractive.

There's a difference of cultural opinion here. In one culture a woman may have 30 people chasing her, or seducing her, or dating her, and it makes her feel that she is very desirable. In another culture, she thinks she's a whore. Same woman, same action. It's all mental training.

Once I counseled a couple, the lady said, "He's never home."

He frowned at her and said, "I am home, but you are sleeping with so and so." She thought he never knew. You know who does that? Animals. It is only in the animal kingdom where a female is in heat and she goes for a man. We are humans. Sometimes you get mad at me that I don't want to interfere. I say, "Go ahead. It's time to go." Because there's nothing to counsel with an animal. Should I tell a goat about Kundalini Yoga? Should I start teaching goats and zebras Kundalini Yoga? Do I need humans blinded by passion, with no compassion, totally dragged by desire, with no elevation? Everything is a make-up. Where is reality?

Our fears are there to spoil our lives. It is not you who betray the soul. It is your fear which betrays the soul. Fear is Earthly, and has nothing to do with the Heavens. Your fear is that you must hassle, and only you can make it. It is never true, never was, nor is, nor shall be. The guiding hand in this world is the Hand of God.

We have waited twenty-eight years to teach the knowledge of the Age of Aquarius. We say there's no such thing, "To be, not to be." The only thing is, "To be, to be." We are saying we are born spiritual for a human experience. We are not born human for a spiritual experience. We say, "God and me, me and God, are One." We say, "We come from the Infinite to the finite, and we must merge back into the Infinite." We say, "God is within us. In God we dwell." This is different from the Age of Pisces where we said, "You are born in sin, you have to worship God, you have to do hard work to please the Almighty, and obey the commandments." How many Jews and Christian obey the commandment, "Thou Shalt Not Kill"? "Oh, get me a well-done, juicy steak." It came without killing? Kabir was a Sufi saint. He said: "Mullah, oh Muslim priest, on one hand you say *Allah* is everywhere in everybody. Then why do you take the chicken and chop off its head? Is *Allah* not there?"

The Piscean religion was, "Which suits me." The Aquarian religion is, "Will I suit it?" Our idea to teach this course is not for making money and pleasing the Europeans. Our idea was to touch you and tell you, "If you are willing to carry the weight, you are welcome. If not, sit home and enjoy yourself." It is our time, we shall be here and we shall prevail. It is destiny. Nine hundred sixty million we shall be. It cannot change. But those who have taken the first step, because they have taken the first step, they can't stop.

What is healing? Look at this Sat Nam Rasayan: does Guru Dev Singh give you a massage and all that? All he does is put his hand on you. Sometimes he doesn't even touch you. Actually it is the "*Sat Naam*" which does the healing. You don't see God working.

You decide everything with your head. You are so ugly, so unwanted, so cruel, so negative, that even the matters of heart you decide with your head. Folks, you are your own enemy. This is the time to get awakened. This is the time to look at yourself. You can't even read another man's face. Is he hurting or pleasing, is he traightforward or not, is the person believing, or not believing? Nothing. You have your own thing. And you happen to be here to learn to be Teachers.

Drop your prejudice against yourself —Number One. Drop your limitation against yourself, and drop your insecurities against yourself. Drop your self unto the Altar of the Creator. You will never need an alternative. God shall come through in your case, in person.

God is everywhere, waiting for you to call. His zip code is His mantra. Mantra is just like that: you take a stone and you throw it in the water, and constant waves go. That is what mantra is all about. It is to be remembered, remembered, remembered; it is to be chanted inside of you with your heart, your mind, your body. The only longing you have is to repeat it. It may be difficult to begin with, but soon God will come through and work for you.

You can be contained, content, and conscious or you can be totally competing and confused, and cry for the rest of your life. "A" is "A." "A" has the destiny of "A." "B" has the destiny of "B." They must meet on a common ground to become "AB." But if "A" wants "B" to become "A," and "B" wants "A" to become "B"— a war has started.

For twenty-five years I have counseled couples. Nobody admits they are wrong. It's "B's" fault. Ask "B"— it's "A's" fault. They never admit, "It is our fault." Once you say it is "our fault," then there is no fault, then there's no blame. But what do you do? In your life you marry 28 times and have 20 men as your husband, then what? One has 26,000 mistakes, the other will have 24,000 the third will have 32,000. Men are men. Men are not vegetables that you can buy and cook.

So what are we fighting? We are fighting against the rule of nature. The rule of nature is, when two people meet they must understand where the other is coming from. When you make a mistake, you always know where you are coming from. Always understand where the other person is coming from, what they are doing. Amazing cases have been reported where woman, because of insecurity, ruined not only the man, but the household, the children, everything.

You have come here to know each other. You're all very important. It is my desire that you should meet everybody, see everybody, impersonally for personal purposes. Let us not look at each other as a woman, or a man, or a Teacher, or a student—we are all Teachers for tomorrow, and we must meet as humans, with grace. The only thing in your life which will serve you is manners. The only thing which makes you great is your commitment. If you are not dependable, nobody will depend on you. You will fall apart.

Money will never give you character, if you do not give yourself character. It is your character and characteristics which people trust—not you. Nobody trusts you. Your sociological concept is totally wrong. You think, "I am needed by people." No. If you cannot chisel and uplift a person, if you just hob-job, chisel a person and don't uplift, you'll be a failure. If you keep on lifting and not cleaning the person, you are a failure as a Teacher. You must know a student personally and treat him impersonally. That's a fundamental law. You'll be staying out of trouble forever. You'll be very popular. But some of our Teachers think nobody sees what they are doing. No, my dear, nobody is looking at you, but the Heavens do. What can the Heavens do? Block your horizon. Then you can't see all. What kind of life is that?

Another category of people is those who blame everybody. If you cannot see God in all, you cannot see God at all. Claim God and stop blaming, that is the way of life. Try to help. Try to be. You will find that the fantastic situation is, God will come through. Our beauty is, we are beautiful, bountiful, and blissful. We are householders. Hold your house.

Leave a person alone. God has created all people equal, beautiful, thank you. If they want to jump off the balcony, let them go. But don't jump with them. Never, ever participate with an unconscious act. Never. In that way, you will automatically become rich, saintly, and glowing. Have a mission in life: be kind, compassionate and caring, peaceful and serving. I can bet you that God will serve you personally. Folks, where there's an ego, there's no amigo.

We have known that we are a genetic electromagnetic field, and that the universal pulse throbs as our impulse. Mind you, there's a difference. The universal pulse carries us as an impulse. That is something which nobody wants to speak about, because once you say you have universal pulse, then you have to identify that pulse, so that you can compare it with your impulse and find out if you are right or wrong. But what you do is, you want it to be *given* to you: "Hello Sir, Yogiji, I have come to you and I want you to give me the Heavens."

Some of you who are sitting here will become great Teachers of the Age of Aquarius. You must understand that you have to build your character first. Care for yourself, be kind to yourself, be compassionate to yourself. That is what you have to do.

The greatest thing you can do as a Teacher is to give without question so that you can take without question. When the whole world falls, you must stand as a lighthouse. When there comes a great great great destructive typhoon of temptation, you must bless it, and walk out of it. There is only one definition of a Teacher: A Teacher is a person or body of persons who stand, walk tall, when everything fails.

You are the last hope of humanity. When things are down and darkest, we walk the tallest. It doesn't matter who you are. What matters is whether you are trustworthy or not. If you are not worthy of your trust, why do you expect anyone to trust you?

It's a very funny world. People do what they want to do. Some people think that teaching Kundalini Yoga—the most powerful science of human strength and chakras—is a business. The first thing Jesus did is that he destroyed all those who were trading around the Temple. Temples don't trade. An altar never has an alternative. If your life becomes an altar, if you worship your altar as a Teacher, if you *be* as a Teacher, the world shall bow to you. When there's an alternative altar to any altar, neither is the alternative right nor is the altar right.

So you must understand, a Teacher is not a human. I gave you the definition of a Teacher the other day. *(YB is referring to the shabad Gurdev Mata.)* That is in the words of Nanak. The faculty, the facet, the quality, the power, the strength, the projection: All that of a Teacher is well-written.

It's a big thing to become a Teacher. People come, touch your feet, bow to you, get your blessing, give you presents—that's all true. But there's an expectation: When everything fails, a Teacher won't fail the student.

You do not understand; you as a tiny human are supposed to carry the will of all humanity. A Teacher carries the will of all humanity, *plus* the Will of God, *plus* the Self, *plus* everybody's destiny. It's a whole load. A Teacher is not just, "Put your legs this way, put your hand this way." What is knowledge? There are libraries full of knowledge. Why does anybody want you? What is richness? There are millions of millionaires suffering and rotting. A Teacher is a glory: glowing, shining, and prevailing, better than God. Because the best of God *is* the Teacher. Nanak sang the song of what a Teacher is. You see, after twenty-eight years I have introduced you to the definition of a Teacher, which I knew all along. I thought, "Now you are okay. You may not understand me at all, but at least you won't hate me."

☺

The only thing which never dies is the Teacher. All the rest shall go. It is your one chance to become Immortal. To become a Teacher, your strength is not your sex, not your money, not your gender, not your wisdom, not your intelligence, nor your resources. Only one thing will always keep you up: that you are full of grace and you are graceful.

☺ You shall never be in a position to command the 108 elements of the universe, until you know perfectly how to obey. It's a simple law: Every action has a reaction, equal and opposite. Some people want students to obey, yet those Teachers do not obey one damn thing. Not only that, they openly violate humanity's basic rules: Once, twice, three times, ten times. In the end, the day will come when you will be in a position to do nothing, and nobody on that day will stand with you. That is the judgment, deciding day. When you leave this Earth friendless, penniless, and without any environment to tell you, "you were here." Maximum you can get is a headstone, "Born such and such, Died such and such."

But one simple guy, Jesu, born out of Fatima, obeyed the law of nature, obeyed the law of God, fought with the entire Roman Kingdom. He's remembered. Whether he was good or bad, we are not discussing here, but he received immortality. A mortal must achieve immortality. The only thing which I want you to do today is to forgive yourself. Forgive yourself of your own corruption. You don't like what I'm saying, right? It's okay. In this life, life is a "lie-if" you have not found your personal truth. Your wife, your children, your house will not go with you. You have to go with them if you can carry them. So become a carrier. Carry everybody. A Teacher is a Teacher—everything else into the world is students.

You see too many things. Your thoughts are scattered. You are yourself scattered. And the tragedy is, you have not understood what death is. When at night you sleep, you are not a man, not a woman, not a time, not a space, and not yourself. Then when you get up the next morning, again you pick up this robe of ego. Every twenty-four hours God gives you a chance to get rid of your ego; you are totally in the bliss. Why can you not remain in that all of the time?

There's a process to achieve that. As in real estate they say, "location, location, location," in spirituality they say, "kindness, kindness, kindness." A man without kindness and a woman without grace are animals—they are not human. You have to understand this once in your heart, and you have to follow it in your heart. You have to be Teachers by your own grace, and through your own kindness to yourself. We can only tell you the technology, we can only share with you our heart; we cannot force you. Those who shall rise to serve the Age of Aquarius shall live forever, in the memory of the generations to follow them. Those who shall betray shall not stay here and hereafter. It's a simple law. It's not something complicated or difficult to understand.

Once upon a time in 1984, the Golden Temple was attacked by the army that was supposed to protect it. Many innocent lives lost their way. But this was a place where no one ever thought this could happen. It sent a lot of pain the world over. The Pope protested from the balcony of the Vatican. The Dalai Lama protested from Indian soil. All that was appropriate. Guru Dass, through the Grace of God and Guru, wrote a song which will live forever. On this special day I ask him to sing that to you. It is the most beautiful song which describes the Golden Temple, the altar of consciousness where God dwells. This is the only one place in the world which is made with gold and marble, to represent sun and moon, and it is in the center of a pool of water, which is said to heal people for the last five thousand years. People visit this sacred place from all walks of life. Something which we have adopted, is that we go every year to clean the surrounding *perkarma* of that Temple, hoping somebody divine must have walked there and we can share the blessings.

I will ask Guru Dass to sing that song. This song will live. The Government of India may not live, the army may not live, and the people who manipulated it may not live. But this song will live and remind us what we have to do when we shall be ruling the Earth. The basic thing to remember today is never ever attack anybody's altar. Never ever interfere with worship. And never break anybody's heart—the humble cry of an injured man in faith can change the universe. One Christ went on the cross and the Roman Empire lost itself. It's a fact. The British put five hundred men who they knew were innocent, before cannons. They lost their British Empire. In the Spanish world, they started putting people on the stake during the Inquisition—they were lost. The Ottoman Empire—you can count all of these and what they have done. When a government attacks the innocent, and mocks Divinity, it is shattered into destruction.

This November we'll go to the Golden Temple again. Mostly it's going, visiting, enjoying the beauty. But the one thing we do is, we clean the *perkarma* at night. The tradition is, when I was a yogi, I used to do very many rotten things. It was the way of life to put a person upside down, stop a car, make a man pee for nothing. But I learned my lesson in one way, and I got posted, through my manipulation, to Amritsar. I was the worst rebel a religion could have. Then I was there for four and a half years and I washed the *perkarma*. God and Guru blessed me, and gave me the sense of joy, my inner feeling, and my happiness. That is what we'll share this November again, when we go. It is a pilgrimage which we do. It is not for any other happiness but to understand three things: your discipline, your endurance, and your faith. There's no other promise. You will be washing the *perkarma* as I washed. You'll be miserable the whole night, in the morning you will love to sleep, and maybe you'll gain a few pounds because you'll eat too much. But the idea is to test your discipline, your endurance, and your faith. That's what we do.

I am personally very grateful that Guru Dass felt those feelings in his heart and these words came from him and he sang them. But when he brought the lyrics to me, I changed the last two. With a very heavy heart, I didn't want to do it. But I said, "These two lines will complete it." I'll ask Guru Dass to come and sing that song. Please listen to this, and sing with it, if you know it. You must sing this song to your children, to your students, to the generations. This song shows human bankruptcy of manners, faith, reality, and character. You must know it. You must understand that this can happen, and this *did* happen.

When Will I Walk On The Cold Marble Again?

by Guru Dass Singh Khalsa, Spain

When Will I walk on the cold marble again?
When will I feel the golden light in my eyes?
Bathe in the holy waters, dress your altar with flowers.
When will I walk on the cold marble again?

When will I walk on the cold marble again?
When will I feel the golden light in my eyes?
Bathe in the holy waters, dress your altar with flowers.
When will I walk on the cold marble again?

The silence of death has killed that song so ageless,
The turning of the pages, the prayers of the pure.
The waters turn red, the sky above has darkened.
Amidst these walls of silence, our prayers can be heard.

When will I walk on the cold marble again?
When will I feel the golden light in my eyes?
Bathe in the holy waters, dress your altar with flowers.
When will I walk on the cold marble again?

The Earth cries in pain, her heart has been broken.
Her sons have been stolen, imprisoned and slain.
Yet those who remain, the spirit grows stronger,
They suffer no longer, sheltered in the Name.

Soon we will walk on the cold marble again.
Soon we will feel the golden light in our eyes.
Bathe in the holy waters, dress your altar with flowers.
Soon we will walk on the cold marble again.

We shall rise again, in grace and strength together.
Sing our songs forever, and righteousness will reign.
The banner of the Name will wave in skies of glory,
Time will tell our story. We say, "Never Again."

Soon we will walk on the cold marble again.
Soon we will feel the golden light in our eyes.
Bathe in the holy waters, dress your altar with flowers.
Soon we will walk on the cold marble again.

A Personal Servant of Infinity

A Teacher uses his little will, his personal private will to let God's Will flow.... Each one has to resurrect, resurrect, resurrect, every day, every moment, against every odd. Jesus did it once—you have to do it all the time.

Nature and God can only give you a chance, but it is you who have to come out on the right side of it. You are very important to you. It's very important that you should know you, and it's most important that everybody should know you as trustworthy, honorable, graceful, steadfast, serviceful, kind, and compassionate. These are a few faculties of a Teacher.

A Teacher shall never, ever ask a man to help, because his God is alert, aware, and consistently constant, and shall always lead the way to protect His servant. A Teacher is a personal servant of Infinity, Lord of the Divinity, Master of the Grace, and he commands the destiny.

Never ever ever control a student. Otherwise you will drag a weight, and that will drag you down—it doesn't matter who you are. When someone needs your counsel, tell them what it is, and walk on. Never stop, otherwise you will stink. Running water is always pure. Yes, people are very attractive, but nobody cares who you are. They want to know that you are learned, that you are clean in character, and that you are uplifting in your being. It's called "vibration." A woman can be a prostitute or a graceful woman. Both are women, but put them together, and you will feel the difference.

But the height of your personality are your divine manners. Manners are your life, and to understand the life is nothing but a mutual existence. That will guarantee your peace, and your service and smile will bring your prosperity.

When everything is so evident, why do you lie? Do you think you are blinded by passion, and the world doesn't know about it? Do you know what passion does to you? Do you know about this mental masturbation that you do? Your mind doesn't work for you any more. You are not in yourself. You are somewhere else. Is this a human? Is this a life?

Do you know why God gave you free will? So you can mess yourself up. It's like having one penny and thinking, "I am a millionaire." You are here to have one thing only—to be clear. If you, as a human, cannot open your heart, you are just a book in a library. You can talk about God, hear about God, but you do not know what God is. Is it your God which is negative, bad, terrible, horrible, miserable? Is it your God which is happy, wonderful, playful, blissful, nice? These are your two sides of God in judgment. God is God—neither good nor bad, right nor wrong, real or not real. Those who belong to God, they elevate themselves. They don't go left and right, they go higher and higher, until they touch Infinity and then beyond. They know the path of God, have beauty, bounty, bliss, containment, consciousness, and contentment. "God is my Lord. Guru is my guide. Let Him guide me."

The world is action and reaction. In this world you need clearance. What is your clearance? It doesn't matter if two hundred came to this course. The only one who matters is the one who will study, understand, and grow upwards. The rest is a compensation.

The teacher is a pure form of a human who's impersonally personal, and personally impersonal, and which nothing affects. Teachers dwell in such a vast dimension, their Father has such a huge mansion, that they can't even count the rooms. A Teacher has no territory, no jurisdiction, no control, and no communication but the Will of God. He uses his little will, his personal, private will to let God's Will flow. But in society he or she keeps himself or herself clean, so people can see through. A Teacher who's blinded by passion and sets up the misery and the tragedy, tortures his or her life, and the life of others. Each one has to resurrect, resurrect, resurrect, every day, every moment, against every odd. You have to resurrect, resurrect, resurrect. Jesus did it once—you have to do it all the time.

If you want to learn about life, watch whales. The whale is a huge monster, very vegetarian, but HUGE! It goes down, it comes up, it goes down, it comes up, it goes down, it comes up. Simply when time puts you down, come up, it puts you down, come up. The whales swim from Mexico to the North Pole. But some are unfortunate. They get stuck in man's nets. That is ego. They never make it. They are left behind.

To me you are the most unfortunate human beings. Look what God has done. He has brought you here, so now you will have knowledge, but you will go and not act. Before that you were innocent, and you never knew what to do. Now you know what to do, and if you don't deliver, then you will be miserable. God did His job; somehow you all came here—not for one day, two days, three days—but for seven days! Now you are being told what a Teacher is. Before you were just teachers. "I am a teacher. I am a creature who becomes a Teacher." But who is going to work for you, Mr. Teacher?

Each student who comes to a Teacher is his personal, infinite responsibility. To a teacher, everyone is a student, and it's his or her responsibility to deliver. What you cannot deliver will destroy you.

What is our language? "I am great. I have great students. I have many centers. I, I, I."

The only thing which says "I, mehhhh" is a goat. I always say, "This looks like a man, but a goat lives in this person."

"Mehhhh." Have you seen that? That's the biggest "I" in the world. Those who say, "I, I, I," they never open their Third Eye. They miss the trip. Because "I" and "Thou" never meet.

ਹਉਮੈ ਨਾਵੈ ਨਾਲਿ ਵਿਰੋਧੁ ਹੈ ਦੁਇ ਨ ਵਸਹਿ ਇਕ ਠਾਇ

Homai naavai naal virodh hei, du-eh naa(n) vis-eh ik thaa-eh

-Guru Amar Das, *Siri Guru Granth Sahib*, page 560

The ego has animosity with the identity of God. Both will not live in one place.

I don't care how many students you have. All I want to know is, how many Teachers have you created? I don't care what a big house you have—you can enjoy it. But how much of a sense of justice have you created? If along with wealth, a sense of justice is not there, life is a living hell. Remember, every good action or bad action has a reaction, equal and opposite. Your salvation lies in detachment of mind. When the call comes, you can go detached.

Some of you are Teachers, and you are afraid of being leaders. A leader leads by presence, by example, by word, by wisdom, by care, by compassion, and by kindness. A Teacher is a person who has a place in the heart of the student, not in the head.

Now you will all sing, *"Bahotaa karam likhiaa naa jaa-eh."* This song will change your poverty into prosperity. Singers, come, come, come, come. Sing with them. Sing, sing, sing.

ਬਹੁਤਾ ਕਰਮੁ ਲਿਖਿਆ ਨਾ ਜਾਇ ਵਡਾ ਦਾਤਾ ਤਿਲੁ ਨ ਤਮਾਇ
ਕੇਤੇ ਮੰਗਹਿ ਜੋਧ ਅਪਾਰ ਕੇਤਿਆ ਗਣਤ ਨਹੀ ਵੀਚਾਰੁ
ਕੇਤੇ ਖਪਿ ਤੁਟਹਿ ਵੇਕਾਰ ਕੇਤੇ ਲੈ ਲੈ ਮੁਕਰੁ ਪਾਹਿ ਕੇਤੇ ਮੂਰਖ ਖਾਹੀ ਖਾਹਿ
ਕੇਤਿਆ ਦੂਖ ਭੂਖ ਸਦ ਮਾਰ ਏਹਿ ਭਿ ਦਾਤਿ ਤੇਰੀ ਦਾਤਾਰ
ਬੰਦਿ ਖਲਾਸੀ ਭਾਣੈ ਹੋਇ ਹੋਰੁ ਆਖਿ ਨ ਸਕੈ ਕੋਇ
ਜੇ ਕੋ ਖਾਇਕੁ ਆਖਣਿ ਪਾਇ ਓਹੁ ਜਾਣੈ ਜੇਤੀਆ ਮੁਹਿ ਖਾਇ
ਆਪੇ ਜਾਣੈ ਆਪੇ ਦੇਇ ਆਖਹਿ ਸਿ ਭਿ ਕੇਈ ਕੇਇ
ਜਿਸਨੋ ਬਖਸੇ ਸਿਫਤਿ ਸਾਲਾਹ ਨਾਨਕ ਪਾਤਿਸਾਹੀ ਪਾਤਿਸਾਹੁ

Bahotaa karam likhiaa naa jaa-eh, Vadaa daataa til na tamaa-eh
Kaytay mangeh jodh apaar, Kaytiaa ganat nahee veechaar
Kaytay khap tuteh vaykaar, Kaytay lai lai mukar paa-eh, Kaytay moorakh khaa-hee khaa-eh,
Kaytiaa dookh bhookh sad maar, Eh bhe daat tayree daataar
Band khalaasee bhaanai ho-eh, Hor aakh na sakai ko-eh
Je ko khaa-ik aakhan paa-eh, Oh jaanai jetiaa mu-eh khaa-eh
Aapay jaanai aapay day-eh, Aakheh se bhe kay-ee kay-eh
Jisano bakhashay sifat saalaah, Naanak paatishaahee paatishaaho

-Guru Nanak, *Siri Guru Granth Sahib*, page 5 (from 25th *pauree* of *Japji Sahib*)
His Blessings are so abundant that there can be no written account of them.
The Great Giver does not hold back anything. There are so many great, heroic warriors
begging at His Door. So many contemplate and dwell upon Him, that they cannot be counted.
So many waste away to death engaged in corruption. So many take and take again, and then
deny receiving. So many foolish consumers keep on consuming. So many endure distress,
deprivation and constant abuse. Even these are Your Gifts, O Great Giver! Liberation from
bondage comes only by Your Will. No one else has any say in this. If some fool should pre
sume to say that he does, he shall learn, and feel the effects of his folly. He Himself knows,
He Himself gives. Very few are those who acknowledge this. One who is blessed to sing the
Praises of the Lord, O Nanak, is the king of kings.

Meditation to Change
Poverty into Prosperity

Part I

Mudra: Sit in Easy Pose with a straight spine, chin in, chest out. Bring both hands into *Giaan Mudra* (touch the tip of the index finger to the tip of the thumb, other fingers straight). Place the right hand next to the right shoulder, palm facing forward. The fingers point up towards the ceiling, and the hand is up at the level of the face. The left elbow is bent into the side, and the left hand is resting, palm up, on left knee.

Eyes: Closed.

Mantra: Chant 25th *pauree* of *Japji Sahib* aloud.

Time: The meditation was done for nearly 28 minutes, then he gave the class a break to ask them to "raise the energy higher," and they resumed for another 6 minutes.

End: Inhale, hold the posture, and move immediately into Part II.

Comments/Effects: "This shabad will change your poverty into prosperity." Yogi Bhajan made this comment before the final 6 minutes: "Go higher in notes and now sing, energizing the electromagnetic energy of the Earth, and passing it on to the Heavens. Don't be here. Pull the electromagnetic energy from the Earth by your will. You are ready now. You have a blue arcline, so push it into the Heavens."

Part II
Mudra: Same as above.

Breath: Breathe very long, deep, and slow through the nose. In the silence, hear the sound of the mantra in your inner ear.

Time: 4 minutes, 45 seconds.

End: Inhale deeply, squeeze your entire spine, all 26 vertebrae, from bottom to top, bringing the energy from the Earth to the Heavens. Hold 15-20 seconds. Fire the breath out. Repeat 3 times total.

Comments/Effects: Breathing in this posture will reorganize your *pranic* energy. Breathe long and deep, and change the dimension of your being into the beyond.

Bhangara Dance was done to a tape for a few minutes, after this meditation. Yogi Bhajan said it was important to dance before everyone went home to sleep, in order to balance out the energy and keep the nervous system strong.

Serve the Future

Come to me with your head in your hand and merge
in the Universe, which I enjoy. You can't come to my
Home with your stiff, neurotic, pig-headed situation.
This is a home of love, relaxation, service, upliftment,
and rejoicing.

The first lesson you must learn is that when you are in the presence of a Teacher, you don't speak—you meditate. It takes about thirty-one minutes for a student to prepare to listen, analyze, and perfectly understand what a Teacher is going to say. If your brain cannot analyze what you hear, it is no knowledge for you. The purpose for coming here is to become teachers, and to become 10, 20, 100, 1000 percent more than what I am. You can run around as a Teacher with thousands of students, but if you do not produce a better Teacher than you, your lineage will stop, and that is your real death. The real death belongs to those who cannot keep up the legacy.

To you, everything is emotion, feeling. Fine with me. But there's a world beyond feeling, emotion, neurosis, and desires. And that is a free world, and that is where humans experience ecstasy. Solving the problem, living in problems—anybody can do it. But what you need is to uplift yourself. One line will describe it:

ਜੇ ਸਉ ਚੰਦਾ ਉਗਵਹਿ ਸੂਰਜ ਚੜਹਿ ਹਜਾਰ ॥
ਏਤੇ ਚਾਨਣ ਹੋਦਿਆਂ ਗੁਰ ਬਿਨੁ ਘੋਰ ਅੰਧਾਰ ॥

Je sa-o chandaa ogav-eh sooraj char-eh hazaar.
Aytay chaanan hoodiaa(n), gur bin ghor andhaar.
　　　—Guru Nanak, *Siri Guru Granth Sahib*, page 463
If a hundred moons rise and a thousand suns appear,
even with such light, there would be pitch darkness without the Guru.

If there are a hundred thousand moons and a hundred thousand suns, and all are shining—without the Teacher, the world is dark.

Do you understand how poor you are when you have no one person in this whole world who can tell you what to do? If we remove the stop signs from the roads, all you will find are accidents. So what you live is from incident to accident, accident to incident. Because you are one small part of the universe. When you do not harmonize with the universe, you do not know harmony. Without harmony you are N-O-T-H-I-N-G. Nothing, nothing, nothing.

You all have nicknames that are given by friends because of their experience of you. And what we do is, we consider what your past is, calculating your destiny, and give you a target name, a spiritual name. That is the journey you have to travel. It sets the standard, the base.

Then we ask you to remember the oldest language of this world. It's the language of the gypsies. There are eighty-four meridian points on your upper palate, and when you pronounce these mantras, your tongue touches those meridians, it stimulates them. This intercourse creates the sense of opening of the Third Eye. Then after you have rotated your tongue in a certain combination and projection, and you speak to somebody, it consolidates the entire system psyche and becomes organized to work for that person and gets rid of the pain.

In the evening when the sun is down sixty degree on the planet, you sit down and meditate. That's called *Rehiras*. It maintains and contains your wealth. Then, at the end of the night, you recite *Kirtan Sohila*. You hand over yourself unto God, or your Higher Self. In the morning you rise again in that Infinity which gave you the breath of life.

You don't know how to live, even. I'm so sorry to tell you that. You do not rise in the morning unto the Infinity of God and say, "Thank you, I am part of it." You do not know the language of "we." Even in the word *small*, "S-M-A-L-L," "A-L-L" is contained.

Come to me with your head in your hand and merge in the Universe, which I enjoy. You can't come to my Home with your stiff, neurotic, pig-headed situation. This is a home of love, relaxation, service, upliftment, and rejoicing. There's no nonsense here. If you cannot reach your Teacher and merge with him, how can you merge with the Teacher of the Teacher of the Teacher—the Super Teacher, God? I'm not suggesting you start sleeping with your Teacher, and screwing up and doing all those weird things, which is normal with you. I'm not suggesting that you do things which you are not supposed to do. I am asking, "Can you reach into his heart?" There are four chambers of a Teacher's heart: one pumps out information, one pumps out blessing, one receives all the faculty of negativity, and one chamber is strong enough to cleanse it. Why should the matter of heart be different for anybody else?

You come to a Teacher and ask him, "What is in it for me?" Why not reverse the question and have me ask you, "What is in it for me?" Your whole wealth cannot please me, the whole universe cannot give me any satisfaction, if you are not determined that you will bypass me and become ten times stronger. Because sooner or later the world you are going to face is going to be very empty and hard, with extremely neurotic minds. That is your future, in which you have to serve, inspire, love, and help. It's up to you to decide.

Some of you love your ego so much, you can't become a part of Infinite expansion. That is a sad story. Sometimes you are clogged up. Nanak knew that. He knew that we need a jump-start. Sometimes our starter cannot start it. The words of Nanak are only helpful as a jump-start. Those words stimulate the thalamus and hypothalamus, and the neurological cells become active. The dead cells are lost, and the person becomes bright, beautiful, and bountiful. When you start a car, it is the starter which starts it, and then the car goes on its own. But when the starter doesn't start it, you have to jump-start it.

You are all perfect. You are thirty trillion living cells, each of you. Each cell communicates with each cell, perfectly. You are so super-stupid you cannot talk to each other. Thirty trillion cells talk to each other at the same level, except you. Because you don't talk with innocence. You talk with purpose. Greed is your leader. You are not real.

People may call you "whackos," they may call you many names, because they don't understand, but when they see you walking determined, that is where you determine your destiny. When they see you walking tall, then the distance is covered. All I'm saying is, "Give God a chance to love you, to help you, to be with you." Why don't you date God? Why do you date everybody else? Date the One who created you. You'll be better off.

ਘਰਿ ਤਾ ਤੇਰੇ ਸਭੁ ਕਿਛੁ ਹੈ ॥ ਜਿਸੁ ਦੇਹਿ ਸੁ ਪਾਵਏ ॥
Ghar taa tere sabh kichh hei, jis de-eh so paavay.
    -Guru Amar Das, *Siri Guru Granth Sahib*, page 917 (from the 3rd *pauree* of *Anand Sahib*)
Everything exists in Your House. The one to whom He gives, shall receive the same.

"God, everything is in Your House, but to whom You give, that is the one who receives." But who receives the gifts? Who gets congratulations? Those who we feel are our relations. In the cosmic energy, our frequency of psyche at the system at which we are parallel, becomes our permanent relationship. It will be like this: Psyche into psyche shall reflect and merge within the psyche and break the duplication and become unisonness when the mental power of the heart is neutral, and a person reaches out, just for seeking God within the other person or creating psyche connection.

All the rest of the people shall suffer. There's nothing anybody can do. These are the laws of this Earth—they're not going to change. Making a religion and collecting people is not what we need. There are already so many religions. We need reality, we need identity. We need to identify in the millions that we are out there to heal, out there to serve, out there to be in them. Our religion is to merge into the hearts of everybody, and not get bogged down with what their head is doing.

This is the principal difference between the Age of Pisces and the Age of Aquarius. Aquarius quenches the thirst of everyone, while Pisces is symbolized by two fish biting at the tail of each other. Get out of the water, pick up your pot, and quench the thirst of everyone.

Come here as students. Leave your egos outside of the door, hang with it your flirting mind, and your theory of gain and loss. Come to me with your heart and your head at the palm of your hand. You shall learn so fast that you can't believe it. God wants you to be Teachers. He knows the Age of Aquarius is here. These are the first five years—in the next sixteen years it will set in because this is the cusp period. To save His creation, He needs a new Teacher.

All those men who were great Teachers, like Hazarat Abraham, Moses, Jesu, whom you call Jesus, Jesus's mother Fatima, Rama, Krishna, Nanak—they all took a stand for the age. That is why we call them "sage." That's what you have to become.

All that you are is consolidated and standardized into one purity—you. You may say, "What is in it for me?" You are one single person, but you have thirteen servants God has given you to work with—you have nine holes, two hands, and two legs—and you must make those thirteen servants serve God, or you shall suffer. That is the first quality of a Teacher.

Then, in the spirit of Guru Amar Das, you are the place for those who have no place, the home for the homeless, the virtue of the virtueless, and the shelter of the shelterless. You are the support of those who have no support. Then God said, "Those whom I have condemned, you uplift them to Godliness." That is the second lesson for a Teacher.

Third, as he's teaching Infinity, and believes in Infinity, the Teacher must depend on that Infinity. Any teacher who will ever depend on the finite will remain limited and miserable. There are certain cosmic laws which you should know. You don't have to raise a pinkie—things will come to you, brought to you by God, Himself. If you are not prepared to serve His Will, with a silver platter in the Hands of God, you have wasted your trip to this Earth.

It is all a matter of heart, not a matter of head. Head makes you an individual—heart makes you universal. But even beyond the head and heart, it is you. You are not a soul, you are not a mind, you are not a body. You are the controller of all three. You are the driving force of all three, to cover the distance and the destiny. You have a nervous system, a circulatory system, a glandular system, a rejuvenation of the cell system, a liver to rebuild and filter things, and you have a spleen. The whole machine is so complicated, but so simple.

You take your car for a wash, but you don't want to come to a White Tantric Yoga course? There for a day, you are put in a boiling pot, and whether you like it or not you are cleansed. Is your car better than you? If somebody drives your car and scratches it, do you see what your face does? Well, you get scratched, your mind gets scratched, your spirit gets scratched everyday—don't you care? Inside your car, if a seat is broken or torn, or somebody messes up your car inside, you don't give them a ride the next time. But when somebody brings gossip, not the gospel, and messes up your body, mind, and soul, you become friends and you feed them lunch? What kind of living is this?

You don't know what is going on inside of yourself. How can you know what is going on inside of everybody else? And you call yourself Teachers? What is this? You must know your inside, and everybody's inside. A Teacher is inside to inside. Outside is identity. Inside is reality. And life is a factual gift of God. Through the *pranic* energy you have already earned it. It is not that you became human because you wanted to be human. No, no, no. You earned it. It's pre-earned. You have pre-deposited in your *pranic* bank account. You can waste it on drinking, eating chickens, and hunting and killing everything, or you can spend it on sending your soul back home, bright, beautiful, and wonderful. Nanak says it in simpler words than me:

ਜਿਨੀ ਨਾਮੁ ਧਿਆਇਆ ਗਏ ਮਸਕਤਿ ਘਾਲਿ ॥ ਨਾਨਕੁ ਤੇ ਮੁਖ ਉਜਲੇ ਕੇਤੀ ਛੁਟੀ ਨਾਲਿ
Jinee naam dhi-aa-i-aa, ga-ay masakat ghaal
Naanak tay mukh ujalay, kaytee chhutee naal
   -Guru Nanak, *Siri Guru Granth Sahib*, page 8 (from the *Slok* of *Japji Sahib*)
Jinee naam dhi-aa-i-aa: Those who have meditated on their identity.
Ga-ay masakat ghaal: have worked this hard labor.
Naanak tay mukh ujalay: Nanak, their faces are beautiful and bright.
 Kaytee chhutee naal: their accounts are all cleared.
In the words of Nanak, your check will not bounce.

What is your ego? How much money is in your bank? How is your credit line? Is that all? So why don't you care about how much *prana* you have, and how much credit you have with the *pranas*? You are born by breath, you live by breath, you shall die with breath. Breath is your ultimate Master. Do you ever breathe consciously? No.

❀

There is one *shabad* which we are going to recite tonight: *Narayan. (See words page 268.)* It's unique in the whole *Siri Guru Granth*. It's so powerfully worded. It forces God to project and concentrate on the human. Sometime just play it, and see what it does. I'm not asking you to trust me; I want you to experience. If it doesn't work for you, throw it away, along with me. There's no need of hanging in with something which doesn't work for you. But at least give yourself a chance. At least give God in you a chance. At least give your distance and destiny a chance.

There shall be one word and only one word in the Age of Aquarius. People with experience shall live; people with knowledge shall die. You decide what you want. It's all up to you.

❀ Your strength is in your purity and piety; your power is in your projection, in your service; your beauty is in your manners and your understanding; and your bounty is in your openness and love. Without that, you are garbage. So give yourself a chance. God has given you a chance. Take His chance. Don't follow me. You have to lead and I have to follow you. A Teacher's future is in his students. A Teacher is yesterday, the student is tomorrow. Give yourself a chance, and your chance should tell others, "This is true."

Go, grow and glow. Be the Lighthouse, be the answer, not the question. Remove the obstacle in the life of others; God will remove obstacles from your life. Try to know the Unknown, and everybody in the human world, in the animal kingdom, and in the angelic world will know you.

❀

ਏਕਾ ਮਾਈ ਜੁਗਤਿ ਵਿਆਈ ਤਿਨਿ ਚੇਲੇ ਪਰਵਾਣੁ
ਇਕੁ ਸੰਸਾਰੀ ਇਕੁ ਭੰਡਾਰੀ ਇਕੁ ਲਾਏ ਦੀਬਾਣੁ
ਜਿਵ ਤਿਸੁ ਭਾਵੈ ਤਿਵੈ ਚਲਾਵੈ ਜਿਵ ਹੋਵੈ ਫੁਰਮਾਣੁ
ਓਹੁ ਵੇਖੈ ਓਨਾ ਨਦਰਿ ਨ ਆਵੈ ਬਹੁਤਾ ਏਹੁ ਵਿਡਾਣੁ
ਆਦੇਸੁ ਤਿਸੈ ਆਦੇਸੁ ਆਦਿ ਅਨੀਲੁ ਅਨਾਦਿ ਅਨਾਹਤਿ ਜੁਗੁ ਜੁਗੁ ਏਕੋ ਵੇਸੁ
Ayk-aa maa-ee jugat viaa-ee, tin chaylay parvaan
Ik sansaaree, ik bhandhaaree, ik laa-ay deebaan
Jiv tis bhaavai, tivai chalaavai, jiv hovai furmaan
Oh vaykhai ohnaa nadar na(n) aavai, bahotaa ayho vidaan
Aadays tisai aadays, Aad aneel anaad anaahat, Jug jug ayko vays
    -Guru Nanak, *Siri Guru Granth Sahib*, page 7 (the 30th *pauree* of *Japji Sahib*)
The One Divine Mother conceived and gave birth to the three deities. One, Creator of the World; One, Sustainer; and One, Destroyer. He makes things happen according to the Pleasure of His Will. Such is His Celestial Order. He watches over all, but none see Him. How wonderful this is! I bow to Him, I humbly bow. The Primal One, the Pure Light, without beginning, without end. Throughout all the ages, He is One and the Same.

Trikutee Kriya

Part I

Comments/Effects: "Whosoever will chant this mantra, and perfect it, will know everything about the Trinity."

Mudra: Bend the elbows into the sides of the body, and place the hands next to the shoulders, palms facing forward. Make the hands into fists, and extend the pinkie fingers straight up towards the ceiling.

Eyes: Look at the tip of your nose.

Mantra: *Ayka Maa-ee* — the 30th *pauree* of *Japji Sahib*. *(See words on page 265.)*

Time: Practiced in class for 18-1/2 minutes.

Focus: Sing aloud with the tape, projecting from your navel point.

End: Place your hands in the mudra for Part II *(see below)*, and inhale deep, hold 17 seconds. Exhale. Inhale, hold 5 seconds. Exhale. Inhale, hold 7 seconds, exhale. Inhale deeper each time, and focus on throwing the disease out of your body as you exhale.

Part II

Mudra: Keeping the position from Part I, bring the two fists together in front of the face, keeping the pinkies pointing straight up. Bring the tips of the pinkies together so they are forming a triangle, and place this about six inches in front of the nose.

Eyes: Stare at the tip of the nose.

Mantra: Same as in Part I.

Time: 5-1/2 minutes.

End: Inhale deeply. Fold your hands in the center of the chest, palms together, and put the total pressure of the whole body on the hands. Hold 17 seconds. Exhale. Inhale. Hold 2 seconds. Exhale. Inhale. Hold 5 seconds. Exhale. Move into Part III.

Part III

Mudra: Fold your hands at the heart center. Place the hands in prayer pose, palm to palm in front of the heart center. Extend the elbows straight out to the sides, and put a tremendous amount of pressure on the two palms.

Eyes: Unspecified.

Music: *Wahe Guru, Wahe Guru, Wahe Guru, Wahe Jio*, by Giani ji.

Time: 8-1/2 minutes.

End: Inhale deeply, straighten your spine, and hold it for 13 seconds. Cannon-fire out. Inhale deeply again, bring the muscular body into one unit through your nervous system. Hold 17 seconds. Cannon-fire out. Relax.

Comments/Effects: Sing from the navel to the tip of the tongue. Let it open up to God. Open up the chakras. Keep your spine straight, and work hard. With your word, connect, and go up.

Sometimes when the energy goes through the chakras it opens them up and there's a lot of garbage in different chakras, and a person goes through a lot. Don't hold your emotions in. Let them open up.

The purpose of this meditation and this course is to open up the basic chakras. So don't be macho and egomaniac and want to control everything. All you have come here to do is to open up your heart. The rest will be the Will of God.

ਨਾਮੁ ਨਿਰੰਜਨੁ ਨੀਰਿ ਨਰਾਇਣ   *Naam niranjan neer naaraayan*

ਰਸਨਾ ਸਿਮਰਤ ਪਾਪ ਬਿਲਾਇਣ   *Rasna simrat paap bilaayan*

ਨਰਾਇਣ ਸਭ ਮਾਹਿ ਨਿਵਾਸ   *Naaraayan sabh maa-eh nivaas*

ਨਰਾਇਣ ਘਟਿ ਘਟਿ ਪਰਗਾਸ   *Naaraayan ghat ghat pargaas*

ਨਰਾਇਣ ਕਹਤੇ ਨਰਕਿ ਨ ਜਾਹਿ   *Naaraayan kehetay narak na jaa-eh*

ਨਰਾਇਣ ਸੇਵਿ ਸਗਲ ਫਲ ਪਾਹਿ   *Naaraayan sayv sagal phal paa-eh*

ਨਰਾਇਣ ਮਨ ਮਾਹਿ ਅਧਾਰ   *Naaraayan man maa-eh adhaar*

ਨਰਾਇਣ ਬੋਹਿਥ ਸੰਸਾਰ   *Naaraayan bohith sansaar*

ਨਰਾਇਣ ਕਹਤ ਜਮੁ ਭਾਗਿ ਪਲਾਇਣ   *Naaraayan kehet jam bhaag palaayan*

ਨਰਾਇਣ ਦੰਤ ਭਾਨੇ ਡਾਇਣ   *Naaraayan dant bhaanay dhaayan*

ਨਰਾਇਣ ਸਦ ਸਦ ਬਖਸਿੰਦ   *Naaraayan sad sad bakhshind*

ਨਰਾਇਣ ਕੀਨੇ ਸੁਖ ਅਨੰਦ   *Naaraayan keetay sookh anand*

ਨਰਾਇਣ ਪ੍ਰਗਟ ਕੀਨੋ ਪਰਤਾਪ   *Naaraayan pragat keeno partaap*

ਨਰਾਇਣ ਸੰਤ ਕੋ ਮਾਈ ਬਾਪ   *Naaraayan sant ko maa-ee baap*

ਨਰਾਇਣ ਸਾਧਸੰਗਿ ਨਰਾਇਣ   *Naaraayan saadsang naraayan*

ਬਾਰੰ ਬਾਰ ਨਰਾਇਣ ਗਾਇਣ   *Baarang baar naraayan gaayan*

ਬਸਤੁ ਅਗੋਚਰ ਗੁਰ ਮਿਲਿ ਲਹੀ   *Basat agochar gur mil lahee*

ਨਰਾਇਣ ਓਟ ਨਾਨਕ ਦਾਸ ਗਹੀ   *Naaraayan ot naanak daas gahee*

- Guru Arjan, *Siri Guru Granth Sahib*, page 867-68

The Name of the Immaculate Lord is the Ambrosial Water.

Chanting it with the tongue, sins are washed away.

The Lord abides in everyone. The Lord illumines each and every heart. Chanting the Lord's Name, one does not fall into hell.

Serving the Lord, all fruitful rewards are obtained.

Within my mind is the Support of the Lord.

The Lord is the boat to cross over the world-ocean.

Chant the Lord's Name, and the Messenger of Death will run away.

The Lord breaks the teeth of Maya, the witch.

The Lord is forever and ever the Forgiver.

The Lord blesses us with peace and bliss. The Lord has revealed His glory.

The Lord is the mother and father of His Saint.

The Lord, the Lord, is in the Saadh Sangat, the Company of the Holy.

Time and time again, I sing the Lord's Praises.

Meeting with the Guru, I have attained the incomprehensible object.

Slave Nanak has grasped the Support of the Lord.

What is Your Reality?

We are not asking you to become religious. We are definitely asking you to become spiritual. For God's sake, find your soul. Find out where you have come from, what you are doing here, and where are you going. Look at the map of your life.

Each one of you has three minds: negative, positive and neutral. Each mind has eighty-one chakras, which simultaneously process your shortcomings, your fears, and your projection. The question is not which religion you belong to. The question is do you have any idea what your reality is? Are you faithfully aware that God created you, that you are a creature and that you have to be a conscious person? Mostly you are afraid to be spiritual, because the moment you become spiritual, you mess up religion.

There are three billion people who believe in the Bible. Very few believe in the Commandments and live by them. In the Bible there are the Ten Commandments. They are commandments. They are not requests, they are not applications, they are not waiting for your answer. They say, "Do this, this, this, this, this, this, this." Sometime read them, and figure out how much you live by them.

We are not asking you to become religious. We are definitely asking you to become spiritual. For God's sake, find your soul. Find out where you have come from, what you are doing here, and where are you going. Look at the map of your life.

Our mission is simple. The Age of Aquarius is dawning—it can't be avoided. There shall be people who will believe in experience and spirituality, who will need a healing hand, who will need a committed, strong character and heartThey will need a person who is vast like Infinity, who's high beyond the sky and deep beyond the center of the Earth—who's everything. But you don't want to be everything. You want what you want; you don't want what you don't want.

There are two sides to everything. One you like, one you dislike. But you as a Teacher have no choice. You are not correct, you are not right, you are not real. What is this like and dislike? Like the dislike. That is the mastery. Otherwise you are not a Teacher—you are a vagabond made juggler. Let an enemy come before you, and totally blow him away with the flood of your love. It happened to me. We were doing *gatka*, sword fighting, and that year I became the champion. So this guy was very angry with me. One day we were going for a walk in the morning, and he took out his sword. He said, "I want to challenge you."

I said, "I love you. I don't want to challenge you at all. It's not my way of life. But if you challenge me, and I accept the challenge, I am going to snatch your sword, and cut your throat. You don't want that."

He said, "Come on, let me see how good you are. You became champion because you belong to a rich grandfather, and your grandfather gives money to everybody."

I said, "Well, it's a matter of honor. I won by my merits. I am willing to lose to you because of my honor."

He said, "Why? I am stronger than you."

I said, "No, you are very weak. You are angry, you are jealous, you are stupid. You are challenging me on my morning walk. These are not the manners of a martial man."

He said, "You don't understand me, man. If you don't accept my challenge, I am going to kill you."

The next minute he was lying on the ground. I was standing over him with his sword in my hand. Then I gave him my right hand, I said, "Get up, my friend. You couldn't kill me and I won't kill you. You are so angry, and so burned with jealousy, that it will not satisfy my appetite."

Then when he got up I gave him his sword. I said, "Can we go for a walk now?" So we had a walk and we talked. He was telling me, "I, I, I, I, I, I want to be champion!"

I said, "Next year I won't participate. If for one year you learn from me, you will be champion." I taught him for one year. The next year he was better than anybody. But when my teacher pitched me against him, I told him, "I want you to win. But for God's sake, don't be angry and don't be anxious. If you are angry, if you are anxious, and if you want it, you won't get it." I said, "Take my word for it. Fight me fairly."

He said, "I am anxious, I am insecure, I have won it already."

I said, "No, forget about the anger and fear. I have taught you. You know better."

The two swords and two shields created like a thunder in the sky. Every attack was fiercely fearful, and each one wanted to cut through the shield and go right to the heart of the other person. I was kind of smiling like it was fun, and I just played very defensively. My defensive mechanism brought me the victory because he became so anxious and started attacking so viciously, he got tired. So, I just took the sword and hit his hand. I didn't chop off the hand, but he lost the shield. Then I snatched his sword, handed it to him, threw away my sword, took his right hand and raised it as a champion.

He said to me, "You can't do that."

I said, "If I cannot honor my student, I have no honor left in me. You are the champion."

My Master came and said, "You cheated me."

I said, "My Lord, you have shown me compassion, you have shown me service, you have shown me helping. With this he is helped, and he is really a champion. Let's not question this right now. Later on, we'll decide."

He laughed and said, "You are a real champion because today you created a champion."

So when I say to you, "Don't trust the Teacher," I am very correct. The Teacher has a very well-made plan to suck you into the cobweb and kill you before your own consciousness. Don't trust your Teacher. Never. He's always out to see where you can fail. This is his priority. this is his first job. If he cannot show you where you can fail, somebody will fail you. Your failure is his defeat. Your victory is his victory.

Look at what kind of Sikhs we are. Look. We are Christians, we are Jews, we are Muslims, we are Buddhists, we are Shinto, we are Hindus, we have all denominations of those religions which, when put together, call themselves "Sikh." "Sikh" means a student.

You want to know how this Sikh religion became a religion? There was a student of mine who had long golden hair . One day he was stopped on Highway 10 in Los Angeles by the sheriff and thrown into jail. He put a towel from the car on his head, and said to the Sheriff, "I am a Sikh. You can't cut my hair. You can't send me to the county jail." So the Sheriff, who was a friend, called us in.

I said, "Well, what is the matter, Sheriff?"

He said, "If there was one ticket, two tickets, I can understand, but there are a hundred tickets. This guy has never paid a ticket in his life. Plus, he has no insurance on the car. He was speeding, so we chased him, stopped him, and arrested him. We have to send him to the county jail, where they will shave his head. He said, "I am a Sikh, you can't cut my hair, you can't do this, you can't do that." I said, 'Well, if he says he's a Sikh, he's a Sikh, but I want something in writing saying that he is a Sikh."

So we took a letter from one of the Gurdwaras, we put Adi Shakti symbols on it, and made a Sikh Dharma letterhead. We typed out, "So-and-So is a Sikh, therefore it is his right to have hair, etc." We signed it and brought it to him.

So this great Sikh came, and I said, "Hey, you don't have a turban, you have a damn towel." Well, three days later when we went before a magistrate, he had on a full turban and everything—he looked so good.

Our attorney told the magistrate, "Sir, this man has totally reformed. Look at his turban. He has become a monk."

And the magistrate said, "Well, are you changed?"

He said, "Yes, my lord, I'm changed."

He said, "Go."

That is how Sikh Dharma began.

Nobody knew what we were doing, but 20 million people created a revolution against the hypocrisy of the time, space, and the government. It was called the Woodstock Nation. Many got sacrificed, killed, suffered irreparable losses of life. Out of that, there are 8 million people left in the United States. We call them "yuppies." They run the country. America is not the same as it used to be, therefore no country is the same as it used to be. Things have changed, in some places for the worse, in some places for the better.

We didn't participate in anything in any pushy way, because we don't proselytize. Our idea was to prepare people for the Age of Aquarius. The funny part is, Sikhism started in India, and Sikhs from India have spread all over. But they are so shy to shake hands with us, you can't believe it. The difference is, we live it, they philosophize about it. It has become a "Sarbat Dharam," it has become Dharma of all Dharmas. Everybody's welcome, nobody is rejected. Everybody has his own way of calling God: "Allah, Allah, Allah," "Ram, Ram, Ram," "Jehovah, Jehovah, Jehovah." There is one God. Call Him any way you want, just call!

We have come to this planet Earth for *bhugatee*. *Bhugatee* means to pay off the debt. So let us pay it with *Jugatee*, with technical know-how, of how to be free. Let us not talk cheap. Let us not act as a creep. Let us not complain and weep. Let us be strong, with our faith in our God, and our soul as our friend, and let us reach out to everyone we can reach out to.

In the tenth, eleventh Centuries, if one lock of hair got cut, that person was considered dead. Not all the hair, just one lock of the hair. No, I'm not asking you to keep hair, for God's sake. We are not here to educate you to keep hair. But at least it's our privilege to tell you why it is there. At least you should know why there is hair. There are twenty-six parts of our skull. These are medical facts. Each sector of the skull controls the entire nervous system of the brain. You have the longest hair in the world as humans. And your hair is pure protein. It's called "heavy protein." If you want to test it out, take some earth and put in small cut hairs, mix them together, and grow a plant. Take some more earth, put all the manure you want to put in, and grow the same kind of plant in that. You'll be shocked how the plant with hairs will grow stronger, better than the other one, because, as without heavy water, there's no atomic energy, without pure protein you have no control of the neurons and neurological ganglia of your brain. So what do we do? We take all the hair up and cover the crown and, so that it can remain covered, we put cloth over it.

You know how funny you are? That is how the yarmulke was worn. It used to be seven yards long and a yard and a quarter wide. You know what it is now? It's a little thing stuck in the hair with a bobby pin. Have you seen that? Adios. Keep on changing.

I don't know where you get this fear that we are converting people to be Sikhs. We are not. Honest to God. It is not our goal to put turbans on every head. We don't have a boutique shop, and we are not cloth merchants. We have nothing to do with your fears. You cannot have fear if your spirit is elevated. It's not that all those who wear turbans are great. They may not understand that they have crowned their head. After that, they have no blame, no claim, no thought, nothing. They are the first servant of humanity.

We are also not dealers in cotton that we prefer cotton, silk or wool. Nor are we anti-polyester. But we simply do not want to mess up our psyche. We are vegetarians not just by choice, we are obeying. Our Lord said, "Thou Shalt Not Kill." So, we'll not kill to eat. You know, anything which moves, swims or flies or walks away, we don't eat. How can you love a life when you kill a life? How can you justify it? Forget about me, I came from India, I am saying so many things. Why not talk to yourself? Ask yourself a question. You are as intelligent as I am. You are as good hearted as you are.

No, no, no, I have seen you so well. "Ahh, that lobster, that one." The guy pulls it up and throws it in boiling water. Then you put on oil and garlic and butter, and you crack his bone and you eat. What a noble food, what a noble work, what a noble human being. We can't say a thing to you. Your feelings are dead.

There was a little boy who, because his friends wanted to eat meat, said to his father that he wanted to eat meat. His father said, "We don't eat meat."

He said, "Everybody eats it."

So one Saturday, his father drove him out of town and let him play with the cows and the calves on a dairy farm. Then he took him to a slaughterhouse where he saw a cow tied up, saw a big hammer come, hit her head. She fainted, then her neck was cut, and she was skinned.

Then he brought him to a market, and asked him to read what was written there. You can kill that boy, but you cannot make him eat meat, because he remembers it. He's sensitive. We have become insensitive to a lot of things.

 You have come here to become Teachers. The first thing you have to teach yourse is that you are here, not to be just anybody, but to become a Teacher. Simple thing. Second, tell yourself what kind of Teacher you want to be. If you want to be a totally divine Teacher, you have to be a Teacher without duality. Do you want to say something and act something different? Do you want to be a saint outside, and a sinner inside? What do you want to do? Make up your mind. But, if you want to become a Teacher of Kundalini Yoga, then your inside and outside, both have to be saintly. Then the power of your touch, sight, and word must create miracles and will create miracles.

I saw you in the meditation this morning. Sometimes the chakras are clogged up, and when the energy comes, it opens up the obstacles. It's nothing so serious, it just happens. People shake, people cry, people call out. It is real. It happens. But some of you say, "Why didn't it happen to me?" It didn't happen to you because sometimes you do not consistently keep your eyes on the tip of the nose. If the posture is perfect, the net result will be perfect. I said this morning, "Put your eyes at the tip of the nose."

This April at Khalsa Council I have given certain exercises which are the minimum for keeping your chakras open. (See Reference section.) All I can do is open them—to keep them open is your responsibility. I can only play my role—you have to play your role. When the two roles will meet, you will start experiencing what we call the Third Eye, ajna. It's not bad.

It is true, whenever there is a light, a moth comes and wants to get rid of it. So in your life there will be tons of obstacles, ton of objections, tons of fears, tons of questions. Everything out there is to shake your faith. If you rise above it, that is because your Kundalini has risen. There's one line from Gurbani that I want you to remember.

ਕੁੰਡਲਨੀ ਸੁਰਝੀ ਸਤ ਸੰਗਤਿ ॥ ਪਰਮਾਨੰਦ ਗੁਰੂ ਮੁਖਿ ਮਚਾ ॥
ਸਿਰੀ ਗੁਰੂ ਸਾਹਿਬੁ ਸਭ ਉੱਪਰਿ ॥ ਮਨ ਬਚ ਕ੍ਰੰਮ ਸੇਵੀਐ ਸਚਾ ॥

Kundalanee surjhee sat sangat, parmaanand, guroo mukh machaa.
Siri guroo saahib sabh oopar, man bach karm sevee-ai sachaa.
           -*Sawaya* in Praise of Guru Ram Das, *Siri Guru Granth Sahib*, page 1402
Associating with the saints, their spiritual nerve is opened and through the Supreme Guru,
they enjoy the Lord of Supreme Bliss. The venerable Great Guru Is over
and above all, so serve thou the True Guru, in thought, word, and deed.

This is a line uttered by a very saintly *bhagat*, about Guru Ram Das. He said, "Kundalini has awakened, O True Congregation. *Parmaanand*—the Perfect God—is showing through the face of the Guru." This is a dharmic power in all of us. It needs to be awakened, and then it needs to be a guiding power in us. With that infinite power within us, we can always serve, be happy, and we can care.

Meditation for the Arcline

Part I

Mudra: Interlock the fingers of the two hands and place them, palms down, about 8 inches above the top of the head. The elbows should be bent to form an arc over the head. The thumbs should come down and touch tip to tip, pointing down. Make sure the chin is pulled in, and the chest is pushed out slightly.

Eyes: Stare at the tip of the nose.

Mantra: The *Narayan shabad*. Sing along with the music. *(Refer to page 268 for words.)*

Time: 24 minutes.

End: Inhale and immediately bring your hands flat against the heart center, left under right. Hold 15 seconds. Exhale. Inhale. Hold 13 seconds. Exhale. Inhale deep. Hold 8 seconds. Exhale. Move immediately into Part II, keeping this posture.

Comments/Effects: This is for the arcline.

Part II

Mudra: Place your hands flat against your chest, left under, right on top.

Mantra: The *Narayan shabad* . For the first 4 minutes, the *Shabad* is sung, and then the mantra *Narayan* alone is chanted for 2 minutes. Sing loud from the navel.

Time: 6 minutes.

End: Inhale deep. Put a total pressure on your heart center with both your hands, and squeeze your body. Press hard every molecule so the energy is distributed equally. (Held 10-15 seconds.) Cannon-fire out. Repeat 3 times total. Relax.

Part III

Get up and dance to a Bhangara drum tape.
In the class, Yogi Bhajan had a number of different students say a closing prayer in their native languages.

Hail Guru Ram Das and Heal the World!

"Hail Guru Ram Das, and heal the world." It is His problem to heal. Your problem is to insert Him into it. You have nothing to worry about. If He doesn't heal, His Name will be spoiled—what's it to you? Most of the time you do not know what to do, true? There are so many times I don't know what to do. So, I insert Him into it.

Once upon a time the civilization on planet Earth got wiped out. It has happened four times. We are in the run of the fifth time. This is what has always happened, and humanity has never had a choice. I'm not asking you to believe it, or to understand it. But, this time it is a little different. It will kill people and drown them in a flood of information. So, people who live with ego and maya, and who are attached to the Earth shall have no place, because all these walls, and all these personalities, will be publicly known.

The computer will open up the whole world, but there will be diseases called "computeritis." The nervous system of the human will be shattered. People will not become physically impotent, they will become mentally impotent. It will be so fantastic that the human will become a computer—put a program in and act. The inner core of the personality shall go out of this world. During this time, some will change; some are trying to change now. Some yoga teachers have more students, some have no students. This is okay. But tomorrow when the floodgates will open, humanity will reach you like a flood. Remember, at that time, there will be only one thing said, "Save me in the Name of God." You have to come through. At that time your body will beome a lighthouse, and you will jump-start the life of the other person. The impotent, blocked mind has to be reopened and invigorated, and life will start again in many people. That is your job. That is what you are going to do.

There is nothing but you, and there shall be nothing but you. Kundalini shall rise in you. Experience will give you the power to share, and you need the strength to care. Wherever you go—grow and glow. If you cannot sacrifice your personality, you cannot reach reality, because your personality becomes darkness and blackness for you, and it will be your own block. Drop it. This is what we say, that's what He teaches. "Hail Guru Ram Das, and heal the world." It is His problem to heal. Your problem is to insert Him into it. You have nothing to worry about. If He doesn't heal, *His* Name will be spoiled—what's it to you? Most of the time you do not know what to do, true? There are so many times I don't know what to do. So, I insert Him into it.

Hey, let us use something which works. When something of mine gets lost, I ask St. Anthony, "Bring it over," and the next minute we get it. So you have to learn to talk to all saints and sages, all denominations, all divisions, all factions. You have to speak to everyone. It doesn't matter what their faith is, what their color is, what their caste is, what their creed is. You have to heal. That's the only deal you have. *Seva.* Service. Selfless service is *seva.* Once you heal a person and servicefully, selflessly have an infinite jurisdiction, you will always be loved and remembered.

Even now when I travel I meet people who say, "Ahh, Yogi Bhajan, I met you in 1972, in such and such place."

I said, "What are you doing now?"

"I am the CEO of that company."

I said, "You used to run around without pants."

He said, "Oh, that was then."

People don't forget that touch. People don't forget that when they were overdosed on drugs, we took care of them, in spite of what their conditions were.

You have the whole world at your command to be students. Not, "I have two-thousand students, I have one-hundred centers." This is too small. It's a shadow. You are born to remove shadows, you are not supposed to live in shadows. It's time to grow and go to all four corners of the world. It's time to spread not you, but the Word. It's time to become the agents of God, rather than the agents of your ego.

But have patience. Patience pays. Prove it. When the karma of your previous incarnation will be cleansed out, and your courage is steady, then everything will start working for you without saying a thing. That is the state of life we must achieve. We must know, "God and me, me and God, are One" —forever. Not in the morning, "God and me, me and God are One," and in the afternoon, "God and me, no God, me, me, me." Stop doing this "me, me, me, me, me." Get out of all that.

Meditation to Melt Negativity

Mudra: Sit in Easy Pose, with a straight spine. Bend the ring and pinkie fingers into the palm, and hold them down with the thumb. Extend the index and middle fingers straight up, and hold them straight, side by side.

Place this mudra about 2 feet to either side of the face, palms facing forward, fingers pointing up. The forearms and fingers will not be straight up towards the ceiling, but tilted out to the sides, at about a 30-degree angle. Keep the hands up at the level of the face. The elbows are bent, but not pressed into the sides of the body. They should be stretched out about 12 inches, away from the sides. The weight of the hands will be on the armpits. This allows the armpits to be open so they can breathe and be stimulated.

Mantra: *Aap Sahaa-ee Hoaa, Sachay Daa, Sachaa Dhoaa. Har, Har, Har.* Tape by Singh Kaur is played. Chant along with the tape, from the navel.

Conditions: To get the proper effect, as you chant the words *Har, Har, Har*, strike the tongue against the upper palate, and firmly pull in on the navel point on each repetition. This will pressurize the Kundalini, and shake it from the base.

Eyes: Either focus at the tip of your nose, or close the eyes—either way will work. However, if you look at the tip of the nose, then the Third Eye point will become heavy like lead, and if you can stand the pain, the Third Eye will open.

Time: Done in class for 27 minutes.

End: Inhale deep. Hold 23 seconds, and concentrate on the area from your navel to the crown chakra at the top of the head, or *shashaaraa*. This distance is only 27 inches. Exhale forcefully, like cannon fire. Repeat two more times, holding the breath only 5 seconds. Relax.

Comments/Effects: "This meditation melts negativity, enemies, and negative vibrations. It is such a powerful meditation that you can even go after a demon and make him a student.

The armpits are the exhaust pipe of the brain. That's why the sweat in the armpits is very different than the sweat of the rest of the body. If the armpits do not sweat, you will have headaches. If you don't like the smell, put some sandalwood oil in your armpits. You will smell good, and in turn it will keep your brain fresh. If you become physically impotent, you can get an injection to correct it, but when you get mentally impotent, you are useless. Then you can't take care of yourself, your future, your environments, and your sensitivity.

This mantra takes your energy to the *shashaaraa*, the thousand-petalled lotus, the crown chakra. It means, "The True God has come down as the True Helper, to uplift your Truth." The 3-strokes of *Har* represent the "Father, Son, and the Holy Ghost" or the three aspects of God, "Brahma, Vishnu, and Mahesh." This mantra opens you up so the universe will open to you. It's a simple bargain.

When you will become my students, then my radiant body shall flow through your lifeline, and you will become immortal. The time shall be known by your work and by your deeds. If you will serve the humanity, you shall be exalted. If you'll be kind, compassionate and caring, God shall honor you with His own hands, if He has many many hands. This is an expression. Life is waiting for you, and giving you a chance to elevate it. Don't fail.

Heal the world. Go. That's why we started Sat Nam Rasayan. *Just touch not, and heal. You can feel, get it all in you, throw it away, person is healed. The most powerful language of the world is silence. And that is a healer's language. Remember that.*

Give God a Chance

*Give your worries, pain, misfortune, anything, to God,
and take happiness, joy, and smiles back to your
home. What do you have God for if He cannot take
care of Itself? Do you have God for suffering?
There's no such God who suffers. You suffer.
Give your suffering to God and enjoy your life.*

You are always afraid of tomorrow. "Should I become a Yoga Teacher? We will be poor. We will die hungry. My spouse will leave me. Da, da, da, da, da, da, da, da, da, da, da." This is what you do. But if you just think, "God has guided me to this. I'm going to grab it. Unto God it is." Give God a chance to work, then see what happens.

That's why Nanak said:

ਦੁਖੁ ਪਰਹਰਿ ਸੁਖੁ ਘਰਿ ਲੈ ਜਾਇ ॥
Dukh parhar sukh ghar lai jaa-eh.
-Guru Nanak, *Siri Guru Granth Sahib*, page 2 (from 5th *pauree* of *Japji Sahib*)

Give your worries, pain, misfortune, anything, to God, and take happiness, joy, and smiles back to your home. What do you have God for if He cannot take care of Itself? Do you have God for suffering? There's no such God who suffers. You suffer. Give your suffering to God and enjoy your life.

You have to understand one thing. I am not here to make you my students. You are the Teachers of tomorrow. You are not my initiates. I came to this world to serve. I earn my own bread, my own money, and I spend it back on you. I came with thirty-five dollars, and I still have them in a conch on my altar.

You are very rich. Come to Espanola and see your riches. Look at this staff. They serve; they work eighteen hours a day. They can process any problem you have got. It may take a bit long because our mail system is a snail system. Other than that, we are fine. We live in our own small village, but we affect the entire state.

Let us understand: There are a lot of good things said about us, and a lot of bad things said about us. There are horrible things said about us. There are marvelous things said about us. But to a yogi, the pair of opposites do not affect; neither good nor bad means a thing. Every coin has two sides to it—heads and tails. If you don't understand, you will fail. Bad things do not stop you, and good things should not shake you.

Student: You mentioned a few days ago that we shouldn't be dependent on our yoga students. Does that mean that as well as being yoga Teachers, we should have other businesses?

YB: We are not bloody idiots that we depend on our students! What kind of Teachers are we? What is this? This is actually prostitution. A student depends on a Teacher, a Teacher depends on a student. What do you mean by "depending on a student?"

S: I was thinking about those people who make all their money from teaching.

YB: Let them make money. They put in their time, they work. Is your time free? Nobody is like me, I have my businesses, and I can do whatever I want. Some people have to put in their time and money and their household, and this is their business. They have the right to charge money. Money comes because you do work. Our wages may be a little higher than others. Charge what you can. What is wrong with that? But do the job—earn straight, earn honestly, render unto Caesar what is Caesar's, and take the rest home.

You know, any present given to me in the last twenty-eight years has gone to the Archives. People have given me things which are worth hundreds and thousands of dollars. They belong to the people. A Teacher doesn't depend on students, students depend on the Teacher. If you do not learn that basic law, you won't make it.

How can a Teacher depend on a student? I don't understand. It is the job of the student to be shaky, to be negative, to be neurotic; otherwise he's not a student. It comes with the territory. A student is a student—sometimes high, sometimes low, sometimes fast, sometimes slow, sometimes good, sometimes bad, sometimes scared, sometimes very loving. Sometimes they want to have sex with you; sometimes they want to kill you. What do you think a student is? A student is a combination of all negativity—real, imaginative, and fantasy-full—all put together in one cup. Your job as a Teacher is to clean it out, sort it out, and out of that, pull the rabbit out of the mud. If you don't want this job, don't become a Teacher. Who's inviting you? But don't entangle your personality doing so—it will all be easily done. The student only has to do one thing. He comes and says, "Maestro, this is my problem." All you have to say is, "Guru Ram Das will solve it—now go home." If the person trusts, it shall be solved. If the person does not trust, it won't be solved. If he or she wants to get it solved, she doesn't even come. She says, "Guru Ram Das, solve my problem." It will be solved. It is so fast. The words "Guru Ram Das" are the code number of God. Don't you understand that? "Ram" means God. "Das" means servant. When a servant of God is summoned by you, God says, "Who? What? Where? Why?" And job is done.

You don't understand simple things. You want complicated things, confusing things, the ego's things. Why should I tell you that you are very good, when you are already very good? Or, should I tell you, "You are good," does it make you better? Will this make you the best?

You have to learn one thing: If you cannot take tomorrow on your shoulders with your character, and with your commitment, you won't enjoy life.

"Oh, we are German." So what? I told all the Germans last time I was in Hamburg, "You have tried to conquer the world twice, and you got beaten. This time conquer the world with Kundalini Yoga—you will never be defeated."

"Oh, we are French." Are you ever a human? Are you ever people of God? End this, otherwise it will end you. You have sixteen years. Prepare yourself and enter the Age of Aquarius, or destroy yourself and be lost. We are five years into the Aquarian Age, and the next five years you'll see how empty-minded people will be. It's already happening. People will become computers, and computers will become people.

The time is now and now is the time. For prosperity, it is your openness, it is your smile, and it is your greetings which can bring the world to you. Go, grow, and glow, and serve the world, today and tomorrow. Share their sorrow. Make them healthy, happy and holy, and drop your personal agenda—God will take care of you when you take care of people.

This is Raaj Yog. It is an Imperial Yoga. It is the path of a sage and a soldier. The mission is serving people in peace and defending his or her honor. Do not feel sour. Do your part, and leave the rest to God. "What should we do? What will happen to me? I can't think. I have no answer. I don't know." Are you kidding? That's not your job. Just know your Guru. It doesn't matter how bad, ugly, naughty you are, He's going to take you through. No guilt. We didn't eat the apple, we ate the snake. Remember that. We enjoyed this Eve. I asked Adam, "How did you enjoy the sex?"

He said, "Well, great." Oh, he confirmed it. Eve was so shy, she couldn't even speak. We are all the by-product of that sexual action, right? So what are we having guilt for? We got out of the Garden of Eden to eat meat and have arthritis and all that. Dead meat, dead animals, dead life. And if you don't have a consciousness, you drink. Now people smoke so much you can't pass through a group of people smoking. You know, the secondary smoke kills faster than the first one. It's terrible. Now even the airlines won't take the responsibility. One tobacco company gave up; they will give thirty billion dollars plus to get rid of the lawsuit. They have knowingly been selling poison. Four million people will die of tobacco disease.

Things are changing. Now before they eat something, people want to read the label. Nobody just grabs it, buys it, and brings it home. Then they want to know, "How many calories does it have...is it organic or inorganic?" The world is changing—be part of that changing world. Be part of me, I'll be part of you. Let us serve the Age of Aquarius. Get rid of any fear you have. Get ready for service. Carry on. Be the flag bearer.

I will share with you how to chant *"Om."* *"Om"* is chanted in the human conch. Nanak took the secret of the word *"Om"* and taught humanity how to chant it. It is chanted in the Third Eye, which is called the Inner Conch of the Divine. You breathe in, and you chant, *"Ek Onnnnnnnng Kaaar."* *(YB produces the sound by resonating the upper areas of the head.)* Breathe in. *"Ek Onnnnnnnnnng Kaaaar."* *"Ek Onnnnnnnnnnnnng Kaaaar."* Relax, relax. When you chant that way, sometimes the *"Ong"* comes like burning hot air from the nose. So before you practice this, it is very good to oil your nostrils. Just watch how it happens, and watch my nose very particularly. *"Ek Onnnnnnnnnnng Kaar."* *"Ong"* comes through this *(YB indicates the whole length of his nose from the sinuses down to the nostrils.)* *"Kaar"* comes with the open mouth.

These are tools. Let us not be fools. Let us use them.

Meditation to Relate to Your Deathlessness

Through this meditation, you are working to get rid of the id, the ego. In this mantra, we are singing to our own deathlessness. This will make you leave a legacy of perfection.

Mudra: Sit in Easy Pose with a straight spine. Extend the arms straight out to the sides, parallel to the ground, with no bend in the elbows. The right palm is flat and face down. The left palm is flat and face up. The palms and fingers should be very stiff and tough, like iron. "Split the thumbs." Extend the thumbs away from the rest of the palm, so they are sticking out to the sides.

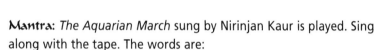

Eyes: Stare at the tip of the nose.

Mantra: *The Aquarian March* sung by Nirinjan Kaur is played. Sing along with the tape. The words are:

   Sat Siri, Siri Akaal, Siri Akaal, Mahaa Akaal
   Mahaa Akaal, Sat Nam. Akaal Moorat. Wahe Guru.

Project from the navel.

Time: 11 minutes.

End: Inhale deeply, raise the hands over the head, no bend in the elbow, and strike the two palms together, forcefully, one time. Exactly when you clap the hands together, let the breath go. Then bring your hands back into the posture. Inhale and repeat the sequence, seven times total. Relax.

Comments: In the end, make sure you strike the hands together over the head only one time, and the breath has to come out at the same time that your hands clap.

Life is a Gift

People are not interested in your complaints, in your tragedies, and in your miseries. Out of sympathy, and apathy, they will listen to you for a while, but after a while, I tell you, people will avoid you. People just want you to be with them with love and affection and elevation.

Science is science and every human being, whether it is a woman or a man, has two undeveloped states: the frontal lobe *(YB puts his fingers to his Third Eye point)*, and the upper palate. That upper palate controls the thalamus and hypothalamus, and the frontal lobe controls the pattern of personality. If you allow them to develop by time and circumstance, there will be no difference between you and an animal. Animal development is by nature, by impulse. Your development has to be by intuition.

If you are intuitively not positively effective, you'll find after a while it doesn't make any sense. The upper palate has eighty-four meridian points. When you speak, it stimulates the meridian points of the upper palate. That stimulates the hypothalamus and thalamus. Then the moon cavity turns around. So we are giving you these tools which, when you chant them, your tongue will touch certain of those points. We have scientifically, by experience, found that the permutation and combination of the words which Nanak spoke have an absolutely positive effect on the human body and the human being. The question is not whether you come along or not. Time never depends on man. It is within time that a man has to surmount it.

Sometimes you meet somebody and you feel you should have not met with that person. There's nothing wrong with the other person, but his neurosis and his anger and his ego. All put together, you just can't handle it. Forget it. God has given you body, mind, and soul, not for torture. Leave those friends who know nothing but offend you. It pollutes the temple. It hurts the soul. It's not good for either of us.

One leaves, ten will come. It will not be a matter of loss or gain. Some people are not fit to elevate themself. They might have a genetic limit, or a psyche limit. It's not good to waste time. The best thing is to move on.

The only saint in this world is the householder. He feeds the police, he feeds the thieves, he feeds everybody and still says, "Almighty God, help me." That's a real saint. With all the divorces, people survive. With all the mess, people survive. With all the abuse, people survive. With all the restrictions, people survive. With all the worst experiences, people survive. They are saints. A saint is not somebody who can do three miracles. What three damn miracles? Every Christian does more than three miracles a day. I think they should declare them all as saints. The condition is that there must be three miracles in order to canonize a person as a saint. Now look at yourself—since you got up in the morning. Until now, how many miracles have you survived?

The challenge of life is very deep and effective. Therefore just remember, life is a gift. Do not waste it.

Whatever starts must come to an end. You have forty-five minutes for individual questions, so you can go home learned.

Student: When you chant "Ong," do you vibrate it at the back of the neck?

YB: No, no, I don't have a neck to vibrate. Don't be foolish. God has provided us with a conch between the nostrils and the throat. It is in that conch that we chant. There are a few chants which can let you know you are chanting correctly. "Ek Onnnnnnnnnng..." It's under your control. It's not a sound you make with your mouth, it is a sound you make with your nose. Ek puts you there. Onnnng goes out, and then you do "Kaar."

Next question.

S: Can you explain broken-down breathing?

YB: You mean the eight-stroke breath? The pituitary is the master gland, the master of intelligence. The cycle of the pituitary is eleven years. The pituitary starts secreting duller and duller, throughout the day. That's why we have some kriyas with eight strokes to put the pituitary secretion in order. If the pituitary does not secrete constantly at a certain average rate, you'll be mostly negative for no reason. So it is better to put the pituitary in shape so you can project and love.

S: When one is teaching class, normally we do the kriya, then relaxation, then we do the meditation. Would it be correct to do the meditation immediately after the kriya, and then relax afterwards? Because students sometimes feel we are breaking...

YB: Students can go to hell. There is an order. That order nobody is authorized, including me, to change. We teach. We are not monopolizing people. The teachings are Infinite. The teachings are not that I made them, or you can make them. That's not right. We are not winning an election and Kundalini Yoga is not a democracy. It is exactly the way it is, and it must be kept pure—that is what it is.

Kundalini is the cycle, the circle, of the entire productivity of this Earth and all there is. In certain kriyas people say, "Should I close my eyes or not?" I never asked the question, so I'm not going to answer. It's up to you. They are all tested out from the last five thousand years and they work. There's no need to change or alter it.

We are not on a "Pleasing the Student" mission. We are here to make them Masters who can stand everything and anything, just with pure strength. If you want to please the student, practice Hatha Yoga. That's fine. Stretch it out, stretch it out, take twenty-two years. There are twenty-two types of yoga. Practice anything else. Here the student is an obedient student, and the Master is a commanding Master. If you do not learn with a commanding Master, tomorrow how can you become a master and command? You'll be a yo-yo. The student doesn't tell you anything. They obey and they experience. In that way their understanding is deep, their head is clear, and Mother Nature and Heavenly Father start serving such a human. Kundalini Yoga is not a democracy and we do not win votes. The crown of spirituality can only be bestowed. It cannot, shall not, will not be conquered. Please know this well.

When you teach, you have only one privilege: *Ong Namo Guru Dev Namo*. That's it. After that, whatever you have remembered, seen and experienced, just share. What do you want? Effect? Effect it shall be. There's no reason that you must not win. When you chant that and you let it go to yourself to God, then you don't fail. God fails, and God doesn't like to fail. He has no such luxury to fail. So have patience, have faith, and learn to give. The only thing you can give to somebody is yourself. With that mantra, you give yourself unto God, and God comes for you. Simple. It's just a love affair. A Teacher and student are dating—they have a relationship—not in the physical sense, but in the spiritual sense. Longing is the same. Do you see? You have left your work, your home, you have come here; because you want to be. You have learned. Now you go back home learned, and expand yourself, spread yourself. That's how it works.

S: Can I slightly vary the melody of the *Ong Namo Guru Dev Namo*?

YB: It is in the back of the conch. If you change it, then it will become vocal. The wrong key will never open the lock. Some things you are free to do; other things you are not free to do. We have kept the teachings of Kundalini Yoga pure from the time we know to the time we are. That's why when some people teach Kundalini Yoga it doesn't work. They teach philosophy, they teach chakras, sometimes they make up *kriyas*. It's a good time, but it will not touch the core. It is as simple as that.

First of all, the Teacher is a dedicated person. He's a channel through which the knowledge flows. He or she is not the knowledge. It's the student who drinks it. The Teacher is not the knowledge, he's the giver of the knowledge. The student is the taker of the knowledge. Why should we mix our ego with it and change it?

S: When we chant *"Ong Namo,"* when we tune in, is that the same as in the Christian religion, when you invoke the Holy Spirit. Is it that the same energy?

YB: *"Guru Dev"* is a very particular word. It means "Oh, All Transparent Knowledge, which takes us from darkness to sunshine." We do not say, *"Nameh."* Normally you will see people chanting, *"Om Guru Dev."* They say, *"Nameh,"* not *"Namo."* And we don't say *"Om,"* we say *"Ong."* "Totality or Reality, come through now and uplift to light." This is a code word. I can't compare it because I'm not supposed to. A Christian will chant it, he will have the same effect; a Buddhist will chant it, he will have the same effect. Whosoever uses the key can open the room. All we teach is the key. We don't enter into the privacy of the room of a person.

When you say *"Guru Dev,"* that is Holy Spirit, the Holy Ghost. *"Ong Namo"* is personified

God, and the self is the son or daughter. That's why in the Khalsa order there's no man, no woman. It's a common gender. Purity and piety are the net result of it.

There is a Jesuit priest who is my student, and one day I gave him a mantra. After all, I sat with him and he got elevated and he said, "Master, give me a mantra." The mantra I gave him was, "Christ, Christ, Christ. No crisis, no crisis, no crisis." "Christ, Christ, Christ. No crisis, no crisis, no crisis."

Yesterday I went to St. Francis's place. They asked me to do a prayer. I did a prayer. I want you to join with me in that prayer. The rhythm is important.

"I offer Thee my ego. Grant me Your light.

Ego against light. Ego against light. Ego against light.

I offer Thee my ego. Grant me Thy light.

Ego against light. Ego against light. Ego against light.

Amigo, Amigo, Amigo. Thank you."

(Class applauds.) What do you give to St. Francis? Give him your troubles. Go home in peace. What is the idea of coming to Assisi?

ਦੁਖੁ ਪਰਹਰਿ ਸੁਖੁ ਘਰਿ ਲੈ ਜਾਇ ॥

Dukh parhar sukh ghar lai jaa-eh.

   -Guru Nanak, *Siri Guru Granth Sahib,* page *2* (from the 5th *pauriee of Japji Sahib)*
You will then obtain joy in your mind and throw away your pain.

Give your discomforts to God, and take happiness home. It is the happiness which you can share, not the troubles. God is interested in your troubles. People are not.

People are not interested in your complaints, your tragedies, and in your miseries. Out of sympathy and apathy, they will listen to you for a while, but after a while, I tell you, people will avoid you. People just want you to be with them with love and affection and elevation. They don't want too much; they don't want too little. You as Teachers should be forewarned. Just be slow, steady, dependable, and honorable in character. Your smiles and your sweetness can win the world. If you have sweet manners and language, you can rule the whole world. It's up to you.

We'll end the day with a little meditation. Now please get ready.

Meditation Set #1

Meditation to Bring Knowledge of "Thou"

Part 1

Mudra: Sit in Easy Pose with a straight spine. Extend the bent elbows out to the sides. Bring the forearms in front of the heart center, parallel to the ground. The palms are flat, face down, right over left for males, left over right for females, with about a 6-inch space between the two hands. The placement of the two palms must be very precise. Imagine there is a line drawn between the two nipples. The right hand should be a few inches above this line, and the left hand should be a few inches below this line.

Eyes: Look at the tip of the nose.

Mantra: The 19th *pauree* of *Japji Sahib* is recited to music:

ਅਸੰਖ ਨਾਵ ਅਸੰਖ ਥਾਵ ॥ ਅਗੰਮ ਅਗੰਮ ਅਸੰਖ ਲੋਅ ॥
ਅਸੰਖ ਕਹਹਿ ਸਿਰਿ ਭਾਰੁ ਹੋਇ ॥ ਅਖਰੀ ਨਾਮੁ ਅਖਰੀ ਸਾਲਾਹ
ਅਖਰੀ ਗਿਆਨੁ ਗੀਤ ਗੁਣ ਗਾਹ ॥ ਅਖਰੀ ਲਿਖਣੁ ਬੋਲਣੁ ਬਾਣਿ ॥
ਅਖਰਾ ਸਿਰਿ ਸੰਜੋਗੁ ਵਖਾਣਿ ॥
ਜਿਨਿ ਏਹਿ ਲਿਖੇ ਤਿਸੁ ਸਿਰਿ ਨਾਹਿ ॥ ਜਿਵ ਫੁਰਮਾਏ ਤਿਵ ਤਿਵ ਪਾਹਿ ॥
ਜੇਤਾ ਕੀਤਾ ਤੇਤਾ ਨਾਉ ॥ ਵਿਣੁ ਨਾਵੈ ਨਾਹੀ ਕੋ ਥਾਉ ॥
ਕੁਦਰਤਿ ਕਵਣ ਕਹਾ ਵੀਚਾਰੁ ॥ ਵਾਰਿਆ ਨ ਜਾਵਾ ਏਕ ਵਾਰ ॥
ਜੋ ਤੁਧੁ ਭਾਵੈ ਸਾਈ ਭਲੀ ਕਾਰ ॥ ਤੂ ਸਦਾ ਸਲਾਮਤਿ ਨਿਰੰਕਾਰ ॥

Asankh naav asankh thaav. Agam agam asankh lo-a.
Asankh kaheh sir bhaar ho-eh.   Akharee Naam akharee saalaah.
Akharee giaan geet gun gaah. Akharee likhan bolan baan.
Akharaa sir sanjog vakhaan.
Jin eh likhai tis sir naa-eh. Jiv furmaa-ay tiv tiv paa-eh.
Jay-taa keetaa tay-taa naa-oh. Vin naavai naa-hee ko thaa-oh.
Kudrat kavan kahaa veechaar.   Vaariaa na(n) jaavaa ayk vaar.
Jo tudh bhaavai saa-ee bhalee kaar. Too(n) sadaa salaamat nirankaar.
      -Guru Nanak, *Siri Guru Granth Sahib*, page 4 (from the *19th pauree of Japji Sahib*)
God, Name, and abodes are countless. Inaccessible and inscrutable are God's realms.
Even to say that they are countless is to carry loads of sins on one's head.
God's virtues and knowledge are sung through words.
The uttered hymns are recorded in letters.
The destiny of a mortal is written on his forehead in letters.
God, Who writes the destinies, has no such letters written on His forehead.
Mortals obtain that which is ordained by God. God's celebrity is as great as
His creation. There is no shelter except God's Name.
What power can describe God and His schemes? I cannot even once be a sacrifice
to God. Whatever pleases God is the only good done, the Eternal and Formless One.

Time: 20 minutes.

End: Inhale deeply. Move immediately into Part II.

Comments/Effects: "Every teacher will be tested in the hands of the great Teacher—Time. We have to conquer time."

Part II

Mudra: Bring the hands into Prayer Pose at the heart center. Separate the hands until there is a 9-inch space between the two flattened palms. The distance must be exactly 9 inches—not less and not more.

Eyes: Unspecified.

Music: Instrumental version of *Ardas Bhaee*. Whistle along with the music.

Time: 9 minutes.

End: Inhale, and move immediately into Part III.

Comments/Effects: Whistling in this position will take away your tiredness and fatigue.

Part III

Mudra: Place the two palms flat down on top of the navel point, right over left. Press hard on the navel point.

Eyes: Unspecified.

Tape: *Ardas Bhaee* version with words. Sing aloud with the tape, speaking from the navel. *(Refer to page 192 for words.)* It is a slow rhythm. As you chant the words, make sure the tip of the tongue touches the upper palate, stimulating the meridian points.

Time: 6 minutes.

End: Inhale very deeply. Press the navel with both hands with all the force you can. Hold 14 seconds. Exhale. Inhale a second time, repeat, holding 13 seconds. Exhale. The third time, inhale deep, press, and bring the spine's muscular system upward, all the way to your neck. Hold for 16 seconds. Relax.

Comments/Effects: When the tip of the tongue does not touch the upper palate, whatever you say is not heard by the other person in the same way you meant it.
Make sure you keep your navel pressed throughout the meditation.

Meditation Set #2

Meditation to Let "Thou" Prevail

Have no thoughts while doing this meditation. Let the Living God come into your heart center. Instead of "I"—let "Thou" prevail.

Mudra: Sit in Easy Pose, spine straight. Bring the hands up in front of the shoulders, and move them a little out to the sides. Palms are flat, with the fingers pointing straight up towards the ceiling.

Hand Mudra: Split the fingers between the middle and ring fingers, keeping the index and middle fingers pressed side by side, and the ring and pinkie fingers pressed side by side. Extend the thumbs straight out, away from the rest of the hand. Try and maintain the finger-split the entire time.

Eyes: Closed.

Focus: Sit calmly and in your heart center, bring in the Living God. Instead of "I" bring in "Thou."

Time: 9 minutes total. The first few minutes were done in silence, then the tape, *Birthday Song,* by Livtar Singh was played.

❀

On this day the Lord gave you life,
May you use it to serve Him.
All of our loving prayers will be with you.
May you never forget him.
May the Long Time Sun Shine Upon You
All Love Surround You
And the Pure Light Within You
Guide Your Way On.
Sat Naam.

End: Finally, Yogi Bhajan recited the following closing prayer, while the students remained in the posture:

Thou, oh Thou in me, and Thou, oh Thou in Thee.
Whosoever dwells in me and that of God, shall be honored to be a Teacher,
beyond time and space, and shall be liberated for the karma of the world.
Those who meditate on the Word, shall have all that there is in the Kingdom
of God. Those who deny it shall seek
His Mercy. Unto the new Age of Aquarius, the saintly
souls are marching to meet the challenge, to serve
and uplift humanity. It is their victory, granted by His light and
His Hand, unto Infinity. With prosperity, reality, and grace.
That the Will of God may prevail,
and our Will may recognize it.
Sat Naam.

All right, now you are free.
(Class applauds.)

Now I am free! Liberated!
I wash my hands. Ha ha ha. It is up to you, now.
I did what I came for, and we'll do it again when we get a chance.
Hey, I have always come to you. Now you should start coming to me in
Espanola, you know what I mean? You are young.

Resources

A.
The Teachers Oath

I am not a Woman

I am not a Man

I am not a Person

I am not Myself

I am a Teacher

This concept is to purify you as a channel and bring the Heavens through you.

◎

The mudra Yogi Bhajan gave to use with this Oath is as follows:

Keeping all the fingers straight up, hold up the left hand next to the left shoulder, palm facing forward, as if you are taking an Oath. Bend the corresponding fingers down as you repeat each segment of the Oath, straightening it back up before you bend the next finger:

"I am not a Woman" • Bend the pinkie finger down
"I am not a Man" • Bend the ring finger down
"I am not a Person" • Bend the middle finger down
"I am not Myself" • Bend the index finger down
"I am a Teacher" • Bend the thumb down

Then close your eyes and concentrate at the *Ayia chakra*, or *Ajna chakra*, the Third Eye; and chant three times, *Ong Namo Guru Dev Namo*. It's called *Naadhi Sodhani Kriya*. *Naadhi* means all the channels. *Sodhanaa* means perfect them. And it's a *Kriya*, an action. Everything which has been given to you is totally pure. Nothing has been added or subtracted. So the purpose is very simple: to give people honestly what we have.

◎

Excerpted from a talk given to Teachers on March 23, 1990 in Los Angeles, California.

B.

Sola Kalyan Sumpuran : The 16 Facets of Perfection of a Kundalini Yoga Teacher

Yogi Bhajan, September 1995

1. A Teacher will never alter the teachings because of personal opinion. You will teach by example.

2. The higher you grow as a Teacher, the more humble you have to be.

3. The Teacher always serves the students, so they can become ten times stronger than you, because every student is a Teacher for tomorrow.

4. A Teacher has to be extremely kind, caring, compassionate, and forgiving.

5. As a Teacher you should always poke, provoke, confront, and elevate your students to excellence.

6. As a Teacher you have to continuously imagine, visualize, believe, and expand in all directions, connect to everything, meditate, practice, and project that you are *Ang Sang Wahe Guru* (with every limb, every part of me, I belong to the Divine), and that the energy of Guru Ram Das is flowing through you.

7. As a Teacher you will always be in Chardi Kala (elevated spirits) and connected to your higher self, never caught in emotional turmoil. Count your blessings, not your curses. Always be graceful. Glow and grow.

8. As a Teacher you will continuously graduate towards the Divinity and Infinity that are the essence of your existence. You are not a human born for a spiritual search, you are a spirit, an Atma (soul), born for an experience as a human. Your purity and piety as an Atma are always maintained, protected, exalted, projected, as a priority over everything, and kept in sight mentally, physically, and spiritually.

9. As a Teacher listen to and obey all righteous teachings. If you read something, you will know it; if you write something, you will understand it; if you teach something, you will perfect it.

It is perfection of your deliverance that gives you grace as a Teacher. Your success as a Teacher lies not in what you know, but in what your student receives.

A Teacher is measured by the growth, dignity, and excellence of the student. If you find any talent, nurture it, teach it, exalt it to the best of your ability and Divinity.

10. As a Teacher do not relate to ego or politics. Always relate to the spirit, soul, and essence of a person. Always relate to the intelligence, talent, and consciousness of a person. Always relate to the manners, methods, and mentality of a person. Pure thoughts are the way to universal knowledge and will make you bountiful, blissful, and beautiful.

11. God and Guru have blessed you with Karma (the law of cause and effect). As a Teacher you must offer yourself in Dharma (lifestyle of righteousness) to honor the gift of God of life. Never create a drift or rift between you and your Atma.

12. A Teacher wears white cotton clothing while teaching. White clothing makes you as a teacher look divine and represent light. The color white represents the seven colors. Cotton is the flower of the Earth. It is good for your psyche, for your energy, and for your nervous system. Your way of dressing should be saintly and make you glow with grace. You should look like a sage and a prince or princess of peace and divinity. A Teacher is a Ph.D.—Prince or Princess of High Divinity.

13. Just as a seed has to wither to become a tree and bear fruit, Teachers who do not become perfect students do not become perfect Masters.

14. The Universal Spirit that rotates the Earth can take care of all your problems. As a Teacher you have to learn trust and faith. Regard every breath of life as a gift. Strive for conscious breathing, breathing one breath a minute.

15. The banner of a Teacher is: "In God I dwell." The standard of arms of a Teacher is: "God within me I trust."
The honor of a Teacher is: "In the Name of God I serve."
The motto of a Teacher is: "Peace of mind and peace within the material world."

16. A Teacher needs to commit to Nam, the God-given identity.
    Without Naam, you cannot have the purity of self and
     the divine projected grace to master all the elements.
    Without commitment there is no character.
    Without character there is no dignity.
    Without dignity there is no divinity.
    Without divinity there is no grace.
    Without grace you cannot sacrifice or serve others.
    Your compassion and presence will not work and you cannot be happy.
Remember once and for all, happiness is your birthright and it is always right to be happy. So be happy, be healthy, and be holy.
We are all holy, because we all have nine holes. Adding two arms and two legs makes thirteen. You are born with thirteen, you will live with thirteen, you will die with thirteen. Thirteen (three and one) makes four—Cup of Prayer. Prayer is your power, your protector, and your provider.

C.
The Alphabets   *by Yogi Bhajan*

Alphabet of a Teacher

A   Always fearless
B   Beautiful in public
C   Concentrated in their action
D   Do as they are told
E   Earth's friend
F   Friend to all
G   Gives all happiness
H   Happy when tested
I   Is a student of God
J   Jumps ahead when behind
K   Keeps up
L   Learns from the best teacher
M   Meditates on God
N   Never negative
O   On the top
P   Prevails through the hardest challenges
Q   Never Questions
R   Ready for anything
S   Soul is pure
T   Teacher teaches others
U   Uses the finest there is
V   Vision, sees God in all
W   Writes from the heart
X   X-rays the aura of the person in need
Y   Yells only at what needs to be awakened
Z   Zaps, then defends

Alphabet of a Woman

A   Able
B   Blessed
C   Compassionate
D   Dharma
E   Exercise
F   Fulfilled
G   Graceful
H   Honest
I   Intellectual
J   Joyful
K   Khalsa
L   Learned
M   Meditate
N   Noble
O   Organized
P   Patient
Q   Queenly
R   Radiant
S   Smiling
T   Thoughtful
U   Understanding
V   Vital
W   Wahe Guru
X   eXcellent
Y   Yoga
Z   Zestful

Alphabet of Self-Esteem

A Attitude
B Botany of Self-Esteem
C Corridors & Conditions
D Distance
E Education
F Faculty
G Grace
H Him
I Identity
J Joy
K Kindness
L Loneliness
M Mother
N Nature
O Option
P Power
Q Quest
R Realism
S Service
T Trend
U Universality
V Variety
W Wisdom
X Xing
Y You
Z Zeal

Alphabet of Marriage

Qualities to Qualify a Man Before Taking Him as a Husband

A Age
B Beauty
C Career
D Discipline
E Education and Excellence
F Fantasies
G Grace
H Handsomeness
I Intelligence and Intuition
J Jovialness
K Kindness
L Leanings*
M Manhood
N Nature
O Optimism
P Patience
Q Quickness, Quietness
R Reverence
S Sweetness
T Temperament, Truthfulness & Tolerance
U Uniqueness
V Variety & Virtues
W Withholdings
X X-ray Intuition
Y Youthfulness
Z Zeal

*Leanings. You must know man's leanings, otherwise you don't know the man. When they build a metal road, there is always a grip in it. Upto a certain temperature it will contract to a point, but it won't crack. At a certain temperature it will expand, but it will not bump up. If any time the weather proceeds more than that, you don't have a metal road. It is called leanings. Don't mesmerize yourself until you know the man's leanings.

The Administrator's Alphabet

A   Administrator I am.

B   I will Bounce off everybody and everybody will Bounce off me.

C   I will Catch but no one will Catch me

D   Diplomacy works for Development.

E   Efficiency, not what you deserve or desire. Not proof or profit. What you Effectively negotiate.

F   "F" is for Future. Harmoniously planning effective discipline. Rational communication will guarantee a prosperous Future.

G   God, Good, and Goods. Administrate with Godly qualities, with Good behavior and by creating Goods for others.

H   Height. I am the scale between high and low. I am the administrator.

I   I am at your service. I am at your call. I am the administrator to answer the call of duty.

J   Every Jerk has to be dealt with a joke. Humor is the way of communication.

K   Kindness effectively controls everything.

L   Longevity of the administration depends on my efficiency and effective negotiation with my subordinates and effective deliverance to my superiors.

M   Manners. Manners guarantee the smoothness of working and make the day.

N   Nature. The Nature of things has to be dealt with and has to be felt. Nurture everybody to adhere to your administrative quality.

O   Opportunity. Good organization brings good Opportunities.

P   Personality. Play pure Personality with power to solve problems.

Q   Quickly understand but never Quickly judge.

R   Rational involvement of others for opinion, problem solving, and decision-making is not a weakness but a strength.

S   Sincere, serious service is the way to be serene, strong and sensible.

T   Trust in good and Trust everybody for nothing. Involve, be inductive, and decide being deductive.

U   Universal, university and you exist in one spot.

V   Virtue. Adopt others' Virtues but value your own grace. That will win the race.

W   Wisdom is the ultimate success. Be Wise to rise in life. Wisdom brings profit; without it you lose a lot. Wisdom is virtuous, Wisdom is a value which nobody can refuse. Wisdom creates the kingdom.

X   X the negative with a positive attitude and with a better substitute. Plan well and swell.

Y   Youth. Talk, look and be Youthful. Youth is an art and a science. It is an essential ingredient of the administrator. Dress well and be well.

Z   Zeal will appeal and heal the wounds. Cause may be any; effect should be harmony.

Alphabet of Qualities of People

Here are the various categories of people and how they function in life:

A   Go and get it. They are restless; they get it.

B   Somebody should get it for them.

C   Get it and give it to me.

D   I was supposed to get it, what are you doing here?

E   Ease out and leave it for me, I am real.

F   Don't confuse me, and don't bother me.

G   God upside down people. I'm God, what I say is real, I am everything, if you don't know me, you don't know a thing. Get out of my life. Normally they are very intellectual, very accomplished, and very studied. They can speak on any subject and be extremely convincing. We also call them coffee-house preachers. They go to the coffee house and drink a lot of coffee and talk until the place closes.

H   These people are fascinating; highly sensitive and highly insensitive. You can never figure them out. They neither make any sense to themselves nor to anyone else. But they look pretty, they dress well and their first appearance is very exciting. They are like beavers; they create dams and stop everything.

I   The intellectuals. Intellectuals are never intelligent, but they feel completely perfect. They drone on and on expounding their knowledge, and after a while you can listen no longer. They sound like a quacking duck, and when people see them coming they avoid them. Intelligent people are those who know intellectually, but they adapt the aptitude. When an intellectual adapts the aptitude for patience, then he conceives the mission.

J   Jokers. They know everything, but they don't know anything. They can be anything. Like water, they have no shape of their own, but take the shape of whatever contains them. They will tell you they are an expert, but they will not stick to anything. Jokers never have the prime role. They are expert trainers, and expert followers, but they will never be the star of the show of life. They are transitory because humor can not last. That is a law of humor. The same is true of joy; you feel it, you enjoy it, you taste it, and the next minute it is something else.

K   They are kind, they are one of a kind, and they kindle love in every heart.

L   Long talkers. They take 60 sentences to convey one little thought. You should run away when you see them coming.

M   There are two types in this category: they mean and they are mean. There is nothing in between. Whatever they communicate, they mean. Or whenever they talk, it burns you to death. They are very mean. There is no third category in this.

N   Neutral people. They are mostly juice people. This is how they talk: "This is fine. This can be fine too. I agree with you, you agree with me. We have agreed on it. It's done. But I can't participate." That will happen after two hours of talking and when everything is set and done. That's all they have, if's and but's.

O   They are the nucleus of our society; they organize everything. They are extremely successful, very joyous, very kind and highly penetrating.

P   If you do not look at their personality and give them a proper pedestal and proper prospective, they shall take one second to pee on you. The majority of them are in control of things. That is the planet Earth's tragedy. They are the source of all suffering and all wars.

They are control oriented. They do anything and everything just to be in control. They can be psychotic, neurotic and obnoxious or sweet and pleasant lovers. There is no facet of life which they can not present under the motivation to control.

Q   It doesn't matter what you say to them, you will have a quick question. They question everything to death and they create duality everywhere. They are trouble shooters; their analytical faculty is invaluable in business. But in normal life, forget it.

R   They are sneaks, they are snakes, they are reserved. You can't get a thing out of them. That's their faculty. They are very good for intelligence work. You shred them, you hang them, you butcher them, they won't say a thing. In normal life you will never know where they are at. Never ever depend on what they say. They are in their own world. Until you penetrate their reserve and find out what is their guiding line, you had better keep your distance.

S   Sincere, serviceful, sanitary and sensible. They have a solution to everything. Tell them a thing, it is solved. Ask them a question, it is answered. Make a deal, it is forever. Great people. Nothing like them.

T   Trampoline-people. These are the only people whose aura moves up and down. Normally the aura expands and contracts with the arcline, but theirs moves up and down. When they talk, you do not know where it is going. You can never figure it out no matter how intelligent and quick you are. Nothing penetrates them.

U   U-people. They are double I's connected at the bottom. This "U" is a rapid cannon fire that never stops. The "U" becomes yo-yo and you run. Their projection is very powerful. They reach and penetrate any psyche to get their point across. They are wonderful public relations people. But living with them is like living on a grill. They will roast you to death.

V   These are very rare people. They come, they see, they conquer, they experience victory. They know the devil, they know the divine and they go to victory. It is in their mind, in their soul and in their being.

W   Working class. If you ever make a working personality a managing personality, you will lose it. Working people do not want responsibility. They are never administrators. They love to work, but after work they don't care if they are human or not. They think they are done. Their limit as a human is just work.

X   They cut everything. They are living human negativity. You can never get from them one word of positivity.

Y   Why-people are the source of every trouble. These are the people who are always asking why and because. Why and because; you can never get out of that.

Z   Z-people are very rare. They have the zeal to inspire themselves and the zeal to inspire others. They are people of infinity. Z-people come once in a while like *avtars,* like guides, like messengers of God. There is no pain which can hurt them. There is no reality which can limit them. There are no circumstances which can deter them. There's nothing which can stop them. Z-people come with the Will of God, they live with the Will of God, they leave with the Will of God. They are like Infinity people. Their zeal penetrates through. Even death can not stop them. Fear of death stops everybody. Fear of family. Fear of poverty. These fears are not imaginary. These fears stop us. These fears stop our intelligence, our creativity, our reality, our personality, our expansion. Fear exists to stop you. Fear is such an imaginary reality that it kills your reality. But in Z-people nothing can stop them.

D. The Art & Science of Liberation

A talk by Yogi Bhajan in 1969

What is a liberated being? And what is the reason we suffer in the hands of time? Every person has two sides. One is a carefree side. The other is a careless side. When one lives in his carefree side, he is guided by his Divine faculty. When he lives in his careless side he is guided by his animal force. It is not the carelessness of breaking a glass or accidentally throwing away something you meant to keep. Materially we are considered careless when we are unable to discharge our material responsibilities. But in reality, we are truly careless when we lose our Divine personality—when that "something" which is very precious, beyond value, is lost just for passion. Emotion and passion are the two buyers of our Spiritual personality. If you analyze this thought you will realize that such a bargain is too costly. For what are we trading our Spiritual Self? This world of ours is a transitory phase of life. It is not permanent, but we always associate ourselves with it as if we belong to it and it belongs to us.

Subconsciously, behind every action is the desire to be recognized. But if you classify your desire for recognition and the way you try to be recognized, you will find that you want recognition without maturity. You want to be recognized as a mature being, but you have not developed the mature attitude of a carefree being.

The only carefree being is that person who is free from negativity. He is liberated. It is a Cosmic Law that such a person is never short of anything. A carefree man doesn't know any misery. He may be humble, but that doesn't mean he is miserable. Ever wise, he sails through time undisturbed. He does not need any correction at the hands of time. His smooth behavior and calmness of personality are the signs that he is a liberated being. In a nutshell, he is the happiest person ever on the Earth.

This does not mean that you should be barred from having worldly goods. Matter is media. It cannot be created and it cannot be destroyed. Similarly, emotion and involvement in desire are also media, but their satisfaction is temporary, not everlasting. If you understand how the addiction to liquor begins, you will understand this Theory of Involvement. This is how it works: A man who does not drink comes under pressure and doesn't know what to do. He goes to the house of a friend for consolation, for a man is a social animal, and by having someone participate in his grief, he feels relieved. The friend offers whiskey for a soothing effect and the man is persuaded to take a drink. The alcohol goes into the body and does its chemical action. It soothes the nerves, and energizes the energy centers so that the man's attitude relaxes and becomes flexible. It is only a temporary relief, but the memory of the first taste sticks in his mind. He can never ever regain the smoothness of that first taste of liquor, but for the lust of that taste and in order to recapture that experience, people become habitual drinkers — alcoholics. They believe that the best way to escape from the pressures of life is to continue drinking and thus drinking becomes a need of the body.

Similarly, whenever you involve yourself in any mode of life, you are going into a channel where you will go on and on and on, and you can never come back to the point from which you originally started. When we forget our original basis of action and become involved, we become a slave.

It has been seen in our entire concept of life, that we are 15% slaves to a routine, to habit. Man must have certain habits without which his life cannot go on. But he can attain liberation by changing the character of these minimum required habits. There are two kinds of habits: Promoting Habits and Demoting Habits. Demoting habits make you unhappy physically, mentally and spiritually. Promoting habits make you happy physically, mentally and spiritually. In your life, if you have all the habits which are promoting habits, you will end up as a Liberated, Divine person. If you have demoting habits, you will always end up as a physical wreck, mentally insane and/or spiritual defunct.

Habit is a must of your personality and mind. For that period when you are acting under a demoting habit, you are totally in the negative personality. It is also a fact that if you get into any one negative habit, you will automatically attract its four sister habits, for they love to stay together. These five demoting habits of behavior and attitude are: greed, anger, lust, attachment and negative ego. When one sister enters the house, she calls the others to join. Each habit is supported on two tripods — 1) Physical, Mental and Spiritual; and 2) Past, Present and Future.

There are two guiding instincts in man. He is either improving his future or blocking his future improvement. If you are conscious of this, an have an honest and sincere urge to improve your future, you will always have promoting habits. Oh man, if you are to care not even for God, at least care for the future. When you care enough for your future to have promoting habits, you will become a liberated person. A liberated person is always a happy person. He does not lack in any material comfort. He does not know any power on earth which can insult him. He lives in grace in this world and when he leaves the body he is respected for generations to follow. Everyone can be like that. Yesterday's greatest sinner can be a Saint this minute. The only thing required is a decision. "Am I to guard my future and choose to be a liberated person, or am I to block my future and go by the material-physical aspect of the world?" For any person who blocks his future, it is a guaranteed fact he suffers in the future. Any person who takes advantage of the "now" causing someone else's loss, blocks his future. Anyone who takes advantage of the "now" invites trouble from Mr. Future.

Maintain a positive attitude with promoting habits for 40 days, and you can change your destiny. This psychological concept of Human behavior is a pattern which can guide you to that goal which is described in our scriptures as Paradise.

In the self one has to sow the seed of Divine vibrations and with the power of these vibrations one has to dwell in the Ultimate which is a Truth, a reality and an ever living primal force. This primal force has been named God by Christians; *Paramatman* by Hindus; and *Allah* by Muslims. Some name has been given it by all, but the Universal Consciousness of this Universal Spirit has one name, that is Truth, so we call it *"Sat"* and we remember it as *"Sat Nam."* *"Sat,"* in the language of Gods, Sanskrit, means "Truth." *"Nam"* means "Name." So without dispute we can say that Universal Consciousness, that Universal Spirit, that creative force in us, has a universal name and that is *"Sat Nam."*

All those who want to liberate themselves and seek to dwell in the Ultimate must cleanse their physical selves and direct their mental beings towards *Sat Nam*, the being of beings. One who dwells on the vibrations of this Holy Nam — *Sat Nam* — in the prime hours of the day before dawn when the channels for vibrations are very clean and clear, will realize the concept of a Liberated Being through the grace of this Beej Mantra which awakens the goddess of awareness in a being. He then lives as a liberated man on the planet Earth.

E.
The Ten Commandments & The Ten Promises

From a lecture by Yogi Bhajan • August 6, 1991

Each Commandment in the Bible is incomplete. The Ten Commandments were given, but not the Ten Promises of God. Every Commandment must bear fruit. That is why the Commandments are incomplete. You are told what to do, but not told what it will do for you.

First Commandment
Thou shalt have no other Gods before me.
Promise
Thou shall conquer the Earth. If the Lord God Creator is pleased with thee, all creation shall be thy servant.

Second Commandment
Thou shalt not take the Name of the Lord in vain.
Promise
Thou shall never be polluted.

Third Commandment
Remember the Sabbath day, to keep it holy.
Promise
Thou shall live in peace and rest.

Fourth Commandment
Honor thy father and thy mother.
Promise
Thy identity shall be perfect. Heavenly Father, Motherly Earth. This whole theory is the same.

Fifth Commandment
I hou shalt not kill.
Promise (Longevity Promise)
Thou shalt not let yourself be killed.
If you spiritually develop in yourself non-killing instincts, then Mother Nature shall protect you and take care of you

Sixth Commandment
Thou shalt not commit adultery.
Promise
Thy purity shall be granted.

Seventh Commandment
Love thy neighbor.
Promise
And the entire neighborhood shall love thee.

Eighth Commandment
Thou shalt not steal.
Promise
All shall belong to thee.

Ninth Commandment
Thou shalt not bear false witness.
Promise
The power to witness My Creation shall be thine.

Tenth Commandment
Thou shalt not covet thy neighbor's wife nor thy neighbor's goods (belongings).
Promise
The Universe shall never question thy will and all good shall come to thee. The real wife of God is the creation; the creation will never question thy will.

F.
The Moon Cycles & How They Affect You

From a lecture by Yogi Bhajan • August 6, 1991

Your biofeedback moves from new moon to full moon, and full moon to new moon. There are three days of the moon, when if you want to take care of your mind and your health, you can fast at these times. In Ayurveda, this is considered to be the mastery of all treatments.Try fasting on lemon and water during these three days in the month, from sun-up until the next morning at breakfast, when you can break the fast.

Full moon—You are naturally accelerated on a full moon; you are at the highest. The secretions in your body will be at their maximum, so you don't want your energy being used to consume food. Save your energy to reconstruct yourself. Try to drink only liquids on this day. If you feel you must eat, drink only milk.

New moon—You are at your lowest. This is a good day to fast on lemon and water.

Eleventh day of the moon (Eleven days after the new moon)—you are in balance, in twilight. The glandular system readjusts itself on this day. Your metabolism is changing, so if you eat very lightly and *sattvic* this day, if you eat light and green things, orif you just live on water and melon, your health will be perfect. Eat very light, very *sattvic* this day. Eat only one meal, and drink lemon and water the rest of the day.

Lemon & Water Mixture
Suggested proportion for the lemon and water mixture is the following:

Use about two cups of lemon juice to about 20 cups of water, and a little sweetener. This will make about three bottles for the entire day.

If you begin to feel very cool, then try adding ginger to it. You can sweeten it with a little maple syrup, black molasses or *ghur* (raw sugar), but don't use too much. Make sure you drink the lemon and water mixture through a straw, to save the enamel on your teeth.

Note: Consult your health care professional before starting any kind of fast.

G.
Yogic Recipes

Yogi Tea

Make at least 4 cups of Yogi Tea at a time. It's a good idea to make large batches at a time, and store it in the refrigerator without milk; then add milk when you want to drink it. It can stay fresh in the refrigerator for about a week.

For ONE cup, the measurements are:
> 10 oz. water
> 3 whole cloves
> 4 whole green cardamom pods (cracked open is best)
> 4 whole black peppercorns
> 1/2 stick cinnamon
> 1 slice ginger root
> 1/4 tsp. black tea (optional)
> 1/4 cup milk

Boil the spices for 10-15 minutes, with the top on the pot(just leave it open a crack to let a little of the steam out). Add black tea and steep for 2 minutes. Add milk, then bring to a boil. Remove immediately from the stove, and strain. Add honey to taste.

For 2 quarts use:
> 20 cardamom pods
> 20 peppercorns
> 15 cloves
> 5 or more slices of ginger root
> 3 cinnamon sticks
> 1 tbs. black tea

Boil at least 30 minutes. Add 1 qt of milk.

Yogi Tea is also available in pre-mixed packages, and in tea bags. *(See References for address of Ancient Healing Ways.)*

Yogi Bhajan says about Yogi Tea: "If you take a really a good amount of Yogi Tea, it will keep your liver very well. It is said to help the liver. And when we started in the sixties, people who had drug habits, who couldn't even move, we put them on Yogi Tea."

Yogi Tea is actually a combination of foods. It is a tonic to the nervous system. It can help to balance your system when you are feeling out of balance. It has been used often as a remedy and preventative measure for colds, flu and diseases of the mucous membranes.

Black pepper is a blood purifier. Cardamom is for the colon. Together they support the brain cells. Cloves help support the nervous system. Cinnamon is good for the bones. Ginger helps strengthen the nervous system and is very good if you have a cold, flu, physical weakness. It can help women when they are experiencing menstrual discomfort, such as cramps or PMS symptoms. You can try making Yogi Tea with extra ginger when you are feeling a cold or the flu coming on. If a man takes a cup of Yogi Tea after intercourse, it can help to replenish his body. In addition, Yogi Tea diluted with milk, can be very helpful to a child who is experiencing the pains of teething.

Morning Drink for Optimal Health

    2 ounces of ginger juice
    2 ounces of lemon juice
    1 teaspoon of flaxseed oil
(Note: you can substitute with olive oil or sesame oil if you don't have flaxseed oil)

Mix together, and drink first thing every morning, after you brush your teeth, and before you drink anything else. Then wait at least 15 minutes until you eat or drink anything else.

Banana Recipe
Especially Good for Women

    1 Banana
    Mango powder
    1 tsp. Lemon or Lime Juice

Peel one banana, slice it length-wise, and place it on a plate. Sprinkle the lemon juice and the mango powder over the banana.

Bananas have potassium, which is necessary for women to maintain their youth. It can help provide energy. The citrus juice provides vitamin C to the body, and the mango powder is very good for providing extra energy. It is especially helpful when a woman is under extra stress.

Black Garbanzos

Here in the west we are used to seeing the white garbanzos. But for nerve energy, there's nothing like those little black garbanzos. The black garbanzos grow in fields in India. During the rainy season there's so much lightening over these fields, that it looks like the fourth of July—electricity goes from the clouds to the ground and from the ground back up to the clouds! It's a very funny natural phenomenon to see. Normally people avoid these fields at this time, because they don't want to be electrocuted. These black garbanzos are very good for the nervous system, and help to control the electromagnetic field of the body. They are the most powerfully energizing food in the world. They are very good for health.

Wash the beans and soak them overnight. In the morning, drain them, and put them into a pressure cooker, and cook until soft. Then make a soup out of them.

Or, you can use the following recipe:

Wash, drain, and soak 3 cups black garbanzo beans overnight. Cook at a slow boil in fresh water, for about 3 hours. Once soft, drain off most of the liquid, and return to the pot with about 1 cup of the cooking water.

In a large, thick-bottomed frying pan, heat on a medium fire:
1/2 cup mustard oil
1/2 cup sliced ginger
2 sliced onions
5-8 cloves chopped garlic
3 chopped jalapenos (optional).

Cook until soft. Then add:
2 pre-boiled potatoes (cut into pieces)
1 tsp. black pepper
1-2 tsp. black salt

Cook for a few minutes. Then add the onion, ginger, garlic mixture to the beans in the original cooking pot. Cook over a low flame, stirring the ingredients for about 10 minutes. Garnish with fresh coriander leaves, chopped. (Note: extra black salt can be added to taste.)

Cherry Sundae

Take some cherries, pit them, and blend them in the blender. Then cut up a pear and an apple, add them to the mixture, and blend again.

Pour this mixture over vanilla ice cream, and eat.

"You talk of energy? You will have to put a weight on your legs to keep yourself on the ground."

Ghee (Clarified Butter)

Simmer unsalted butter for about 10-15 minutes over a low-medium heat. Regular salted butter can be used if unsalted butter is not available. After heating, let it set for a few minutes, and then scoop all of the white foam from the top with a spoon. You'll see the clear, yellow ghee left at the bottom. Pour this into a container, using a strainer, and not letting any of the white sediment at the bottom of the pan slide in. Use *ghee* as you would butter or cooking oil.

Yogi Bhajan says of *ghee:* "Ghee is not an oil, it is a pure protein. It is supposed to melt the fat in your body. When you eat it with your food, you'll find three things:
1. You'll urinate more than usual that day (helps rid excess fluids from the body).
2. Your body will be warmer than normal.
3. You'll look at things more clearly than you normally do. You'll think more clearly. In India if somebody gets obese, they start living on *ghee*. And in Tibet and all these areas, they put *ghee* in their tea, and drink it—they live on it. That's their protein."

Jalapeno Milkshake

3-5 raw jalapenos
8-10 ounces of milk
A little honey (cuts down the heat of the jalapenos)

Put ingredients into a blender. Blend for 20-30 minutes. Pour it in a glass and sip it. Do not drink it straight down. "The spirit will go through you."

Yogi Bhajan's story about this jalapeno milkshake:
"Once I had to go to Mexico and I found a student of mine had been in the hospital. So I went straight to the kitchen, I took the jalapenos and the milk, blended it, and put tons of honey in it, because I knew she would react. Then I started giving it to her with a spoon — it is very difficult to go in. But I think on the fifth or sixth spoon she opened up her eyes. And by the end, when the glass was finished, she got up. She said, 'What was that?'
I said, 'Nothing, nothing, nothing.' I said, 'I have come all the way and you were not there to serve me. I hate it. So you should be up.'
The next day we secretly made it, and told her, 'Bottoms up, but slowly, spoon by spoon, sip it.'
She said, "It is sweet and bitter." She still takes it every day.
Once in a while when you really want to have a trouble-free life, hallelujah and jalapenos are the same. You need that drink."

Lettuce

Lettuce has .1 percent opium. There are many ways that lettuce can be prepared, that we have never even considered!

If you have a problem sleeping, make lettuce soup with milk, and take it with two tablets of 7-R. It's so relaxing, and you'll sleep very soundly. If you don't use milk, you'll be out before you even hit the pillow.

Roasting lettuce with black pepper brings its flavor to life, and the stomach welcomes it. Take lettuce and chop it up. Heat up a grill or heavy frying pan, and roast the lettuce, just as you might roast any other vegetable. You can add black pepper and jalapenos to taste, and add a little *ghee*. These help to bring out the flavor and are very good for the health.

Another way you can take lettuce is to make a *masala. (See recipe below.)* Then take a full head of lettuce, cut it into four pieces, put it in the pressure cooker, and really cook it. Once done, put it on a plate. Next take that beautiful masala with everything, and fill in the leaves and all around with it. Then eat it. You will have energy to work through the day, but you'll also have relaxation.

If you can make a juice out of the lettuce, and drink it at night, it can put you right to sleep. This is a very powerful and very relaxing drink.

Basic Masala

1/3 cup oil (sesame or olive oil is good)
1 teaspoon *garam masala* mixture
2 onions, chopped or sliced
3 cloves garlic, chopped fine
2 T peeled & chopped ginger root
2 medium tomatoes, peeled & chopped

Finely blend the following ingredients:
1/3 oz black cardamom
6 oz coriander seeds
1 tsp. turmeric
3 oz cumin seeds *(Jeera)*
1/4 tsp. cayenne powder (more or less)
1 oz cinnamon stick
1 oz whole cloves
salt to taste
1 oz green cardamom seeds
1 oz whole black peppercorns

Heat the oil in a frying pan. Add onions, ginger root and garlic and sauté until the onions start to brown. Then add the spices and salt. Sauté for 3 minutes, stirring. Add tomatoes and continue to cook until tomatoes dissolve into gravy. Add 1/2 cup water if necessary. You can then use this *masala* mixture as a basis for many vegetable dishes.

Onions, Ginger & Garlic

Onion, Ginger & Garlic are known as the Trinity Roots, and are essential for maintaining a healthy and energetic system. Ginger is for the nervous system, and helps when you are feeling flu or colds coming on, and is very energizing. Garlic enhances semen production and maintains potency. Onions purify the blood.

Parantha (Stuffed Chapati)

Make a dough out of the following flours, mixed together very well:

3/4 cup garbanzo flour
1/4 cup whole wheat flour
1/2 teaspoon salt (optional)
1/2 cup liquid from an onion, ginger & garlic that have been juiced in a juicer

Make a filling out of the pulp of the juiced onion, ginger & garlic. Other spices such as black pepper, red chiles, ajwan seeds, salt, and celery seeds can be added to this pulp mixture.

Directions for making the parantha:
Knead into a dough, about 5 minutes until soft and pliable. Then put the dough into a bowl, cover with a slightly damp cloth for about 15 minutes. Once set, knead a few more times, then break off a piece and roll it into a ball, the size of a golf ball. Place on a lightly floured cutting board and roll out into a 5 inch circle, 1/4 inch thick.

Place about a tablespoon of the filling into the center of the circle. Fold over the sides of the dough to cover the filling, bringing all the sides into the center, to form a little 'sack.' Place the filled dough onto a lightly floured surface and carefully roll it out with a rolling pin until it is looks like a 5" circle.

To cook:
Heat an iron frying pan until hot. Carefully place the stuffed parantha in the middle of the pan and cook on each side for about 45 seconds-1 minute. Then spread a little bit of ghee on each side of the parantha and cook until crispy and golden brown.

When finished:
Yogi Bhajan recommends mixing black pepper oil or black pepper, red chili oil or a little bit of red chili flakes or cayenne, *ajwan* (oregano) seeds, and turmeric with some *ghee,* and spread this on the cooked *parantha.* Traditionally, *paranthas* are served hot and eaten with plain yogurt as a breakfast dish.

Trinity Root Healing Drink

1 medium onion
1-3 inches ginger root, peeled & sliced thin
1/2 bulb garlic, peeled
1 quart milk, preferably goat milk
1 tsp. turmeric

Finely chop 1 onion, peel & slice the ginger, and peel the garlic. Place these into a pressure cooker along with the milk. Bring to full pressure and cook for five minutes. Cool off pressure cooker and strain the milk into an iron frying pan. Simmer the milk for 15 minutes. Strain and serve.

Note: If a pressure cooker is not available, the same mixture can be made in a crock pot overnight. Just add some extra water, and cook on low. In the morning, strain and serve.

Yogi Bhajan's comments on this drink: "I drink it every morning. In the goat's milk we boil onion, garlic, ginger and turmeric at night on a slow fire, and next morning I drink a glass of it. Within minutes you will feel a change. You know how you will feel? Like wings have sprung from your armpits. That's how you feel. The time has come that you must start taking care of yourself. Medical costs have gone so high, you don't want to be sick. These are preventive things. These are very good things."

H.
Herbal References

The following healing herbal formulas have been developed by Yogi Bhajan, and are based on Ayurvedic Medicine Formulas. Ayurveda is a sophisticated science of herbal medicine practiced in India for over 5000 years, which works to strengthen and balance the body. The following herbal formulas were mentioned in this book. For a full listing of all formulas available, contact Ancient Healing Ways. *(See Contacts.)*

Herbal Formulas

1-R. Called 'triphala' in Ayurvedic medicine, is a general tonic, and a bowel cleanser. Best taken at night, with warm milk, it helps with elimination.

2-R. Made up of turmeric & parsley, it is for purifying the blood and keeping the stomach soothed. It can help neutralize indigestion, expel gas, and help inconditions of ulcers. Do not take if pregnant.

3-R. Contains the trinity roots (ginger, onion, and garlic.) and is for your structural balance, like bone marrow structure. It is cleansing as well as energizing, a general tonic to the body. It is good for the digestive system, a blood cleanser & a sexual tonic. It has also helped in conditions of back pain.

7-R. The main ingredient is willow bark which helps to reduce inflammation and pain. It is very good for taking away your fatigue through its relaxant properties. It can reduce fever and has been used in cases of muscle spasms. Note: Do not take if you are pregnant. Most effective taken with milk.

108-R. Is sometimes referred to as "Healthy Heart" and has been used to lower blood pressure levels, cleaning the arteries of the heart, stabilizing your energy, and generally revitalizing your body & mind. It has calming and uplifting effects to the mind. Do not take on an empty stomach. Not recommended for people with low blood pressure.

Young Blood Powder. Also called "Young Blood Great Royal Diet." This formula contains a number of herbs and foods, all formulate together to help reduce weight, stimulate metabolism and cleanse the digestive system. Take two tablespoons each morning in juice or water to balance and strengthen all the five elements of Earth, Water, Fire, Air, and Ether in the body, and to energize all the chakras of the body.

GRD Oil. This is a specially formulated combination of pure, all natural oils designed to promote and maintain a healthy, balanced life. It is a 5000-year-old formula, invented by the Egyptians. They used to put it in the foods of their slaves so they would have the strength to continue working hard without getting sick. It is said to be very helpful to the immune system, but one should only take 3 drops every morning in orange juice, not more, and it has to be taken every day. (Over time you can slowly build up to 5 drops maximum—not more.)

☺ 1.
Books

The following is a list of books referred to during this Course:

Bhajan, Yogi. *The Teachings of Yogi Bhajan*. Hawthorn Books, New York, 1977.

Bhajan, Yogi. *Foods for Health & Healing*. Spiritual Community & K.R.I. Publications, Berkeley & Pomona, 1983.

Bhajan, Yogi. *Furmaan Khalsa: Poems to Live By*. Furmaan Khalsa Publishing Co., Ohio, 1987.

Khalsa. *The Man Called the Siri Singh Sahib*. Sikh Dharma, California, 1979.

Kaur, Bibi Inderjit. *Weight-Loss Diet, a.k.a., The Millet Diet*. Bibiji Inderjit Kaur, New Mexico.

Khalsa, Shakti Parwha Kaur. *Kundalini Yoga: The Flow of Eternal Power: An Easy Guide to the Yoga of Awareness*. Time Capsule Books, California, 1996.

☺

1.
Mantras & Musical Tapes

The following is a list of the Mantras and Musical Tapes used for the Meditations during this Course *(See Contacts for ordering information):*

Espanola Course

Class 1: *Saat* chanted in a long fashion. *Sa* means totality, Infinity. This is the first sound with which God created the universe. *Ta* means life. And *Naam* means Name or Identity. This mantra can give you Heaven and Earth in balance.

Class 2: *Har.* The *Tantric Har* tape by Simran Kaur Khalsa. *Har* literally means "the Creative Aspect of God."

Class 3: *Tantric Har* by Simran Kaur Khalsa. Utter no word.

Class 4: The mantra, *Har,* is chanted in a monotone with the tape *Rhythms of Gatka* by Matamandir Singh Khalsa playing in the background.

Class 5: *Ong Namo Guru Dev Namo* by Nirinjan Kaur & Guru Prem Singh Khalsa.

Class 6: *The Yogi* and *Gobinday Mukunday,* by Matamandir Singh Khalsa, from the musical album: *The Yogi in the Court of Guru Ram Das,* a tape containing mantras and songs. *Listed as catalog #MAS020 from GT Enterprises.*

Class 7: *Gobinday Mukunday,* by Matamandir Singh Khalsa, from *The Yogi in the Court of Guru Ram Das,* a tape containing mantras and songs. *Listed as catalog #MAS037 from GT Enterprises.*

Class 8: *Sounds of the Various Religions,* from the tape *Bharia Hath* (the 20th *pauree* of *Japji Sahib)* by Matamandir Singh Khalsa. *Available from GT Enterprises.*
    Further explanation of this tape: Each religion is based on a specific sound current, and the way they praise God or call on God can be boiled down to one specific syllable or sound:

Yaa =	Yaa-ho-vaah: Jehovah (Judaism)
Haa =	Ha-le-lu-jha — Halleluyah (Christianity)
Laa =	Laa-ay-laa - Allah (Islam)
Raa =	Raa-maa - Rama (Hinduism)
Saa =	Sat Nam = (Sikh)

Class 8 & 9: *Dhuni*
The *Dhuni* tape is an instrumental piece played on a one-stringed instrument, and has a rhythm which works perfectly with the mantra, *Sat Naam, Sat Naam, Sat Naam Ji, Waa-Hay Guroo, Waa-Hay Guroo, Waa-Hay Guroo Ji.* Yogi Bhajan says about this tape, *"Dhuni* is that which accelerates excellence in us." *Listed as catalog #CT130 from GT Enterprises.*

Class 10:
    Reality, Prosperity, and Ecstasy, by Nirinjan Kaur Khalsa, based on an affirmation by Yogi Bhajan.
    Dhuni.

Class 12: Mentally recite *Sat Naam, Sat Naam, Sat Naam Ji, Waa-Hay Guroo, Waa-Hay Guroo, Waa-Hay Guroo Ji,* with the tape *Dhuni.*
    All For You, from a tape of songs of the same name by Ragu Rai Kaur, was also played during the class.

Class 13: *Rhythms of Gatka,* by Matamandir Singh is played while the class chants the mantra *Har.* It is a strong, driving drum beat tape. *Listed as catalog #MAS021 from GT Enterprises.*

Class 14: Mentally recite *Sat Naam, Sat Naam, Sat Naam Ji, Waa-Hay Guroo, Waa-Hay Guroo, Waa-Hay Guroo Ji,* with the tape *Dhuni.*

Class 15: Mentally recite *Sat Naam, Sat Naam, Sat Naam Ji, Waa Hay Guroo, Waa Hay Guroo, Waa-Hay Guroo Jee,* with the tape *Dhuni.*

Class 16: *Aadays Tisai Aadays, Aad Aneel Anaad Anaahat, Jug Jug Ayko Vays.* This mantra is spoken in a continuous monotone.

Class 18:
    Part I: *Har Haray Haree Waa-Hay Guroo.* Chanted in very precise syllables, in a spoken monotone, with a brief pause after each syllable.

    Part II: *Ardaas Bhayee, Amar Daas Guroo, Amar Daas Guroo, Ardaas Bhayee.*
    Raam Daas Guroo, Raam Daas Guroo, Raam Daas Guroo, Sachee Sahee.
    The instrumental version of this mantra is played.

Class 20: *Wahe Guru, Wahe Guru, Wahe Guru Jio,* by Giani Ji.

    Class 11, 19, and 22 had no meditations. Class 17 and 21 used no mantra or music.

Assisi Course

Class 1: *Wahe Guru, Wahe Jio* by Giani Ji
Prabh Joo To Keh Laaj Hamaree by Master Darshan Singh
Rhythms of Gatka by Mata Mandir Singh
Sat Nam, Wahe Guru #3 by Lata Mangeshkar (Nightingale of India)
Flowers in the Rain, sung by Gurudass Singh (sung live)
Birthday Song from the *Khalsa Way* album, by Livtar Singh (played in class)
Ardas Bhaee Healing Sounds album.
Every Heartbeat by Nirinjan Kaur
Aquarian March by Nirinjan Kaur

Class 2: *Bharia Hath—Five Sounds of Religion* by Matamandir Singh

Class 3: *Ong Namo Guru Dev Namo* by Nirinjan Kaur
Gurudev Mata by Guru Jiwan Singh

Class 4: *Reality, Prosperity & Ecstasy*, by Nirinjan Kaur
Humee Hum Brahm Hum by Nirinjan Kaur
Ong Namo Guru Dev Namo by Nirinjan Kaur

Class 5: *Promises* by Sat Peter Singh (played in class)
Birthday Song from the *Khalsa Way* album, by Livtar Singh (played in class)
When Will I Walk On The Cold Marble Again? by Guru Dass Singh (sung live)

Class 6: *Bhauta Karam* performed live by Har Anand Kaur

Class 7: *Aykaa Maa-ee*, by Sangeet Kaur
Wahe Guru, Wahe Jio, by Giani Ji

Class 8: *Ardas Bhaee* — Healing Sounds of the Ancients (played in class)
Narayan performed live by Guru Dass Singh
Bhangara Drum Tape

Class 9: *Aap Sahaaee Hoaa*, by Singh Kaur

Class 10: *Aquarian March*, by Nirinjan Kaur. This is the Mantra *Sat Siri, Siri Akaal, Siri Akaal Mahaa Akaal, Mahaa Akaal Sat Naam, Akaal Moorat Waa-Hay Guroo.*

Class 11: *Asankh Naav Asankh Thaav* by Guru Dass Singh (sung live)
Ardas Bhaee — Healing Sounds album.
Birthday Song from the *Khalsa Way* album, by Livtar Singh

K.
Five-Part Meditation Series
To Keep the Chakras Open

Taught to Khalsa Council • April 2, 1997

We have to learn to penetrate. We have to learn to consciously take our soul to Infinity. We have to practice those practices to create a blueprint, so that when we build on that blueprint we'll become real.

After this series, you will be unable to ask a negative question. You are the temple of God. You simply need to recharge yourself to face the transmission against the obstacles and height of time and space. You have two challenges—time and space. You and your spirit are two dominant forces within you. When the spirit dominantly helps your mind and helps your body, you are successful.

Part 1

Mudra: In Easy Pose, place the left palm flat on the heart center, fingers pointing towards the right, and the thumb extended along the chest, pointing up. The right hand is placed next to the right shoulder, palm facing forward, fingers pointing towards the ceiling. Keep the hand up at the level of the face. Make a fist with the right hand, and extend the index finger towards the ceiling. Hold the posture.

Eyes: Look straight. Do not wink or look left or right. Just look straight forward.

Breath: Clench the front teeth together. Forcefully breathe in, long and deep, through the teeth, and exhale through the nose.

Time: 11 minutes.

End: Inhale deeply and immediately move into Part II.

Comments/Effects: I'll tell you the secret. In this meditation, the saliva will go with the breath. It will give your blood the magnitude to change its genetic cells to a hundred thousand times its power. It's a very pure science. That is what is written. Breathe in through the lock of the teeth, and breathe out through the nostrils, full and deep. Also they say, the breath should be forcefully inhaled. This stimulates your nervous system to get force into it.

One mistake you can do, is to wink your eyes during this meditation. That will dilute the health of your eyes, which this *kriya* is intended to give you. You must use force to breathe in through the lock of the teeth so that the maximum saliva can concentrate with your breath and go into the lungs and enrich you. Breathe out through the nostrils, so that all genetic diseases will leave you.

After six minutes you will enter into a twilight zone, where physically you may try to fail. Your self-essence at that time will depend on your spirit. Have faith, have trust. Understand this is not something that we just manifested today. It has been practiced for centuries and has a proven result. You need your determination, your will, your commitment. Please don't resist—exist! Beat through it.

At seven minutes, your body will start reacting heavily. It is now testing your own will. It's normal. If you experience your own will as united, then you will understand God's Will.

Part II

Mudra: Interlock your hands over your head and make the arms and hands like a circle around your head. The arc should be an arc, not a triangle, not a square.

Breath: Make the mouth into an 'O' and breathe in and out deeply through the 'O.'

Time: 9 minutes.

End: Inhale and move immediately into Part III.

Part III

Mudra: Place your palms flat against one another, fingers pointing towards the ceiling, and the thumbs stretched back towards the body. Place the pads of the thumbs on the sides of the eyes, right under the eyebrows. Hold the posture.

Eyes: Closed.

Music: The instrumental version of *Ardas Bhaee*. Whistle along with the tape.

Time: 4-1/2 minutes.

End: Inhale and immediately move into Part IV.

Part IV

Mudra: Stretch the arms straight out in front, arms parallel to the ground, no bend in the elbow, right palm flat and face up, left palm flat and face down. Sit very straight, and hold your shoulders tight, to get the correct experience.

Breath: Breathe as you please. Begin Breath of Fire for the final minute.

Time: 3-1/2 minutes total. 2-1/2 minutes with long deep breathing, Breath of Fire for the final minute.

End: Inhale deeply and move immediately into Part V.

Comments/Effects: The arms have to be absolutely straight. Keep the shoulders held tight and the spine very straight, otherwise the nervous system will crunch it.

Part V

Mudra: Place your hands flat against your chest, right over left.

Breath: Calm down the breath for 30 seconds, and then breathe long and deep, as best you can, for 30 more seconds.

Time: 1 minute total.

End: Relax.

Comments/Effects: In this part of the meditation, let peace and tranquillity, spirit, mind, and body create a relationship for everlasting bonding. As it is the Will of God, so be it.

L.
Contacts

Ancient Healing Ways. *Call for a free catalog*
Route 3, Box 259, Espanola, NM 87532
Toll Free: 800-359-2940
Inter'l: 505-747-2860
FAX: 505-747-2868
Supplier of books, audio and video tapes, herbal formulas, malas, healing teas, and bodycare
products formulated by Yogi Bhajan.

Sat Nam Versand. *Call for a free catalog*
Freiligrathstr. 14 - 60385 Frankfurt, Germany
Phone: 49-69-43-44-19   FAX: 49-69-43-85-71
Supplier of books, audio and video tapes, (including music used during this meditations),
healing teas, other herbal and bodycare products, and clothing.

Golden Temple Enterprises. *Call for a free catalog*
Box 13 Shady Lane, Espanola, NM 87532
Toll Free: 800-829-3970
Inter'l: 505-753-0563   FAX: 505-753-5603
Supplier of video & audio recordings of classes by Yogi Bhajan, including the music used
during the meditations.

Cherdi Kala Music. *Call for a free catalog*
1539 S. Shenandoah St., Apt #301, Los Angeles, CA 90035
Phone: & Fax: 310-550-6893
Supplier of audio music tapes.

IKTYA (International Kundalini Yoga Teachers' Association)
Contact Person: Nam Kaur Khalsa, Executive Director
Route 2, Box 4 Shady Lane, Espanola, NM 87532
Phone: 505-753-0423   FAX: 505-753-5982   Website: www.yogibhajan.com
Organization of Kundalini Yoga Teachers. Membership includes a listing in the Annual
Teacher's Directory, discounts on selected yoga products, and subscription to Kundalini
Rising! a newsletter for Teachers. It provides a listing of Teachers worldwide.

3HO Events
Rt. 2 Box 132-D, Espanola, New Mexico 87532
Toll Free: 888-340-2420
Inter'l: 505-753-6341, ext. 121   FAX: 505-753-1999
For information on Winter and Summer Solstice gatherings, White Tantric Yoga schedules
around the US, Europe, Mexico, and Canada, special events, and camps.

Glossary

We have included in this glossary terms which, though they may not appear in this book, you may come across while at a Kundalini Yoga Class, a 3HO event, or while reading books on Kundalini Yoga or Sikh Dharma.

Adi Shakti. Literally means "Primal Power." *Adi* means "primal" or "first" and *shakti* means "God's power manifested." The *Adi Shakti* has been worshipped for centuries in the Orient in the form of the goddess, and thus the female energy of Infinity is also referred to as Adi Shakti. Woman is seen as a manifestation of the *Adi Shakti* energy.

Agan Granthi. The heart center cavity. It is the source of all fire-related activites —including digestion and breath. When this center is locked, your ribcage is out of placement, the diaphragm doesn't act correctly, and you lose one third of your life force. That's why in Kundalini Yoga we find so many meditations to open up the ribcage and the heart center.

Ajna chakra. The Third Eye point, or the sixth chakra, associated with the pituitary gland; also *Agia chakra*.

Ajwan seed. Oregano seed.

Akaal. Undying.

Akaal Purakh. Undying Being.

Akaal Takhat. Literally "Eternal Throne"; established by Guru Hargobind as the supreme seat of religious authority for Sikhs, located in Amritsar, India.

Amrit. Spiritual Nectar; the ceremony in which one takes vows as a baptized Sikh.

Amritdhari. One who has taken "Amrit," baptized into the Khalsa.

Amrit Vela. Literally "ambrosial time." The third watch of the day, 2 1/2 hours before the sun rises.

Anand. Bliss, ecstasy.

Anand Sahib. One of the daily prayers of the Sikhs, composed by Guru Amar Das, which connects one to the inherent ecstasy.

Anandpur Sahib. Birthplace of the Khalsa, located in Punjab, India.

Ang Sang *Wahe Guru*. "God exists in every part of me."

Arcline. One of the ten bodies, sometimes it has been referred to historically as the halo. The arcline goes from ear to ear; and is the seat of the *akash*, the ether, in the body. Its color varies with the health and the mental or psychic condition of the person. Women have a second arcline reaching across the chest, from nipple to nipple, which Yogi Bhajan says gets imprinted with the sexual experiences she has had in her life.

Anhad. The sound from deep within the navel point. *Anhad Shakti* is in the navel point. When you speak from the navel, that is the effective infinite process. When you speak from the navel and with the tip of the tongue, you create a sound link between the navel and the tip of the tongue. The mind through the cavity of the subconscious has to balance. The balance comes with your applied consciousness. Anyone who projects with the frequency of the self from the *anhad* at the navel point shall change the rhythmology of the cosmology of the magnetic field of the Earth. What thou shall say, thou shall obey. This universe and the other universes are powered by the power of the resounding sound, *anhad*. Unlimited sound vibrates and creates light and creates life. *Anhad* is the by-product of the Gurmantra, *Wahe Guru*.

Ardas. Prayer; the traditional formal prayer of the Sikhs.

Asa di Vaar. This is a collection of prayers or *shabads*, which can be found in the *Siri Guru Granth Sahib*. It is traditionally recited or sung in the morning hours.

Asan (Asana). Position, seat, yogic posture.

Ashram. A learning center for spiritiual growth.

Atma. Soul.

Aura, Auric Body. There are 7 chakras (energy centers) in the body, and the 8th is the aura, the electromagnetic field of energy which surrounds every living creature. A strong, radiant aura can protect us from many misfortunes and strengthen our mental, physical, and spiritual bodies. Kundalini Yoga *kriyas* and *pranayams* increase the auric field, thus increasing awareness.

Avtar. An incarnation of god in a human body.

Baisakhi Day. For Sikhs the day of the formation of the Khalsa by Guru Gobind Singh which took place at the traditional festival of Spring (Baisakhi), when he first administered the baptism of Amrit.

Bana. The outward projection, usually referring to religious clothing.

Bani. Literally "Word." Refers to the Word of God contained in the Sikh Sacred Writings.

Banis. The Sikh daily prayers.

Beads of Truth. Publication of the 3HO Foundation.

Beej Mantra. Sat Naam is known as the "beej" or "seed" mantra.

Bekhri. Sound made with the tip of the tongue, i.e., aloud.

Bhagat Ravidas. An Indian saint whose writings appear in the *Siri Guru Granth Sahib.*

Bhagwan. Teacher, master.

Bhagautee. Creative power of the universe.

Bhai. Brother.

Bhai Sahib(a). An honorary title which means respected brother (or sister); in Sikh Dharma, the chief priest.

Bhakti. Self-purification. The devotional form of yoga practiced by a Bhakta, a devotee.

Bhat. Minstrel.

Bheta. An offering or donation made in the Name of God.

Bir. Full one-volume of *Siri Guru Granth Sahib* in Gurmukhi.

Black garbanzos. A type of chickpea, black in color, which are very energizing.

Brahma. The Hindu god of creation, one of the three primary manifestations of God.

Brahmgiani. Enlightened person.

Buddha. An enlightened one; founder of the Buddhist faith.

Chakra. An energy center of consciousness associated with the seven nerve centers of the body.

Chanani (Chandoa). Canopy placed over the *Siri Guru Granth Sahib.*

Chapati. Unleavened flat bread.

Charan Japa. Walking meditation.

Chardi kalaa. In high spirits.

Chauree. Fan made of horsehair which is waved over the *Siri Guru Granth Sahib.* It is used to create a positive etheric field and is a symbol of the sovereignty of the Guru.

Chole. A flavorful Indian dish, traditionally made with garbanzo beans (chickpeas) and potatoes.

Chunee. A type of head-scarf, usually silk or silk/cotton, worn by women.

Churidars. Traditional Indian legwear which is tight around the ankles and calves, and loose around the waist and thighs.

Darvesh. A Muslim ascetic, some of whom practice ecstatic dancing and whirling or chanting.

Devas. Gods.

Devtas. Angels.

Dharana. Concentration.

Dharma. A path of righteous living, the law of the universe which binds all things in relationship.

Dhiaan. Meditation.

Fakir. A Muslim or Hindu religious ascetic monk.

Fingers. Each finger on the hand has a special name and is associated with a different energy in

Yogic science:

> Index finger: The Jupiter Finger, associated with the quality of knowledge and intuition.
>
> Middle finger: The Saturn Finger, associated with wisdom, intelligence, and patience.
>
> Ring finger: The Sun Finger, associated with the physical body and physical health.
>
> Little finger: The Mercury Finger, associated with communication.
>
> Thumb: The Id, associated with the ego.

Ganesha. The Hindu elephant god, a symbol for prosperity.

Garbanzos. *See "black garbanzos."*

Ghee. Clarified butter.

Giaan Mudra. A common hand position used in many meditations in Kundalini Yoga: Curl the index (Jupiter) finger under the thumb, and hold the other three fingers straight.

Golden Chain of Teachers or the Golden Link. The long line of spiritual masters who have preceded us. When we chant *"Ong Namo Guru Dev Namo,"* we tune into that flow of spiritual energy and become one with the Universal Teacher.

Golden Temple. The Harimandir Sahib, the most sacred Sikh temple in the world, located in Amritsar, India. It was founded by Guru Ram Das, the fourth Sikh Guru. Constructed of marble and gold. It is surrounded by a pool of healing water.

Gootka. Small book containing prayers from the *Siri Guru Granth Sahib.*

Gopis. Consorts of Lord Krishna; milkmaids.

Granth. Literally: knot; book.

Granthee. One who performs priestly duties in a Gurdwara.

Gunas. The three conditions of matter: *sattvaa*—pure essence (saintliness), *raajaas*—active, creative or initiating energy (imperial), and *taamaas*—inertia or decay.

Gurbani. Word of the Guru. Refers particularly to the words from the *Siri Guru Granth Sahib.*

Gurbani Kirtan. Devotional singing of Gurbani.

Gurdwara. Sikh place of worship; literally, "Gate of the Guru."

Gurmukh. Literally, one whose face is always turned toward the Guru, or one whose mouth always repeats the Guru's words; a perfectly devoted person.

Gurmukhi. Literally "from the Guru's mouth"; refers to the script in which the *Siri Guru Granth Sahib* is written.

Guru. That which takes us from darkness to light. Literally *"Gu"* meaning darkness; and *"Ru"* meaning light. In Sikh history, a succession of ten Gurus revealed the Sikh path over a 200-year period. They were:

1st Sikh Guru:	Guru Nanak
2nd Sikh Guru:	Guru Angad
3rd Sikh Guru:	Guru Amar Das
4th Sikh Guru:	Guru Ram Das
5th Sikh Guru:	Guru Arjan
6th Sikh Guru:	Guru Hargobind
7th Sikh Guru:	Guru Har Rai
8th Sikh Guru:	Guru Har Krishan
9th Sikh Guru:	Guru Teg Bahadur
10th Sikh Guru:	Guru Gobind Singh

The 10th Sikh Guru, Guru Gobind Singh, passed the Guruship to the Siri Guru Granth Sahib, which embodies the writings, teachings, and sound current of the Gurus.

Gutka. Indian martial art of sword fighting.

Harimandir Sahib. Often referred to as The Golden Temple. *(See Golden Temple.)*

Hukam. An order from the Guru.

Hydrotherapy (ishnaan). A system of water-therapy referred to in the west as "hydrotherapy" and in the east as "ishnaan"—involving bathing in cold water to open up the capillaries and flush the system, thus increasing the circulation and improving the glands and the general health of the body.

Ida. Left nerve channel *(nadi);* relates to the left nostril, moon energy.

Ishnaan. *(See Hydrotherapy.)*

Isqbal. Sometimes referred to as "Sat Isqbal"—an intestinal cleanser. A mixture made from an Indian plant fiber similar to psyllium seeds—swelling up in the intestinal tract and pushes out all the old debris. Taken as a 3-day fast to improve health, beauty, and energy.

Jaap Sahib. A prayer written by Guru Gobind Singh which gives one conscious awareness of one's grace; one of the daily prayers of the Sikhs.

Jahangir. Moghul Emperor of India at the time of Guru Arjan's martyrdom.

Japji Sahib. A prayer written by Guru Nanak which relates the conscious mind to the soul; one of the daily prayers of the Sikhs.

Jetha. The name of the Fourth Guru, Guru Ram Das, when he was a student of his father, the Third Guru, Guru Amar Das.

Jatha. Group.

Ji. Literally meaning "soul," used as a term of endearment, or sign of respect.

Jumna. A river in Northern India, flowing SE from the Himalayas to the Ganges at Allahabad, 860 mi. long.

Kaalaa Jeeraa. A spice related to cumin and caraway but thinner and darker; known as "black cumin."

Kaam. Desire. One of the five obstacles to enlightenment.

Kaamanaa. Desire for higher values. *Kaam* should be converted into *kaamanaa*. You can't get rid of desire, but you can turn the desire towards the desire for higher values. You can desire desirelessness. To be desireless is a desire.

Kakaars (5 Kakaars). The five symbols (Five K's) worn by baptized Sikhs.

Kaliyug. The Iron Age, Steel Age, or Age of Darkness, the current Age.

Kanga. Wooden comb; one of the Five K's worn by baptized Sikhs.

Kara. Steel bracelet; one of the Five K's worn by baptized Sikhs.

Karma. The cosmic law of cause and effect, action and reaction.

Kathaa. Spiritual discourse.

Kesh. Uncut hair; one of the Five K's worn by baptized Sikhs.

Khalsa. Literally means "pure one."

Kirtan Sohila. One of the evening prayers of the Sikhs.

Khanda. Double-edged sword.

Kheer. Rice pudding.

Kirpan. Small, single-edged sword; one of the Five K's worn by baptized Sikhs.

Kriya. Literally: completed action; a particular yogic posture or series of postures linked to mantra and breath to produce a particular effect.

Krodh. Anger. One of the five obstacles to enlightenment.

Kundalini. Comes from the word "kundal"; coiled energy; the creative potential of an individual.

Kutcheras. Special cotton underwear. One of the Five K's worn by baptized Sikhs.

Lakh. 100,000.

Lakshmi. Goddess of wealth, good fortune and plenty; heavenly consort of Narayan.

Lehna. The name of the Second Guru, Guru Angad, when he was a student of the First Guru, Guru Nanak.

Lobh. Greed.

Lord Krishna. An Avtar who is one of the great teachers in the Golden Link, who lived in a human form.

Lord Rama. An Avatar, incarnation of God, who lived in human form.

Lungar. Free kitchen associated with Sikh worship service.

Mahabharata. Classical Hindu epic poem.

Mahan Tantric. Master of White Tantric Yoga; title which is held by Yogi Bhajan, was bestowed upon him in 1971. There is only one Mahan Tantric at any given time alive on the Earth.

Manmohan version. An English translation of the *Siri Guru Granth Sahib*, also containing the original Gurmukhi script.

Maryada. Code, practice.

Masala. A special blend of spices, usually cooked into Indian dishes, such as curries.

Master. A person held in high esteem, considered to be an authority in his or her field.

Maya. The illusion of the reality of sensory experience of one's self and the world around us. Usually thought of as what takes us away from, or blinds us from perceiving God.

Mian Mir. The Sufi Pir who is associated with Guru Arjan, the Fifth Sikh Guru.

Miri/Piri. Temporal/spiritual balance of the universe; concept introduced by Guru Hargobind of secular/spiritual sovereignty.

Mound of Mercury. The fleshy portion or mound on the palm, just underneath the pinkie or Mercury finger.

Mudra. Yogic hand position.

Mukhia Sardarni Sahiba. Title for a female regional minister in Sikh Dharma.

Mukhia Singh Sahib. Title for a male regional minister of Sikh Dharma.

Mullah. A learned Muslim.

Naad. The sound current, or inner sound.

Naam. The vibration or essence of God; identity.

Nadi. Energy channels for the flow of *prana*.

Narayan. A Name of God in the aspect of Sustainer, Preserver; Name of Lord Vishnu.

Nitnem. Literally "repeated every day"; referring to the daily Sikh prayers.

"O" breath. A special breath used in Kundalini Yoga. Make an "O" of the mouth and breathe through it.

Ojas. Spinal fluid.

Ong Namo Guru Dev Namo. Translated as, "I bow to the Divine Creator, I bow to the Divine Teacher Within." This is the mantra always used to "tune in" before teaching a Kundalini Yoga class.

Oshu. A Japanese title of a respected holy man or spiritually elevated being.

Paap. Sin; more literally "that which one gets for oneself."

Panj Piare. Five Beloved Ones. Historically those first five persons who received the Amrit.

Panth Khalsa. The ordained Ministry of Sikh Dharma; also refers to the general body of the Khalsa worldwide

Paramatma. The Supreme Self, the Highest Atma, the Highest Godhead.

Parantha. A type of Indian flatbread.

Patanjali. Rishi Patanjali, author of the famous yoga teachings, The Yoga Sutras, thousands of years ago. He wrote the *Push Puran*, predicting the coming of Guru Nanak, and first recited the mantra *Wahe Guru*.

Pauree. Literally "step" or "ladder." Refers to a particular poetic form used in the *Siri Guru Granth Sahib*.

Pavan Guru. That which carries the prana is called "pavan."

Perheraavaa. Dress.

Perkarma of Golden Temple. The walkway surrounding the Golden Temple, made of marble, on which people walk, often as a prayer or meditation, as they prepare to enter the Golden Temple itself.

Phulkaris. Colorful woven cloth of the same pattern worn by Guru Nanak.

Pingala. Right nerve channel *(nadi);* related to the right nostril, and the energy of the sun.

Prakirti. The creation, the creativity, the matter that has been created by the Creator. Earth is Prakirti.

Prana. Subtle ambient life energy; incoming breath of life given by God.

Pranayam. Yogic system of breathing exercises.

Prashad. Blessed food; refers to sweet food passed out at the end of Sikh worship service; gift of the Guru.

Pratyahar. One of the eight "limbs" of yoga, as described in the Yoga Sutras of Patanjali. Yogi Bhajan says on *pratyahar:* "Pratyahar is the control of the mind through withdrawal of the senses. The joy in your life which you really want to enjoy is within you. There is nothing more precise than you within you. The day you find you within you, your mind will be yours. In pratyahar we bring everything to zero (*shunia*), as *pranayam* brings everything to Infinity."

Purkha. The Creator.

Pundit. A Hindu who is learned in the scriptures.

Raaj Yog. The Royal Path of yoga.

Raag (Raaga). A traditional melodic mode of the Indian classical music system.

Raajas. One of the three conditions of matter—creative (*see guna*).

Radha. Beloved of Lord Krishna.

Rehiras. One of the daily prayers of the Sikhs, recited in the evening; adds energy to one's being.

Rehit. Code of Conduct.

Rishi. Enlightened being; yogi.

Rishi knot. Top-knot of the hair traditionally worn by yogis (*rishis*), and other spiritual practitioners.

Rukhmani. Wife of Lord Krishna.

Saag. Curried mustard greens.

Sach Kandh. Realm of Truth.

Sadhana. Spiritual discipline; the early morning daily spiritual practice.

Sadh Sangat. Literally "congregation of the disciplined ones"; company of the holy.

Sadhu. A disciplined spiritual person.

Samadhi. The state of consciousness in which the mind is free from reacting to thought waves.

Samskaras. Patterns of behavior brought from past lives.

Sanchar. Ceremony.

Sanskrit Sloks. Part of the structure of the *Siri Guru Granth Sahib.*

Sant Hazara Singh. Yogi Bhajan's Spiritual Teacher; previous Mahan Tantric.

Sanyaasi. Renunciate.

Sat. Infinite Truth.

Sat Naam. "*Sat*" means "Truth" and "*Naam*" means Name. It is sometimes translated as "Truth is my identity," and when someone says "*Sat Naam*" to another person, it means "Your Truth is your soul."

Sattvic. A state of purity; One of the three conditions of matter—purity (*see guna.*)

Seva. Selfless service.

Sevadar. One who does *seva.*

Shabad. Sound current. Word of God. Refers to the poems in *Siri Guru Granth Sahib.*

Shabad Guru. Sound which transforms your consciousness. The *Siri Guru Granth Sahib* is a *Shabad Guru.*

Shabd Hazare. One of the daily Sikh prayers.

Shakti. Universal creative energy; one's self-projection; feminine aspect of God; God's power in manifestation; woman.

Shushmanaa. Central spinal channel.

Shuniaa. A stage of consciousness wherein one brings his or her ego to a "zero" state. It's not quite the act of surrender, which is involving "you" using "your" energy to engage in the act of surrendering. But once you become *shuniaa*, zero, then the One will carry you. There are certain rules of Mother Nature. When you fold your hands, God will open up His arms. It's a natural law. The first principle of a Teacher is, "I am not." The power of a Teacher of Kundalini Yoga is in his zero, in his *shuniaa*.

Siddhas. Beings who are perfect beings, masters, and have aquired siddhis.

Siddhis. Occult powers.

Sikh. Sikh means a seeker of truth, and refers to one who follows the Sikh religion.

Sikh Dharma. A living experience of values as taught in the *Siri Guru Granth Sahib* and exemplified by the 10 Sikh Gurus.

Simran. Constant remembrance and repetition of God's Name. Replacing a negative thought with a positive one, as a meditative process.

Siri Guru Granth Sahib. A written compilation of the words of the Sikh Gurus, as well as Hindu, Sufi, and Muslim saints, expressing the Truth experienced while in a state of divine union with God. Written in *naad,* an elevated sound current, the ecstasy of their consciousness is transmitted through the vibration of their words—the *Shabad Guru.* Not a scripture nor a bible, these 1430 pages of poetry can elevate the reader to higher consciousness. Siri Guru Granth Sahib, therefore, is revered and worshipped as the Living Guru of the Sikhs, the emodiment of the consciousness of the Ten Gurus.

Siri Sahib. Sword.

Siri Singh Sahib. Title given to the Chief Religious and Administrative Authority of Sikh Dharma of the Western Hemisphere. This position is currently held by Yogi Bhajan.

Sohung. "I am God, God is me."

Spiritual name. A name that describes the spiritual destiny a person should strive for in life.

Subtle body. The subtle body is one of the ten bodies; the body which carries the soul to God at the time of death.

Sukhmani. Peace Lagoon; a prayer written by Guru Arjan; Song of Peace.

Sutra. Section from scripture.

Swami. Master.

Tabouleh. A middle Eastern salad made of bulghar, parsley, tomato, scallions, mint, olive oil, and lemon juice.

Taamas. One of the three conditions of matter—inertia or decay (see guna)

Tantric Yoga. There are three forms of Tantric Yoga: White Tantric, Black Tantric, Red Tantric. White Tantric Yoga is a profoundly deep, meditative experience, done in pairs as a group, and only led by the Mahan Tantric. In this group meditation a powerful energy force is created. This "life -force energy" is directed through the subtle body of the Mahan Tantric The subconscious mind is uplifted and cleansed of hidden tears, phobias, and restraints. White Tantric Yoga enables you to break through these subconscious blocks so you can enjoy life. White Tantric Yoga should not be confused with Black or Red Tantric. Black Tantric directs the energy to manipulate and control another human being, and Red Tantric directs the energy solely for sexual purposes.

Tattvas. The elements of fire, air, earth, ether, and water of which all creation, including the human body is composed.

Teerath. Sacred place

Ten bodies. According to Yogic science, we consist of ten bodies. They are: 1) Soul Body; 2) the Three Mental Bodies—2) Negative Mind, 3) Positive Mind, and 4) Neutral Mind); 5) Physical Body; 6) Pranic body; 7) Arc body; 8) Auric body; 9) Subtle body; 10) Radiant Body. For a good explanation of each of these, see Chapter 25 of *Kundalini Yoga: The Flow of Eternal Power*, by Shakti Parwha Kaur Khalsa.

Tenth gate. The center of consciousness located at the top of the skull.

Thaakur. In the Hindu religion, Stone idol; in Sikh Dharma, "powerful one."

Third Eye Point. *Ajna,* the sixth center or chakra. Associated with wisdom and intuition.

Tiaaga. Renunciation, abandonment.

Traysha Guru. Three-fold Guru; trinity.

Trinity Herbs. Onion, ginger, and garlic.

Trinity of God. Father, son and Holy Ghost; or Brahma, Vishnu, Mahesh; or One who Generates, Organizes or Destroys and Delivers (G-O-D).

Turmeric. An orange/yellow spice, which is said to have many health benefits.

Wahe Guru. A mantra of ecstasy, expressing the excellence and magnificence of God.

Yogi. One who has attained a state of yoga, mastery of one's self. One who practices the science of yoga.

Wahe Guru. Ecstasy of God Consciousness.

Wahe Guru Ji ka Khalsa, Wahe Guru Ji ki Fateh. "My purity belongs to God, all victory belongs to God!"

Yam. Yams/Niyams "do's and don'ts"; the ethical precepts defined by Patanjali.

Yarmulke. Skullcap worn by members of the Jewish faith.

Chapter Notes

Chapter One
1 This poem appears in *The Man Called the Siri Singh Sahib*, Khalsa, Sikh Dharma, California, 1979.

Chapter Two
1 *Communication: Liberation or Condemnation*, by Harbhajan Singh Khalsa Yogiji, 1980.
2 Gurucharan Singh Khalsa comments on this passage: "He means always connect the tip of the tongue to the navel energy. That energy calls on the Kundalini or basic force of your original self. It activates the *shabad brahm* of Kundalini, and the hiss of that activity is the power of the Word. Always invest your word with that power. It is the power of *laya* that accelerates the impact of mantra. You may then project the empowered word through any chakra depending on the impact and effect you want."

Chapter Four
1 Genghis Khan (1162-1227) was a Mongol conqueror. Kublai Khan (1216-94), grandson of Genghis Khan, was Founder of the Mongol dynasty in China).
2 Debris from threshing grain.

Chapter Five
1 A river in Northern India, 860 mi. long, flowing SE from the Himalayas to the Ganges at Allahabad.
2 Any of a group of peptides, resembling opiates, that are released in the body in response to stress or trauma and that react with the brain's opiate receptors to reduce the sensation of pain.

Chapter Seven
1 Quote from Matthew 22:21.12

Chapter Eleven
1 Guru Singh was the first non-Indian Sikh to wear a turban.
2 All the Gurus were considered to be Nanak. This particular shabad was from the Fifth Channel of Nanak, Guru Arjun.
3 *Kundalini Yoga: The Flow of Eternal Power*, by Shakti Parwha Kaur Khalsa, Time Capsule Books, California, 1996.

Chapter 12
1 *Communication: Liberation or Condemnation*, by Harbhajan Singh Khalsa Yogiji. University for Humanistic Studies, San Francisco, 1980. Available from Ancient Healing Ways. *(See Contacts for address.)*

Chapter 17
1 This poem can be found in *The Man Called the Siri Singh Sahib*, page 51.
2 Yogi Bhajan was often call "Yogi Bahan" in India.

Chapter 18
1 It is said that the soul enters the body of the mother on the 120th day after conception.

Chapter 20
1 Nirvair Singh and Kaur Khalsa went to Anchorage, Alaska during the 1970s to teach Kundalini Yoga. At this printing, they are living and thriving there.

Index

A

Abraham 128,159
Adam and Eve 14,281
agan granthi 23,25
Age of Aquarius 3,6,7,13,112,153,225,226,235,239,250,
    253,263,281
    cusp of 180
Age of Pisces *(See Piscean Age.)*
ahangkaar (see pride.)
Air element 17
ajna chakra *(See 6th chakra.)*
akasha (See Ether element.)
akashic records 123
Allah 271,304
Alphabets
    administrators 300
    marriage 299
    qualities of people 301
    self-esteem 299
    teacher 298
    woman 298
altitude and attitude 5,9,29,54,120,150,171,216,249
ambrosial hours 146
Amen 113
Amritsar 255
Ancient Healing Ways 323
anger *(krodh)* 156
Ang Sang Wahe Guru 123,296
aradhana 6
arcline *(See also radiant body.)* 150,205,208
Ardas 32,201
Ardas Bhaee 290
argument 4,8,11,42
Asa di Var 207
astrology 135
attachment *(moh)* 156
attachments, five 154
Atma *(See also soul.)* 296
attitude *(See altitude.)*
aura *(See also radiant body.)* 13,30,65,79,123,150,180
avtar 121
awareness 3,4,51

B

banana recipe 309
beast, human, angel 163
bharat roop (multiple self) 53
bhugatee 272
bindi 204
blessing 34,124,227,228
bliss 237

body, mind, soul 5,10,155,235,264,285
bone structure and marrow 39,40,188
bountiful, blissful, beautiful 252,258
Brahm 5,215
breaths in a lifetime 111
Breath Formula, Healing 198
Breath of Fire 64,66,73,77
breath, cannon fire 47
Buddha 30
business of life 47

C

caliber 146,157,187-191
cannon-fire breath 47
cats 33,42,238
cause and effect *(See also karma.)* 37,79,125,127
central nervous system 23,29
chakra, 2nd 121,244
chakra, 3rd 13,21,37
chakra, 4th 21,23,25
chakra, 5th,21
chakra, 6th 21,46,121,151,244
chakra, 7th 14,41,60,74
chakras 5,17,23,117,267
character 3,297
chardi kala 296
Cherdi Kala Music 323
clothing, white 297
cockroach 29,31,33
command 27,30,37,194,245,253
command center *(See 6th chakra.)*
Commandments, Ten 128,146,234,305
commitment 3, 4, 250,297
commotion 11,42,55,67,93,194,390
communication 17-22,36
communication, definition 17,34
Communication: Liberation or Condemnation 137
compassion 67,69,221,229
complexes 59-66,69
compulsion 42
computeritis 275
concentration 21
confrontation, necessity of 145,173
Contacts 323
consciousness 221
consciousness, cycles of 70
consciousness, moral 146
consciousness, workings of 43,145,146
courage 14,37
cotton 272,297

higher self 199

hookery, art of 19,22,45

holes (9 and 13) 297

householders 124,215,286

Houses of Knowledge, 190,191

Humeh Hum Brahm Hum 14,33,139,247

Human being 23,37,63,64,69,79,101,153,235,236,244

human, definition of 180

humans, as pets 42

humility 67

hydrotherapy (ishnaan) 172

hypocrisy 115

hypothalamus 285

I

I am, I am. 11,20

ida, pingala, shushmanaa 12,23-25

Individual Personality Impact IPI 42

Infinity, the Infinte 3,4,6,11,14,25,57,108,154,155,
    221,234,238,245,257

information overload 36

innocence 133

insecurity 6

intellect, danger of 43,145

intellect, intelligence 6,171

intellectuals 171, 217

intelligence, cycle of 70

intercourse 104

International Kundalini Yoga Teachers' Association
    (IKYTA) 323

intuition 6-8,40,51,60,69

J

jalapenos 196,311

Japji Sahib 16,34,67,95,101,111,127,147,167,174-177,219,
    245,259,260,264,266,279,288,289

Jesus, Jesu 202,244,254,263

judgment 3,4,7,60,68,74

K

Kabir 106,251

karma 64,67,151,167,205,208,276

karma, Law of 24

karma, surrendering 172

Khalsa, Guru Dass Singh 254-256

Khalsa, Shakti Parwha Kaur 121

kindness 11,69,254

knowing 4

Krishna 30,52,159,263

Kublai Khan 41

Kundalini 96,124,275,277,279

Kundalini Yoga 5,11,28,36,49,51,115,119,193,241,253,286

Kundalini Yoga Teacher, 16 Facets of Perfection 296

Kundalini Yoga Teacher, Oath of *(See Oath.)*

Kundalini Yoga, Laws of 28,49

L

latitude *(See longitude and latitude.)*

Law of Avagan 125

Law of Diminishing Returns 209

Law of Final Destination 29

leadership *(See Obedience and leadership.)*

lettuce recipe 312

liberation 164,303

life, cycle of 70

life force *(See prana.)*

lifestyle of righteousness (See also Dharma.) 297

limitations 249,251

logic 8,11

Long Time Sun 222,292

longitude and latitude 5,10,29,46,54,68,120,150,226,249

love 18,19,42,75,153,167,234

love, definition 172,180

M

magnetic field *(See electromagnetic field.)*

Mahabharata 104

Mahan Tantric 169

Mahesh *(See Shiva.)*

mantra 113,288

mantra and musical tapes 317

mantra, definition 243,251

marriage 42,105,168

masala 197,312

Master 10,25,49,50,95,101,108,122,132,168,180,
    191,211,296,297

Master of Kundalini Yoga 108

master and servant 49

mastery, over time 9

maya 28,31,108,182,183,275

meditation, at dusk 262

meditation, definition 234

meditation, evening 262

meditation, importance of 145,209

Meditation Series for chakras 320-322

men 160

men, lifecycle 39

menstruation 41

Mercury mound, Mercury point 13

meridian points 285,290

Mian Mir 83,120

mind *(See also body, mind, soul)*

mind, neutral 117,237

Mohammed, 30,159,203

moon cavity 285

moon center 151,152

moon cycle and diet 195,307

Moses 128,159

Mukunday 141

Mul Mantra 98